ETHICS IN AN AGE OF SURVEILLANCE

People increasingly live online, sharing publicly what might have once seemed private, but at the same time are enraged by extremes of government surveillance and the corresponding invasion of our private lives. In this enlightening work, Adam Henschke re-examines privacy and property in the age of surveillance in order to understand not only the importance of these social conventions, but also their moral relevance. By analysing identity and information and presenting a case for a relation between the two, he explains the moral importance of virtual identities and offers an ethically robust solution to design surveillance technologies. This book should be read by anyone interested in surveillance technology, new information technology more generally and social concepts like privacy and property.

ADAM HENSCHKE is an applied ethicist, working on areas that cross over between ethics, technology and security. He is a lecturer at the National Security College (NSC) in the Australian National University, Canberra, Australia and a research fellow with Delft University of Technology in The Hague, The Netherlands. His research concerns ethical and philosophical analyses of information technology and its uses, military ethics and relations between ethics and national security. He has published on surveillance, emerging military technologies and intelligence and cyberspace. He is the secretary of the Asia-Pacific Chapter of the International Society of Military Ethics (APAC-ISME).

Ethics in an Age of Surveillance

PERSONAL INFORMATION AND VIRTUAL IDENTITIES

ADAM HENSCHKE
Australian National University

CAMBRIDGE
UNIVERSITY PRESS

CAMBRIDGE
UNIVERSITY PRESS

University Printing House, Cambridge CB2 8BS, United Kingdom

One Liberty Plaza, 20th Floor, New York, NY 10006, USA

477 Williamstown Road, Port Melbourne, VIC 3207, Australia

314-321, 3rd Floor, Plot 3, Splendor Forum, Jasola District Centre, New Delhi - 110025, India

79 Anson Road, #06-04/06, Singapore 079906

Cambridge University Press is part of the University of Cambridge.

It furthers the University's mission by disseminating knowledge in the pursuit of education, learning and research at the highest international levels of excellence.

www.cambridge.org
Information on this title: www.cambridge.org/9781107570474
DOI: 10.1017/9781316417249

First published 2017
First paperback edition 2018

A catalogue record for this publication is available from the British Library

Library of Congress Cataloging in Publication data
NAMES: Henschke, Adam, 1976– author.
TITLE: Ethics in an age of surveillance : personal information and virtual identities / Adam Henschke.
DESCRIPTION: 1 Edition. | New York : Cambridge University Press, 2017. |
Includes bibliographical references and index.
IDENTIFIERS: LCCN 2017009170 | ISBN 9781107130012 (Hardback)
SUBJECTS: LCSH: Intelligence service–Moral and ethical aspects. | Electronic surveillance–Moral and ethical aspects. | Confidential communications–Moral and ethical aspects. | Personal information management–Psychological aspects. | Online identities. | Privacy, Right of. | BISAC: LAW / General.
CLASSIFICATION: LCC JF1525.I6 H455 2017 | DDC 170–dc23
LC record available at https://lccn.loc.gov/2017009170

ISBN 978-1-107-13001-2 Hardback
ISBN 978-1-107-57047-4 Paperback

To my parents and siblings, real and theoretical:
Pam, Jurgen and Chris. CAPPE's staff and students.
Without you all I would not be myself.

Contents

Acknowledgements

The list of acknowledgements for a first book is difficult; it feels like everyone from a primary school teacher, to someone who I had a drunken conversation with at 3am, to PhD supervisors, to current colleagues deserves some kind of recognition. But to write down everyone who helped form this book in some way or another would be both tedious and confusing. So, in an effort to be specific, a large number of people won't be listed but deserve acknowledgement; my apologies to you.

First, I thank the staff and colleagues at the National Security College at the Australian National University (ANU). Their willingness to give me fairly free rein, intellectual motivation and economic support while I converted my PhD dissertation into something more book-like is greatly appreciated. Within the ANU, the University House Early Career Fellowship programme funded research and travel opportunities.

I also thank the Brocher Foundation and the Hastings Center, who both hosted me as a research fellow at different points in the book's progress. The time spent at both institutions was absolutely essential in giving me the focus to develop some of the key concepts and in giving me the space to develop the larger structure of the book. This research was supported by U.S. National Science Foundation grant #1318126. Any opinions, findings and conclusions or recommendations expressed in this material are those of the author and do not necessarily reflect the views of the persons or organisations above.

Though it is a number of years between the book as it is and the PhD that it was, the lion's share of the research and conceptual development was done for my PhD at Charles Sturt University's Centre for Applied Philosophy and Public Ethics (CAPPE). I sincerely see CAPPE's staff as my theoretical parents, having raised me from an immature academic and CAPPE's fellow students as my theoretical siblings who grew up with me. While John Weckert, as my primary supervisor, played the biggest role in this, the academic environment of CAPPE is something that was quite special and hopefully wove itself into my DNA.

Early arguments, concepts and ideas for the book appeared in 'Making Sense of Animal Disenhancement', *NanoEthics*, 6:1, 2012, 'Did You Just Say What I Thought You Said? Talking about Genes, Identity and Information', *Identity and the Information Society*, 3:3, 2010 and 'Computer Ethics and Applied Contexts' (with John Weckert) in Floridi, L., (ed.) *A Philosophical Introduction to Computer Ethics*, Cambridge University Press, 2009, as well as many conference papers and public seminars.

I gratefully acknowledge Matt Gallaway at Cambridge University Press for showing an interest in the project early on and maintaining his interest in the time that followed. It's absolutely certain that without his willingness to take a risk on a first-time author that the book would not exist. I also recognise the work of the other people at Cambridge University Press; Meera Smith, Rebecca Jackaman and the rest of the production team who shepherded my words into an actual book. I also thank Ana Stiparu, whose help in the final stages of production saved me from intellectual collapse.

Finally, I wish to thank my real family and a stellar set of friends. When I first said that I was going to study ethics, though many were confused, my family and friends never wavered in their faith that I could make something of this: despite the fact that my typically deranged ranting gave little idea of what I was actually doing or why. My parents, Pam and Jurgen and my brother, Chris, not only encouraged me in keeping on working but also took an interest in what I was doing. Thanks also go to my various housemates and friends in Canberra, who put up with me for the duration and my friends in Melbourne and elsewhere, who motivated me by asking questions about my work and challenging me when the answers made no sense.

Looking back, this book had its inception while I was studying in Sweden in late 2006. In the ten years that followed, I have been so very lucky to have been exposed to so many great and wonderful people inside and outside of academia who helped in so many different ways to bring this book into being. Without this global village of colleagues, friends and family, what was a tiny idea conceived at the beginnings of a Linköping winter would not have emerged. And while I am hardly able to offer anything objective about the quality of what follows, my heartfelt appreciation goes out to everyone who helped bring this tiny idea, that identity and information may have some relation, into the world.

PART I

Surveillance Technologies and Ethical Vacuums

1

On the Project and Its Motivation

1.1 THE PROJECT: USHERING IN THE AGE OF SURVEILLANCE

We are all targets in the age of surveillance.[1] Imagine that you buy the following items: Cocoa-butter lotion, a large purse, vitamin supplements (zinc and magnesium) and a bright blue rug. Now imagine that these purchases tell someone that there is an 87 per cent chance that you are pregnant and due in six months. The company Target did this – used these and other pieces of data to produce a 'pregnancy score' for its customers. This surveillance became public knowledge when Target sent a family a 'pregnancy pack', congratulating the shopper on their pregnancy. The shopper was a teenage girl, living at home and her parents were unaware that their child was sexually active, let alone pregnant (Hill, 2012). Having trivial information such as purchase of cocoa butter produce Personal Information such as pregnancy is a fact of the age of surveillance. Coupling our behaviour with this focused attention reveals information for those who would want to target us. And while many would see such use of Personal Information as problematic, explaining why the purchase of cocoa butter is something of deep moral importance is far harder and more complex.

Information communication technologies (ICTs) have revolutionised the ways we live our lives. They are ubiquitous – firmly integrated into our working habits and our social lives – and play an ever deeper role in the exercise of basic political rights. From its initial introduction to the public in the early-mid 1990s, internet access has become

[1] I will not seek to define surveillance, as opening with a definitional discussion can tend to obscure the larger points being made. That said, this description by David Lyon will serve as a functionally useful account of how I generally use the term. 'Literally, surveillance means to "watch over" and as such it is an everyday practice in which human beings engage routinely, often unthinkingly … In most instances, however, surveillance has a more specific usage, referring to some focused and purposive attention to objects, data, or persons' (Lyon, 2009). My interest is with this sustained and focused attention to a target or set of targets. This is returned to in Chapter 3, where I talk about surveillance operators as epistemic actors.

comprehensive in many developed countries (The World Bank 2015)[2] to such a point that the UN Special Rapporteur on the Promotion and Protection of the Right to Freedom of Opinion and Expression held that internet access could be considered a basic human right (The Human Rights Council 2011). Social networking defines many people's social lives and is used by researchers, marketers and governments to shed light on and assist in, provision of essential services like healthcare (Chambers et al., 2012; Househ, 2013; Moorhead et al., 2013).

Our behaviours are evolving in parallel with these ubiquitous technologies. Whether it is the drive to photograph and broadcast our meals, the role played by Twitter in the social uprisings in the Middle East in 2011 (Lotan et al., 2011),[3] the push to have police officers wear body cameras while on patrol (Belluck, 2009; Pearl, 2015) or the live webcasting of brain surgery (Belluck, 2009), we use ICTs to communicate a wealth of Personal Information. Underneath the ubiquity of ICTs is the huge range of different information technology types, connected through their capacity to produce, collect, store and communicate information. As David Lyon notes, the evolution of our social practices runs hand in hand with the development of surveillance technologies:

> Although as a set of practices it is as old as history itself, systematic surveillance became a routine and inescapable part of everyday life in modern times and is now, more often than not, dependent on information and communication technologies (ICTs). Indeed, it now makes some sense to talk of 'surveillance societies', so pervasive is organizational monitoring of many kinds.
>
> (Lyon, 2009)

Combine the near invisible presence of ICTs in our lives with their informational capacities and we have *the age of surveillance*: a social epoch marked by informational technologies which endorse, encourage and enable us to live lives under constant surveillance.

What marks this age as one of *surveillance* is our own role in this – it is not simply that there are these new information technologies that target us for observation. We are complicit in this observation – we are often the willing sources of this information, happily uploading selfies, buying wearable surveillance technologies, actively publicising vast amounts of Personal Information like no other time in history. These ICTs are not just invasive; they are changing our very behaviours. What's so unique is that ICTs afford the ability to make ourselves the subject of observation. Facebook's value comes from the fact that its users are the active suppliers of Personal Information. This involvement in our own surveillance is unique in history.

[2] Note here that such coverage and access is patchy both globally and within different sectors of the community.

[3] At least in its initial stages. As Evgeny Morozov notes, social media alone was not enough to continue and close off a full revolution (Morozov, 2013, pp. 127–128).

What is interesting about this age of surveillance is our ambivalence to the treatment of this Personal Information. Compare the responses to a new smart phone with the revelations of widespread government surveillance: when Apple released their iPhone6, a colleague told me glowingly that it will remind him of things on his shopping list, can use the GPS to send text messages to his wife when he's almost home from work and can monitor his patterns of sleep. In the same conversation, he spoke with anger of how various governments around the world have been exposed for widespread spying and ubiquitous surveillance (Greenwald, 2014; Harding, 2014). His concern about government overreach seemed justified, but it was hard to reconcile this with his willing encouragement of commercial technology that watches him while he sleeps. Imagine if the government was involved in surveillance at this level of intimacy, watching him while he sleeps. This ambivalence is confusing – should we continue to embrace these surveillance technologies, further involving them in our most intimate of behaviours? Or should we be deeply worried, offended at the very thought of strangers watching us at every turn?

At first glance, our ambivalent responses suggest revealed preferences:[4] though we say we are opposed to such widespread surveillance, our behaviours reveal that we don't actually care so much. If anything, our willing *involvement* in surveillance shows that we actively endorse this age. Part of the explanation for this is that so much of this Personal Information is *insignificant*: who honestly cares whether I roll over in bed at 3:48am on Monday the 10th of August? Any worry about such insignificant information is likely to be paranoid and self-obsessed. However, as the responses to Edward Snowden's revelations of government surveillance show (Greenwald, 2014), there are deep concerns for many people about such omnipresent surveillance.

A sustained ethical analysis of these ICTs and of our behaviours surrounding them, will show that the arguments of involvement and insignificance are wrong-footed: by looking more deeply at just what Personal Information is and the ways that ICTs produce, collect, store and communicate this Personal Information, we can recognise the rise of *Virtual Identities*. These Virtual Identities carry with them special moral importance. As we will see, framing the discussion of surveillance in relation to Virtual Identities not only explains *why* our concerns are justified, it also gives some direction as to *how* to respond to those concerns, in ways that allow us to retain many of the desirable aspects of these ICTs. By looking at the age of surveillance in reference to Virtual Identities, we can both better understand the limits of the arguments of involvement and insignificance and the ambivalence to these technologies.

[4] As Daniel Solove points out, the arguments that our actions betray our real preferences are quite weak when looked at closely (Solove, 2004, pp. 76–92).

1.2 THE MOTIVATION: FROM INTIMATE TO INNOCUOUS INFORMATION

The motivation of this book is to understand how we should be treating Personal Information. Our ambivalence to Personal Information presents a challenge: should we care about privacy and control over Personal Information or perhaps there simply is no real moral problem – the sorts of information that surveillance technologies produce are innocuous, of no moral weight. Any worry about such information is mistaken. However, if we think of intimate Personal Information such as medical information, we see that there are legitimate concerns about the collection, use, storage and communication of medical information. If Personal Information collected by surveillance technologies shares some trait with medical information, then perhaps we ought to be taking more care with Personal Information more generally.

The differential uptake between government and private information services illustrates a general public ambivalence to surveillance technologies. In the past decade, many countries have attempted to roll out electronic patient medical records, but have had limited success. Australia passed the *Healthcare Identifiers Act 2010* (Australian Government 2010), described by the then Minister for Health Care and Ageing, Nicola Roxon, as 'a key building block of the Government's plans ... to revolutionise healthcare delivery through the introduction of personally-controlled electronic health records' (Nicola Roxon, 2010). The Australian eHealth programme began in July 2012.[5] To date, this 'key building block' has had limited uptake by the community (Ley, 2015). In early 2009, US president Barack Obama committed to 'a goal of computerizing all of America's medical records within 5 years as a means of improving efficiency, quality and safety and ultimately saving money' (Tang and Lee, 2009). The roll out in the United States has been plagued with a host of problems (Bowman, 2013). While some efforts have been more effective than others, the overall trend seems to be limited community engagement in these government initiatives.

At the same time, private industry is releasing an increasing range of services and products that collect, store, analyse and distribute Personal Information. Wearable health informatics technologies like Fitbit promise to 'empower and inspire you to live a healthier, more active life. We design products and experiences that fit seamlessly into your life so you can achieve your health and fitness goals, whatever

[5] As of July 2012, the Australian eHealth programme has been released, see ehealth.gov.au. However, it is operating on an opt-in system to enrol users and as of the date of writing, has been unsuccessful in getting people to enrol in the programme. While this lack of enrolment is due to a host of reasons, it certainly indicates considerable scepticism in such projects – including whether the Australian people trust the government with their data and whether such programmes will actually be useful or not. It should be noted that these eHealth programmes have generally been problematic: the United Kingdom attempt to convert medical records to electronic formats, proposed in 2002, had cost £10 billion by 2013 and was largely abandoned (Syal, 2013).

they may be' (FitBit, 2015). They produce information about the wearer's physical activity, in order to better inform the individual wearer about their lifestyle. As the technologies have advanced, 'informational ecosystems' have evolved into a suite of technologies and services. Apple's informational services are being bolstered by physical instruments such as the iPhone, iPad and the iWatch. The iRing (currently under patent application) involves 'an advanced ring-style wearable that uses voice, motion and touch input to control and interact with larger computing devices' (Campbell, 2015). What's notable about information harvesting products and services like those released and offered by Apple is that people actively seek them out and in many cases will queue up for hours or days to be the first to purchase the product. This is no minor subsection of the community either – Apple's position as the world's most highly valued company is built on the success of their informational ecosystems. Compared to government-provided services, these personalised information devices show people's willingness and genuine excitement to engage in self surveillance.

Perhaps recognising this ambivalence, the United Kingdom has sought to open up public access to medical data in order to stimulate new ways of producing and using aggregated medical data and new ways of producing data that is relevant for healthcare. Vast amounts of anonymised National Health Service (NHS) data have been made available for public access as of September 2012.[6]

One response is to point out the difference between government and private actors by saying that government services are about intimate *medical* information, whereas commercial products and services simply use innocuous Personal Information – we're talking about apples and oranges here. However, whether governmental, private or a mixture[7] of both (Solove, 2004, p. 3), a key goal of the informationalisation of our lives is to *integrate* different information to produce new information.[8] In addition to making medical data easier to communicate and access, what's essential to recognise is that by integrating this innocuous information, surveillance technologies are expanding what qualifies as morally relevant information.

To show how innocuous information becomes morally weighty, consider the problem of aging populations in the developed world. As the number and proportion of aged people in populations increase, dementia is also likely to increase in

[6] A summary of the motivations outlined in §1.1 of a recent UK Government White Paper, where it is stated that the release of government data is 'enabling people to make better choices about the public services they use and to hold government to account on spending and outcomes. Transparency is also providing the raw material for innovative new business ventures and for public service professionals to improve their performance.' (U.K. Government 2012).

[7] I refer here to the idea that a clear distinction between international state actors and global non-state actors is not a clear distinction. This point is borne out by the third motivation of the United Kingdom's Open Health programme, which is but one example of an expressly public/private partnership involving the use of personal information.

[8] The notion of new information and emergence is discussed in detail in Chapter 5.

number of sufferers and possibly in severity (Malloy et al., 2007, pp. 77–78). Remote patient monitoring and early detection may not only decrease economic costs (Tegart, 2010, pp. 8–9) but can also, hopefully, increase the quality of life for sufferers and carers:

> Near the end, my parents were spending about $180 day for home nursing. For just a fraction of their monthly nursing bill, they could have thrown enough blinking sensors and networking gizmos into their house to record and transmit every step, bite, breath, word and heartbeat in their Portland house.
>
> (Baker, 2007, p. 157)

As the need for treatment and support of those with conditions like dementia increases, there will likely be a corresponding growth in markets interested in exploiting these opportunities by developing novel ways and means of identifying and treating sufferers and supporting their carers.[9]

Personal Information, understood as 'information that relates to a person or group of people in some way'[10] that is non-intimate and innocuous, is a key tool in strategies to mitigate the impacts of aging populations. Consider the length of time between hearing a close friend or relative's voice on a phone and the recognition of who is speaking. This lapse between hearing the voice and recognising who is speaking is being investigated as a potential flag for dementia in elderly people (Baker, 2007, p. 168). Another novel method looks at word and grammar use through time. Over a long enough time, one's writing patterns may indicate a decline of cognitive ability. '[W]ith advanced statistical analysis of different writings, from blog posts to e-mails, researchers (or even employers) may pick up the downward trend of our cognitive skills long before we even suspect it' (Baker, 2007, pp. 177–178). In the near future, homes may be filled with sensors and monitors recording our behaviour (Albrecht and Mcintyre, 2005, p. 114; Baker, 2007, pp. 154–181; Tegart, 2010, pp. 11–35). Similarly, the success of Barack Obama's re-election in 2012 was credited in part to his team's use of Personal Information to reliably predict voting intention and willingness to contribute money to the campaign (Scherer, 2012). Likewise, the revelations by Snowden of national security agencies' mass collection and use of things like metadata (Greenwald, 2014) show just how interested government institutions are in our innocuous information.

These examples show that the realm of what could be classified as 'intimate information' is expanding far beyond what a patient shares with their doctor in a consultation or treatment. Moreover, intimate knowledge such as the cognitive decline of a person is drawn from fundamentally innocuous information – split second gaps between answering the phone, the form of our sentences, the way we

[9] For a recent overview of technologies associated with longevity, see: (Tegart, 2010).

[10] I discuss information in detail in Chapter 5 and in §7.4 develop an account of 'personal information' as 'information that relates to a person or group of people in some way'.

move our feet in the kitchen. The Snowden revelations underpin a larger claim that what we consider to be important Personal Information is changing in the age of surveillance, the technologies making the distinction between intimate and innocuous information dependent on the way that information is used.

What are the causal factors through which technology can change information? There are (at least) two separate, but related, factors. First is the rise of surveillance technologies and our changing behaviours. This is afforded by the 'the synergistic combination of four major "NBIC" (nano-bio-info-cogno) provinces of science and technology' (National Science Foundation and Department Of Commerce 2003). These converging technologies not only produce more relevant information about things and people but are also being developed with the capacity to *share* information across the different technological domains. Advances in nanotechnology produce information that supports cognitive technology and, when coupled with biotechnology, produce a wealth of transdisciplinary data, ready for analysis by advanced informatics (Cheshire Jnr, 2008; Hook, 2008).

The second causal factor is that this information, gleaned from a host of different disciplines, can now be collected and shared between people that were once separated from each other, either by discipline, geography, language or time (Nissenbaum, 2009, pp. 21–35). The development of surveillance technologies is astounding because of the wealth of information that it may use, the diversity of sources of this information and the incredible range of people who can access, use and ultimately benefit from this information. In the United Kingdom, the Open Health programme is a paradigm example of the ways in which Personal Information is being used for population health.[11] In parallel, another UK government agency, Government Communication Headquarters (GCHQ) has been collecting massive amounts of information. In a 2010–2011 review, GCHQ 'stated that in one 24 hour period the agency had been able to process and store "more than 39 billion events" ... [meaning that] GCHQ had managed to collect 39 billion pieces of information in a single day' (Harding, 2014, p. 161). This shows just how much information we produce and how much is collected.

Focusing attention on the informational element in the age of surveillance is important, as technological and behavioural shifts mean that the standard ways that we have dealt with Personal Information may no longer be able to provide us

[11] For example, three services arising from the UK Open Health initiative and already available through the 'data.gov.uk' website, are *Dr Pocket*: 'Dr Pocket is a company that uses public information about hospitals, doctors and organisations in health to help people find the best GP for them', *The London DataStore*: 'Available for free use and reuse, however people see fit, the London Datastore has joined up with 4iP to create a development fund to encourage developers to use the raw data to develop apps, websites and mobile products' and *Health iQ*: 'Health iQ is an analytics consultancy that works across healthcare and life sciences, who helped Healthcare for London to develop a specialist stroke service.'

with clear guidance. Consider informed consent,[12] a central issue in medical bioethics.[13] If an important factor in informed consent is that a health care professional give information of any conflict of interest (Beauchamp and Childress, 2001b, p. 75), how can a remote private company accessing the UK Open Health platform meaningfully meet this requirement? These concerns become even more complex when thinking of issues arising from in-house remote monitoring, dementia and meeting the standards of patient competence necessary for informed consent to be meaningful (Beauchamp and Childress, 2001b, pp. 73–77). And in a world where the data trails we leave wherever we go and whatever we do (Nissenbaum, 2009) are being used in massive state surveillance programmes (Greenwald, 2014; Harding, 2014), concerns about Personal Information and informed consent extend to deep-seated concerns about the impact of surveillance technologies on our basic political freedoms.

Further, these records about medical visits, shopping habits, where we drive (Ramli, 2011) and who we interact with (Greenwald, 2014, pp. 160–164) are digital, so are typically[14] neither reduced by use nor limited by use-by dates: an electronic database can be accessed perpetually without any decline in the information. Assuming that the database remains stable and the technology is accessible and reliable, repeat use and access have no necessary effect on the information quality. Compare information to a pie. For each piece of pie eaten, there now remains one less piece of total pie. Likewise, as time passes, the pie gradually becomes less edible, losing flavour, nutrition, probably becoming toxic and ultimately ceasing to be food. Information in databases should not face such degradation through access or time. '[I]nformation doesn't wear out. It [can] be endlessly recycled [and] repackaged' (Drahos and Braithwaite, 2002, pp. 58–59). Given this, there is a large amount of uncertainty about what Personal Information in databases[15] may be used for, in the near and distant future. As such, those who request and provide the source information surely cannot know what they are consenting to; technologies are impacting on how we apply a principle like informed consent and can alter the fabric of our political culture.

[12] Rather than framing this as in issue of informed consent, this could be equally covered by reference to patient confidentiality. The basic issue about redundancy of key concepts in medical bioethics remains the same.

[13] Tom Beauchamp and James Childress describe informed consent as typically having seven elements; competence, voluntariness, disclosure, recommendation, understanding, decision and authorisation (Beauchamp and Childress, 2001b, p. 80).

[14] This claim is perhaps controversial, as it presumes that the technologies have stable software and hardware that do not alter the information when it is accessed and remain accessible through time. Further, as I argue in Chapter 5, *semantic* information is multirealisable, so the information can change depending on its use. However, the general claim of 'non-depletion by use' stands.

[15] This is not a new concern – people working with DNA/biobanks have had to confront it (Clayton, 2005).

The impact of these technologies on informed consent and political communities displays a larger concern about simply applying standard ethical principles to broader issues arising from surveillance technologies: the basic worry is that as the traditional patient-professional relationships and political processes break down and reconfigure themselves in the face of new technology, do we simply say that the key bioethical principles[16] are now outdated? Should we simply accept that we are under state surveillance no matter where we go or what we do? Perhaps the problem is not that the principles are wrong or outdated, but in light of technological changes, a new analysis is required of these existing ethical theories.[17]

Instead of jettisoning well-developed ethical and political principles, perhaps these changes in information technologies mean that we need to rethink[18] the moral values that underpin the principles? If so, how do we actually go about doing this? A first step in the rethinking is to be clear what we are actually talking about, 'for the way we conceptualize a problem has important ramifications for law and policy' (Solove, 2004, p. 27). These changes arise not from new moral concerns, but new ways these moral concerns are encountered in response to changes brought about by surveillance technologies. As it stands, this does not clearly describe the problem. It is not simply the convergence of the technologies and not even the informational richness coming from the technological convergence. As this book will argue, essential to understanding ethics in the age of surveillance is that the new technologies afford[19] informational aggregation, which produces an emergent Virtual Identity.[20]

This is a central claim of the book and the justifications are expanded throughout Chapters 4, 5 and 6. For now, I will simply describe what I mean by 'emergent Virtual Identity' as it relates to Personal Information. As cognitive agents, we can understand aggregated and integrated Personal Information as *an* identity: a particular identity emerges from the aggregation of Personal Information. Surveillance technologies function by bringing information together, aggregating it from a host

16 I refer here to autonomy, non-maleficence, beneficence and justice, discussed in detail in (Beauchamp and Childress, 2001b).

17 Unsurprisingly, this is not the first such attempt. Take Helen Nissenbaum's description of her recent research: 'The primary mission of this book is to confront and give a moral and political account of this pileup of technologies and practices, to pinpoint and understand sources of concern and to provide a framework for expressing and justifying constraints' (Nissenbaum, 2009, p. 6). My arguments, however, differ from Nissenbaum's, discussed in Chapters 2 and 8.

18 This use of 'rethink' here is a reference to Neil Manson and Onora O'Neill's book *Rethinking Informed Consent* (Manson and O'Neill, 2007), where they argue that the model of informed consent, like that described by Beauchamp and Childress, needs to be revisited.

19 I talk more about affordances and their special significance to identity and information in Chapter 6. In anticipation of that discussion, I will simply state here that affordances, as used in this book, relate to the ways in which technologies can make certain behaviours and/or results easier or harder.

20 As mentioned in §1.5, throughout this book I develop a number of key terms and use them in reference to a particular set of meanings. Typically, unless otherwise mentioned, I will indicate this by use of capitalisation; Virtual Identity is one such term.

of different sources and integrating it into a Virtual Identity. 'In the Information Age, personal data is being combined to create a digital biography of us . . . In short, we are reconstituted in databases *as a digital person composed of data*' (Emphasis Mine, Solove, 2004, pp. 44, 49). While Daniel Solove and I differ in the terms we use,[21] we are both concerned about the same process, 'where a multitude of dots juxtaposed together form a picture, bits of information when aggregated paint a portrait of a person' (Solove, 2004, p. 44). The aggregation and integration of information about a person produces something new, a rich and detailed portrait of the person, a Virtual Identity. The time one gets out of bed, the way one walks into their kitchen, the time taken to recognise a voice on the phone, shopping habits, one's attraction to George Clooney: as independent data points they will tell little of interest about the person. But when large amounts of data are accumulated through time and these separate data streams are aggregated, a highly detailed and potentially intimate 'portrait' of this person emerges: being attracted to George Clooney was part of a profile used by Obama's re-election team (Scherer, 2012).

This Virtual Identity is not simply an aesthetic entity; it can be highly revealing about that person and/or can be used to harm the person. For instance, certain repeated behaviours may set off a series of triggers, indicating that the person is losing cognitive ability and may be developing dementia. However, once we consider aggregated and integrated Personal Information as a morally reactive Virtual Identity, the scope of the information that we ought to be concerned about expands dramatically: aggregated and integrated Personal Information suddenly becomes relevant far outside of the field of bioethics. We have now moved from discussing intimate information like that produced in a medical context to the moral importance of innocuous Personal Information like minor changes in speech patterns. And, assuming that we ought to treat like cases alike, given our concern about the intimacy of medical information, I suggest that we ought to be similarly concerned about the potential for innocuous information to be equally intimate. This concern extends into the fabric of our political culture. The revelation of state activity in the age of surveillance is an indication of just how important these Virtual Identities are – what's at stake is life and death and the core values of our liberal democracies.

1.3 VIRTUAL IDENTITY IN AN ETHICAL VACUUM?

Recognising parallels between medical information and that produced by surveillance technologies is important: if there's something morally important about medical information, then perhaps surveillance technologies produce similarly important information. And insofar as like cases should be treated alike, consistency may demand that we treat surveillance information similar to the ways we treat

[21] Solove favours 'digital person', while I favour 'Virtual Identity'. The explanation for this is given in §4.7.

medical information. Standard medical practice typically[22] assumes patient confidentiality, which means that what information the patient gives to the medical professional will be treated with due consideration and care. Two standard complementary justifications offered are a duty to respect patient autonomy and to reduce bad consequences (Beauchamp and Walters, 1994, pp. 123–130). If a medical professional wants to disclose intimate patient information to others, they ought to display respect for the patient by maintaining confidentiality until the patient has consented to disclosure: some people may simply not want intimate information about them shared.

Consequences need to be considered for two reasons. First, because 'violations of confidentiality make patients unwilling to reveal sensitive information' this reduces efficacy of diagnosis and cure and 'in the long run, [this] is detrimental to the health of patients' (Beauchamp and Walters, 1994, p. 129). The second consequential concern is the harms[23] that arise from unequal treatment or discrimination arising from disclosure of Personal Information: consider the disclosure of a person's HIV status to the public or to an employer (Beauchamp and Childress, 2001b, p. 293; Solove, 2004, pp. 66–67). In short, intimate information, like that collected in a consulting room, is treated confidentially to respect patient autonomy[24] and harmful consequences. Further to this, given the ways in which this Personal Information can be so easily transferred to the political sphere, the impacts of informational misuse can extend beyond the personal to have great weight on the political (van den Hoven, 2008). Basically, we ought to treat other Personal Information with consideration and due care.

Yet these justifications do not clearly explain why *medical* information ought to be protected. There are all sorts of Personal Information that we disclose to others on a regular basis, yet these non-medical forms of Personal Information typically don't receive anywhere near the same attention as medical information. We need a story of why *medical* information is special.[25]

[22] It should be noted that some, like Mark Siegler, see confidentiality as a fiction (Siegler, 1994).

[23] Similar to the preceding footnote, for the ease of reading, I will typically refer to 'consequences' or 'harms'. §1.5 explains that this is in reference to a common intuition about moral value, that people ought not to be harmed. A taxonomy of informational harms is given in §9.3.

[24] For ease of reading, I will typically refer to 'respect for autonomy' or just 'autonomy'. As I explain in §1.5, this is in reference to what I consider a common intuition about moral value, that people ought to be respected qua people. Issues of autonomy, basic respect and personal information are covered in §8.5.

[25] There is a considerable body of work that argues that there is some special relationship between a medical professional and a patient (Alexandra and Miller, 1996, 2009; Beauchamp and Childress, 2001b; Oakley and Cocking, 2001a, b). Perhaps this special relationship is the reason for heavy emphasis on and special treatment of, personal information in medical contexts. However, we need to explain the special nature of these relations to see if they, in fact, justify special treatment. This book explains this by looking at the sort of information that is produced in such relations.

Andrew Alexandra and Seumas Miller claim that professional confidentiality is 'derived from the notion of privacy' (Alexandra and Miller, 2009, p. 151). Which brings us to the question, *should* medical information be private?[26] As described at the end of §1.2, the aggregation of information produces a Virtual Identity. Aggregated Personal Information produces a representation of a person; this book argues that the Virtual Identity that emerges is morally relevant. Yet, following the recognition that what is important is not the 'medicalness' of the information, but its capacity to reveal the person and/or harm them, moral concerns similar to those regarding medical information could arise anywhere there is aggregation of Personal Information. And with the ubiquity of surveillance technologies, this information can be found everywhere: shopping practices, driving habits, web browser history, court records, employment information, school histories (Nissenbaum, 2009, pp. 36–50).

What makes the age of surveillance particularly challenging is that with the explosion in social media such as Facebook and Twitter, we are not simply *passively* implicated in announcing our lives to the world; many of us are *actively* involved, willingly uploading Personal Information for public digestion. Given our own complicity in this public life, is it any wonder that Facebook's co-founder Mark Zuckerberg once declared that privacy was no longer a social norm (Johnson, 2010) and that Google CEO Eric Schmidt recommended that people should just change their name if Google searches won't allow them to distance themselves from past action (Hearn, 2010)? So, though medical and surveillance information might be similarly revealing, our own willingness to make such Personal Information public might suggest that notions like informed consent, confidentiality and indeed privacy are of limited value now. What's more, by being actively involved in publicising our lives, it makes claims about the political devolve into hyperbole and paranoia. It's hard to say we are at risk of becoming a police state when we are such active participants in the surveillance.

This seems to present two options – either the past forty years of attention that ethicists paid to intimate Personal Information was foolish and there is no *moral* concern about such information, or, given the sheer range and amount of Personal Information being produced and communicated by surveillance technologies, there may be no clear way of developing a robust *ethical* theory to deal with Personal Information generally. Instead, we must deal with problems in an *ad hoc* or *post hoc* manner, by reference to what people want at a given time.

This is, however, a false dilemma. Note that 'moral' and 'ethical' can be used to relate to two different things. 'Moral' concern refers to situations where someone makes an 'ought' sort of statement that is, we *ought* to care about intimate information. Ethical theory, however, is intended to mean a robust and well-considered set of theories that explain *why* we ought to care about something, how we ought to care about something and when we ought to care about something. Though they both track to the same thing, 'how should one live' (Kagan, 1998a, p. 1), 'moral' is the

[26] Chapter 2 covers privacy issues in depth.

answer to the question, while 'ethics' is the working out of the answer.[27] This moral/ethical distinction is important to make when considering the changing understandings of Personal Information, as the claim that (a) there ought to be *no moral concern* about Personal Information is fundamentally different to the claim that (b) there is *no robust ethical theory* to deal with Personal Information. Take Facebook as a case in point: as mentioned, the CEO of the popular social networking website proclaimed in January 2010 that privacy was no longer a social norm (Johnson, 2010). Yet there was a backlash against him and Facebook and in May 2010, Facebook announced it was making it easier for users to protect information they felt was private (Arthur, 2010). And in the following years, there have been many controversies about Facebook and its respect for Personal Information (Farrell, 2015), from its research into manipulating the emotions of its users (McNeal, 2014a; McNeal, 2014b) to its involvement in state-sponsored surveillance programmes (Greenwald, 2014, pp. 108–111). These examples suggest that there *is* moral concern about how Facebook treats people's information. So, though we may not have a *moral* vacuum, there exists an *ethical* vacuum: people do care about how Personal Information should be treated, but what they lack is a robust and principled set of reasons justifying *why* Personal Information should be treated with concern. This ethical vacuum is similar to what James Moore refers to as 'policy vacuums' (Moor, 2001, 2005). I have already referred to respect for personal autonomy and consequentialism as the likely foundations of things like informed consent and confidentiality. Maybe the case of surveillance technologies is the same – we can simply apply autonomy and/or consequentialist concerns to Personal Information and we'll have sorted out our problem. However, as the next section shows, this is not so simple.

1.4 PERSONAL INFORMATION AND THE FAILURE OF SIMPLE ETHICAL THEORIES

If ethics is the explication of morality and if there is already a moral position on new technology, then what the new technology has produced is not a new sort of concern; rather, it is a gap in the existing ethical systems to deal with the new situations that technology throws at us. There may already exist ethical frameworks which we can apply to the new situations. In order to apply them, three steps must be taken to deal with the new situation: (a) identify the problem, (b) locate foundational moral principles[28] that can tell us how to deal with the problem and (c) show how the foundational principles produce pragmatic answers to these new-seeming problems.

[27] I discuss my account of a moral/ethical distinction in §1.5.

[28] By foundational moral principles, I am referring to some principle or principles that typically figure at the foundation of a moral 'ought statement'. For the purposes of this book, I assume that respect for autonomy, minimising harms and the need to treat like cases alike sit at the base of the majority of moral statements. I discuss this in §1.5. Further, I use terms like 'foundational', 'basic', 'primary' and so on interchangeably.

1.4.1 *The Problem: Breaking Information Down*

To identify the moral problems with Personal Information, let us start with a simple claim like 'good moral behaviour requires respect for other people's autonomy and limiting the bad consequences of actions'. The basic principles of autonomy and consequences are the moral foundations of ethical systems like informed consent and confidentiality, discussed earlier. The problem is that simplistic references to broad and vague terms like autonomy or consequences achieve very little.[29]

To explain this, let us grant that Personal Information is important; as Personal Information is relevant to either respect for autonomy or consequences it ought to figure in one's ethical reasoning. Even granting this premise, simply referring to autonomy or consequences does little to offer any justification as to *why* we should care about the information produced by surveillance technologies: if I buy cocoa butter, this piece of information is so morally innocuous as to be irrelevant. Looked at as a discrete data set about one single action, one can hardly think of a less interesting act than the purchase of a single item.[30] Moreover, I've likely made this purchase by choice. Simply talking about autonomy and consequentialist reasoning to Personal Information fails because ICTs break information down into small discrete units and we then reason that each discrete informational unit is irrelevant to autonomy or produces no or negligible harms. In short, discrete units of information become insignificant in any moral assessment.[31]

1.4.2 *The Problem of Involvement: Beyond Simple Autonomy Claims*

Consider the case of technology and Alzheimer's disease again: software that can analyse a person's writing patterns through time as a way of monitoring and possibly alerting one to their cognitive decline. With the rise of social media, this sort of

[29] In a similar vein, though discussing human rights, James Griffin states 'we need far more than a *list* of human rights. We need more than just their *names*. We must also know their content. But how do we decide it? And we need to know how to resolve conflicts between them' (Emphases Original, Griffin, 2008, p. 5). Like Griffin, my point is that making simple reference to 'respect' or 'negative consequences' is not, in itself, enough. I suggest that the role of ethics is to clarify, explain and justify what we mean when we refer to some autonomy violation or undesirable consequences. I explain this more in §1.5.

[30] This claim is, of course, dependent on what I'm doing – if I'm just buying typical shopping products, it is of no moral relevance. If, however, the purchase is of large amounts of fertilizer, the information gathered at this point is linked to geo-spatial and temporal metadata *and* I am subsequently in the same location and time as a bomb made from fertilizer, then the purchase information might be quite relevant. I discuss the national security issues in detail in Chapter 9. The point here is that that the single data set about a purchase, considered by itself, is of no moral concern. It is only when it is aggregated with other data that it becomes interesting.

[31] I recognise here that Nissenbaum makes the same observation (Nissenbaum, 2009, pp. 241–243). However, my account picks up where Nissenbaum leaves off. I make more of this claim in Chapter 2.

analysis may not involve any information typically recognised as private: if open to the public, a person's blog history or their activity on Twitter[32] can be accessed and analysed. Consider also a writer for a newspaper: their writings for the past thirty years may be entirely in the public domain. Their writings can be analysed and if the analysis works,[33] the writer's cognitive status can be guessed at. In both situations – call them 'Blogger' and 'Writer' – the possibility arises for a third party to guess at the cognitive status of Blogger and Writer. Further to this, the third party could foreseeably make public announcements on the cognitive status of Blogger or Writer.

Now, insofar as publicly disclosing medical records about a person's cognitive decline seems like a violation of privacy expressed as autonomy,[34] then doing similar also seems to be a violation of Blogger or Writer's autonomy: neither has asked nor consented to public disclosure of their cognitive status. So treating like cases alike would hold that the third party has indeed committed some transgression of Blogger's or Writer's autonomy. The intuition that Blogger or Writer has been wronged by the third party deserves attention.

However, to uphold such a claim, one would need to show *how* this was a transgression of the autonomy of Blogger or Writer. Second, one would need to show *why* this was a *morally* concerning transgression[35] of their autonomy. Now, if one can show how and why we ought to be concerned for a person's right to control knowledge of their cognitive status generally, one may feel the we (as the 'moral community') ought to intervene on the wronged individual's behalf.

Yet this intervention may be unwanted by Blogger or Writer and may be seen as unjustified interference, the bad end of paternalism. '[N]ot all individuals want privacy. For example, people may want their names sold to other companies' (Solove, 2004, p. 91). If people willingly and knowingly want their information shared, then it is interference in their autonomy to *prevent* this from happening.

The morally concerning transgression of autonomy can be missed if we see each instance of blogging or writing as a freely chosen action. I call this the trap of involvement – we will not likely see autonomy concerns if we look only at individual data points. The trap of referring to *simple* autonomy is that the third party can point to the fact that each individual data point about Blogger or Writer was made publically available by Blogger or Writer – they were *involved* in making it public;

[32] An interesting point on this: in early 2010, Twitter donated its archive to the U.S. Library of Congress (Stross, 2010). So individual tweets will now be recorded for the foreseeable future, offering a massive resource for analysis.

[33] Note that the concerns raised by this example are not dependent upon the software actually being able to accurately predict or diagnose a person's cognitive status. If it is publicly assumed to work as its proponents describe, the moral concerns remain.

[34] For the purposes of this example, I am assuming that many people would find the non-consensual disclosure of a person's cognitive status as a violation of a right to privacy.

[35] For instance, as Griffin writes, '[t]he decisions relevant to autonomy, the specific moral and political value that I want to explain, are decisions about the life to pursue and of course not all decisions are about that' (Griffin, 2008, p. 152).

it is obviously their choice. This allows the third party to ask: 'how have I wronged them? There is nothing especially private about a blog, a tweet, much less about an article they published in the local paper.' Further to this, the third party may continue: 'anyway, how have I compromised their autonomy? If autonomy relates to the free will and Blogger and Writer freely and willingly put their words in the public space, how have *I* transgressed their autonomy?'

Finally, with a note of contempt for well-wishing paternalists, the third party may conclude: 'and who are *you* to interfere with their wishes? If these people don't see it as a transgression, they actively put their Personal Information out there, how dare you tell them otherwise?' Joel Feinberg puts this concern eloquently:

> [W]hen manipulative techniques are used to open a person's options and thus increase his freedom on balance, but without his consent . . . [h]ere indeed a person is "manipulated into freedom," not with his own connivance, but without his knowledge, and perhaps even against his will . . . [and] insofar as we force a person against his will into a condition he did not choose, we undermine his status as a person in rightful control of his own life . . . *we nevertheless violate his autonomy if we force our better conception of his own good upon him.*
>
> (Emphasis Mine, Feinberg, 1985, pp. 67, 70)

By looking at individual data points, there appears to be no significant transgression of autonomy and in an effort to protect against such transgressions, it turns out that we may in fact be undermining Blogger or Writer's autonomy. The trap of involvement sees each discrete act, whether blogging, writing newspaper articles or buying cocoa butter, as an expression of the person's autonomy.

If, however, we focus attention at the level of aggregated Personal Information we begin to recognise *what* has happened and *why* we ought to care: it is at the level of aggregated information that the privacy of Blogger and Writer has been breached – their cognitive decline is the product of the aggregation and analysis of their public works. This call for attention to aggregated information needs a further step to track to a moral foundation – a story needs to be told *why* we ought to consider Personal Information in aggregate. We need to have a story, a set of reasons, that explains just why information needs to be considered in aggregate. This book tells the story of aggregation.

1.4.3 *The Problem of Insignificance: Beyond Simple Consequentialism*

Now, if simple autonomy cannot offer an explanation, maybe we can use consequences instead. Indeed, as Jeroen van den Hoven has pointed out, many people and cultures do not value autonomy as highly as liberal cultures typically assume (van den Hoven, 2007b, pp. 319–320). Let us instead work from the premise that Personal Information can be harmful[36] – public knowledge of Blogger's or Writer's cognitive status can cause them substantial reputational, economic and emotional

[36] A taxonomy of harms arising from personal information is given in §9.3.

harms. So, at a quick glance, consequences seem to offer a way of explaining why we ought to be concerned about Personal Information. However, like autonomy, breaking Personal Information into discrete units provides a powerful challenge to this claim of harms arising from the use of Personal Information. Simply knowing someone's blogs, tweets or newspaper articles does not seem to be harmful. In fact, this information is so innocuous that Blogger and Writer willingly placed this information into the public sphere. Social network websites display a great deal of Personal Information for anyone with an internet connection to access. So, not only does it seem like Personal Information is something that people don't worry about, perhaps it is something that they ought not worry about.

In *It Makes No Difference Whether or Not I Do It* (Glover, 1986), Jonathan Glover presents 'the argument from insignificant difference'. His basic point is that if each *individual* action or event is morally insignificant, then it would seem to follow that an assessment of the actor or the action as a whole should describe them as insignificant: what we can call 'morally innocuous'. In these situations, an individual transgression of autonomy is so innocuous that it doesn't deserve to be included in moral calculations. Looking at consequences, the difference that each individual consequence makes is insignificant, so the total consequences must also be insignificant. As before, what does it matter if someone knows that I bought cocoa butter?

Extending this line of reasoning, Derek Parfit presented underdetermination as a 'mistake in moral mathematics' (Parfit, 1987, pp. 67–86). The moral importance of a particular action is undervalued as a result of considering it independently:

> It is not enough to ask, 'Will my act harm other people?' Even if the answer is No, my act may still be wrong, because of its effects. The effects that it will have when it is considered on its own may not be its only relevant effects. I should ask, 'Will my act be one of a set of acts that will *together* harm other people?' The answer may be Yes. And the harm to others may be great. If this is so, I may be acting *very* wrongly.
>
> (Emphasis Original, Parfit, 1987, p. 86)

Rather than thinking of the insignificance of a single blog post, consider the impact that revelation of Blogger's or Writer's cognitive decline has on their life. Similarly, consider the impact of revealing to a family that their teenage daughter is sexually active and pregnant. It is only when they are aggregated do we recognise the possible consequences of such insignificant data points.

> The problems of digital dossiers do not consist merely of a series of isolated and discrete invasions or harms, but are systemic in nature, caused by a particular social or legal structure ... In isolation, a particular piece of information may not be very invasive of one's privacy. But when pieces of information are combined, they may form a detailed account of an individual. The whole may be greater than the sum of the parts.
>
> (Solove, 2004, p. 95)

As before, the problem is that if we can't offer a story of seeing *why* the data should be viewed in aggregated form, that we should be viewing the whole rather than the parts, then the piece-by-piece consequences seem to argue against the moral importance of Personal Information.

The point here is that a simple claim that consequences are important will not be persuasive: the particular consequences need to be spelled out and the way that the Personal Information ought to be conceived will need to be argued for. The following chapters put forward an argument that the relation between identity and information not only provides a way of conceiving Personal Information but also justifies why we ought to be concerned about Personal Information at an aggregated level. This exposition of the relation between identity and Personal Information lifts the discussion beyond *simple* consequentialist handwaving to present a detailed examination of what harms have occurred and how to deal with them.

To be clear, I do not want to say that autonomy or consequences are vacuous terms, unable to offer any substantive advice on what we should do and why. Rather, the claim being made here is that *simple* appeals to autonomy and/or consequences don't offer much in the way of detailed *ethical* justification. To fill the ethical vacuum opened by these new surveillance technologies and behaviours, if we are to properly attend to autonomy and/or consequentialist related concerns we need to develop a fine-grained analysis of how these terms are relevant in the age of surveillance.

1.5 ON MY METHODOLOGY AND TERMINOLOGY

How do autonomy and consequences fit into my story, what do I mean by them and why are they relevant? To explicate my approach, in this section I give a brief outline of the ways in which I am using particular terms and how I denote uses of specific terms perhaps in contravention of standard grammatical conventions.

1.5.1 *On Ethical Explanations*

The terms 'morality' and 'ethics' are often used interchangeably. Wherever possible, I keep to a convention mentioned earlier: I use 'morality' to refer to certain judgements of right and wrong and/or good and bad actions, agents, intentions and so on, whereas I use 'ethics' to denote a systemised set of explanations for why an action, agent, intention and so on is judged to be right or wrong, good or bad. For instance, I might say that burning a cat is *morally* wrong and then offer an *ethical* appraisal of that judgement by reference to a set of reasons and explanations.

On this convention, ethics is the set of reasons applied to a given state of affairs. Following Michael Smith, not just any reasons will do – rather than explaining an action,[37] ethics is concerned with reasons that *justify* why we ought to act or not act

[37] For ease of reading, I will refer to actions, acts and sometimes intentions here. However, as I have written elsewhere (Henschke, 2012), I generally intend 'action' to refer to a full set of

in a given way (Smith, 1987, p. 38, 1994, pp. 94–98). Offering a reason for acting is not enough: if it is to be judged as ethical or not, such judgement needs to be justified.

In this book, ethics refers to a systemised public justification for an action, founded on, or derived from, some moral value: an ethical justification should, at the very least, relate to some morally weighty value. Another way of putting this is that for a judgement to track properly and publicly to something moral, at the very least, it should go to something that is commonly held to be wrong or right and/or bad or good. Passing judgement on some use of particular information is not enough – an ethical explanation explicitly tied to key moral values is required for the judgement to be justified.

To give an example, consider this: 'If you round a corner and see a group of young hoodlums pour gasoline on a cat and ignite it, you do not need to *conclude* that what they are doing is wrong; you do not need to figure anything out; you can *see* that it is wrong' (Emphasis Original, Harmann, 1977, p. 4).[38] Most of us in this situation would agree that the burning of the cat is morally wrong. Yet in seeking to justify why this is wrong, we may struggle in finding or articulating our reasons. In response, I hold that there are three sorts of 'moral reasons' which are typically held to be foundational: that people[39] are due respect in virtue of them being people, that we ought to minimise/avoid people's suffering and finally, that we ought to treat like cases alike.

These three accounts are intended to track to standard ethical systems. First, in a nod to deontology, there is a set of rules about how someone ought to be treated in virtue of the fact that they are a person.[40] Clearly, what those rules are, exactly how they are expressed and if/when they can be justifiably overridden are the hard questions for a given ethical system. Second, in reference to consequentialism, unnecessary suffering should be avoided or minimised. Utilitarianism, the most obvious such decision theory, has a range of different forms and of course there are non-utilitarian consequentialist systems that count things different to/in addition to suffering and/or pleasure. Finally, equality has the 'golden rule': that we should treat like cases alike. For instance, we could ask the hoodlums if they would like to

considerations liable to ethical judgement: an agent's intention, the act itself and the purposive aim of the act.

38 I recognise here that Gilbert Harmann is making a different point about ethics and observation and how to test and confirm moral principles.

39 I use 'people' here in a deliberately open sense: depending on what counts as a person, the set of things included in what ought to be respected can be as broad or narrow as one needs. In an account like Tom Regan's (Regan, 2004), animals like cats may count; on other accounts only fully developed adult humans would count. However, in line with the approach taken here, one would have to offer some justificatory reason why something should or should not count as a person and/or for moral consideration.

40 Griffin's *On Human Rights* is one such example, whereby he locates human personhood as the foundation for human rights (Griffin, 2008).

be set on fire and then demand some explanation to show why it is justified for them to set someone else on fire.

Do we hold such foundational beliefs? My reply is to appeal to a common morality. By common morality,[41] I mean that in most situations, most people, most of the time would agree that people deserve respect,[42] that unnecessary suffering should be avoided or minimised and that we ought to treat like cases alike. Most ethical systems express moral value for people with reference to three sorts of descriptions that track to the three foundations mentioned: autonomy/liberty,[43] utility/efficiency[44] and equality/justice.[45] This book spells out the content and limits of these values as they relate to the Personal Information derived from and used by surveillance technologies.

I am not attempting to offer a complete normative theory here: to do such a thing would be to write a fundamentally different book: Instead the book will articulate how I see these different normative factors interacting, having developed the reasons why we need to consider Personal Information in aggregate, Chapters 7, 8 and 9 look to the moral relevance of such aggregated information. Second, while there is certainly significant disagreement in normative ethics about what the right thing to do is, at a practical level these disagreements may not be so important. That is, despite different foundational moral values, sophisticated ethical systems are likely to converge on many their practical conclusions.[46] This is because, in part, they acknowledge the importance of other moral values.

41 I note here that my use of 'common morality' is different to – though consonant with – that of someone like Bernard Gert (Gert, 2004; Gert, Culver and Clouser, 2006). It is different in that his account specifies a particular set of rules. However, the rules he derives come from a similar approach as to the one I advocate here. As he says 'the moral system that thoughtful people use, usually implicitly, when they make moral decisions and judgments. It is the only guide to behavior affecting others that all rational persons understand and upon which they can all agree' (Gert, 2004, p. v).

42 At the very least, most people would probably hold that they, their loved ones or those they consider important deserve respect.

43 I here mean to refer to accounts like Griffin's, in which autonomy and liberty are seen as importantly different (Griffin, 2008, pp. 142–175). Griffin's account seems to follow, in part at least, Joel Feinberg's two concepts of autonomy, *de jure* autonomy, 'the sovereign right of self-government' and *de facto* autonomy, 'the actual condition of self-government' (Feinberg, 1985, pp. 62–68). Griffin's sense of autonomy seems to track closely to Feinberg's *de jure* autonomy, while Griffin's sense of liberty seems to track to Feinberg's *de facto* autonomy. This autonomy/liberty distinction sits below some of the discussions in Chapters 2 and 7.

44 I here mean to show that 'maximising the good' can refer to things like utility, commonly expressed in some form of welfare or other good maximisation (Kagan, 1998a, pp. 25–69), but is also commonly considered in reference to efficiency, such as economic efficiency. This economic efficiency point sits below some of the discussions in Chapter 3.

45 I here mean to bring attention to practical and moral differences between simply treating like cases equally and a need to be difference-sensitive (Appiah, 1994; Gutman, 1994; Habermas, 1994; Jones, 2006; Kymlicka, 1995; Modood, 1998; Okin et al., 1999; Wolf, 1994). This point is also implicit in some of my discussions in Chapters 7 and 9.

46 This point is argued, for instance, by James Sterba: 'traditional theories of ethics, be they Aristotelian, Kantian or Millian, or whatever, have come to be revised and reformed in such a

For instance, a sophisticated deontological theory will be concerned with consequences. 'Deontological theories are defined as non-teleological ones, not as views that characterize the rightness of institutions and acts independently from their consequences. All ethical doctrines worth our attention take consequences into account in judging rightness. One which did not would simply be irrational, crazy' (Rawls, 1971, p. 30). Some deontological theories hold that in some situations if a threshold is breached, large goods/harms can justifiably take precedence over individual rights.[47]

A final note about this pluralist approach is on the nature of disagreement. In most situations, most people will agree on their moral appraisal of a situation: we typically hold that setting a cat on fire for fun is wrong. However, there is considerable, perhaps intractable,[48] disagreement on *why* such an action is wrong. That is, while there may be ethical disagreement, we can often find an overlapping consensus[49] in our conclusions. This convergence on judgements, despite highly divergent moral theories, is nicely captured by a comment from two members of the U.S. National Commission for the Protection of Human Subjects of Biomedical and Behavioral Research, Albert Johnson and Stephen Toulmin. They say that the commission usually agreed over practical conclusions and only faced '*serious differences* of opinion . . . when confronting *the reasons why* members concluded the way they did' (Emphases Mine, Jonsen and Toulmin, 1988, pp. 16–19). This book's pluralist approach aims to find a set of mutually useful justificatory reasons as to why and how we should care about Personal Information in the age of surveillance: some of the reasons may be more appealing than others, but it should be clear by the end of the book that, whatever one's moral orientation, we all ought to care about Personal Information.

1.5.2 *On Terminology*

This book introduces a number of particular terms and taxonomies. Often, the use of these terms is spelled out quite particularly as I have a specific intention in mind, denoted by the term's capitalisation. For instance, Numeric Identity, Character Identity, Group Identity, Essentialised Identity and Virtual Identity and in Chapter 5,

way that, at least in their most morally defensible formulations, they no longer differ in the practical requirements they endorse' (Sterba, 2005, p. 1).

[47] This might be considered a form of ethical exceptionalism, which certainly has problems in application: (Griffin, 2008, pp. 76–79). I talk more about when and why some exceptions to moral rules are sometimes justified in Chapters 7 and 9. For more on exceptionalism, see (Allhoff, 2012; Fiala, 2006; Marks, 2006).

[48] Rosalind Hursthouse gives a nice overview of the difference between supposed and legitimate dilemmas (Hursthouse, 1999, pp. 43–87).

[49] This reference to an overlapping consensus is a reference to Rawls, whereby a central element of the role of public reason is to find areas that we can agree upon (Rawls, 1999b, pp. 172–174, 1999a, 2001, pp. 26–37).

Thin Information and Thick Information and so on. These terms are used to pick out certain particular points and their particular use is denoted through capitalisation. A list of these words, with their intended meanings, is given in Appendix 1.

1.6 STRUCTURE

This chapter has outlined the rise of the age of surveillance and then traced a shift from a moral vacuum to an ethical vacuum and advocated the position that we value autonomy, consequences and equality. In order to develop ethical frameworks that explain the relevant foundational moral claims we need to shift from simple moral references to substantive theoretical analyses in ethics. We need a theoretically grounded way of dealing with the problems that arise from technology and Personal Information. This book provides such a theoretical framework.

At its most general, the question that the book will answer is 'are surveillance technologies changing our moral world and if so, how?' The book answers this question in a novel way by looking at the relation between identity and Personal Information. I have already shown, in part at least, that much Personal Information is currently *not* treated as morally serious. My position is that Personal Information *is*, in fact, morally serious. Simply stated, the argument of the book is this: *identity and Personal Information are linked in a strong, mutually causal relation. Given that identity is something of moral importance, we ought therefore to treat Personal Information as something also of ethical importance.* While such a claim might seem unproblematic, these new information technologies of surveillance present us with something truly novel: the capacity to collect, store, analyse and distribute information with great speed, largely free of geographic limits, often with the active participation of those who would criticise those conducting the surveillance. The book frames the problem by reference to the capacity of information technologies to produce a Virtual Identity from innocuous Personal Information.

Surveillance technologies create these ethical vacuums because they create 'morally innocuous' information. That is, Personal Information that seems either devoid of moral content or that is so minimal that an argument about its impact on rights or harms seems absurd. Yet now, because of changes in technology, such data becomes ethically important when aggregated. We now have the potential to easily use this innocuous information in ways that can infringe on people's rights, could potentially harm them and/or could lead to some unfair treatment of that individual, or an individual like them.[50] As the Target example from the start shows, these new technologies can reveal highly intimate information about people from the most innocuous of sources.

[50] These points are all expanded and explained in Chapters 7, 8 and 9.

The notion of identity here presents a novel analysis of surveillance technologies and behaviours. It builds from a specific and new normative foundation: I develop the notion of the 'Identity/Information Dyad', a concept where identity and information are in a mutually causal 'dyadic' relation. Having created this new tool, I can point to the notion of the Virtual Identity to both give reasons as to just what is wrong with the use of seemingly innocuous Personal Information and also offer ways to avoid the moral problems associated with uses of surveillance technologies. Furthermore, applying this Identity/Information Dyad to specific technologies allows us to retain many of the reasons why we might want such surveillance in the first place.

The overall topics and shape of the book are as follows. Chapter 1 frames the discussion by reference to new and converging surveillance technologies that produce Personal Information which, at first glance, seems morally innocuous: that is, posting a comment to a public website. From this I have said that we need a fine-grained ethical analysis that can give a set of principled reasons as to why we ought to care about such innocuous information. Yet perhaps this call for a fine-grained ethical analysis is premature? We are not in a moral vacuum. So perhaps there are conventions that currently exist that can regulate technology and information? This is true. Privacy and ownership present two conventions commonly codified into law, which deal in part with Personal Information. Is it possible that these two conventions can deal with the issues raised, in a way that does not necessitate a *de novo* ethical theory?

While privacy and ownership do offer a starting position, the next two chapters show that they do not do this sufficiently. Because common conceptions of privacy are typically viewed in isolation from each other, such approaches are of limited use in dealing with surveillance technologies. Exploring the case example of workplace surveillance, reasons are given why a non-reductionist account of privacy is better able to respond to access and use of innocuous Personal Information. Chapter 3's contention is that ownership's usefulness is constrained when it comes to innocuous Personal Information because the common moral foundations for ownership claims, instrumental value and intrinsic rights, cannot properly capture the value of innocuous Personal Information that is produced by surveillance technologies. Instead, I develop a foundation which ties information production to identity and presents us with a stronger conceptual and normative foundation for ownership over Personal Information.

To explain why Personal Information is a morally relevant concern, Chapter 4 develops an account of identity that focusses on the people's cognitive processing of information. I present a taxonomy of identity types and demonstrate how these identity types ultimately impact on a person's self-development and quality of life. This chapter sets a foundation for a principled analysis of new technologies by demonstrating connections between identity and the common moral foundations of basic respect and the obligation not to needlessly harm others. Chapter 5 goes on to explore philosophic approaches to information as 'data that is well ordered and meaningful'. This chapter shows how existing states of mind affect how a person constructs information. The basic argument of this chapter is to say that information is not epistemically inert: it is reactive to a person's existing beliefs and emotions.

Chapter 6 brings the discussions of identity and information together. Importantly, the claim in this chapter is that identity and information stand in a relation of mutual causation to each other, a relation I call the Identity/Information Dyad. This Identity/Information Dyad is a novel concept, allowing for a new analysis of problems of surveillance technologies.

Bringing the discussion back to ethics, Chapter 7 suggests that the Identity/Information Dyad, with its capacity to draw out the moral importance of Virtual Identities, presents a principled way of demonstrating why we should be morally concerned about the ways that surveillance technologies produce and use innocuous Personal Information. By applying the analytic tool of the Identity/Information Dyad, we can give a set of principled reasons why Personal Information is not morally innocuous. Instead, by recognising the relation between identity and information, instantiated as Virtual Identities, we can come to see just how Personal Information is relevant to discussions of basic recognition and harms. That is, why Personal Information is morally important. We follow this argument by reference to metadata, the paradigm example of information that seems morally innocuous, but as the Identity/Information Dyad shows, is in fact morally laden when aggregated and used.

Having established the moral importance of Personal Information by reference to identity, Chapter 8 then explains how we can weight that importance. It focuses on individual concerns, particularly, when an individual is a data source – when they are willing in creating and distributing this information. This chapter frames the discussion broadly in bioethics terms by focussing on the rise of wearable health technologies. Chapter 9 then presents an alternative moral foundation, to weight Personal Information by reference to the possible negative impacts on a person when they are the target of information. With reference to the political and social fall-out from the revelations by Snowden and evolving counter-terrorism surveillance methods, the discussion is framed around the roles and responsibilities of governments and the problems of weighing national security against individual liberties.

The final chapter brings the discussion full circle by making clear that the Identity/Information Dyad offers some advice on how convergent technologies should be designed to reduce the moral problems discussed. Much of the book is spent focussing on reasons to limit the production and use of Personal Information, but there is certainly a great deal of good that can be gained from such information. Chapter 10 looks at value-sensitive design in parallel with good public policy as a way of accessing those benefits whilst protecting and limiting the problems raised in previous chapters.

By giving a sustained and pluralistic ethical analysis, the aim is to convince people that innocuous information is relevant to serious moral discussion. Moreover, by linking information to common moral foundations, this approach should complement and strengthen existing arguments about human rights, harms and desserts, whilst ensuring that the benefits of such information are achieved. Ideally, the new information world we live in will evolve in a way that sidesteps and minimises the ethical concerns with surveillance technologies whilst reaping as many of the rewards of the age of surveillance as we can.

2

On Privacy

2.1 PRIVACY'S LIMITS IN AN AGE OF SURVEILLANCE

In 2012, a contractor for the US National Security Agency caused the greatest security breach in US intelligence history. Edward Snowden, distressed by government surveillance of US and international citizens, decided to go public with what he knew about the levels of state surveillance.

> My sole motive is to inform the public as to that which is done in their name and that which is done against them. The U.S. government, in conspiracy with client states, chiefest among them the Five Eyes – the United Kingdom, Canada, Australia, and New Zealand – have inflicted upon the world a system of secret, pervasive surveillance from which there is no refuge.
>
> (Greenwald, 2014, p. 23)

The amounts of information gathered by these surveillance programmes are staggering: '[B]etween 8 February and 8 March 2013, the NSA [National Security Agency] collected 124.8 billion telephone data items and 97.1 billion computer items' (Harding, 2014, p. 266). It is hard to overstate the impact of what he revealed. For those in the national security realm, it constituted the most 'massive and damaging theft of intelligence in our history' (Simeone, 2014). For those already distrusting of government overreach, it confirmed the notion that there is a global police state that has the world's populations under constant pervasive surveillance (Greenwald, 2014, pp. 174–178). For information handling companies like Google, Facebook and so on, it was a discomforting revelation of their own involvement in government surveillance, destroying their promises about privacy: 'pretty much all of Silicon Valley was involved with the NSA, Snowden said – Google, Microsoft, Facebook, even Steve Job's Apple. The NSA claimed it had 'direct access' to the tech giant's servers' (Harding, 2014, p. 11). For many citizens around the world, it was a deeply uncomfortable warning that these information technologies and our own behaviours were fodder for those who wanted to watch us. And for those interested in the notion of privacy, it showed one clear thing – the age of surveillance means the end of privacy.

This chapter begins by looking at surveillance technologies that challenge current privacy conventions: most common theoretical approaches to privacy are of limited use in the age of surveillance because they view privacy as a singular concept.[1] That is, that there is only one way to understand or value privacy. Such an approach is unable to recognise the moral weight of innocuous Personal Information. §2.3 'Privacy's Recent History' presents the recent history of privacy conceptions, looking at descriptive conceptualisations of privacy and the ways it has commonly been justified. §2.4 'Privacy Questions' argues that there are practical limits arising from understanding privacy as a singular, independent concept. §2.5 then develops a pluralistic position on privacy to advance a position that, despite the differences between them, the different conceptions need to be viewed in relation to each other. Importantly for this book, this relational approach draws out the need to recognise and elucidate the relations between common elements of all privacy discussions, which start to point out the importance of Virtual Identities. §2.6 then shows the relevance of a pluralistic account of privacy in the age of surveillance. The chapter then closes out with a demonstration of how the pluralistic approach responds to the motivating case example.

This follows from Chapter 1 by looking at how surveillance technologies impact existing conventions – in this case, privacy. The next chapter follows a similar pattern by looking at how new technologies challenge existing conceptions of ownership, again showing that there is an important relation between identity and information. The later chapters then attend to this relation and its moral importance.

2.2 SURVEILLANCE AND PRIVACY IN PUBLIC: THE CASE OF KATE AND KARL

Consider this scenario: Kate is at work one day, having a particularly bad day. Nothing seems to be going right. In desperation, she starts swearing at her computer, hitting the keys and generally expressing her frustration. Like any good manager, her

[1] Concept and conception are used in this chapter to make a distinction between how we understand the notion of privacy and what content that notion takes. At the level of concept, I consider that we can understand privacy in three ways – as a singular monistic thing, as plural but independent ideas, or as plural and interacting ideas. At the level of conception, this is the content of what one takes privacy to be. Secrecy, intimacy, information control and so on. If one takes privacy to be a singular concept, then one might hold that privacy is secrecy and secrecy alone. However, if one takes privacy to be a plural but independent concept, then one might hold that privacy is secrecy or intimacy. Finally, if one takes privacy to be a plural and interacting concept, then one might hold that privacy is secrecy and intimacy in relation to each other. The chapter will argue that privacy is best understood as a plural and interactive concept.

supervisor recognises that Kate is struggling and approaches her: 'Hey Kate. I couldn't help but notice your behaviour and can see that you're having a bad day. How about I shift you off this project onto something a little more enjoyable?' Kate nods despairingly and thanks the supervisor for their concern. Now imagine this: Karl is at work one day, having a particularly bad day. Like Kate, he abuses his computer, pounding away at the keys, generally expressing his bad state of mind. Instead of a supervisor coming over to talk to him, however, a friendly virtual office assistant pops up on Karl's computer screen: 'Hey Karl. I couldn't help but notice your behaviour and can see that you're having a bad day. How about I shift you off this project onto something a little more enjoyable?' Karl nods despairingly and thanks the computer for its concern. In Karl's situation, rather than a supervisor recognising and attending to his distress, these tasks are done automatically by computer software. What I have described is an automated response triggered by workplace surveillance software. Workplace surveillance software refers to a cluster of related technologies designed specifically for the purposes of 'watching, listening to, or recording of an individual's activities' (Solove, 2008, p. 104). In Karl's situation, the surveillance technology is 'keylogging software,' which utilises data analysis to assess people via their typing patterns. As recent articles show (Lohr, 2014), Joseph Kizza and Jackline Ssanyu are correct (Kizza and Ssanyu, 2005, pp. 1–18) in their prediction of such technologies being integrated into many workplaces.

In his book *The Numerati*, Steven Baker sees workplace surveillance like keylogging software as problematic:

> At work, perhaps more than anywhere else, we are in danger of becoming data serfs – slaves to the information we produce. Every keystroke at the office can now be recorded and mathematically analyzed. We don't own them ... From [this surveillance, employers] can draw powerful conclusions about our productivity, our happiness at work, and our relations with colleagues ... Microsoft even filed in 2006 to patent a technology to monitor the heart rate, blood pressure, galvanic skin response, and facial expressions of office workers. The idea, according to the application, is that managers would receive alerts if workers were experiencing heightened frustration or stress. Such systems are in early stages of research. But even with today's technology, if your company is not scouring the patterns of your behavior at the keyboard, it's only because it doesn't choose to – or hasn't got around to it yet.
>
> (Baker, 2007, pp. 18–19)

Data serfs, under the watchful eye of a capitalist Big Brother. Is Baker overstating the need for moral concern about these new technologies or is there something more substantial occurring, some serious privacy violations which we ought to be concerned about?

Baker's concerns seem dependent on whether there is some relevant moral difference between cases like Kate and Karl. §1.5 mentioned that we should treat like-cases alike and at first blush, both examples seem morally innocuous, displaying good management even: a supervisor is actually recognising the emotional state of their workers and is taking enough interest to do something about it. Yet in the second case, perhaps there is something amiss. While we would generally allow, if not expect, a supervisor to take an interest in their worker's emotional states, having a computer monitor and respond might represent a privacy violation. But, if claims like Baker's are to have any substance, we require a more detailed moral analysis of how Kate's and Karl's cases differ. As per the idea of ethics being a systemised account of just what is wrong and why we ought to be concerned, we must understand what factors are involved, which factors are morally relevant and why they ought to concern us. What is morally different between Kate and Karl and why we should care?

Looking closely at the keylogging software, as a workplace surveillance technology, we see that it is used in order to produce two kinds of valuable information about workers. It is a type of biometric technology[2] which assesses an individual's behaviours. By analysis of an individual's keystroke patterns, it is claimed to do one or both of the following tasks:

(1) Identify the particular worker and/or;
(2) Identify the emotional state of the worker.

Claim (1): *Identify the particular worker*. This claim holds that each person produces a unique signature with their keystroke patterns. In this instance, keylogging software is claimed to be able to identify individuals and produce what we may call a 'personnel identity'.[3] For example, Ahmed Awad E Ahmed and Issa Traore,[4]

> [p]resent a keystroke recognition scheme based on free text detection that goes beyond the traditional approach of using keystroke dynamics for authentication or employee performance evaluation, and consider using such information for dynamic user profiling. The generated profiles can be used to identify reliably perpetrators in the event of security breach. By observing, recording and checking

[2] Biometric technologies involve 'the collection with a sensoring device of digital representations of physiological features unique to an individual ... and may also involve typical behavioral patterns' (van der Ploeg, 1999, p. 295).

[3] This is a slight play on words here, as the specific identity concept that Claim (1) tracks to is concerned with numeric/personal identity. This is a different identity concept from character identity, which figures in Claim (2). The term 'personnel identity' seems to fit both the workplace context and the philosophic concepts of numeric/personal identity. I describe and discuss numeric/personal identity in §4.5.

[4] This example provided by Ahmed and Traore is a case of 'free text identification.' That is, the person typing can be identified without the need for them to type a particular word or phrase. Free text identification relies on the 'ability to enroll a user using a non-predefined set of data. This allows both monitoring the user on the fly and non-intrusively by totally hiding the detection process from the user' (Vizer, Zhou and Sears, 2009). The point here is that, given an existing database of known user keylogging patterns, new possibly unauthorised users can be identified by the text they type.

> an individual worker's keystroke patterns against an existing database of employee records to confirm a worker's identity.
>
> (Ahmed and Traore, 2008)

Claim (2): *Identify the emotional state of the worker*. Claim (2) runs on the premise that surveillance technologies will be used in workplaces to identify the worker's emotional state via their behaviour. Generally, these surveillance technologies can identify emotional states either by physical or behavioural means. Physical measurement involves monitoring the worker's physical state: changes in blood pressure, heart rate and so on can indicate a different emotional state of the worker. A patent submitted by the Microsoft Corporation, mentioned by Baker (Baker, 2007, p. 19), details one such set of biological measurements:

> [A] help request can be triggered in at least two different ways: implicitly or explicitly. When a parameter is violated or a threshold is satisfied or exceeded, the system can automatically initiate the help request in order to identify the target activity and target user and determine the type or source of assistance most suitable for Joe and his activity. Parameters or thresholds can relate to the particular activity, to the user's physical state, or to the user's environment. For example, sensors can monitor the user's heart rate, blood pressure, body temperature, galvanic skin response, EMG, brain signals, respiration rate, movement, facial movements, facial expressions, etc.
>
> (Macbeth et al., 2006)

Direct measurements are likely to be intrusive, cumbersome and most probably unpopular amongst employees.

Non-invasive behavioural measurements seem more practical for application in the workplace. Surveillance technologies can monitor a person's eyes in order to make assumptions about their emotional state.[5] Another method is keylogging software. Lisa Vizer, Lina Zhou and Andrew Sears describe their research, which uses keystroke patterns to assess stress in elderly patients:

> [T]he use of a combination of timing, keystroke, and linguistic features to detect stress and possibly assess cognitive and physical function . . . This research explores the detection of cognitive and physical stress with the ultimate goal of continuous monitoring of keyboard interactions to detect acute or gradual changes in cognitive and physical function. The primary contribution of this research is to highlight the potential of leveraging everyday computer interactions to detect the presence of cognitive and physical stress.
>
> (Vizer, Zhou and Sears, 2009)

[5] 'According to one synergistic embodiment of the invention, the emotional response information can be detected based, at least in part, on the subject's eye properties (e.g. eye movement, blink rate, pupil dilation and or other eye properties). Advantageously, this enables (if desired) the same eye tracking device that is used to collect visual attention data to collect emotional response data' (Lemos, 2007).

In terms of workplace surveillance, my focus will be on non-invasive behavioural technology like keylogging software. There are two reasons for this. First, assuming that it works as described,[6] it is the least intrusive, can be retrofitted and activated by installing the software on a computer. Second, at first glance, it seems to pose the least moral concern. Ahmed and Traore state that '[b]y collecting only user keystroke dynamics instead of actual keystrokes data, our technique *limit[s] the amount of personal information gathered*. This protects to some extent the privacy of the monitored individuals, compared with existing surveillance technologies' (Emphasis Mine, Ahmed and Traore, 2008).

Their point has some merit. Compared to monitoring an employee's heart rate, keystroke dynamics are not physically invasive and so seem to be far less of a privacy concern. If we can identify a moral basis for concern with a non-invasive technology that only attends to behaviours not typically seen as private, where the privacy concerns seem fairly limited like keylogging software, more invasive cases would raise similar and likely stronger concerns.

Having described the keylogging software technology, we are now in a better position to begin assessing the two cases. Does Karl's case hold any aspects relevant to privacy not found in Kate's? The first response is to say that there is some relevant difference – the technology in Karl's situation has violated his privacy and done so in a way that Kate's supervisor hasn't. However, given the apparent similarity between Kate's and Karl's situations, something needs to be said to justify the assertion of a privacy invasion: if Karl's privacy has been violated, it has not occurred in an immediately obvious manner. Like the concerns raised in §1.4, a simple appeal to privacy will not suffice – Karl is at work, on work property, producing work and surrounded by workmates. A standard response to a claim of privacy invasion is to call attention to the facts that Karl is in public, doing mundane activities, such that an expectation of privacy is unreasonable. Privacy 'does not assert a right never to be seen, even in a workplace'.[7] In short, privacy claims made in relation to public spaces are just plain wrong.

This response points to two things. First, this response relies on privacy to be understood with respect to a distinction between private and public, to be discussed in §2.3.2. Second, that technology can change our expectations of what counts as private. Where employees of many different industries once had a measure of workplace privacy – out of the boss' line of sight typically meant a greater scope for employee

[6] For the purpose of this chapter, I am going to presume that this keylogging software actually meets both claims – that it can reliably and accurately produce a personnel identity for a given employee and that it does actually reliably and accurately correlate with the worker's emotional state. If it turns out that this software does not meet the stated expectations, I believe that the arguments put forward in this chapter about keylogging software remain relevant to the general discussions of privacy.

[7] This is a deliberate paraphrasing of Jeffrey Reiman's claim that privacy 'does not assert a right never to be seen even on a crowded street' (Reiman, 1976, p. 44). I mention more about Reiman's approach to privacy later in this chapter.

privacy – technologies now observe and report back on all forms of work: keylogging software tracks an employee at the desk, smart cards monitor and limit an employee's movements while at work (Want, 2006) and Global Positioning Systems (GPS) track company cars (Wang et al., 2008) outside of the office. This trend is continuing: the 2007 report from the American Management Association states that '45% of employers [tracked] content, keystrokes and time spent at the keyboard ... and ... 43% store[d] and review[d] computer files' (Association 17 November 2014).

This expansion of technology into areas and practices once assumed to be private goes much farther than the workplace. In many countries, Closed-Circuit Television (CCTV) Cameras dot[8] the public landscape (Norris and McCahill, 2006), clothes have been released that contain Radio Frequency Identification Devices (RFIDs) (Beres, 2015). Further to this, as mentioned in the opening chapter, many people around the world are willing participants in this – whether at work, home or driving, many people wilfully and happily post Personal Information to publicly accessible internet and social networking sites. Anywhere there is internet or mobile phone access is now a potential public space. And anytime you're online or on the phone, you're now potentially under surveillance by a government agency such as the UK Government Communication Headquarters (GCHQ) or the US National Security Agency (NSA) (Greenwald, 2014, pp. 90–170).

Given these trends, the need to compare Kate's and Karl's cases seems even more important to resolve: if there is nothing of moral relevance between them, then we have little reason to be concerned about the rise of other surveillance technologies. However, if there is something morally relevant between Kate's and Karl's cases, then perhaps other non-invasive surveillance technologies are also involved in morally substantive privacy invasions. If we can locate something morally problematic about non-invasive workplace surveillance technologies, then this distinctive feature can help us understand if there's something to be morally concerned about with regard to surveillance technologies more generally.

2.3 PRIVACY'S RECENT HISTORY

Following from Chapter 1, the focus is on how surveillance technologies challenge our understanding and valuation of privacy. This technological challenge is central to current discussions of privacy and requires not only ethical analysis, but one that

[8] While London is often referred to in relation to CCTV cameras, it is important to note that the numbers of CCTV cameras and the number of times one is captured on them have been challenged. Clive Norris and Michael McCahill estimated that there was about one CCTV camera for every fourteen Londoners, (Norris and McCahill, 2006, p. 101), amounting to a possibility of being captured by a CCTV Camera 300 times a day, statistics which have received much coverage in popular and academic literature. More recently, however, these statistics, particularly the '300 times a day' have been challenged by David Aaronovitch (Aaronovitch, 2009). That said, the human factors and limits of CCTV surveillance add levels of complexity to the reality of how CCTV surveillance operates in practice (Smith, 2015).

is concerned with technology and history. For instance, consider that we conceive of privacy as something secret, necessarily kept out of the public sphere. Given that so many people willingly and consensually[9] put details of their lives online, it seems to indicate either that the given information is not private, or that privacy itself is no longer important.[10] Why is this? Perhaps people simply no longer care about privacy: Facebook's Mark Zuckerberg has said that privacy is no longer a social norm[11] (Johnson, 2010). On a more extreme analysis, it may no longer be possible to expect privacy: in 2010, Google's CEO, Eric Schmidt,[12] suggested that we shouldn't even entertain the thought of keeping our past private and if we don't like what Google tells the world about us, our best response is to change our name and move our house (Hearn, 2010). Facebook shows us that we don't really care about privacy and Google tells us we can't do anything even if we did care. And, lest we forget, Snowden has shown us that governments are using information technologies, exploiting our behaviours, to engage in surveillance at a level unprecedented in human history. Has technology killed privacy?

2.3.1 *Privacy and Surveillance Technology*

Before we consider privacy a dead concept, we can learn some interesting things about the recent history of privacy. The seminal paper *The Right to Privacy*, written by Samuel Warren and Louis Brandeis in 1890, was written *in response* to new technologies: in the late nineteenth century, cameras had become portable, could take photographs practically in an instant and could be used by almost anyone who could afford one. Foreshadowing current debates about the explosion of surveillance technologies more than a century later, Warren and Brandeis were concerned about the ways that the new technologies were invading personal space. They wrote their article in response to the wrongs allowed by the development of photographic technologies that 'rendered it possible to take pictures surreptitiously' (Warren and Brandeis, 1890, p. 211). This 'new technology made it important to explicitly and

[9] The claim that people consensually put their information online is contestable, (Solove, 2004, pp. 82–85). However, the point is that the information is treated *as if* people had given informed consent when putting their information online.

[10] This could indicate a case of revealed preferences: despite saying that privacy is important, people reveal their true preferences when they show that they are happy to trade Personal Information for some benefit, a claim strongly rejected by Daniel Solove (Solove, 2004, pp. 80–81).

[11] 'Norm' here is deliberately ambiguous, in that Mark Zuckerberg's use is in reference to a popular convention, that is, it is normal that people *act like* they don't care about privacy anymore. His use also implies that this *is* a social norm, that is, people *don't* actually care about privacy anymore.

[12] Eric Schmidt's stance seems to be one of 'technological fatalism' – this technology and the changes it brings are happening regardless of what you want and we can do nothing to resist it. Such fatalism about technology, I suggest, is problematic. Chapter 10 explores some ways we can use technological design to limit the problems caused by these technologies.

separately recognize this protection under the name of privacy' (DeCew, 2006). The relevant points here are that technology and privacy have, at least for the past century, had a close relationship and that technological changes do not necessarily mean the death of privacy. Indeed, in Western tradition, a right to privacy was actually conceived as a *response* to technological change. This chapter's purpose is to rethink privacy such that we do not discard it wholesale in the face of modern technologies.

In order to determine whether privacy is a redundant concept, we need to understand what we mean when we refer to privacy. The following two sections look at different ways that people have sought to conceptualise privacy: by describing what it does and/or justifying its moral importance.

2.3.2 *Privacy Described*

This section summarises five common ways that people have conceptualised privacy in privacy literature: as a right, as something secret, as a space, as control over information and as a realm free of government intrusion. These concepts cluster together as they track to ways in which people *describe* privacy; they seek to answer the question of 'what counts as private?' In contrast, §2.3.3 explores privacy by reference to its *justifications*. That is, the concepts in §2.3.3 seek to answer the question of 'why *should* X be considered private?'

In recent Western tradition, privacy is often said to have crystallised as a singular concept (DeCew, 2006) following the 1890 publication of Warren and Brandeis' seminal article *The Right to Privacy* (Warren and Brandeis, 1890). 'What Warren and Brandeis achieved was nothing short of magnificent. By pulling together various isolated strands of the common law, the authors demonstrated that creating remedies for privacy invasions wouldn't radically change the law but would merely be an expansion of what was already germinating' (Solove, 2004, p. 58).

This first shows that there was already a moral position on privacy within US society, even if it had not been coherently organised in a specific legal sense – there was a moral position but an ethical vacuum, or at least a legal vacuum. Second, it shows that Warren and Brandeis' account was powerful, as it presented a case for privacy to be seen as a singular and individualised right.

Sidestepping the need to enter a detailed description of what a right is,[13] or why privacy *itself* is a right (justifications are offered in §2.3.3), describing privacy as a right captures its importance and gives a recognisable point of reference to grasp onto. This is not to say that merely asserting something as a right makes it so,[14] rather that the description of privacy as a right had a practical force, then as now.

[13] Rights are covered in §3.3 and throughout Chapter 8.

[14] Unless you are a legislature, or perhaps a court, with the authority to create or recognise legal rights.

On top of its historical significance, Warren and Brandeis' article is important as it identified the individual as the locus of moral concern for privacy. It did this through reference to an *individual's* right to privacy, in particular 'the enforcement of the more general right of the individual to be let alone' (Warren and Brandeis, 1890, p. 205).[15] In the article, they make clear that the individual was the focus of moral concern: 'the protection of society must come mainly through *a recognition of the rights of the individual*' (Emphasis Mine, Warren and Brandeis, 1890, pp. 219–220). Following Warren and Brandeis, the individual took centre stage in privacy discussions, at least in places[16] where an individualist approach was well received.

A second point which developed, in part at least, from Warren and Brandeis[17] is that it sets up a distinction between the public and the private.[18] Privacy has been an important concept in human relations probably as long as there have been human relations. In some form or another, privacy traverses the temporal and cultural spaces of human society.[19] That said, certain Western conceptions of privacy can trace their lineage back to ancient Greek thought,[20] particularly the idea of privacy

[15] This formulation is in line with a more general right to liberty as non-interference. The relevant aspect here is that the non-interference comes from the recognition of privacy. This leaves the justifications for why something would count as private unexplored. Common justifications are explored later in this section.

[16] As noted by van den Hoven (van den Hoven, 2007b), this individualist focus limits the application of privacy in places with a more communitarian emphasis.

[17] This is perhaps most evident in Warren and Brandeis' account when they say '[t]he right to privacy ceases upon the publication of the facts by the individual, or with his consent' (Warren and Brandeis, 1890, p. 218).

[18] The public/private distinction has been criticized for a host of reasons. For instance, where exactly does one draw such a division? Mirroring the polis/oikos division, as Patricia Meyer Spacks notes, this public/private divide is often confused with a public/domestic divide:
'[P]rivacy can ally itself with the "public" side of the public/private dichotomy by its frequent opposition to the domestic ... The debate about private versus public of course bears on privacy, but the "private life" does not necessarily entail privacy ... Discussions of "private" versus "public" characteristically concern the operations of the state, the relation between members of the state in their communal and their individual functioning. The subject of privacy, in contrast, especially if considered historically, often demands focus on the ways people expose and guard themselves in relation to limited numbers of others' (Spacks, 2003, pp. 1, 4). Catherine MacKinnon captures the sentiment well: '[T]his right of privacy is a right men 'to be let alone' to oppress women one at a time ... It keeps some men out of the bedrooms of other men' (MacKinnon, 1987, pp. 101–102). I cannot do justice to this field of discussion, as it is extremely broad and detailed, covering various fields of philosophy from multiculturalism, post-modernism and feminist thought to name a few. Chapters 8 and 9 of the Second Edition of Will Kymlicka's *Contemporary Political Philosophy* provide an initial overview (Kymlicka, 2002). Anita Allen's *Uneasy Access* and Patricia Meyer Spacks' *Privacy* then enter into detailed analysis of privacy as criticised by different views in feminist philosophy (Allen, 1988; Spacks, 2003).

[19] Unsurprisingly, there are many different cultural and historical approaches to privacy, from Chinese (McDougall and Hansson, 2002), Islamic (El Guindi, 1999) and Greek/Christian trends in Europe (Moore, 1984).

[20] The use of the terms 'public' and 'private' in Athenian culture are discussed in detail by Barrington Moore (Moore, 1984).

as a binary conception, to be understood in relation to the non-private. The ancient Greeks made reference to a distinction between political and domestic life, the *polis* and *oikos* and also between what is one's own and what is communal, the *idion* and *koinon* (Arendt, 1958, p. 24).

What we now have as a common binary conception is the public/private distinction. This rests upon 'the secrecy paradigm', under which 'privacy is tantamount to complete secrecy and a privacy violation occurs when concealed data is revealed to others' (Solove, 2008, pp. 21–24, 111). The relation between the public/private divide and the secrecy paradigm is that what is private is, by definition, not public. Likewise, if a secret becomes public knowledge, it is no longer private. Under the secrecy paradigm, 'when others know the information, it is no longer completely secret' (Solove, 2008, p. 139). The examples of Blogger and Writer discussed in §1.4 speak directly to this: if something is made public, it is no longer secret. Further, if a person willingly publicises something it them seems strange for them to claim that people ought to respect their privacy on that matter.

The public/private distinction then affords[21] another conception of privacy as a space, or boundary.[22] Privacy 'is a set of boundaries we create between ourselves and others' and '[p]rotecting privacy involves reducing the extent to which individuals, institutions and the government can *encroach* on people's lives' (Emphasis Mine, Solove, 2008, pp. 74, 93). Julie Inness states that 'control-based definitions of privacy function by giving the individual control over a *certain area* of her own life, in other words, they give the individual *a specified realm of autonomy*' and later '[w]e have every reason to embrace the idea that privacy provides people with *control over some area or areas* of their lives' (Emphases Mine, Inness, 1992, pp. 47, 53).[23]

Think also of the language used when referring to the loss of privacy. Perhaps one of the most frequently used terms is a 'privacy violation'. In her article *The Right to*

[21] Nissenbaum makes a stronger point that the public/private distinction has guided privacy discussions into conceptualising privacy as a 'dichotomy of spaces' (Nissenbaum, 2009, p. 94).

[22] Joel Feinberg states that '[d]escriptions of the right [to privacy] vary from case to case, but one common element it seems to share with "personal sovereignty" is the notion that there is a *domain* in which the individual's own choice must reign supreme' (Emphasis Mine, Feinberg, 1985, p. 87). Thomas Scanlon states 'that these [privacy] rights have a common foundation in the special interests that we have in being able to be free from certain kinds of intrusions' (Scanlon, 1975, p. 29). Jeffrey Reiman: '[i]t is sufficient that I can control whether and by whom my body is experienced in some significant places and that I have the real possibility of repairing to those places' (Reiman, 1976, p. 44). James Rachels states 'if we are able to control the relationships that we have with other people, we must have control over who has *access* to us' (Emphasis Mine, Rachels, 1975, p. 331). Finally, W. A. Parent states that a person 'may not be concerned that a few close friends, relatives or professional associates know these [personal] facts, but they would be very much concerned if the information passed beyond this limited circle' (Parent, 1983, p. 270). The boundaries conception is found in the reference to Parent's 'limited circle'.

[23] Note that in the original source, the author had different emphases: 'control-based definitions of privacy function by giving the *individual* control over a certain area of *her own* life, in other words, they give the individual a specified realm of autonomy' (Inness, 1992, p. 47).

Privacy, Judith Jarvis Thomson uses violation, or some cognate, 116 times, in a 21-page paper: on average more than 5.5 times per page (Thomson, 1975). Other terms frequently used are a 'privacy breach', an 'invasion of privacy' or a 'privacy transgression'. The frequent references to boundaries, zones, spheres, regions, territories of privacy and the corresponding references to invasion, transgression, breach and violations of privacy, suggest that boundaries are a common way of describing privacy or its loss.

Describing privacy as a space or bounded zone may refer to physical space, or a non-physical space, like an informational space, prompting a description of privacy as information and its control. Alan Westin states that '[p]rivacy is the claim of individuals, groups, or institutions to determine for themselves when, how and to what extent information about them is communicated to others' (Westin, 1967, p. 7). Others[24] offer varying conceptions of privacy as control over Personal Information. On these accounts, privacy is seen as the recognition that an individual has some legitimate claim to control their Personal Information. That is, speaking of privacy recognises that a person can and should control their Personal Information.

A final point in favour of describing some types of privacy as information control, raised by van den Hoven, seems to receive little coverage in privacy discussions: the right to be let alone from *other people's* information:

> When a man who enters an almost empty restaurant picks the table next to me, there are several things I may object to. First, I may not all be concerned with *my* personal data, but rather with *his* personal data. I may in other words not be concerned with what this person is learning about *me*, but with what I am learning about *him*.
>
> (Emphases Original, van den Hoven, 2008, p. 306)

While van den Hoven's focus is on other privacy concerns, see §2.5.3, his example further shows the centrality of information in privacy: we may not only seek to keep our information private, but to also keep other's information out of our personal space.

A final way that privacy is described is an extension of the conception of privacy as keeping others out of our space. Rather than, or perhaps in addition to, simply being the idea of control over personal space, this last descriptive conception takes it that privacy is the realm where one specific actor cannot enter. That actor being 'the government'. When thinking of it in this explicitly political sense, privacy is seen as the opposite to government intrusion: the private describes that zone that the

[24] Solove quotes Arthur Miller 'the basic attribute of an effective right to privacy is the individual's ability to control the circulation of information relating to him', Charles Fried 'rather it [privacy] is the *control* we have over information about ourselves' and US President Clinton's Information Infrastructure Task Force: 'an individual's claim to control the terms under which personal information – information identifiable to the individual – is acquired, disclosed and used' (Emphasis Solove, Solove, 2008, p. 24).

government is not permitted to interfere in. 'Protecting privacy involves reducing the extent to which individuals, institutions and the government can encroach on people's lives' (Solove, 2008, p. 93). A person's home, for example, is private. And whatever happens there is none of the government's business – 'abnormal' sexual activity, drug use, religious or political gatherings. Insofar as they occur behind closed doors, they occur in a zone or space that is sheltered from government scrutiny.

These examples show there is some overlap between descriptive approaches: privacy describes some space – physical or informational – in which an individual is typically recognised as having a claim to exclude others, such as the government. The descriptive accounts, however, miss something important. In order to answer 'does X count as private', we may need to ask '*why* does X count as private'. Why should government be stopped from observing what a person does behind closed doors? This point is mirrored by Luciano Floridi:[25] 'A theory of informational privacy needs a criterion of discrimination to be able to explain why some information processes do *not* count as violations of privacy' (Emphasis Original, Floridi, 2006, p. 116). Further to this, Helen Nissenbaum notes that 'there are virtually no uses of privacy with a purely descriptive meaning, one should assume that the normative intent is integrated into its core meaning' (Nissenbaum, 2009, p. 69).

2.3.3 *Privacy Justified*

The common element in the following set of privacy conceptions is that they all seek to understand privacy by reference to some morally distinctive relevant feature. That is, they conceptualise privacy by the ways it is justified – this might be because privacy is essential for democratic freedom, for the development of personhood or because of the importance of intimacy.

Picking up from the 'privacy is the space free from government' conception, one set of justificatory conceptions is that privacy can be understood through the explanations that it is either a necessity for liberal democracies or, without it, people's behaviours and their beliefs are 'chilled' by the fear of government reprisals. On the necessity for democracy, justification argues that 'the political role of privacy is not a matter of empirical contingency but has the status of a necessity. Moving beyond the arguments that present privacy as facilitating forms of political participation and increasing the effectiveness of the decision-making process ... privacy [is] constitutive of the liberal

[25] Luciano Floridi develops an account that is wholly focused on describing privacy in relation to information. His account is derived from the 'thesis that the minimal condition of possibility of an entity's least intrinsic value is to be identified with its ontological status as an information object' (Floridi, 2002, p. 287). Floridi's account is an extreme approach whereby an informational analysis not only changes what privacy means, but 're-ontologises' the agent themselves (Floridi, 2005b, pp. 188–189) and changes the very conception of privacy and agents into informational notions. Given that his approach sits at the margins of privacy discussions, I instead focus on Floridi's philosophy of information in detail through Chapter 5.

model of political legitimacy ... privacy is implicated in the idea of public justification that liberals place at the core of legitimate political order' (Mokrosinska, 2014, p. 375).

Parallel is the chilling justification: if we know or think that we are being watched, our behaviours will change. While this may be good – knowledge of surveillance in bathrooms is shown to increase the likelihood of handwashing (Greenwald, 2014, p. 180) – such changes can be detrimental to political freedom. If I know the government is likely to be watching me, then I am less likely to engage in behaviours that might be seen by the government as contrary to their interests. 'Merely organizing movements of dissent becomes difficult when the government is watching everything the people are doing' (Greenwald, 2014, p. 177). In short, the idea of widespread government behaviour 'chills' free political behaviour and association.

Such chilling is perhaps concerning not simply because of its chilling effects on political culture: it is not just that a police state chills certain political behaviours; it destroys political culture as it chills a person's freedom of beliefs. And it is this negative impact on personal development that is of moral concern. Jeffrey Reiman concludes *Privacy, Intimacy and Personhood* with:

> [t]he right to privacy, then, protects the individual's interest in becoming, being, and remaining a person. It is thus a right which *all* human individuals possess-even those in solitary confinement. It does not assert a right never to be seen even on a crowded street. It is sufficient that I can control whether and by whom my body is experienced in some significant places and that I have the real possibility of repairing to those places. It is a right which protects my capacity to enter into intimate relations, not because it protects my reserve of generally withheld information, but because it enables me to make the commitment that underlies caring as *my* commitment uniquely conveyed by *my* thoughts and witnessed by *my* actions.
>
> (Emphases Original, Reiman, 1976, p. 44)

Privacy is seen as a right, justified by reference to agency and choice over intimate decisions.[26] Reiman argues these are necessary for personhood. On a strong reading, insofar as a society is to respect agents' capacity to develop and maintain personhood, society *must* respect privacy. Other authors[27] also recognise a link between personhood and privacy. What personhood means is a vague term; for some,[28] this may be a problem.

26 I note here that Griffin's account of privacy is relevantly similar to the role that 'central' decisions play in his account of human rights generally and privacy in particular (Griffin, 2008, pp. 152, 225 – 241).

27 Solove lists Warren and Brandeis' reference to 'inviolate personality', Paul Freund, Edward Bloustein, Stanley Benn as well as a number of decisions in the U.S. Supreme Court which cite personhood in privacy cases *Griswold v. Connecticut*, *Einstadt v. Baird* and *Roe v. Wade*, where privacy is founded in personhood, understood as the right of an agent to choose (Solove, 2008, pp. 29–31).

28 As Solove states '[t]heories of privacy as personhood, however, fail to elucidate what privacy is, *because they often to do not articulate an adequate definition of personhood*' (Emphasis Mine,

An excerpt from Anna Funder's book *Stasiland* on the former East Germany's state surveillance illustrates this point of privacy being necessary for personhood:

> 'At the time, I criticised other things – not being allowed to study or have a career. But looking back on it, it's the total surveillance that damaged me the worst. I *know* how far people will transgress over your boundaries – until you have no private sphere left at all. And I think that is a terrible knowledge to have.' She flicks her hair as if to get rid of something. 'At this distance, I understand for the first time what he did to me in that room . . . It was the loss of everything until I had disappeared too'.
>
> (Emphasis Original, Funder, 2002, pp. 113, 115)

Repeated minor transgressions into personal space can be as damaging as and maybe more damaging than a single major breach in privacy. 'Each particular instance of [data] collection is often small and innocuous; the danger is created by the aggregation of information' (Solove, 2004, p. 59). While Solove cashes out the problem here in terms of harms, it mustn't be overlooked that, like the *Stasiland* example, there is something about multiple small privacy breaches that threatens and undermines the person *qua* person. For example, James Griffin holds that for most of us, most of the time, privacy is an empirical necessity[29] for human development: 'Without privacy, autonomy is threatened . . . It takes rare strength to swim against strong social currents . . . The richness of personal relations depends upon our emerging from our shells, but few of us would risk emerging without privacy' (Griffin, 2008, pp. 225–226).

Privacy-as-intimacy is a conception that holds that it is not the particular content of something that determines its privacy; rather it is the relation between the private thing and the person. As a way of making it distinct from individual development, intimacy is interpersonal. 'This theory appropriately realises that privacy is essential not just for individual self-creation, but also for human relationships' (Solove, 2008, p. 34). This idea developed in the mid-1970s, when privacy was dependent upon intimate relationships between people:

> [T]he revealing of personal information takes on significance. The more one knows about the other, the more one is able to understand how the other experiences things . . . The revealing of personal information then is not what constitutes or powers the intimacy. Rather, it deepens and fills out, invites and nurtures, the caring that powers the intimacy . . . it is of little importance who has access to personal information about me. What matters is who cares about it and to whom I care to reveal it.
>
> (Reiman, 1976, p. 34)

Solove, 2008, p. 31). Note that Solove's argument is not a knockdown argument against privacy justified by personhood, as one 'merely' needs to articulate an adequate description of personhood. To take one example, Griffin builds his concept of a generalised human right, which includes a right to privacy, from an explication of what personhood is and why it matters (Griffin, 2008). Chapter Four also tackles this problem by developing an informational account of identity.

29 I say 'empirical necessity' here, as Griffin points out that privacy is not conceptually necessary for human agency – some 'supermen' and 'exhibitionists' can live without privacy. His point is that most of us need privacy at some point, in order to develop as persons.

This intimacy account clearly overlaps with privacy-as-personhood. Intimacy is important as it is a necessary component for a person to become and maintain their personhood, their agency, but is formed through our relations with others.

Julie Inness takes Reiman's privacy-as-intimacy conception and expands it (Inness, 1992, pp. 19–22). Stating that 'privacy's content covers *intimate* information, access and decisions', Inness describes privacy as 'the state of an agent having control over a realm of intimacy, which contains her decisions about intimate access to herself (including intimate informational access) and her decisions about her own intimate actions' (Emphasis Original, Inness, 1992, p. 56). The source of moral concern is not based on a public/private division; rather it is invasions of, or unwanted access to, intimate Personal Information: 'We must look at the *type* of information disseminated; it is the *intimacy* of this information that identifies a loss of privacy' (Emphasis Original, Inness, 1992, p. 58).

Simply referring to intimacy as the source of privacy's moral importance would be replacing one word with another and prompts a further question: 'what constitutes intimacy?' (Inness, 1992, pp. 9–10). Delineating between intimate behaviour and intimate motivations, Inness argues that it is not behaviours that form the basis of privacy concerns. Rather,

> intimate decisions are identified by their motivation dependent content. When an agent characterizes an act or activity as intimate, she is claiming that it draws its meaning and value from her love, liking or care. Intimate decisions concern such matters and, thus, involve a choice on the agent's part about how to (or not to) embody her love, liking or care.
>
> (Inness, 1992, pp. 74–75)

On Inness' account then, privacy is an attitudinal state, whereby those decisions, actions or facts about a person which *they* love, like or care about are what form the core of privacy. Illustrating her case with an example of a love letter, Inness points out that it is not the content of the love letter that makes it important. Rather it is the fact that a love letter conveys the importance of a particular relationship between two people. When showing another a love letter, this act 'draws its meaning and value as an *intimate act* from its tie to our love, liking or care' (Emphasis Original, Inness, 1992, p. 79). While the intimacy argument has its detractors,[30] the intimacy discussion points out that our relations with Personal Information produce different 'moral meanings', a major point made in Chapter 5.

[30] Solove argues that the broad terms of identity and autonomy 'could apply to almost every action or decision an individual undertakes ... Without limitations in scope, the word "intimacy" is merely a different word for "privacy" and is certainly not sufficient to determine which matters are private' (Solove, 2008, p. 36). Following this, Solove then argues that intimacy is too narrow, as it can't deal with things that are normally private but non-intimate (Solove, 2008, p. 36). Yet, as I show in §2.5, this lack of sufficiency is not the knockdown argument that Solove believes it to be.

2.4 PRIVACY QUESTIONS

The issue now is how to respond to privacy. We have a range of different conceptions to choose from. Should we choose one as *the* definition of privacy? If we cannot settle on one conception, what happens if we considered all equally? Both approaches come with problems. The approach I suggest is pluralistic and interactive: we should see the different conceptions as relevant, but that they must be understood as standing in relation to each other.

2.4.1 *Problems with Singular Concepts*

Of the different conceptions described so far, which one should we choose as *the* best conception? There are two major concerns with such an approach. First, any given conception has its problems and detractors. Second, assuming that there is a single concept of privacy, we risk discarding privacy entirely when that conception is no longer useful. On the first point, Solove's *Understanding Privacy* is an example of looking at each conception, finding fault with it and then proposing an alternative conception. Solove offers criticisms of each conception, that they are all too vague, too narrow, too broad or all three. Instead, he proposes that privacy ought to be understood by reference to social goods. However, this approach is as open to criticism for being too vague, broad or narrow as the other conceptions. So, if Solove's criticisms are correct and his own theory is equally vulnerable to such criticisms, then it seems we have reasons to discard each conception.

The second concern is that if we cannot find privacy's 'one true answer', we may throw the baby out with the bathwater: we find fault with each conception and so reject the notion of privacy entirely. This could occur because of the concern just described, or could occur when people's behaviour no longer tracks to that definition. Thus, like Facebook and Google's responses described in §2.1, we conclude that our behaviours reveal our true preferences, or that new technologies have ended the possibility of privacy altogether. We end up discarding privacy as we think it no longer serves any practical purpose. Popular discussions about privacy are often underpinned by the secrecy paradigm and an assumption of a public/private divide. Faced with the end of secrecy and assuming that secrecy is the only proper conception, privacy gets abandoned altogether. Though we could instead look at the other conceptions, we're likely to confront a similar problem.

2.4.2 *Problems with Multiple Concepts*

Instead of assuming that there is a single conception, perhaps reasonable people can disagree about which conception is right. Perhaps privacy is an essentially contested concept.[31] That is, there are a number of privacy conceptions that could be said to

[31] After Gallie (1956), the idea is that 'the claim that debates about concepts can never reach closure as invariably good theoretical, methodological and moral arguments can and will be made in favor of one or another definition' (de Haan, 2008, p. 29).

be reasonable; on this concept, there's a plurality of different ways to think of privacy and we can choose which one seems most sensible. However, I think that part of the reason why people might think that Facebook's Zuckerberg and Google's Schmidt were right in their assertions that privacy is no longer useful is the profusion and separation of different privacy conceptions. If each is right, how do we select between them and what happens when they are in conflict? By allowing multiple *independent* conceptions and no interaction principle,[32] we end up more confused than ever.[33] Consider the opening paragraph from *Privacy, Intimacy and Isolation*:

> Exploring the concept of privacy resembles exploring an unknown swamp. We start on firm ground, noting the common usage of "privacy" in everyday conversation and legal argument. We find intense disagreement about both trivial and crucial issues . . . we find chaos . . . the ground starts to soften as we discover the confusion underlying our privacy intuitions.
>
> (Inness, 1992, p. 3)

Certainly, disagreements about which concept is correct are nothing new. However, if each new analysis of privacy offers *the definition* and *the explanation*, which one are we to choose? Further, by accepting multiple independent conceptions, we retain all the problems identified by Solove with each individual conception. 'Privacy is too complicated a concept to be boiled down to a single essence. Attempts to find such an essence often end up being too broad and vague, with little usefulness in addressing concrete issues' (Solove, 2008, p. 103).

Rather than listing the different conceptions and selecting amongst them, another solution is to take a pluralistic line but recognising that the conceptions *ought to be viewed in relation to each other*: The reason why none of the single descriptions or justifications work is that they do not function independently.

2.4.3 *Privacy as a Cluster of Related Conceptions*

The proposal is that we look at the different descriptions and justifications, but consider them in relation to each other, understanding privacy as an organising principle that clusters the different conceptions together and offers some explanations of their relations. The virtue of this approach is that the descriptive elements are justified by reference to moral values such as intimacy, personhood and/or

[32] This is a reference to concerns raised by Shelly Kagan in reference to moral pluralism: 'A complete normative theory must include more than a *list* of normative factors. It will also have to include *interaction principles* – principles specifying how the various factors interact to determine the moral status of particular acts' (Emphases Original, Kagan, 1998a, p. 183).

[33] This point was brought home to me at a conference I attended where one presenter began his paper saying that he had read many different philosophical positions and, given their perpetual disagreement, concluded that the philosophers were not saying anything useful at all. His response was to go and ask people to find out what privacy *really* was. Unsurprisingly, he found that such an approach did not uncover what privacy really was either, as people either had no idea or offered multiple conceptions.

harms. At the same time, we can explain the justifications by reference to secrecy and the flow of information from one space to another.

More than simply offering plural meanings, seeing privacy as a cluster allows the different elements to both explain and limit each other. The point here is that the problem with the different conceptions viewed so far is that, in seeking to reduce privacy to a single conception, they lose the utility of the other conceptions. My point is that rather than looking for 'the one true meaning of privacy', we should instead look to the different elements that each conception brings to privacy discussions. Importantly, we recognise that in some situations, certain conceptions will be more relevant, others less so.

Is such an approach workable? In discussions of ownership, 'ownership' is typically seen to refer to a range of related concepts. I discuss ownership in detail in the next chapter, but relevant to this discussion is that ownership is often seen as a 'bundle of rights' (Honoré, 1961). That is, ownership relates to a range of interpersonal different rights and duties, which vary depending on the owner and the thing owned. Importantly, despite the obvious fact that owning a handgun means very different things to owning a stock portfolio, approaching ownership as a bundle recognises that we do not throw away the idea of ownership. Nor do we say that we must limit 'ownership' in reference to either a handgun *or* a stock portfolio. Such a cluster of related concepts has proved highly useful in other areas, so why not approach privacy in a similar way? Indeed, Solove's approach begins similarly by viewing privacy in terms of 'family resemblances'[34] (Solove, 2008, p. 9). Thus, clustering different conceptions is neither novel in legal discussions generally or privacy more particularly.

For instance, talking of privacy as *only* informational control is problematic as information might be non-private. For instance, the fact that a person has two eyes is information about that person, but it hardly seems private.[35] Likewise, talking *only* of intimacy is problematic. For instance, a wedding is a public statement that two people like, love and care for each other, yet is conducted in public. However, a wedding may also be considered a private function. Instead, if we see privacy as referring to some connection between information *and* intimacy, privacy talk makes more sense: we rule out non-intimate information like 'having two eyes'. How do we deal with a public-but-private event like a wedding? The pluralistic approach allows for discussions of spaces, capturing the intuition that privacy typically involves some

[34] Ludwig Wittgenstein's 'family resemblances', found in his *Philosophical Investigations*, §65–§71 (Wittgenstein, 1958), presents a way of recognising and understanding people, things and particularly concepts in philosophy that is different to 'necessary and sufficient' conditions. Rather than saying that 'X is an essential to Y, a necessary condition of being Y', Wittgenstein clusters concepts by how they resemble each other. For more on family resemblance, see (Bambrough, 1968; Khatchadourian, 1968; Pelczar, 2000; Pitcher, 1968).

[35] Other information might not refer to people at all, that is, the public disclosure of a viral genetic sequence might be socially harmful, so should be kept secret. But to talk of privacy here makes no sense.

space or boundary. A wedding ceremony is conceivably conducted within a private space: consider a large celebrity wedding where the public and the press are not allowed. Privacy is maintained if no unauthorised photographs of the wedding are released. Privacy is maintained as long as the flow of information across this boundary is appropriate.[36]

This prompts the question: what makes a given information flow appropriate? Nissenbaum's argument is that appropriateness is dependent upon the given context (Nissenbaum, 2009, pp. 140–147) and I discuss her approach in §2.5.2. As per the approach to ethics as justification, we limit appropriateness by justifying what counts as appropriate in relation to the moral values that people commonly hold, like basic respect, harms and equality. This coheres with the pluralistic morality advocated by van den Hoven, §2.5.3, allowing us to limit what counts as appropriate, whilst speaking to the individual wrongs of privacy violations as well as the group and social harms that can arise when privacy is violated. Chapters 8 and 9 have detailed discussions on these points.

2.5 PLURALISM IN PRIVACY

What I am arguing for here, given the challenges posed by surveillance technologies, is not especially controversial. People like Daniel Solove, Helen Nissenbaum and Jeroen van den Hoven are equally concerned about the impacts of technology on privacy. Each of them offers a pluralistic approach, similar to what was discussed in §2.4. Despite the virtue of their approaches, I think that each needs a little more detail to be maximally useful. This section presents the three approaches, offers criticisms as to their current shortcomings and offers some suggestions as to how the approaches can be improved.

2.5.1 *Privacy as Social Good and Its Limits*

In the past ten years, Solove has developed a pragmatic methodology to build privacy up from a cluster of related problems.

> [M]y approach to conceptualizing privacy understands it pluralistically rather than as having a unitary common denominator ... Following philosopher John Dewey's view that philosophical inquiry should begin as a response to dealing with life's problems and difficulties, I argue that the focal point should be on privacy *problems*.
>
> (Solove, 2008, Emphasis Original, p. 9)

Starting with problems rather than theories, Solove attempts to step around the problems he identifies with other accounts: 'My taxonomy's categories are not based

[36] I use 'appropriate' here as a direct reference to Nissenbaum's approach, which holds that privacy is *appropriate* information flow (Nissenbaum, 2009, pp. 129–157).

upon any overarching principle. We do not need overarching principles to understand and recognise problems' (Solove, 2008, p. 105). Solove instead offers an account of privacy that is grounded in the 'social good'. 'I contend that privacy has a social value and that its importance emerges from the benefits it confers upon society ... [p]rivacy certainly protects the individual, but not because of some inherent value of respect for personhood. Instead, privacy protects the individual because of the benefits it confers upon society' (Solove, 2008, pp. 79, 98). For Solove, the social good is fundamental to why we should care about privacy.

There is a tension within Solove's approach. He clearly states that his account is built from recognising privacy problems and understands these problems in relation to the social good. However, by doing this, he seems to be repeating the mistakes that he criticises in others (Solove, 2008, p. 103). His account, however, defines the problems in reference to society, particularly in reference to the harms that a lack of privacy causes for society. One of his motivations was to avoid structuring an account of privacy around an essentialist theory, yet his account is derived from such a theory: That privacy problems just *are* harms: in particular, harms to society.

One concern with Solove's references to society is that his account is framed by and founded upon, references to society, so the harms that he presents become vulnerable to the same criticisms that he uses against the other conceptions of privacy. His standard criticism is to show that the other conceptions are too broad, too vague or too narrow. So what counts as 'society' in Solove's description? By defining privacy simply in reference to 'social harms', we can see that Solove is too vague; without offering a clear and usable explanation of what he means when he refers to society, we are left with an amorphous and shapeless idea, one that 'fails to provide much guidance about what privacy entails' (Solove, 2008, p. 17). Without guidance, we are left without a justifying reason as to why social goods are to be favoured over individual goods and ultimately have no way of balancing conflicts between the interests of society and individuals: the standard problem for any consequentialist theory founded in maximising the social good.[37]

Further, Solove's account is too broad in that he seems to allow that privacy is that which is deemed private by a particular society, 'privacy is not simply a subjective matter of individual prerogative; it is also an issue of what society deems appropriate' (Solove, 2008, p. 25). On this, it would seem that if a particular society deems X thing appropriately private, then X becomes private (Solove, 2008, p. 173). However, this does not help us as we have no clear idea of what he means by society. Is this a simple cultural group? Is it a linguistic group, a nation or all people everywhere? Without further guidance as to what should be/should not be

[37] This is not to say that maximising the social good is to be discarded as a legitimate moral theory. Rather, that making reference to 'maximising the social good' is merely the start of the story of justification, rather than the end.

deemed appropriate and what counts as society, Solove's foundation of social harms rehashes the points made in §1.4: simple references to consequentialism are not enough. In short, Solove's own account has the same limits that he finds in other theories.

2.5.2 *Context Relative Informational Norms (CRINs) and Their Extension*

As with the pluralistic move and in accord with Solove, Nissenbaum recognises that '[n]o single principle seems perfectly suited; yet each embodies themes that are importantly related to privacy' (Nissenbaum, 2009, p. 125). Seeing a need to respond to the technological challenge (Nissenbaum, 2009, pp. 21–64), she argues that we should respond to privacy concerns not by reference to some particular conception of privacy. Rather, we should instead focus on determining appropriate information flows. 'Usually, when we mind that information about us is shared, we mind not simply that it is being shared but that it is shared in the wrong ways and with inappropriate others' (Nissenbaum, 2009, p. 142). Accordingly, she develops a heuristic which aims to explain what has gone wrong and can tell us how we ought to respond. She calls these context relative informational norms (CRINs). These CRINs are 'characterized by four key parameters: contexts, actors, attributes and transmission principles' (Nissenbaum, 2009, p. 140).

For Nissenbaum, the CRIN model can both explain why people feel concerned about some privacy violation and how to respond to it. Take social networks like Facebook. Many people feel that these social networks violate privacy, but when asked to explain how, they can find themselves at a loss. The CRIN model says that what people feel is that these new technologies are affording practices that are different to the prevailing informational norms: traditionally, we only shared Personal Information with those spatially, temporally and/or emotionally close to us, those that we had a direct relation with. New technologies allow for sharing of this Personal Information beyond the traditional spatial, temporal and/or emotional limits. As such, we are now operating under a new informational norm.

I agree with much of what Nissenbaum says: her critique of privacy is accurate and informational flow is an appropriate focus of concern for surveillance technologies. Further, in line with Nissenbaum, we need to assess the social-institutional contexts in which information is being produced, communicate and used. While agreeing with much of Nissenbaum's approach, I think there is more that needs to be added. In short, we need to establish just how surveillance technologies disrupt CRINs and *when* we should care, that is, we need *moral* explanation and *moral* motivation. We need a story to establish a link between practice and relevant moral norms such that we know why something is morally problematic.

Consider Nissenbaum's example of why we should be concerned about social networks; she says that this new technologically mediated practice

> is morally troubling because it threatens to disrupt the delicate web of relationships that constitute the context of social life, injecting into workplace and business contexts information of the wrong type, under inappropriate transmission principles ... [but] for substantive conclusions to be drawn, one would need to elaborate and demonstrate key dependencies.
>
> (Nissenbaum, 2009, p. 228)

We need to be able to say just why we should be concerned about such disruptions to relationships, to go beyond saying that relationships are important and that disruptions to these relationships can be bad for people. This is what I mean by moral explanation and moral motivation: by showing just *how* the surveillance technology disrupts the relations between people, we can hopefully explain the moral weight of this disruption. And, presuming that morality has some motivational feature, by explaining the weight of this disruption, we can further say *why* we ought to care about such a disruption.

Chapters 8 and 9 return to these disruptions by exposing how changes in information flow afforded by new technologies change how a person sees themselves, how they see others and how they see others see themselves. Succinctly stated, surveillance technologies are morally concerning because of the ways that they can impact on identities. If these impacts are shown to result in some deep misrecognition and/or to cause harms to people's self-identity and/or their treatment of others then, in line with Nissenbaum, we should be morally concerned about such technologies. '[H]aving demonstrated that some of the practices performed in social network sites ... [are violations of] contextual integrity, can we further demonstrate that they are morally problematic?' The goal of Nissenbaum's approach is to fill out '[t]he evaluative step ... to compare entrenched and novel flows in terms of values, ends and purposes of respective contexts' (Nissenbaum, 2009, p. 227). What my analysis adds to Nissenbaum's is detail on a particular set of entrenched values – basic respect, harm reduction and equality – and a detailed explanation of how the novel flows of information impact these values.

2.5.3 *Giving* Oomph[38] *to Data Protection*

Van den Hoven's account raises concerns similar to Solove and Nissenbaum, but takes a different approach. In a series of papers (van den Hoven, 2007b, 2008; van den Hoven and Manders-Huits, 2006; van den Hoven and Weckert, 2008), he and others develop a theory of 'data protection' in response to the question 'why should we protect personal data; what moral reasons do we have to protect personal data?' (van den Hoven, 2008, p. 466). The data protection account seeks to avoid

[38] *Oomph* is used here to capture the need for moral motivation, that is, why we should care about data protection. Richard Joyce uses oomph to refer to the story as to why a certain thing has moral weight or authority (Joyce, 2006, pp. 170–171).

unnecessary conceptual debates about what privacy *is* and instead focuses on the *ends* of privacy. It asks what privacy is actually doing for us and why access to information should be constrained (van den Hoven, 2007b, p. 320). He does so by identifying four key moral justifications for protecting data.

1. Information-based harms;
2. Informational inequality;
3. Informational injustice;
4. Encroachment on moral autonomy (van den Hoven, 1999, p. 33, 2008, pp. 477–491).

Information-based harms arise when someone is harmed by the use of Personal Information, like identity theft resulting in financial and physical damages (van den Hoven, 2007b, pp. 321–322). Informational inequalities occur when a person has unequal access to a service or product as the result of handing over or giving access to their Personal Information. Informational injustices build from Michael Walzer's *Spheres of Justice* (Walzer, 1983) and occur when information intended for use in a particular context is used in another context. A paradigm example would be using surveillance information gathered in a national security context for economic gain: the original context of the information was national security and it is an injustice if this information is then used for economic benefit.

What does my account do that van den Hoven's doesn't? The main strengths of van den Hoven's account are that he avoids the need to define privacy and so can focus on pluralistic discussions of privacy. The limit to the data protection account is that the relations between the information covered by data protection and its moral foundations are not entirely clear. This concern is made evident when considering innocuous Personal Information.

Consider the keystroke information described in §2.2. Speaking of data protection independent of the data itself and its specific relation to moral foundations provides little on what data should be protected: is surveillance of a single keystroke the same as the surveillance of a day's, a week's and so on. If not, why not? When we talk of privacy concerns just as a moral problem of harm, inequality, injustice or as an autonomy violation, we risk making informational misuses and transgressions true but trivially so. Further, they can become lost amongst the world's other harms, inequalities, injustices and violations of autonomy: any concern about Karl's privacy being violated from keystroke logging programs seems insignificant contrasted with all the world's other harms. Yet with the rise of so many informational technologies, these harms may be significant – §9.3 spells out the range of different harms that can arise from misuse and abuse of information technologies.

To prevent data protection from shrinking in importance, we need to explain the connection between data and their moral foundation. This point is clear when considering innocuous information, which is only troubling when considered in aggregate. We cannot simply talk of harms or other moral problems; we need to give a principled reason why certain data need to be viewed in aggregate. Having detailed the reasons why we need to see innocuous information in aggregate, Chapters 7, 8 and 9 return to data protection, giving it its 'oomph'.

A further virtue coming from an explication of the relations between data and why we should protect it will not only tell us *why* we should care about such things, it may also help guide us in *how* to respond and prevent the problems that data protection is attending to. A standard problem of pluralistic approaches is how to respond to conflicts between the different values. For example, if we need to update a research participant's name and contact details, such that their medical data is not used outside of the original contextual spheres, we will be faced with a potential conflict between informational autonomy and informational injustice. Offering a detailed explication of the relations between data and the moral foundations, we have a mechanism that can balance conflicts *within* data protection.

The general point of this section is not that Solove, Nissenbaum or van den Hoven are wrong: I agree with their positions to a great degree. The goal is to add to their accounts. The later chapters that explore the relations between identity and information fill out the pluralistic approaches and begin to find a way to balance conflicts. Building from this clustered approach to privacy, the basic rule of thumb offered is that the more revealing information becomes, the more we ought to consider it a threat to privacy, a claim substantiated in Chapter 8.

2.6 SURVEILLANCE TECHNOLOGIES AND PRIVACY'S RETURN

The age of surveillance is not the end of privacy. Instead, what surveillance technologies challenge is the public/private distinction and largely destroy the idea of easy secrecy. Bearing in mind that the Western notion of privacy, crystallised by Warren and Brandeis, came into being in response to the rise of new surveillance technologies we should be a little circumspect about declaring privacy dead. Instead, in line with Nissenbaum's position, what's shifting are the informational norms, the practices – including moral practices – around how we handle, treat and value Personal Information. In line with seeing privacy as a concept that has multiple interactive conceptions, these surveillance technologies and new behaviours shift and reduce emphasis on some elements in the privacy cluster like privacy as secrecy and increase emphasis on others, like privacy as intimacy.

To illustrate this point, let's return to the case from Chapter 1 – where Target produced a pregnancy score for a teenage shopper. This is an invasion of her privacy. That said, none of what she was doing in the store could be said to be secret. Still, the intuitive pull is that some wrong has occurred here. Note that this is the case even if she was not harmed by the revelation to her family that she was pregnant and sexually active. The intuition that something morally problematic has occurred points to an ethical vacuum – we know something problematic has occurred, but need a story as to how.

Descriptive: Privacy is	*Normative:* Privacy justified by reference to	*Plural:* Privacy elements organised by
A right	Freedom from chilling	Social Good
Something secret	Personhood	CRINs
A space	Intimacy	Data Protection
Control over information		
A realm free of government intrusion		

FIGURE 2.1 List of privacy conceptions

The first part of this story is that privacy is not just secrecy; it covers a range of interactive conceptions beyond the secrecy paradigm. Second, we've got the twin challenges arising from publicly available information: involvement and innocuous information. We are often actively involved in making this Personal Information public, so claims of a violation of our right to privacy seem false and the information itself is often so innocuous that we ought not be worried about it. The pluralistic concept of privacy can respond to this – first, on involvement, though we may have freely allowed our Personal Information to be collected, but we've not consented to it being used to reveal intimate information like sexual activity or whether we're pregnant. This can be captured by the information injustice and intimacy conceptions. In terms of its innocuous nature, in addition to the informational injustice and intimacy, if such innocuous information is aggregated and used by the state, we have an example of a government in overreach.

Taking the pluralistic and interactive concept as a practical approach to privacy issues, we can map out a basic methodology: for each case, look at the range of conceptions that are involved or not and see which are relevant to the case at hand (Figure 2.1):

The next step is to see how they interact. In order to do this, we can follow Nissenbaum's idea of CRINS, to see how they are currently weighted by (a) individuals in specific cases, (b) the relevant community more broadly and (c) yourself. Then, as per ethics being a systemised set of reasons, see if a, b and c are reasonable, that is, what is their justification for weighting the conceptions in a given way. Such an approach is complex and messy, but allowing for such fine-grained detail avoids the pitfalls of the reductionist approach found in the singular concept of privacy and uses the strengths of the recognition of privacy as a plural concept, whilst ensuring that the conceptions are properly seen as interactive. While this is not as neat as some would like, what the analysis shows is that rather than being the end of privacy, if anything, the age of surveillance heralds its return.

2.7 KATE AND KARL REVISITED: PLURALISM IN PRIVACY

§2.2 described keylogging software. Recalling the characters from that case, both Kate and Karl were having a bad day in the office and after this was recognised, both were assigned to different tasks. The difference between the two cases was that it was Kate's supervisor who recognised she was having a bad day and reassigned her, while in Karl's case it was an automated computer program that did this. This computer program recognised Karl's state of mind through software that logged and analysed the patterns which he typed; keylogging software twigged to the behavioural clues supposedly embedded in Karl's typing patterns. So what can pluralism tell us about Karl's case? Is there any privacy violation going on in Karl's case? If so, is it relevantly different from Kate's case? Finally, even if it is morally different from Kate's case, is the breach of Karl's privacy something that we should be worried about?

Karl's case is significantly different from Kate's and it is something that is morally concerning, as explained by the cluster of privacy conceptions. To show how this relates to Karl's case, first we need to look closely at the information produced by the keylogging software. Can this information be described as intimate Personal Information about Karl? If the information is intimate, would Karl have reasons to restrict access to it; does it deserve protection? Finally, does this show how Karl's case is different from Kate's?

Has the information produced something that someone could reasonably be expected to like, love or care about? Recall from §2.2 that there are two types of information that are produced by keylogging software: (1) Information that can identify a particular worker and (2) Information that can identify the emotional state of the worker. Given that the information of type (1) is equivalent across both Kate's and Karl's cases, information of type (2) is what is most relevant. Information of type (2) is behavioural information and what's more, it is aggregated behavioural information. '[W]e are reconstituted in databases as digital person composed of data' (Solove, 2004, p. 49). If accurate, the keystrokes present a record of Karl's emotional states the entire time he is logged in at work. This record of one's emotional states is something that contains information that most people would like, love or care about – it is intimate information.

Second, consider what this information is about. It is not simply the bland details of how Karl types, but it is capable, or at least claimed to be capable of, producing information that 'can open a window into people's minds' (Solove, 2004, p. 24). One's own mind is a place that would be considered within a zone of the most private things about a person. The description of the deleterious effects of the pervasive surveillance in the former East Germany speaks to this lost space within one's mind: 'I *know* how far people will transgress over your boundaries - until you have no private sphere left at all … It was the loss of everything until I had disappeared too' (Emphasis Original, Funder, 2002, pp. 113, 115). Privacy as personhood connects to the concern about Karl's case: the information produced by the keylogging software exposes Karl's state of mind and can do so without his knowledge or full consent. By stepping into the zone of Karl's state of mind, keylogging software has stepped into a space typically reserved for the self and close others.

Is this any different from Kate? Note that the keylogging software produces a virtual identity for Karl that is not comparable when Kate's supervisor attends to her. While both examples involve the production of and access to, employee behavioural information, in Karl's situation this information is digital. What this means is that it will not degrade with time or use, it is accessible to staff beyond the immediate supervisor and it can be aggregated with other information. It is this, I suggest, that makes Karl's case relevantly different from Kate's: not only is it producing private information, but the Virtual Identity produced by keylogging software can be accessed by many different people, at many different places and times and it also has the potential to be aggregated with other information about Karl. '[T]he increasing digitization of documents enables more documents to be retained by eliminating storage constraints, increases the ability to access and copy documents and permits the transfer of documents en masse' (Solove, 2004, p. 132).

So in Karl's case, we have intimate Personal Information. This would be a set of information that Karl could legitimately consider private, where unwanted access would be an invasion of Karl's privacy. This information produces a Virtual Identity for Karl, so it is relevantly different from Kate's case. By explaining Karl's case in reference to Virtual Identity, I hope to pull into focus not only the real practical concern – the construction of a Virtual Identity from aggregated Personal Information – but to also present a set of ethical justifications as to why this is a problem special enough to warrant due care and attention. Finally, is this a cause for moral concern? If I can show why Karl should have a claim to limit other's access to this information, that the use of the information could be harmful or lead to substantial inequalities, I would be able to justify a claim of why such information should be treated with care. These claims are substantiated later in the book.

3

On Property

3.1 PROPERTY'S FAILURE IN AN AGE OF SURVEILLANCE

Perhaps the effort to rethink the concept of privacy is misguided as we have another well-established set of norms governing people's relations with Personal Information – the institution of property. Insofar as property is about morally legitimate claims of control and access to certain resources, then it may offer us a way of resolving moral issues arising in the age of surveillance. However, as this chapter shows, when looking into the ethical explanations of property, particularly when considering property and intangibles like information, we see that the current institutions of property fail those who have morally legitimate claims.

It may seem strange to enter into a detailed examination of property when considering surveillance: surely privacy or other traditional moral concerns like informed consent cover the issues and problems of surveillance and Personal Information in a far more relevant way? In contrast, I suggest that property is not only a relevant frame of analysis, but that the age of surveillance makes it fundamental to any meaningful ethical discussion. There are two claims that justify the importance of a discussion of property. First, that information is a product, arguably *the* product, of surveillance. Second, that any comprehensive ethical analysis of surveillance must seek to locate who owns that product.

This chapter develops these points by proposing that the end product of surveillance is information. §3.3 looks at property's recent history. It introduces information technologies to draw out the fact that the recognised owners of that information are typically neither those from whom the information is derived, nor those to whom it is applied, nor even those who 'create' the information. Rather, in the age of surveillance it is typically some external group or institution that has the legally recognised property claims. The conceptual analysis of property begins by describing what we mean by property and then looking at rights-based and social good-based justifications for property. §3.4 presents an ethical analysis of property and intangibles, §3.5 then looks at surveillance products and property claims. §3.6 completes the discussion by looking at the ownership of the products of surveillance and the need to relate any moral claims of property to people.

3.2 OWNING THE PRODUCTS OF SURVEILLANCE: THE CASE OF CCTV

Closed Circuit Television (CCTV) was perhaps the first surveillance technology to achieve substantial integration in our social lives. CCTV cameras are largely ubiquitous through our built environments – found in public spaces like town squares, in commercial spaces like shopping malls, in professional spaces like the workplace and in semi-private spaces like apartment elevators.[1] Beside the familiarity and integration, the reality of CCTV operation presents an intriguing and illuminating case example of just what it is that surveillance technologies *do*.

CCTV technologies are close to omnipresent, typically justified as a practical and cost effective technological solution to crime and feelings of insecurity. In his detailed sociological analysis of the introduction and implementation of a large CCTV network in a British city, Gavin Smith argues that the publicly stated reasons for CCTV were to decrease crime and increase economic activity through increased security (Smith, 2015, pp. 64–83). The former UK Home Secretary Jack Straw captures the sentiment well: 'The evidence is clear. In the right context, CCTV can significantly reduce crime and disorder . . . Not sure of house style here When used properly, CCTV can deter criminals, greatly assist the police and others in bringing offenders to justice and to help reduce people's fear of crime' (Jack Straw, quoted in Smith, 2015, pp. 37–38).

The problem, as Smith's work shows, is that CCTV is not a technology that can be set up and then simply left to run. It requires care and consideration in where and how the cameras are located, substantial resources for maintenance and standard operation (Smith, 2015, pp. 76–95). And most relevantly, CCTV needs a workforce of human operators to make sense of the incoming and collected data: images or footage taken of an assault remain data until a human has watched them and made sense of them. Nowhere is this more clearly stated, than a quote from one of the operators: 'What I do [when bored] is make up stories for people I watch on the cameras and call them names' (Smith, 2015, p. 115). What surveillance systems require, therefore, is a mental 'buy in' from the operators. They don't simply sit and stare; as a watcher, they have to make sense of the scenes in front of them. That

[1] Though I suggest that their ubiquity is a reasonable claim, we need to take care in just what this means. An oft-cited report in the UK claimed that the average British citizen was observed by CCTV cameras an average of 300 times a day. David Aaronovitch has shown the '300 times a day' figure is far from accurate (Aaronovitch, 2009). However, the general claim about the ubiquity of CCTV as a widely distributed surveillance technology still holds.

is, it is only through engagement with a human that the input can be understood as an assault, a theft, an event of importance or relevance.

In contrast to Smith's position that the purpose of the CCTV operators is as 'social order keepers' (Smith, 2015, p. 135), what I suggest instead is that these operators are there to produce knowledge. That is, the CCTV operators are engaged in a process of epistemic action. An epistemic action is an action that is conducted to bring about information. They are '[a]ctions designed to change the input to an agent's information processing system. They are ways an agent has of modifying the external environment to provide crucial bits of information' (Kirsh and Maglio, 1994, pp. 541–542). Chapter 5 presents a detailed account of what I mean by information, but let me stipulate here that information is meaningful, that it has a semantic element.[2] Without a layer of meaning, what surveillance is doing is merely collecting data. CCTV operators are trying to make sense out of what's happening on the screen in front them: they are involved in locating the actions of strangers within a context of social meaning 'this guy is about to hit that guy'. That is, they are making the scenes understandable such that others *know* what's going on. The point here is that CCTV technology has a specific product as its output – information, something meaningful.

This idea that CCTV is engaged in producing information with a necessarily meaningful element extends to all surveillance technologies. Consider when surveillance technologies are used as part of a policing investigative strategy. Seumas Miller and Ian Gordon argue that 'the investigative role is essentially an epistemic or knowledge focussed role; that is, the principle role of detectives is to acquire knowledge with respect to the who, what, when, where, how and why of crimes' (Miller and Gordon, 2014, p. 48). Further to this, beyond surveillance in the criminal justice context, any *useful* surveillance is going to require some human input to give it a semantic element. Big data, for example, is just a collection of bytes in a computer until an algorithm analyses it for things of interest and some person acts upon that analysis. The algorithms at the start contextualise the data and start to give it meaning, but those algorithms are developed by humans with the aim of producing useful information out of the data. When something is flagged, when some connection is brought out or the analysis produces something of interest, much like with CCTV, an operator will respond to that, giving further meaning to the data. In short, the point of surveillance is creating a product and that product is *meaningful* data.

What does this have to do with property? What has been described so far is the idea that surveillance is concerned with producing information as a product. In order for property to be relevant to this chapter, I have to show that it is relevant to the discussions of the products of surveillance.

[2] The source of this claim is Luciano Floridi's General Definition of Information (GDI), which is 'ordered, meaningful and true data' (Floridi, 2011a, pp. 80–84). Again, this is spelt out in detail in Chapter 5.

3.3 PROPERTY'S RECENT HISTORY

This section exposes the relevance of property to a comprehensive discussion of the ethics of surveillance. Continuing the point that surveillance is an epistemic action, something concerned with producing information that has a semantic element, we now look to what is done with that information. Specifically, we see that Personal Information can be owned and that the owners are 'external' to the information. What I mean by this is that the recognised owners are not the people who provided the information in the first place, nor are they the people for whom the information is most relevant, nor even are the owners those actively engaged in the process of creating the information, the epistemic labourers. To make sense of these points, this section covers what property is and the moral justifications that underpin the legitimacy of any claim to property.

3.3.1 *Property and Information Technologies*

To begin, we find demonstrations of property over Personal Information in the medical realm: the cases of 'Canavan disease' and 'Catalona'. The point of discussing the two cases is to show not just that Personal Information can be owned, but the precedent is that the owner is not necessarily those from whom the information was derived, nor those to whom it is most relevant, nor even those who created the end product.

Canavan disease[3] is a genetically inherited autosomal recessive disorder that typically results in mortality of those afflicted by four years of age.[4] In the late 1980s, community members approached a researcher, Dr Reuben Matalon from the Miami Children's Hospital Research Institute (MCHRI). Matalon and the group used donated patient blood, tissue samples and familial pedigree information to successfully isolate and identify the genetic sequence for Canavan disease. In 1997, Matalon and the MCHRI were granted a patent on this identified genetic sequence, giving Matalon and the MCHRI the legal right to 'restrict any activity related to the Canavan disease gene, including without limitation: carrier and prenatal testing, gene therapy and other treatments for Canavan disease and research involving the gene and its mutations' (United States District Court, 2003). The Greenberg family, representing families with Canavan disease, challenged the patent, but it was upheld, allowing Matalon and the MCHRI the right to limit testing, gene therapy and commercial research on the genetic sequence responsible

[3] The relevant legal case is *Greenberg v. Miami Children's Hospital Research Institute* – Case 264 F. Supp. 2d 1064 (S.D. Fla., 2003), for court proceedings, see (United States District Court, 2003).

[4] For information on the disease see (Surendran, Matalon, et al., 2003; Surendran, Michals-Matalon, et al., 2003).

for Canavan disease. That is, those who provided the information were not recognised as the legitimate owners.

The second example, 'Catalona', concerns a medical researcher, Dr William Catalona, his former employer, the Washington University (WU) and ownership of samples and information relating to patients with prostate cancer.[5] WU formed a 'biobank' known as the Genito-Urinary (GU) Biorepository, which Catalona was 'instrumental' in establishing (United States District Court, 2006) – this biobank had in excess of 30,000 tissue samples from research patients, 100,000 serum samples and 4,400 DNA samples. In 2003, Catalona changed jobs to work for North-Western University (NWU) and tried to take samples and linked medical records with him.[6] Though many research subjects consented to Catalona taking their samples with him, WU claimed property over the samples and sued Catalona and the patients that he represented to maintain exclusive property over the samples. In 2006, the court found that the samples remained under WU's control, despite the content of informed consent forms and the explicitly stated intention of the research subjects (United States District Court, 2006). Again, as with the Canavan case, those who provided the information were not recognised as the legitimate owners. And in this example, neither is one of the key people involved in the creation of the database.

Though there are important legal differences in both cases (Andrews, 2006), in each case research subjects and patients were denied property claims over Personal Information.[7] Instead, institutions and their current employees were the legally recognised owners of the samples and information. Granting the property claims to the institutions resulted in limiting the access of other patients or sufferers of the disease to information relevant to their disease and treatment. By recognising the institutions as the owners, the legal system advanced a position that the sources of information – those who provided the initial information – are not owners and those to whom the information is most relevant – those who are either suffering from a given disease or those caring for the sufferers – are not the owners either. Moreover, we see in the case of Catalona that even those who laboured to create the new information are not the owners.

The relevance of this is that surveillance technologies allow for vast amounts of Personal Information to be collected and aggregated about us: think of the data trails

5 (United States District Court, 2006).
6 Note that this case was not only about ownership of raw materials – patient samples and so on, but also about the information pertaining to these materials – linked medical records. Such 'pre-existing' knowledge about the samples is essential to producing useful information from the materials. The reasons that sit under this claim are given in Chapter 5.
7 As Peter Drahos and John Braithewaite have shown, the particulars of property evolve and shift through time. Recent developments in the ownership of human DNA, such as the recognition and latter rejection of patents on the human breast cancer gene BRCA1, have perhaps shifted recognition in favour of the source and targets of information. But the point of the Canavan and Catalona cases remain – it is possible and likely for the legally recognised owner to be some person or group distinct from the source, targets or creators of information.

we leave in our online activities. Much of the control over these is governed by End User Licence Agreements (EULAs): the text boxes that we invariably click 'agree' to when downloading new programs or accessing new websites. Information companies and the state (Greenwald, 2014, pp. 108–111, pp. 90–170) collect vast amounts of information about us. We are typically ignorant about what they do with this Personal Information. Further, if a company sells off, closes down or merges with another company, then some other group gets that information and we're even more ignorant about what's being done with that information (Solove, 2004, pp. 38–41). Likewise, the 'Five Eyes' agreement between the United States, United Kingdom, Canada, Australia and New Zealand (Walsh and Miller, 2015) means that intelligence information is being shared between different countries.

The point here is twofold. First, we have no effective control over our Personal Information; we cede that to some external people or institution. Second, we typically have no idea what's being done with that information. In his *The Digital Person*, Daniel Solove (Solove, 2004, pp. 27–55) hits this point exactly: he points out that many discussions about Personal Information focus on George Orwell's *Big Brother* trope to explain our worry about surveillance. A better lesson is found in Franz Kafka's *The Trial*: more often than not, our information is being collected, analysed and used by a faceless bureaucracy. The Kafka lesson is that the problem is not so much a *Big Brother* police state; it is instead the lack of knowledge we have about what's being done with our Personal Information, by whom and what for. The problem comes from the powerlessness produced by our ignorance about our Personal Information. Moreover, in true Kafka fashion, when trying to get access to our own information, the bureaucratic and legal institutions act as road blocks:[8] impediments rather than helpers. If we were to have a story, a detailed ethical explanation, about property of Personal Information, we would be in a better place to justify why ceding control to other people and faceless institutions is problematic. The ensuing discussion of property's moral foundations draws out the core of the problem – 'external' ownership of the products of surveillance does not take into account those from whom the information comes, to whom it is most relevant, nor those who created the meaning. What this section has shown is that surveillance technologies are designed to generate information as a product: that product can be owned. However, the owners are typically not the source, target or creators of that product.

3.3.2 *Property Described*

It is common to say one has property rights, but what are rights? (Kagan, 1998a, p. 170). There are ways of describing rights without writing a full book on the topic

[8] A recent example from Australia shows this – a journalist was pursuing a telecommunications company to get access to metadata about his own activities. There has been a drawn out legal battle as the company had been seeking to prevent him accessing his own information (Farrell, 2016b).

or descending into a 'horrible ambiguity' (Kagan, 1998a, p. 170). Common to most rights talk is the primacy of the individual. 'To have a right is to have something that overrides other considerations in both moral and legal discourse ... In their typical expression, rights are attractive because they express the great moral significance of every individual human being' (Campbell, 2006, p. 3). The 'the language of rights and claims [shifts] the focus of our attention from the agent (and what she is required to do) to the right holder (and how she has a right to be treated)' (Kagan, 1998a, p. 172). Given the importance of the individual, their right 'trumps'[9] other considerations like maximising wellbeing (Dworkin, 1978, p. 269; Mulgan, 2001, p. 17).

Jeremy Waldron's *The Right to Private Property* takes the foundation for private property to be rights based. That is, on his account, when considering the moral basis for property, the object of moral concern is the agent qua rights holder. From these rights, a correlative set of duties are generated in other people to observe and respect the agent's rights.[10] He proposes that '[i]n a system of private property, the rules governing access to and control of material resources are organized around the idea that resources are on the whole separate objects each assigned and therefore belonging to some particular individual' (Waldron, 1988, p. 38). The point here is not to say that Waldron's account is necessarily correct. Rather it is to provide some guidance as to what is meant when someone says that 'Person Y owns X': there are likely a system of rules governing access to and control over, X, organised around the idea that the X is a separable object assigned and belonging to the named owner, Y. As Y is the legitimate rights holder, another party, Z, must respect Y's rights or face sanctions for taking X. In line with rights, so described, the individual's property claim is seen as something special and important.

Like the concept of privacy being a related cluster, property is typically considered to be a bundle of rights. This bundle traditionally consists of eleven rights and/or duties: the right to possess, the right to use, the right to manage, the right to income, the right to the capital, the right to security, the power of transmissibility, the absence of term, the prohibition of harmful use, liability to execution and residuary character (Honoré, 1961, pp. 112–124; Waldron, 1988, p. 49). And parallel to the

[9] This idea of 'rights as trumps' is often associated with Ronald Dworkin's naturalistic account of rights, particularly *Taking Rights Seriously* (Dworkin, 1978). The Dworkinian 'rights as trumps' position is not being advocated here. Rather, it is showing that, for whatever justification, the individual is seen as especially important in rights talk.

[10] Note here Jeremy Waldron's point that rights and duties have different moral foundations and speak to different moral concerns. That is, 'X has a right (against Y) to do A ... is regarded as logically equivalent to, indeed as a mere notational variation on, something like ... Y has a duty (owed to X) not to do B' (Waldron, 1988, p. 68). He goes on to point out that this logical equivalence is not necessarily accurate, as rights and duties take different things to be the location of moral concern. Rights are typically concerned with the patient, with duties to the patient being generated from the right. Duties, however, have their primary concern in the agent's action towards the patient, with the patient's rights being generated from the agent's duty (Waldron, 1988, pp. 70–73).

concept of privacy as a cluster of different interacting conceptions, depending on the circumstances, different rights will be in play, in different ways and in different configurations: owning a house, a car, a lion or a handful of grapes will entail different rights and different duties.

A driving force for property is the condition of scarcity: 'In all times and places with which we are familiar, material resources are scarce relative to the human demands that are made on them ... Scarcity, as philosophers from Hume to Rawls have pointed out, is a presupposition of all sensible talk about property' (Waldron, 1988, p. 31). According to Waldron, the situation of scarcity generates a 'problem of allocation' – who gets what and why? If this problem is not dealt with properly, then conflict is likely to arise (Waldron, 1988, p. 32). Consider grapes – if there was a location where grapes naturally grew in abundance all year around, without the need for cultivation, in amounts so great that everyone who liked grapes was able to eat to their fill without noticeably reducing the abundance of grapes, there would seem[11] be no need for property. Yet if any of these conditions was to change, if the grapes required cultivation to grow, demand exceeded supply, or they only grew in abundance at particular points in time, there would be scarcity. It is in this scenario of resource scarcity where problems of property arise: there needs to be some way of allocating the grapes such that conflict between grape lovers does not break out.

Imagine Louise has a plot of land with an abundance of grapes and a situation of scarcity arises. Louise now says that she owns these grapes. When Louise says 'I own these grapes', what does that mean? First, her property claim arises between people. Property does not simply require scarcity but another person or thing to lay a claim of property against – and it need not be (though typically will be) another person or people; Gods or thieving insects will suffice.[12] This point of the intersubjective nature of property, often overlooked, is recognised at the very beginning of Peter Drahos' *A Philosophy of Intellectual Property*: 'Like other property rights, intellectual property rights are relations between individuals ... property rights entail relations between two people *and* between a person and an object' (Emphasis Original, Drahos, 1996, pp. 1, 4). A claim of property will state or imply who the owner is, what they own and who they are claiming property against.

Following this, I call attention to four things in Louise's statement 'I own these grapes': first, the claim identifies an owner (Louise), second, it identifies the thing

[11] The language is deliberately vague here, as this is a contentious claim. However, to get the discussion started, Waldron's claims in *The Right to Private Property* about scarcity are assumed to be correct (Waldron, 1988, pp. 31–32). Later sections explore ownership of intangibles, situations where property is invoked beyond material scarcity.

[12] This is an obscure claim, but imagine if natural forces take something away from you. It seems appropriate within common language to say 'damn you God, that was *my* house you washed away' or 'hey ants, stop eating *my* ice-cream sandwich'. The point here is that the agent is expressing some property claim against another agent and that second agent does not necessarily have to be a human for language of the property claim to make sense, though it remains to be seen if the claim is justified.

that is owned (these grapes), third, it is a claim against everyone else and finally, Louise's statement implies that her claim is morally justified.

3.3.3 *Individual Rights: Labour Investment and Historical Entitlement*

How then do we justify a claim property of objects? One way is to identify the first occupant: Louise might say, 'I own these grapes because I got to them first.' There are two immediate problems with this justification. First, what happens if Sean takes grapes from Louise's crop that she has not touched or grasped? Sean is the first occupant, so he attains rights of property over these *particular* grapes. Yet this reduces property to 'finders/keepers' and does not track to most legitimate justifications of property. More substantially, this does not justify property; instead it is a claim to *identify* the owner. Even if we are to recognise Sean's claim, in order to justify property, a story needs to be told *why* first touch equates to property.

One approach of justifying property is to locate the moral foundation in the rights of the individual. Perhaps the most discussed account is Locke's labour investment theory,[13] presented most clearly in §27, book two, of his *Two Treatises of Government*:

> Though the earth, and all inferior Creatures, be common to all Men, yet every Man has a *Property* in his own *Person:* this no Body has any right to but himself. The *labour* of his body, and the *Work* of his hands, we may say, are properly his. Whatsoever then he removes out of the State that Nature hath provided, and left it in, he hath mixed his *Labour* with, and joyned to it something that is his own, and thereby makes it his *Property* . . . for this *Labour* being the unquestionable Property of the Labourer, no man but he can have a right to what that is once joined to, at least where there is enough, and as good, left in common for others.
>
> (Emphases Original, Locke and Laslett, 1963, pp. 328–329)

Locke's idea is that people have ownership over themselves. When they work on something, they invest themselves in this thing and so become mixed with it. By extension, they come to own the thing worked on. For example, consider Louise. She has now dug the ground, planted seeds, watered and harvested grapes. By investing her labour in these grapes, she mixes some part of her person with the grapes. She has property over her person and so gains property rights in the fruits of her labour: in this case, grapes.

[13] Labour investment, though perhaps the most common way to read Locke, is not the only way to understand his account. For instance, Peter Drahos holds that 'Locke and the natural law tradition of which he was a part, remind us that the choices over property forms are choices about the nature of community' (Drahos, 1996, p. 68). On this account of Locke, in a negative commons all things are 'open to anybody to make the subject of exclusive belonging', whereas in a positive commons all thing are jointly, rather than individually, owned (Drahos, 1996, p. 57). So, if Locke had in mind a positive communal space, then things could be owned by labour, but jointly.

While much can be discussed about Locke's account,[14] two important things to note are that the rights generated from the labour are *special* or *contingent* rights and not *general* rights. Second, these rights must be understood in the larger context of Locke's work – in particular, property's lexical inferiority to a general right to subsistence.

On the first point, the generation of *special* rights as opposed to *general* rights, the investment of labour means that Louise gains property over the grapes as a result of her activity on the given grapes. Waldron[15] describes special rights as rights 'we have because of what has happened – because of the occurrence of some events, apart from which, we would not have the rights in question' (Waldron, 1988, p. 109). Louise's property of the grapes 'arises out of a particular *contingent* event in which [she] was involved – namely the event of [her] labouring on the field' (Emphasis Mine, Waldron, 1988, p. 108). The special right is contingent upon a particular event – labour, which separates Louise from other people.[16] Sean has not laboured in the field so has no such right (Waldron, 1988, p. 111). Contrasting special rights, general rights are not dependent upon a special set of circumstances, 'but attributes the [moral importance of the right] to the interest itself, in virtue of its qualitative character' (Waldron, 1988, p. 116). This distinction is relevant because the labour investment theory generates only special rights; only those who labour have a right to property, 'there is nothing in Locke to support the proposition that private property is something which all persons have a general right to; his position is that provided each person's subsistence is taken care of there is no cause for moral concern if anybody happens not to have acquired any resources as his own private property' (Waldron, 1988, p. 139).

This reference to subsistence brings us to the second point: the need to understand labour investment theory within the context of Locke's work. Waldron argues that an understanding of Locke's work prioritises the right to survival above the right to property (Waldron, 1988, pp. 137–252). The relevance comes from considering libertarians who strongly emphasise a property rights position. Will Kymlicka describes this position where property rights trump survival rights: '[n]o one has the right to take [resources] from me, even if it is to keep the disabled from starving' (Kymlicka, 2002, p. 104). The libertarian reading holds that Louise owns her plot of land and all the food stuffs that it generates. Further, she has no moral obligation to

[14] Waldron's *The Right to Private Property*, especially chapters 6 and 7, present a thorough examination of Locke's theory. Waldron discusses Locke within the historical and religious context that Locke was writing in (Waldron, 1988).

[15] Note that Waldron follows the distinction between special and general rights developed in H. L. A. Hart's *Are There any Natural Rights*, (Waldron, 1988, pp. 106–109).

[16] As I understand Waldron's take on Locke, property rights expressed in Kantian terms would be perfect but non-universal as the owner is specified in contrast to all others as non-owners, but the rights are only generated by the owner's labour (Griffin, 2008, p. 96).

feed Sean, even if Sean is starving.[17] If he steals Louise's food, even if it is for his survival, he commits a serious wrong against Louise. His action is impermissible and the state ought to intervene on Louise's behalf.

Yet according to Waldron, on a complete Lockean account, the special rights to property 'are themselves constrained by a deep and, in the last resort, more powerful *general* right which each man has to the material necessities for his survival' (Emphasis Original, Waldron, 1988, p. 139). In §42 of the *First Treatise*, Locke states:

> As *Justice* gives for every Man a Title to the product of his honest Industry, and the fair Acquisition of his Ancestors descended to him; so *Charity* gives every Man a Title to so much out of another's Plenty, as will keep him from extream want, where he has no means to subsist otherwise.
>
> (Emphases Original, Locke and Laslett, 1963, pp. 205–206)

So, on a full Lockean account, property rights are trumped by a general right to survival.

Under Locke's theory, the 'mixing' of one's labour with material objects presumes a directionality of property. We gain property over the new thing, rather than simply losing our labour. However, Robert Nozick asks:

> Why isn't mixing what I own with what I don't a way of losing what I own rather than a way of gaining what I don't? If I own a can of tomato juice and spill it in the sea so that its molecules . . . mingle evenly throughout the sea, do I thereby come to own the sea, or have I foolishly dissipated my tomato juice?
>
> (Nozick, 1974, pp. 174–175)

For Nozick, this presents a challenge to standard Lockean property rights. Instead, he offers a different interpretation of property rights generated from the Lockean proviso to leave 'enough and as good, left in common for others' (Locke and Laslett, 1963, p. 329). Nozick states '[t]he crucial point is whether appropriation of an unowned object worsens the situation of others' (Nozick, 1974, p. 175). On Nozick's account, justice in holdings is 'exhaustively covered' by three steps:

1. A person who acquires a holding in accordance with the principle of justice in acquisition is entitled to that holding.
2. A person who acquires a holding in accordance with the principle of justice in transfer, from someone else entitled to the holding, is entitled to the holding.
3. No one is entitled to a holding except by (repeated) applications of 1 and 2 (Nozick, 1974, p. 151).

[17] This strong position described by Kymlicka could be associated most clearly with Robert Nozick. However, to be charitable to Nozick, he does not explicitly say that people should starve. Perhaps where his account is most similar to that described by Kymlicka is in a footnote in *Anarchy, State and Utopia*, where Nozick states 'a right to life is not a right to whatever one needs to live; other people may have rights over these other things . . . one *first* needs a theory of property rights before one can apply any supposed right to life' (Emphasis Original, Nozick, 1974, p. 179). The account presented in *Anarchy, State and Utopia* holds that property rights are more important than a right to remain alive.

These three features are central to Nozick's account: '[A] principle of (initial) acquisition, a principle of transfer and a principle of rectification. Its central tenet is that any configuration of holdings that results from the legitimate transfer of legitimately acquired holdings is itself just' (Scanlon, 1976, pp. 4–5).

Thomas Scanlon notes that Nozick's account offers no more than a 'skeletal framework of rights derived from Locke' (Scanlon, 1976, p. 4): Nozick offers no explanation for the original acquisition. The most he says is '[w]e shall refer to the complicated truth about this topic, which we shall not formulate here, as the principle of justice in acquisition' (Nozick, 1974, p. 150). This lack of justification of initial acquisition is troubling, as it is the foundation of Nozick's argument and justifies entitlement and a right of transfer.[18] Waldron states that Nozick's Principle of Just Transfer 'operates on material provided in the first instance by the [Principle of Just Acquisition]', yet 'Nozick does not tell us what his favoured [Principle of Just Acquisition] is' (Waldron, 1988, p. 257).

Perhaps the reason for the lack of elaboration of any principle of just acquisition in Nozick stems from a fundamental problem within Locke's own justification of property rights. Locke's justification was built from the premise that one gains property over the thing laboured on by mixing one's labour. 'The idea that labour is literally *mixed with* an object is crucial to this argument. Without it we cannot explain how the force of the labour entitlement is transferred to the product of one's labour' (Emphasis Original, Waldron, 1988, p. 184). Locke's justification stands on two things: self-ownership and the extension of that self-ownership into other things via the mixing of labour (Waldron, 1988, p. 177). Waldron argues that labour is an action, not a thing and one cannot own an action, which leads him to say that the notion 'that the object thereby comes to contain something the labourer owns – is left completely mysterious' (Waldron, 1988, p. 185). Waldron concludes that Locke's labour investment theory, 'the best known [special rights] based theory fails to provide an adequate defence of private property' (Waldron, 1988, p. 252).

So, a Lockean account of property rights like that described by Nozick fails as it offers no justification of initial acquisition. Locke's own account fails as it cannot explicate what is central to Locke's justification: mixing labour with an object. While somewhat involved, recognition of the justifications and their weaknesses are important. First, if labour investment and historical entitlement, some of the most common justifications offered for property claims, have a weak or non-existent foundation, then any property claims based on these justifications are weak at best. Second, it prompts us to investigate different moral foundations of property.

[18] Thomas Nagel states that Nozick's book, '[d]espite its ingenuity of detail … is entirely unsuccessful as an attempt to convince and far less successful than it might be as an attempt to explain to someone who does not hold the position why anyone else does hold it' (Nagel, 1975, p. 137).

3.3.4 *Individual Rights: Psychological Individuation*

An alternative account for individual property rights is developed by Georg Hegel,[19] and is drawn from people's need for psychological individuation.[20] On individuation, Hegel argues that a person can only[21] develop their personality, or 'individuate', through an expression of their will. We are born with a mind that is free and infinite: 'There is no external limit to the range of the mind's capacity; there is nothing which it cannot know' (Reyburn, 1921, pp. 77–78). However, if we were to leave the mind at that we would be empty: the mind needs the external world to give it substance. 'Mind obtains its substance from the outer world; the details of its contents have been found [by the mind] and can all be traced to 'natural' sources ... By apprehending the object and taking it as content, mind articulates and determines itself' (Reyburn, 1921, p. 84). For Waldron, this means that '[f]ree will must proceed out of its initial embodiment in [the subject] into the external world where a genuinely universal embodiment can be established' (Waldron, 1988, p. 354). This expression of the will in the world is a dynamic interaction, where the mind and the world show themselves 'not only opposed to but identical with its opposite' (Taylor, 1978, p. 15).

Hegel's writing is often dense and obscure: the 'mind has emerged as the Idea that has reached its being-for-self. The *object* of the Idea as well as the *subject is the concept*. This identity is *absolute negativity* ... this externalization of the concept has been sublated and the concept has, in this externalization, become identical with itself' (Emphases Original, Hegel and Inwood, 2007 §381, p. 9). This is a dialectic model where things become themselves through their opposite.[22] Stepping past the complexities in Hegel's language, his basic point is that the mind individuates itself

[19] Given the range of subjects that Hegel covered in his writings and the breadth and depth of Hegel scholarship, I cannot do justice to his ideas here. Most of the relevant material is taken from his *Philosophy of Right* with some supporting material from his *Philosophy of Mind* (Hegel, 1967; Hegel and Inwood, 2007). Secondary sources like Charles Taylor, Hugh Reyburn and Alan Patten are also helpful (Patten, 1999; Reyburn, 1921; Taylor, 1975, 1978). Amongst other places, this account of Hegelian property rights is spelled out in detail in chapter 4 of Drahos' A *Philosophy of Intellectual Property*, by Margaret Radin in *Property and Personhood* and Waldron in chapter 10 of *The Right to Private Property* (Drahos, 1996; Radin, 1981; Waldron, 1988).

[20] Some may disagree that psychological individuation is an accurate description: '[a]lthough [Hegel's account] resembles a psychological account of personality and property, it is closer to a teaching of an understanding of property and personality' (Drahos, 1996, p. 78). However, note that Hegel states that '[b]y resolving itself, the will posits itself as the will of a specific individual and as a will *separating itself off against another individual*' (Emphasis Mine, Hegel, 1967 §13, p. 26). So, on this, it seems fair to describe Hegel's approach as one of psychological individuation. Either way, the major point of relevance of Hegel to this book is the relation he establishes between identity and information.

[21] Note that, in contrast to Locke's system where labour investment generates a special or contingent right, psychological individuation is a *general* right, possessed by all people.

[22] Though obscure, this revealing of the self through the other can be summarised as follows: Hegel's dialectic of identity 'presents us with something which cannot be grasped in ... a series

by exercising its capacity to will in the world. By expressing itself in the world, the mind externalises itself and so it becomes substantiated. The elements of this relationship – in this case, the mind and the external world – interact with each other and mutually influence each other.[23]

The first stage of becoming a person occurs when the individual's will is externalised by its embodiment. In this early step, the agent's mind acts within and upon the agent's own body (Taylor, 1978, p. 20). Waldron claims that 'the first step in this process of externalization is the establishment of the bare principle of [the agent's] personality in the public world of material objects' (Waldron, 1988, pp. 355–356).[24]

While there is an issue of mental causation[25] in explaining *how* the will actually expresses itself in the body, it seems reasonable to say that an agent's will manifests itself in some way through their body: rejecting such a position would result in the absurd idea that all humans were automatons or accidents, stumbling through the world chaotically.

Bringing the discussion back to Hegel, personal development requires exercise of the will in the world, via embodiment. Through the will's expression in the world, our personality begins to develop.

> 'Through this positing of itself as something determinate, the ego steps in principle into determinate existence' (Hegel, 1967, p 22).

According to Waldron, this embodiment of the will in the body and in things in the world is not a mere a capacity for agents, but a fundamental psychological *need*: Agents 'need to be able to "embody" the freedom of their personalities in external objects so that their conceptions of themselves as persons cease to be purely subjective and become concrete and recognizable to themselves and others in a public and external world' (Waldron, 1988, p. 353). Hegel makes this need of the will to express itself beyond the boundaries of the body an *absolute* natural right: 'A person has as his substantive end the right of putting his will into any and every

of propositions which [do] not violate the principle of non-contradiction . . . [that is] A is A, that A is also –A; and that –A shows itself to be after all A' (Taylor, 1978, p. 15).

23 Chapter 6 presents the argument that identity and Personal Information are in a 'dyadic' relationship, built around a process of continuous reciprocal causation.

24 In early development, infants develop an understanding of their physical body through movements that correspond with the way organs and sensory inputs relate to each other. This is called 'body babbling', where 'infants move their limbs and facial organs in repetitive body play . . . What is acquired through body babbling is a mapping between movements and the organ-relation end states that are attained' (Meltzoff and Moore, 1997, p. 184). Waldron has missed, or at least obscured, a vital step. The first step of embodiment is the expression of the will in the agent's *own* body. For the will to develop, it must first come to grips with actual embodiment in its body.

25 Mental causation, the problem of how the mind as a non-material thing can interact with the body, which is a material thing, is another massive area in philosophy that can't be covered here. For an introductory overview, see the entry in the *Stanford Encyclopedia of Philosophy* on *Mental Causation* (Robb and Heil, 2009).

thing and thereby making it his, because it has no such end in itself and derives its destiny and soul from his will. This is the *absolute* right of appropriation which man has over all "things"' (Emphasis Mine, Hegel, 1967 §44, p. 52).[26]

Combining this capacity of things to express a person's will with the absolute right of appropriation, we come to have property rights in external things:

> Since my will, as the will of a person ... becomes objective to me in property, property acquires the character of private property; and common property of such a nature that it may be owned by separate persons acquires the character of an inherently dissoluble partnership in which the retention of my share is explicitly a matter of my arbitrary preference.
>
> (Hegel, 1967 §46, p. 42)

Summarising Hegel's account, a person's will is expressed through things and as a person has the natural right to their 'private personality' and to their 'self-consciousness' this right extends to those things that their will has occupied.

While the Lockean and Hegelian justifications are similar, they differ in their mechanisms. Recall that in labour investment Locke relied on the *actual* mixing of labour with a given thing. Hegel's account differs in that it is not the *mixing* of labour with external things that grants a property claim to the labourer, but an *expression* of an agent's will in the external thing. A response to this could be 'if Locke's account failed, as it relied on a strange mixing of labour, how could Hegel's account succeed, where it relies on a similarly "spooky" embodiment of the will in external things?' Note that the process is referred to as being an *expression* of the will in external things rather than an actual *embodiment* of the will in the external thing.

To explain, assume that people have a will, which they can express through their body. Problems of mental causation aside, if the will can express itself in a physical entity like the agent's body, it seems to follow that that the will can also express itself in physical objects beyond the boundary of the body. Importantly, I am not saying that the object actually takes on the agent's will; there is no 'spooky' transference of will into the object. Instead there is an expression of the agent's will in (or through)[27] the object: the argument is not that there is embodiment of a person's will in something external, but that others can recognise the person's will through its expression in external things. If Fred watches Georgie walk to a window and open

[26] As an aside, note that things without an expressed will can receive an agent's will; however, things and especially people, which have a will expressed of their own cannot take in a new will without some diminution of their own will. Taking human slavery, for example, this diminution of one's will by another is a grave moral injustice (Waldron, 1988, pp. 357–358).

[27] 'In or through' is used here as, depending on the form of expression and the type of object, some expressions may be said to be in the object, while some will be through the object. For instance, one could argue that an artist's will is expressed *in* a painting, while the artist's will was expressed *through* the act of painting. To say more on this issue is beyond the scope of this book, as the point being made is about the object and its relation to the expression of will.

it with her arms, it does not seem odd or spooky for Fred to say that Georgie willed the window to be open, that her physical actions expressed this will.[28]

Importantly, on the Hegelian justification, there must be some relation between the will and the object, '[t]here has to be some physical relation between the body inhabited by the will in question and the external object in which that will is to be embodied' (Waldron, 1988, p. 363). Returning to the relation between the will and the world, the will acts upon the world and in doing so, the world gives substance to the will. 'My will is reflected in the object inasmuch as there is this *dual line of effect from my will to the object and back to my will*' (Emphasis Mine, Waldron, 1988, p. 370). If we consider a chair that I have built, 'the embodiment involves something like a *conjunction* of *two* relations between my will and the chair. There is (1) the relation constituted by my having built the chair and (2) the relation constituted by my being in a position to use or modify the chair' (Emphasis Original, Waldron, 1988, p. 369). What Waldron sees in Hegel is a reflection between the will and the object: a relation of mutual causality[29] between the will and the external world. The object of the will's embodiment is the 'nexus' of this relation (Waldron, 1988, p. 370).

3.3.5 *Social Good*

One alternative way of justifying property rights is that they promote social good: whether it is the institution of property generally, or property rights in a set of given things, some hold that such rights maximise the good for all in a given society, what I'll refer to as 'social good'.[30]

Consider Thomas Hobbes' famous line that the 'warre of every man against every man', makes 'the life of man, solitary, poore, nasty, brutish and short' (Hobbes, 1968, pp. 188, 186). This state arises when people are 'without a common power over them to keep them in awe, [so] are in a state of war of every person against every other ... Hobbes contends that, in the state of war, there is so little security of life and property, that all live in constant fear and productive work is pointless' (Kavka, 1983, p. 292). Without an authority of some sort to secure life and property, everyone's life is bad. While Hobbes' account is centred on the importance of authority for security in general, Gregory Kavka points out that the securing of property is one of the fundamental roles for the given authority (Kavka, 1983). We all benefit by having secure property, as part of the bulwark against a war of all against all.

[28] This attribution of beliefs and desires to other agents relies on a folk psychological explanation of behaviour and is discussed in §4.6.3.

[29] Mutually causal relations are discussed in §6.5. To summarise, they are relations in which two things mutually impact each other.

[30] In this section, when I talk of 'social good' I mean something that is held to be good for a given society. Unless otherwise specified, I do not mean to refer to *a* good that can only be realised by a given society – public healthcare, education, road infrastructure and so on.

David Hume presents a case for property founded on social good and self-interested agents. The 'principal disturbance in society arises from those goods, which we call external and from their looseness and easy transition from one person to another' (Hume, 1985, p. 541). Like Hobbes, Hume locates the importance of conventions to fix property to an owner as a way of promoting security, '[I]t is by that means we maintain society, which is so necessary to their well-being and subsistence, as well as to our own' (Hume, 1985, p. 541). The support for a set of social conventions recognising property arises from enlightened self-interest: 'I observe, that it will be for my interest to leave another in the possession of his goods, provided he will act in the same manner with regard to me' (Hume, 1985, p. 541). On Hume's account, rational self-interested agents all benefit from a stable society and property rights are needed to secure such stability.

Similar to arguments from social stability, another justification comes from the increased welfare[31] that property promotes. This argument holds that property encourages production of goods which are directly beneficial to people's wellbeing. For example, property encourages Louise to grow more grapes than she needs and these grapes can be distributed. This way, Louise's land not only increases her wellbeing by providing her with grapes but also increases the wellbeing of others.

The flip side to this argument is that people are harmed by *not* having a system of property rights. This is often referred to as the 'tragedy of the commons', in which all are harmed from individual overexploitation of natural resources (Hardin, 1968). Allowing open access to natural resources, each agent benefits by use, but all suffer when the natural resources run out or are polluted. 'Ruin is the destination toward which all men rush, each pursuing his own best interest in a society that believes in the freedom of the commons. Freedom in a commons brings ruin to all' (Hardin, 1968, p. 1244). Despite Hardin's idea that private property can be detrimental to protecting the commons,[32] the 'tragedy of the commons' is often used as an argument in support of individual property rights:

> What the private owner holds, he protects, cares for, betters. The environment gains ipso facto. This corollary is worthy to be heeded by those who these days are anxious about the fate of the elephant, the rhinoceros and the fish stocks of the ocean. While these remain in the state of ferae naturae (free ranging and wild) there are first cousin to nes nullius (nobody's thing). Trammel them round with a private property fence and Lo! There are at once and henceforth safe from marauders,

[31] Welfare here does not refer to state support of individuals, like the 'welfare state'. Instead it refers to Shelly Kagan's description of 'welfarism', which 'claims that well-being is *all* that matters' (Emphasis Original, Kagan, 1998a, p. 48). On Kagan's description, a strict welfarist holds that wellbeing (however described) is the only value to be considered and so this ought to be maximised.

[32] 'Indeed, our particular concept of private property, which deters us from exhausting the positive resources of the earth, favors pollution' (Hardin, 1968, p. 1245).

> predators, free-riders and the madding crowd. Not only so; they are open as never before to the democratic interchanges of the free market in property, the acquire value, it pays to bred and rear them – the species is safe.
>
> (Denman, 1997, p. 166)

Looking at social good and property rights, an institution of private property reduces the harms arising from overexploitation of resources held in common.

A related, but different, strand to the 'property as wellbeing' argument is the concept that people benefit from some institutional recognition of property, as this property forms the basis for economic development and growth: '[E]conomic growth occurs if output grows faster than population ... economic growth will occur if property rights make it worthwhile to undertake socially productive activity' (North and Thomas, 1973, p. 9). While there are different mechanisms operating within this, the basic argument is that economic growth is a good thing, property rights encourage economic growth[33] and therefore, property rights ought to be recognised.[34]

'Property as stability', 'property wellbeing' and 'property as growth' arguments all recognise a need for property and institutionalise this need in terms of property rights. However, the moral justification of the rights claim is not in the individual's property rights: the rights are contingent on property leading to some other good – social stability, economic growth, overall wellbeing and so on. As they are contingent upon these other goods, the rights might be justifiably overridden when the other goods demand it. An economic libertarian, in contrast, may hold that an individual's property rights trump any social goods that may be gained by overriding the individual's claim.

In summary, this section started with the relations between property and surveillance technologies, introduced the idea of property and looked at three different justifications for property rights: labour investment and historical entitlement, psychological individuation and social good. Locke's labour investment theory seemed promising, but ultimately lacked a clear mechanism to justify why something like first occupancy could be sustained. Hegel's psychological individuation, however, develops an argument in support of a general and non-contingent right to private property. Following Waldron, 'property is something which it is important for every individual to have, so that there is a basis for overriding ethical concern if some people are left poor and property*less*' (Emphasis Original, Waldron, 1988, p. 342). That is, if one takes the Hegelian system seriously, all people have a property claim

[33] I note that some people hold that economic liberty is a right in itself – Milton Friedman (Friedman, 1970), for example, presents an extreme end of this view.

[34] Of course, there are a number of important moral and empiric claims contained within this economic growth argument – is economic growth necessarily a good thing? Do property rights actually incentivise innovation? Do more goods always mean economic growth or does it depend on the type of good? The argument at its most simple is economic growth is morally good and that if you want economic growth, you need property rights.

in things that are necessary for individuation, those things central to self-development. Finally, we saw that while the social good arguments were internally sound, they have the limitation that property rights could be overridden in the face of greater social good.

3.4 INTELLECTUAL PROPERTY: OWNING THE INTANGIBLE

We have so far looked at owning tangible things. This section looks at ownership of the intangible – intellectual property. To describe intellectual property, let's revisit Louise. She now has grapes in abundance. In fact, she has too many grapes; each year many rot on the vine. Sharon, Louise's enterprising neighbour, has developed a way of preserving grapes by crushing them, collecting the liquid and storing it in large watertight barrels. Having spoken with Sharon and tired of losing all her uneaten grapes, Louise decides to follow Sharon's method. A few months later, Louise tastes this liquid, finds that it is extremely tasty. She tells people in the village and within days is selling her product to villagers. Sharon realises that Louise is likely to make large amounts of money and becomes annoyed. She tells Louise that it was her idea, so considers that she is entitled to some of the money that Louise is making. 'Why?' asks Louise, 'it was my *effort* that grew the grapes and that made the juice. It is mine. You did nothing to make this wine'. Sharon looks at Louise with surprise 'Nothing? It was my *idea* to do this. Without my idea you would have nothing. Given that *I* first expressed this idea, I own it. Until you pay me what I deserve, I will appeal to the city council to stop you from selling any more wine.' We now have Sharon claiming property rights over an idea, the intangible.

The dispute between Louise and Sharon is not about tangibles like grapes or products like wine. The dispute is about intangibles like ideas, 'products of the mind'. Intellectual property allows things like songs, stories, movies, invention designs, genes (Drahos and Braithwaite, 2002) and perhaps even colours[35] to be owned. How does this come about? First, intellectual property relies on active institutional support of the claimant's rights. Robert is likely to know if someone has taken his car without his consent. It is much harder for him to know if someone else is using his idea. Importantly, it is even harder to stop them using his idea than his car: even when it is in public, he can lock his car to prevent someone taking it. How can he lock up an idea?[36] To limit access to ideas, legal institutions are needed, so intellectual property typically refers to the *institutional* recognition of a creator's rights.

[35] In an example of owning a colour, a confectionary company attempted to prevent another confectionary company from using a shade of purple similar to their own (Gillies, 2009).

[36] One way is to keep the idea private, like a trade secret. But if Robert wants to profit from his idea, then it would likely need to be in public in some way. And if it is in public, it is no longer secret.

These rights are controls over ideas and their expression.[37] The two main forms[38] of intellectual property protection are copyright and patents. Copyright relates to the expression of an idea,[39] while patents relate to the idea itself. In contrast to copyright, patents grant the recognised owner a monopolistic right of exclusion over an idea. A patent on a pharmaceutical, for example, can exclude non-owners and/or non-licensees from producing that pharmaceutical. As David Koepsell points out, the patent is a rights claim over the universal form of the item, a set of controls over the type, not the token (Koepsell, 2009, p. 10). One typical practical difference between patents and copyright is that copyright requires recognition of the original author, while a patent can prevent use of the idea:

> Patents restrict the actual usage of an idea (in making a physical object), while copyrights restrict only copying an expression of an idea. One can freely use the ideas in a copyrighted book in one's own writing, provided one acknowledges their origin. One cannot freely use the ideas a patented invention represents when developing one's own product.
>
> (Hettinger, 1989, p. 52)

For a patent to be valid, generally it must meet four criteria: accurate description of manufacture, novelty, inventiveness and utility (Ricketson and Richardson, 1998, p. 627).[40] Importantly, this validation allows for the institutionally recognised owner to restrict others' use of the idea. 'The right to exclude can be a very significant ... right and may be sufficient to turn what, previously, would have been collective property into private property' (Lever, 2001). Institutional recognition of intellectual property, like in the Canavan and Catalona cases, represents a significant restriction on how people access and use Personal Information. It is therefore important to see how such property rights over the intangible are justified.

If intellectual property is the institutionalised prevention of someone accessing or using an idea, we may ask: 'Why should one person have the exclusive right to possess and use something which all people could possess and use concurrently?' (Hettinger, 1989, p. 35). Owning a Cadillac is very different from owning an idea:

[37] Making a clear distinction between what counts as an idea and an expression is hard. However, I will use this distinction given that it is standard in discussions of intellectual property.

[38] There are other forms of intellectual property, like design, trade secrets and plant breeder's rights, but they are not particularly relevant to the current discussion.

[39] To illustrate copyright, consider the story of Romeo and Juliet: the idea has two star-crossed lovers from different families whose lives and love end tragically. Now, consider West Side Story: the idea has two star-crossed lovers from different families whose lives and love end tragically. The idea between the two is the same (or at least, relevantly similar), but the expression differs: clearly Shakespeare's story uses different language, different characters and a different setting to those in West Side Story: the same idea is expressed differently.

[40] 'Generally' is used here, as different legal jurisdictions will take different factors into account for assessing the validity of a patent application. For one detailed introduction to the history and requirements of valid patents within the Australian legal system, including many case examples, see (Ricketson and Richardson, 1998, pp. 543–767).

only one person can use the Cadillac at one time while an idea can be used by many people at once (Drahos and Braithwaite, 2002, p. 26). The general position on intellectual property is one of moral pluralism, balancing the interests of individual creators with society's interests: a creator is encouraged to make their idea known to the public and in return they get a monopoly over that idea or its expression for a limited period of time,[41] at which point the idea becomes open and free for all. 'Our society gives its inventors and writers a legal right to exclude others from certain uses of their intellectual works in return for public disclosure of these works' (Hettinger, 1989, p. 36). This way, the copyright and patent owners get to profit from the creation and then the ideas enter the common pool of ideas to benefit society at large. Similar to the pluralistic approach to privacy advocated in Chapter 2, intellectual property is typically justified by four plural interacting values: Lockean style labour investment, Hegelian personhood, economic/utilitarian and social planning[42] (Fitzgerald, 2003, p. 180).

We saw in the previous section three justifications for property rights: labour investment, psychological individuation and social good. How do these relate to intellectual property arising from surveillance technologies? We can start with natural rights justifications for ownership of Personal Information. Yet, recalling the previous section's discussion, labour investment alone does not offer a stable foundation for property. Following Justin Hughes, if Locke's view is to be used, it needs to be combined with Hegel's (Hughes, 1988, p. 329). From Hegel, we justify an owner's claims by reference to psychological individuation, where the creator's will is made substantial through its expression (Waldron, 1988, pp. 369–370), or on the need for social recognition (Patten, 1999, pp. 157–161). Hegel, perhaps in conjunction with Locke, can justify natural rights for a creator – in this case, the person who created the product of surveillance. However, justifying property claims of the products of surveillance in natural rights means that other individual needs trump intellectual property: recall that in Locke's system, subsistence trumps property rights (§3.3.3). Similarly, 'Hegel does not believe that property rights are absolute anyway against the demands that might arise out of higher stages of ethical development' (Waldron, 1988, p. 387). Staying alive is a necessity for higher ethical development, so – all other things being

[41] Copyright and patents differ in the length of exclusivity that they grant: copyright is something in the vicinity of seventy years following the author's death, while patents are fourteen to twenty-one years following invention or application submission, depending on the jurisdiction. However, these time periods can change: the US 'Sonny Bono' Copyright Term Extension Act of 1998, further extended the term length of copyright protection (Merges and Reynolds, 2000) and patent 'evergreening' allows for patents to be extended beyond their initial terms (Faunce and Lexchin, 2007). Some, like Richard Posner, argue that there are important economic benefits coming from long terms for intellectual property rights (Posner, 2005, pp. 58–62).

[42] To give an idea of this, social planning is given as a justification for intellectual property based on 'reasons of cultural enhancement' (Fitzgerald, 2003, pp. 183–184). Similar to the economic/utilitarian justification, the idea of social planning is that by fostering a creator's rights, we develop a rich informational and cultural landscape which is ultimately a good in itself. Given that much of the discussion about the justification of intellectual property is on utilitarian and natural rights, I do not talk about social planning.

equal – it would trump an information owner's holder's rights. As we will see in Chapter 9, this circles back to discussions of national security.

Given this pluralism of foundations, or perhaps despite it, economic/utilitarian justifications, the social good, often take precedence over other interests:

> Arguably, the guiding premise of American copyright and patent law is the utilitarian ethic that legal protection of intellectual property (especially copyright and patent) is needed to advance public welfare because it fosters creative genius/product which can in turn be distributed for the good of the general public.
>
> (Fitzgerald, 2003, p. 180)

Further supporting this view, Edwin Hettinger states: 'Natural rights to the fruits of one's labor are not by themselves sufficient to justify copyrights, patents and trade secrets, though they are relevant to the social decision to create and sustain intellectual property institutions' (Hettinger, 1989, p. 51). Justifying intellectual property in natural moral rights is hard.[43] So hard that rather than saying that the inventor or creator has such natural rights (either by Lockean or Hegelian justification), the social good justification is typically used.

This is directly relevant to surveillance technologies: when thinking of control over Personal Information, if utilitarian reasons are to take precedence over individual rights, then it means that the social good of surveillance programmes trumps individual claims to control their Personal Information. This would then suggest that a collective good like national security ought to be chosen over individual rights. However, as we will see in Chapter 9, it is incumbent on those making national security claims that a given surveillance programme will actually protect the collective good. Moreover, in addition to the necessity to justify why individual rights of privacy, property and recognition are outweighed (§8.3–8.6), as §9.3 shows, any claims would need to take seriously the set of harms that arise from use and misuse of aggregated Personal Information.

A further complication comes in at the core of utilitarian reasoning: that the social good can trump individual rights.[44] If we couch social good in terms of utility and if widespread surveillance regimes are detrimental to people's wellbeing,[45] then

[43] For instance, Thomas Pogge writes: 'The difficulties of defending (legal) intellectual property rights by appeal to (moral) natural rights are so overwhelming that most defenders of the ongoing intellectual property initiative appeal to the beneficial consequences of protecting property rights ... such rights incentivize intellectual innovation, or so we are told' (Pogge, 2008, p. 230).

[44] In line with my discussion in §1.5, I do not want to be understood as saying that a consequentialist system is unable to recognise rights, or that a rights system is unable to respond to extreme consequences. Some accounts of consequentialism may be able to recognise rights (Pettit, 1988) and some deontological theories, like threshold deontology (Alexander, 2008, pp. 85–90), respect individual rights but only up to a given threshold. The point is that there is a lot of effort and sophistication needed for a consequentialist ethics like utilitarianism to retain the individualist protections found in deontological ethics.

[45] For example, Greenwald argues that state-based surveillance programmes can be highly detrimental to society at large (Greenwald, 2014, pp. 170–210).

should institutional claims of property over Personal Information be upheld? If utilitarian reasons are used to justify the moral claims on external ownership of Personal Information, then this utilitarian reasoning can also limit property, whether at a specific or more general level.[46]

Of direct relevance to surveillance technologies is the recognition of those whose intellectual labour was necessary in creating the products of surveillance. Drahos and Braithwaite argue that the original creator is often not the owner of the patent or copyright (Drahos and Braithwaite, 2002, pp. 48, 166, 176). So, on this, it would seem that the Hegelian justification is weakened, as it was based in the development of self by reflection and recognition of that will's expression.[47] If – as is the case in institutional ownership of Personal Information – the owner is not the creator, then that institutional owner does not have that strong connection via psychological individuation. Note also that for the products of surveillance there are likely to be many contributors: who amongst these is identifiable as the owner in a Hegelian sense?

Second to this, 'ideas have fuzzy boundaries' (Drahos and Braithwaite, 2002, p. 26): we may not even be able to properly identify the thing owned. Like Nozick's tomato juice in the ocean, how do we actually identify the boundaries of a given idea, such that we can see it in relation to Hegel's need for individuation or social recognition of the will? Finally, perhaps, with the four foundational values of intellectual property (Fitzgerald, 2003, p. 180) there is a pluralism between them, where no single value trumps the others. Balancing or trade-offs between foundational principles would likely mean that intellectual property rights themselves are not trumps; any property claims over the products of surveillance need to be considered alongside other values.

The key point is that, on any justification, intellectual property rights are not absolute. Either they are contingent and become subsumed under the social good or are non-absolute claims, so in particular situations get outweighed or traded off against other rights, interests or values. Further, as we have seen, in order to get a proper justification for a property claim over an intangible like meaningful information, we need to see who has the strongest connection to that information and who is impacted most by its use and exclusivity.

3.5 SURVEILLANCE PRODUCTS, PERSONAL INFORMATION AND PROPERTY

To make the links to surveillance technologies explicit, given that Personal Information is intangible, the justifications discussed will help us identify who has a moral claim to the Personal Information. By looking at the concept of Personal

[46] At the more general level, for instance, advocates of intellectual property rights regimes hold that without patents there would be no innovation. However, this was not historically the case (Johnston and Wasunna, 2007) and as Pogge points out, there may be alternative forms of incentivisation (Pogge, 2005a, b, 2008, pp. 230–261).

[47] As discussed in §3.3.3.

Information, we get a better understanding of such information so that we can make sense of moral claims of ownership over it.

To draw in the moral importance of surveillance products, what I am most interested in is surveillance products that are about people: while surveillance as a process might involve producing meaningful information about non-humans, animals in their natural habitat, for instance, people are the focus here. As introduced in §3.2, surveillance produces information, stipulated as 'data that is well ordered, meaningful and judged to be true'.[48] Given the focus on people, we are thus concerned with Personal Information, stipulated as 'information that relates to a person or group of people[49] in some way, signifying that there is some relation between a person and some information'.[50] Under this description, what counts as Personal Information? Any data set about a person – their name, age, birth date, hair colour. Note that this set can be as broad or specific as one wants – it could potentially include something as general as the fact that a person is a human, or could be something so specific as an individual's physical location over a period of time collected from a car's Global Positioning System (GPS) (Ramli, 2011).

To anticipate the conclusion, in line with the pluralism of property justifications, Personal Information which is morally relevant[51] is information that either (a) was derived from their labour via Locke, (b) is an expression of their will, from Hegel and/or (c) has some substantial impact on wellbeing such that it ultimately maximises social good. In short, a property claim over information is most strongly justified by the person that is strongly tied to that information and/or the person that is most vulnerable to uses of it and/or the social good.[52] This means that if we want to identify justified claims of property over Personal Information, we must seek to identify who is most strongly identified with that information and those whose welfare will be most affected by that information. In short, we must locate those from whom the information came, the sources of the information and those to whom the information is most relevant: the targets of the information.[53]

On individual rights justifications, both Locke's and Hegel's justifications are relevant to Personal Information. Given that Hegel's justifications were deemed stronger than Locke's, Hegel is the focus here. The same general conclusions hold

[48] This general description of information is taken from Luciano Floridi's general definition of information, discussed in detail in Chapter 5.

[49] For ease of use, I will simply refer to a single person unless otherwise stated. However, all that is said about an individual person here is applicable to groups of people.

[50] This description of Personal Information is explained in Chapter 7.

[51] As a way of focusing upon important Personal Information, what is relevant to this book is the need to consider *morally relevant* Personal Information. Obviously though, reference to morally relevant Personal Information is vacuous unless there is a way to determine which Personal Information is morally important and why it should be considered morally relevant. Chapters 6 and 7 are focused on these problems.

[52] See Chapters 8 and 9 for a deeper development of these ideas.

[53] §7.4 gives a detailed account of how we can understand Personal Information as it relates to people, which I describe as people as the source and target of information.

for labour investment. Consider again the fundamental importance of personality to the Hegelian justification of property:

> [T]hose goods, or rather substantive characteristics which constitute my own private personality and the universal essence of my self-consciousness are inalienable and my right to them is imprescriptible. Such characteristics are my personality as such, my universal freedom of will, my ethical life, my religion.
>
> (Hegel, 1967 §66, pp. 52–53)

This draws out two morally important features of property and Personal Information. First, Hegel's inalienable link between a person's 'universal essence of self-consciousness' tracks to personhood. Second, some things are fundamentally important to a person. Recalling §2.3.3, intimacy was an attitudinal state towards things that a person likes, loves or cares about. Hegel's description of the importance of the relations between a person and characteristics central to them explicates the arguments about personhood and intimacy, which overlaps with the conceptions of privacy as personhood and intimacy.

However, to legitimately claim that *Personal Information* is central to a system of psychological individuation, two further steps are needed. The particular mechanism or mechanisms that relate Personal Information to personhood must be developed. Chapters 4–6 are detailed expositions of this mechanism. Second, central to this mechanism, we need a way to identify what Hegel calls the 'substantive characteristics which constitute my own private personality'. On this point, consider Waldron's description of Hegel's system: 'A person's will is embodied in an object to the extent that (1) his will has made a difference to the object and (2) the object, affected in this way by his will, itself makes a difference in turn to his willing' (Waldron, 1988, p. 370). That is, how has the expression of the person's will impacted the object and how does the object in turn impact the person's will?

Waldron's discussion of the will and object outlines a dyadic relationship. A dyadic relationship is one where two things have the capacity to mutually influence each other.[54] From Hegel, the will affects the world and the world affects the will. This is not simply a fact about agency, but the essence of freedom. Moreover, it has an intrinsically social element: Allen Patten's interpretation of Hegel stresses the importance of the agent's public recognition of their capacity to act upon the world (Patten, 1999, pp. 148–162). Patten argues that this capacity manifests itself not just as self-recognition of agency (Patten, 1999, p. 148), but also recognition by others that

[54] Dyadic relationships are discussed in §6.5. A point to note is that I have chosen the term 'dyadic relationship' rather than calling this a dialectic relationship. The reason for this is that the Hegelian dialectic is a particular concept taken from Hegel's philosophy and carries with it particular philosophical assumptions, positions and discussions which are beyond the scope of this book. I use the term dyadic relationship to be a concept similar to the Hegelian dialectic, but without the baggage. For more on Hegel's Dialectic, see (Bencivenga, 2000; Pinkard, 1988; Rosen, 1982).

they are an agent (Patten, 1999, pp. 157–161). Patten concludes that a 'social world that lacks the institution of private property could not be one in which individual personality is able to develop and flourish, because it could not be a community of mutual recognition' (Patten, 1999, p. 161). A person expresses their will and it becomes known to others. Insofar as people deserve respect,[55] property is a system by which society respects people by recognising their will. Hegel states: '[m]y individual right, whose embodiment has hitherto been immediate and abstract, now similarly becomes embodied in the existent will and knowledge of everyone, in the sense that it becomes recognized' (Hegel, 1967 §217, p. 139). Patten's description of Hegel stresses that property is a necessary element for an agent's recognition as an agent within a society (Patten, 1999).

This social recognition becomes especially important when considering intangibles like Personal Information. Whether it is the recognition of a relation between personality and the world or the particular value that a particular society places on a set of Personal Information, the relation between 'my own private personality' and its 'substantive characteristics' is something fundamental both to the wellbeing of people and peoples and to recognition of basic rights of a person or people, points elaborated in §8.5.

Finally, note that Waldron's interpretation of Hegel is dynamic. The relation between the will and the world is responsive *to the extent that* the will and its expression in the world are related. This substantiates a conclusion of Chapter 2, where privacy claims were given an importance *to the extent that* a person stood in an intimate relation with Personal Information and/or *to the extent that* a set of information could impact on them. Likewise and paraphrasing Waldron,[56] in a psychological individuation system of property, a person's claims over Personal Information will be recognised 'to the extent that (1) his will has made a difference to the Personal Information and (2) the Personal Information, affected in this way by his will, itself makes a difference in turn to his willing'. The more a particular person's development of personality is involved in the development of a set of Personal Information *and* the way in which that person is affected by a set of Personal Information, the greater their claims of property over that set of Personal Information. In order to apply this rule of thumb to a property claim, one needs to identify the set of Personal Information and identify the people from whom the information was derived and to whom the information relates. The more intimate that relation, the greater the importance of the need to recognise the property claims.

This becomes especially important when considering Personal Information as; 'substantive characteristics which constitute my own private personality and the universal essence of my self-consciousness are *inalienable*' (Emphasis Mine, Hegel,

[55] Recognition and respect are discussed in §8.5.

[56] This is a paraphrasing of Waldron's original quote: 'A person's will is embodied in an object to the extent that (1) his will has made a difference to the object and (2) the object, affected in this way by his will, itself makes a difference in turn to his willing' (Waldron, 1988, p. 370).

1967 §66, pp. 52–53). Consider that Iomelda is under surveillance and a set of Personal Information is produced about her: her date of birth, her place of birth, her parent's names and her blood type at birth. This set of Personal Information is *inalienable*; Iomelda cannot change this set of information about herself. Also note that even if this set of information is anonymised and cannot be used to identify Iomelda qua Iomelda, the information set itself still relates directly to Iomelda. Thus any property claims about this information need to take Iomelda's interests into account. §8.4 and §8.5 explain the moral importance of this.

While the moral relevance of such a set of information may be innocuous, consider the importance of social recognition of inalienable Personal Information: skin colour, for example, is mostly unchangeable. If a community judges that people with darker skin are to be targeted for increased surveillance due to a belief that they are potential criminals or terrorists, they are being valued differently than people with lighter skin; despite the contingent nature of the value, the process of valuing can serve to harm and/or disrespect those with the darker skin. The relevance is that because of the inability to change skin colour, those with the darker skin may end up internalising the social disvalue associated with their skin colour, a point made in more detail in §8.5. In short, a person can become alienated from themselves as a result of negative social recognition of Personal Information arising from surveillance and the ways its products are put to use. This alienation is not because there is no longer a relation between a person and their Personal Information. Instead it is alienation with key facts about themselves, because they, the people from whom the Personal Information comes and to whom the Personal Information relates, do not have *control* over the ways that given Personal Information is recognised. While this may not seem to directly relate to rights of property, if Hegel's account of property has moral substance, then it can go some way to justifying why a person or people should have some, albeit limited, recognised rights of control over the inalienable Personal Information that comes from and goes to them.

On the point of information and welfare, this is a claim built around the social good justification for property discussed in §3.3.5: Personal Information can be used to increase pleasure or suffering,[57] either in individuals or generally. The social good justifications for property can be cashed out in at least three different ways. First, to see if Personal Information should be owned at all. Second, to determine if particular sets of Personal Information should be owned. Finally, to identify whether a particular person or people have a justified property claim over a particular set of Personal Information. The first question is largely an empiric matter: to determine whether a general system of property over Personal Information increases or decreases the social good is dependent, in part at least,[58] on whether it *actually*

[57] §9.3 is a taxonomy and set of descriptions of different types of informational harms.

[58] 'In part' is given here, as there is a harder issue within normative ethics of what counts as social good – is it just maximising welfare as utilitarians would argue, or are there other factors that need to be included? Even on a utilitarian welfare maximisation calculus, we confront

promotes or reduces the social good. Of special relevance to the production and use of surveillance products is when a state justifies surveillance programmes by reference to a social good like national security. Chapter 9 focuses on this issue.

The second question, should *particular* sets of Personal Information be owned, has a number of different perturbations. For instance, some Personal Information like an epidemiological database might best promote social good if the information it contains has no owner and is available and accessible to all interested parties, while a forensic DNA database might best serve the social good if access is strictly controlled by an independent arm of the respective government.[59] In contrast, private property may incentivise parties to develop socially beneficial uses for aggregated Personal Information (Posner, 2005, pp. 66–69).[60] A counter-argument to this is that private property will not incentivise innovation but instead raise costs for access to Personal Information, resulting in lesser social good overall and/or greater social harms overall.[61]

The third question to answer is whether a particular person or group has justified property claims, based on the social good produced by owning a particular set of information. For instance, consider that a private company has a database on geospatial location such as international travel, social network information that shows with whom people are in contact, as well as updates about people's health status and information about emerging disease outbreaks and the risk of pandemics. The company may be able to claim that their ownership of the given set of Personal Information *maximises* the social good by providing an important global public health service. However, if they used the recognition of their property claim to charge for access to the information and such costs prevented general access, this might ultimately increase overall harms by preventing the spread of general knowledge about emerging pandemic preparedness and responses.

This brief discussion of different social good justifications confirms two things. To make any clear decision on ownership of particular sets of Personal Information based on the social good, a great deal of particular information is needed – we need to know the Personal Information set in question, the claimants and counter-claimants, the expected benefits and harms of recognising/not recognising property and any further empirical evidence to justify or challenge the respective claims.

problems of whether we should be maximising mind states or world states and whether we need to look at individual wellbeing or take the total wellbeing view (Kagan, 1998a, pp. 29–48). These particularly hard issues of what counts as social good are beyond the scope of this book to look at in detail. Perhaps the modern classic text on this is Parfit's *Reasons and Persons* (Parfit, 1987). A more general set of discussions around utilitarianism can be found in Glover (1990).

59 For instance, the U.S. Combined DNA Index System Forensic DNA database CODIS could be an example of the second kind www.fbi.gov/about-us/lab/codis. Further discussion of biobanks is given in *Harnessing the Benefits of Biobanks* (Andrews, 2005).

60 Recalling the UK's Open Health\Open Governance programme from §1.2, one of the motivations was to incentivise private innovation.

61 See arguments raised by Drahos and Braithwaite, Pogge and Selgelid and Sepers, amongst others (Drahos and Braithwaite, 2002; Pogge, 2008; Selgelid and Sepers, 2006).

Second, to make a sensible claim of ownership of Personal Information, the information needs to be seen in aggregate: many of the harms and benefits of applications of Personal Information can *only* be recognised and understood when the information is aggregated, a point raised in §1.4 and discussed in detail in Part III of the book. In short, we can only properly understand justifications from social good if we see the information in aggregate. Again, later chapters explore these points in more detail.

3.6 CCTV REVISITED: RELATING INFORMATION TO PEOPLE

§3.2 presented CCTV as a set of technologies and practices that were paradigmatic of surveillance technologies more generally – a set of technologies that had information as an end product. Importantly, the CCTV example drew out the role of humans in this process. Surveillance technologies do not simply create data, humans are necessary components of the system's epistemic activity; humans are needed to make the data meaningful. So, with the idea that surveillance is a socio-technical system, a hybrid of technology and human operators, where does the extended analysis of the moral foundations of property leave us?

In relation to both labour investment and psychological individuation, recall that the people with the strongest claims of property are those people from whom the Personal Information comes and to whom the Personal Information relates. In the case of the CCTV, the people from whom the information came would be the individuals under surveillance, those captured by the cameras and witnessed by the operators. Those to whom the information relates would be those people whose lives are impacted by the use, misuse or non-use of the surveillance products; a victim of a crime, a suspect in a case, maybe the larger community. In both situations though, if we take property claims to be generated from a foundation of labour investment or psychological individuation, the weakest set of claims comes from the institutional owners: the company, the government agency or the state at large are not the ones from whom or to whom the information is most directly relevant. Moreover, such institutions are not people – any moral claim derived from an individual's rights cannot be applied to an institution.

However, there are two counter-arguments to the source's and target's property claims. First, as it was the individual CCTV operators who produced the relevant information, perhaps these operators have the strongest rights claims: by their efforts, the camera information was aggregated, producing the new and valuable information. In fact, from §3.2, I made it explicit that these operators were necessary to the epistemic action. Countering this, we can note that this argument is mostly a labour investment argument, which we have seen is the weakest of the property arguments investigated. Instead, perhaps the psychological individuation argument applies to the operators, as it was their will as expressed that produced the relevant Personal Information. This might be true, but this only looks at one side of the relationship – the people to whom the information relates would have at least an equivalent property claim as the operators. This would mean that that the source and targets of surveillance information would have at least *some* justified property claims over the information: the creators' rights are not absolute.

A different argument comes from the right of contract. On this, the rights of contract held between the institutions and the operators trump the source and target people's claims. This is, in essence, Nozick's historical entitlement thesis.[62] However, recall from §3.3.3 that Nozick gave no principle of initial acquisition. As we have seen, the most substantive moral justifications for initial acquisition are psychological individuation or social good, which mean that the contracts that transferred ownership from the operators to the institutions ought to be recognised as weak claims at best. Again, looking closely at the justifications, the reasons favour the source's, target's and operator's claims over the institution's exclusivity claims.

Turning to the social good justifications, they seem to count *against* the institutional property claims: A potential social good produced by CCTV and surveillance more generally is that the community under surveillance benefits from reduced crime and a stronger sense of security. However, as Smith points out, this is simply not the case with CCTV; there is very little evidence that CCTV does actually reduce crime rates (Smith, 2015, p. 47). And while controversial, much of the analysis of the global surveillance programmes revealed by Snowden suggests that these massive open-ended surveillance programmes have had negligible outcomes in reducing the threats of terrorism (Review Group on Intelligence and Communications Technologies, 2013). Where such surveillance programmes have been useful, they have by and large been a small part of much larger targeted investigations. The point here is that the social good justifications of CCTV and other expansive and open-ended surveillance programmes are limited.

A different line of argument against individual property claims to the products of surveillance is raised by Margaret Everett, in that individual ownership over Personal Information can lead to harms of commodification (Everett, 2005). This might be the case, but note that this is an argument *against any ownership* of Personal Information: any form of ownership of information can lead to commodification and if commodification is a harm then we ought not recognise *any* property claims over Personal Information like that produced by surveillance.

Two final points to note about the property claims over the products of surveillance: we are unlikely to find an *absolute* right of property. On justifications by labour investment and psychological individuation, other factors need to be taken into account when considering property claims. Again, what this means is there is a possibility for an individual's property rights to be outweighed by other interests. Some property claims may increase harms or interfere with the promotion of the

62 'A person who acquires a holding in accordance with the principle of justice in transfer, from someone else entitled to the holding, is entitled to the holding' (Nozick, 1974, p. 151).

good; there may be situations in which the social good is advanced by not recognising particular property claims.

As a set of concluding remarks, three main points can be mentioned. First, the two most substantial arguments for property rights come from Hegel's need for individuation and the promotion of the social good. Depending on one's particular moral tastes, one might support property claims justified by the need to express and recognise one another's will or by maximising the social good. Second though, if one is to take the moral systems that justify claims of property seriously, then one needs to recognise that there are likely to be situations where an individual's claims of property may well need to be considered in reference to other moral concerns. Likewise, any institutional claims must also be compared and weighed against a range of other moral considerations.

Finally, in reference to Personal Information, in order to properly respect the moral claims of property, one needs to see who is most connected to and affected by the Personal Information. Further, recalling the introductory discussion from Chapter 1, if one is to take property claims about Personal Information seriously, one needs to consider Personal Information in aggregate. Later chapters of this book show that identity presents a way of viewing claims about Personal Information that is responsive to individual claims of property, as well as fully recognising the importance of Personal Information in aggregate. However, in order to substantiate this claim, I need to spell out what I mean by identity, by information. Further, I need to show how identity and information relate to each other. Chapters 4, 5 and 6 do this.

PART II

Identity and Information

4

On Identity

4.1 IDENTITY IN A WORLD OF INFORMATION: AN AGE OF SURVEILLANCE

Our information is everywhere – we leave data trails whenever we are online (Singer and Friedman, 2014, pp. 12–31), CCTV cameras look down on us in public places (Smith, 2015), Global Positioning Systems (GPS) track our movements via cars (Ramli, 2011) and phones (Maas and Rajagopalan, 2012) and the incoming 'Internet of Things' (IoT) promises a future 'where everyday objects can be equipped with identifying, sensing, networking and processing capabilities that will allow them to communicate with one another and with other devices and services over the Internet to accomplish some objective' (Whitmore, Agarwal and Da Xu, 2015). Once-private places like the home are on their way to becoming informational environments. The question is, what does the age of surveillance mean for us?

This book's motivation is to understand how we should be treating the information produced by surveillance technologies. In order for any judgements about the treatment of this information to have moral weight, there needs to be some moral basis for these judgements. The discussion picks up from the concept of privacy as a cluster of related conceptions and the idea that property claims over surveillance products are both individual and social. Understanding the age of surveillance involves recognition that information is the product of surveillance and appreciation of the arguments about involvement and innocuousness of the information: we willingly make our Personal Information public and much of that information is morally innocuous. Responding to involvement and innocuousness, the core argument of this book is that identity and information are in a relation of mutual causation – each impacts the other. However, in order to expose the mechanics of this relation we need to understand identity and information.

This chapter develops an informational account of identity. Surveillance technologies that produce and distribute innocuous Personal Information create ethical vacuums, raised in Chapter 1. Chapters 2 and 3 have explored the problems posed by technologies to existing conventions of privacy and ownership that have been used to deal with the practice and products of surveillance. Again though, we need some explanation of the links between the moral foundations of privacy and property and Personal Information to show why innocuous information should be viewed as morally weighty. However, in order to fill the ethical vacuums opened in the age of surveillance, identity needs to be conceptualised in a way that is directly relevant to information. This chapter develops the conceptual tools to consider identity in an informational context. Information is discussed in Chapter 5 and the relations between identity and information are explicated in Chapter 6.

§4.2 sets the stage for talking about identity in informational terms. §4.3 introduces the parts played by information in cognition and perception and places experience as a necessary element of perception in §4.4. Having shown the centrality of information to perception and experience, a range of identity concepts are summarised and bring out a common element of identity: relative equivalence, §4.5. Bringing together the discussion of perception and experience and the relation of equivalence, §4.6 develops a taxonomy of identity elements to produce a general perceptual concept of identity which allows relations between identity and information to be recognised. The chapter concludes in §4.7 with a discussion of Virtual Identity, to make clear how identity is relevant to surveillance technologies.

4.2 WHAT ARE WE DOING WITH OUR LIVES? THE CASE OF SALLY ONLINE

Consider that Sally is online, visiting a social networking site like Facebook. She posts photos, status updates and so on. Personal Information about herself. By looking at her page online, her brother Harry now has an idea what she looks like day-to-day, her status and what else she does through the day. Others also access Sally's page and learn about her despite these third parties not knowing her and Sally not knowing that they are learning about her. This is not limited to Facebook, or social networking sites. Whenever a person is online, they leave a data trail about what they have looked at, how long, what they have bought, how much they paid and so on. With the rise of smartphones that integrate GPS with online access, third parties can find out where Sally is when she logs in to change her status.[1] Read an

[1] For example, in 2011, in the United States, cellphone companies reported at least 1.3 million data requests from law enforcement agencies (Maas and Rajagopalan, 2012). This data includes 'location data, calling records and text messages' (Editorial, 2012). While certain agencies may have justifications for such access to Personal Information, other agencies lack such justifications. For instance, 'the National Measurement Institute wants warrantless access to Australians' metadata to help them hunt down supermarkets skimping on lamb chop portions' (Farrell, 2016a). Whether they are justified or not is covered in Chapters 8, 9 and 10. The point here is that our Personal Information is being accessed and such practices are long established (Bowcott and Norton-Taylor, 2016).

eBook and a third party may now know how quickly Sally reads the book, what time of day she reads, if she finishes the book and how long she stays on a given page (Flood, 2012). This sort of information is being used to suggest to political parties the likelihood of Sally voting for them, what sorts of policy foci she would prefer, when to ask for political donations and how much to ask for.[2] Repeating the common theme of the book, we are under near constant surveillance and quite frequently are active participants in this surveillance. In order to have a sensible moral appraisal of how we live and share our lives in the age of surveillance, we need to understand what it is we are actually doing with all this Personal Information.

4.3 FROM INFORMATION TO IDENTIFICATION

In order to develop a systematic account of ethics in the age of surveillance, we need to effectively understand the role of information in identity. One way of doing this is to see how information forms identity. By starting with the idea of cognition, we begin to build up the story of how information relates to identity.

4.3.1 *Human Cognition: Thoughts about Thoughts*

This section develops an account of cognition to present a case that cognition, in particular, human cognition, can be understood as 'thoughts about thoughts'. This cognitive approach in which the informational aspects of identity are investigated allows for identity and information to be related, ultimately producing the conceptual tools to assess surveillance technologies.

We begin with the bacteria *Escherichia Coli*. These bacteria receive information about attractant and repellent chemicals and can move towards or away from the chemicals (van Duijn, Keijzer and Franken, 2006, p. 161). This allows us to propose a minimal account of cognition, built on three key factors – there is some information about the world (presence of attractant/repellent chemicals), there is some response to that information (the bacteria move towards/move away) and the response must be coordinated with the input in some way. This coordination presents the basis for minimal cognition. Marc van Duijn, Fred Keijzer and Daan Franken take pains to stress minimal cognition is different from the E.coli's metabolic controls: the bacteria do not directly manipulate metabolism, but instead change the environment such that the metabolic processes change (van Duijn, Keijzer and Franken, 2006, p. 164). The bacteria display a biological function *about* a biological function. It is this 'aboutness' which grounds the basic form of cognition.

[2] Following the 2012 US election, some credited the Obama campaign's use of data to follow and target voters with the Obama victory (Scherer, 2012).

Increasing the complexity of organisms, Alvaro Moreno and Arantza Etxeberria consider neural networks as an example of a cognitive system within an organism, proposing that the nervous system is 'decoupled' from the basic metabolic system: '[W]hen we say that the nervous system is a dynamically decoupled system, we mean that nervous interactions obey a dynamics (or a set of rules) *not governed by the general metabolic organization*, although it is structurally maintained by it' (Emphasis Mine, Moreno and Etxeberria, 2005, p. 167). Similar to van Duijn et al.'s bacteria example, the nervous system displays a control *over* metabolism: '[I]n the organisms endowed with a nervous system . . . instead of through metabolic mechanisms of self-control, adaptation takes place through an informational meta-control on metabolic–motor functions' (Moreno, Umerez and Ibañez, 1997, p. 113). Neural systems present a system that is concerned with attending to and responding to, metabolism in a way that is not direct control over metabolism itself. Neural control is *about* other biological processes.

In relation to human cognition, a higher level of control marks our form of cognition as something beyond that of bacteria and animals (Kornell, 2009). Humans display a capacity for decoupled representation;[3] a process where we take in and process information about the world, where the inputs do not produce a single automatic response. 'That is, we have internal cognitive states which (a) function to track features of the environment and (b) are not tightly coupled functionally to any specific type of response' (Sterelny, 2003, pp. 30–31). To have a decoupled representation means that the stimulus does not determine the response; the response has been 'decoupled' from the stimulus.

For instance, consider that you see a bear: you have a visual representation about the world: 'there is a bear standing in front of me'. Having capacity for decoupled representations means that you have mental processes *about* that representation: 'I see a bear, crap, I hope it doesn't kill me, I'd better run away, wait, do I run away, or run at it, or curl up into a ball, why didn't I read that bear safety brochure?' Seeing[4] the bear is a 'coupled' representation – if your eyes are open, you can't choose not to see.[5] However, your *responses* to the visual stimulus, ranging from 'I recognise that that shape in front of me is a bear', to 'why didn't I read that bear safety brochure', are thoughts *about* the visual stimulus being represented. '[W]e have internal states that track aspects of our world, but which do not have the biological function of controlling particular behaviors. Beliefs are representations that are relevant to many

3 Sterelny's use of 'decoupled representation' is in reference to the response being decoupled from the stimulus. This is compatible with but a slightly different use from the way that Moreno and Etxeberria mean it, where one system is not governed by another.

4 This is a simplification of seeing, as seeing is more complicated than presented here. For example, things within our field of vision may not be seen at all (Mack, 2003). This 'inattentional blindness' is discussed in §4.4.2.

5 This point, that certain aspects of our sensory process are 'cognitively impermeable', is made by Jerry Fodor (Fodor, 1983, pp. 52–55) and is discussed in Chapter 5.

behaviors, *but do not have the biological function of directing any specific behaviour'* (Emphasis Mine, Sterelny, 2003, p. 29).

From this, an account of cognition becomes apparent – it is not the representation formed when our senses transmit information about the world – it is the thought *about* the representation: a mental process about a mental process. In short, a thought about a thought. Like Nate Kornell's 'metacognition' (Kornell, 2009), cognition involves thoughts about thoughts. The idea here is that in evolving these decoupled representations, humans started to have thoughts about thoughts and as our cognition evolved, these thoughts became increasingly abstracted[6] – that is, our thoughts became further and further decoupled from the original source representations.

Consider that when a person reads Romeo and Juliet, they are likely not thinking about the black and white symbols in front of them: typically, people do not think about the letters, the words, the sentences or perhaps even the story, but the psychological state of Romeo or Juliet. We produce thoughts about thoughts about thoughts and so on. Note that this increasing abstraction does not necessarily mean that the thoughts about thoughts are lacking in detail. Clearly, when thinking about the psychological state of characters in a novel, the reader constructs highly detailed representations of those characters. The increasing level of abstraction here refers to the increasing levels of thoughts accessing different representations, possibly integrating multiple representations and beliefs together and responding to them. Cognition,[7] so described, is the process of having thoughts about thoughts, often involving complex interactive networks of representation and belief.

4.3.2 *Dual Process Scheme of Perception: Feed Forward Perception (FFP)*

This account of cognition moves to our perception of the world. Sense organs receive information about the world and through transducers and input systems, transform that information about the world into a format that the brain can use:[8] *'what perception must do is to represent the world as to make it accessible to thought'* (Emphasis Original, Fodor, 1983, p. 40). In what is called the dual processing scheme, two perceptual processes 'feedforward processing' (FFP) and 'reverse hierarchy theory' (RHT) occur simultaneously. This dual processing scheme, originally

6 For more on human evolution and decoupled representations, see part 1 of Sterelny's, *Thought in a Hostile World* (Sterelny, 2003, pp. 1–96).

7 On the model of cognition presented here, even sub-personal thoughts, that is, those thoughts that a person has about the world of which this person is not conscious, can influence the way that this person thinks. What a person thinks about themselves and about others will influence how they think about their selves and others.

8 I recognise that I use information in two different ways here. The first, 'pre-processed information', tracks to a thin conception of information as 'ordered data', while the second, 'processed information', refers to a thicker concept of information as 'ordered meaningful data that is judged to be true'. Chapter 5 discusses information.

proposed for visual perception by Shaul Hochstein and Merav Ahissar (Hochstein and Ahissar, 2002), has been proposed for other sense modalities like auditory perception (Shamma, 2008). Dual process perception operates in two directions. Hochstein and Ahissar make a distinction between FFP and the RHT as follows: '[p]rocessing along the feedforward hierarchy [FFP] of areas, leading to increasingly complex representations, is automatic and implicit, while conscious perception begins at the hierarchy's top [RHT], gradually returning downward as needed' (Hochstein and Ahissar, 2002, p. 791).

In FFP, incoming data is transformed for use by being broken down into fine detail. The finest visual detail about the world comes at recognition of an object's edges (Sterelny, 1990, pp. 62–80) and auditory recognition of specific frequencies (Rauschecker and Scott, 2009). In voice recognition, specific brain regions and specific neurones are involved in recognition of different auditory object classes (Rauschecker and Scott, 2009, p. 719). The sense inputs are broken down into very general types, known as '*what* and *where*'. The *what* type is concerned with what is being looked at, what is making a noise, while the *where* type is concerned with location of the input source.[9]

When observing other people, different regions in the brain process different object classes.[10] The visual processing of the human body, for example, occurs in the extrastriate body area of the brain, while facial processing occurs in the fusiform face area of the brain (Downing *et al.*, 2001). When processing the face, different parts of the face are processed differently too: '[V]isual perception and cognition appear to be served by distinct mechanisms for at least a select few categories, including faces, places and bodies' (Downing *et al.*, 2001, p. 2472). These different regions also process learned information about things like another's emotional states.[11]

Incoming information must be processed into something that the brain can use, some form of representation of the world: it has been transformed from *input about* an object or event to a *representation of* that object or event. However, at this level of

9 In visual perception, sense data is carried from the eye to the primary visual cortex. The *what* data travels to the inferior temporal region, while the *where* data travels to the posterior parietal cortex (Mishkin, Ungerleider and Macko, 1983, p. 415). For auditory perception, the sense data is carried from the ear to the primary auditory cortex, the *what* data then travels to the superior temporal region, while the *where* data travels to the posterior parietal cortex (Rauschecker and Scott, 2009, pp. 718–719).

10 Despite scientific literature lending support to the domain-specific view of facial recognition (Kanwisher, 2000), this is not to say that particular brain regions are necessarily limited to specific perceptual functions. Valerie Hardcastle and Matthew Stewart argue that though specific forms of perception are regionally, perhaps neurally, specific this does not mean that a given brain region is only limited to one form of perceptual processing (Hardcastle and Stewart, 2005). Further to this, Andy Clark, describes a series of technological developments where blind people have been given 'sight-like' representations of the world via touch (Clark, 2008, pp. 35–37).

11 For example, the neocortical regions of the brain interact with the left and right hemispheres of the amygdala to produce socially contextualised fear reactions in response to the direct gaze of others (Skuse, 2006).

detail, the world is still not recognisable, it must be built up. The transformed information is processed upwards through series of neural processes to produce representations of ever greater informational complexity. The processed information converges and is integrated by neuroanatomical computational hubs (Rauschecker and Scott, 2009, p. 720; Sporns, Honey and Kotter, 2007). Through convergence of processed sensory inputs, the observer constructs an integrated representation of the object or event being perceived.

Visual recognition is obtained by integration of neural information to produce an emergent visual representation of the perceived face, body and ultimately of the whole person. An observer constructs a rich representation for another by integrating perceptual information about that person, a composite of visual representations producing a comprehensive set of observations for a given subject of observation. Likewise, auditory sense data is also sorted into different object classes, 'auditory objects coexist based on many attributes, such as timbre, pitch and loudness, that give each its distinctive perceptual identity' (Rauschecker and Scott, 2009, p. 719). Auditory perception also does not simply relate to *what* and *where* questions, but also *who* is talking.

This shows how a cognitive approach to identity exposes relations between identity and information: the convergence of processed sense data produces not only recognition of *what* is being looked at, or *what* spoken words are being heard, but also *who* is being seen, *who* is talking. By integrating fine-grained detail, the observer constructs a representation of what a person looks and sounds like, which they use to identify that person. These integrated representations are cognitive processes, a vast array of thoughts about thoughts. Unless something goes wrong in our cognition, we do not even know that we are constructing these integrated representations. As a person experiences more about the world, they develop a set of dynamic cognitive frameworks, a complex set of interacting thoughts about thoughts that form, frame and focus how that person understands the world.

4.3.3 *Dual Process Scheme of Perception: Reverse Hierarchy Theory (RHT)*

This brings us to the RHT. Rather than attending to fine detail and building up a complex representation, the RHT takes the object of perception to be the whole complex scene:

> [RHT] proposes that the … forward hierarchy acts implicitly, with explicit perception beginning at high-level cortex, representing the *gist of the scene* on the basis of a first order approximate integration of low-level input. Later, explicit perception returns to lower areas via the feedback connections, to integrate into conscious *vision with scrutiny* the detailed information available there. Thus, initial perception is based on spread attention (large receptive fields), guessing at details … Later vision incorporates details.
>
> (Emphases Original, Hochstein and Ahissar, 2002, p. 792)

The dual process model, involving both 'bottom up' processes of the FFP and 'top-down' processes of RHT, explains perception in terms of an integrated system modelled on the most efficient method of *identification*. If an observer has already encountered a given input – a visual cue or noise – it will be more beneficial to recognise the input as the higher level abstracted object rather than the low-level cue. The RHT:

> postulates that a parsing decision is first based on the highest available level of ... representation (e.g., objects). If the discrimination task is poor at that level, it proceeds down the representational hierarchy to benefit from more detailed, lower-level cues that participate in generating the percept. If the high "objects" and their "low-levels cues" are congruent, the feed-forward process is rapid, and use of all available salient cues is effective and comprehensive.
>
> (Shamma, 2008, p. 1141)

So, rather than needing to process all the fine detail of an incoming predator, an observer need only recognise the rapidly moving object as 'possible lion'.[12] Consider an observer in a crowd who is searching for a particular person. Recognition will be more likely and efficient if anticipating meeting this person. The higher level abstracted representations will enable Harry to rapidly recognise his sister Sally if he anticipates that she will be in the crowd. Likewise, the dual processing account explains why Harry thinks he saw Sally, despite knowing she is overseas – a stranger's facial structure, body shape or tone of voice may call to Harry's mind the complex representation of Sally, despite knowledge that she is not in the country. Harry's existing cognitive framework accesses the general abstraction of Sally despite the inaccuracy in the incoming information.

4.3.4 *Informational Processing, Cognition and Identification*

Perception of others involves the transformation of information into a set of representations, involving both FFP and RHT processes. These complex neural interactions produce detailed composite representations of what and who, a person is seeing and hearing. Like the construction of complex sentences,[13] we perceive others through the integration of fine-grained detail about a person to give the observer an informationally rich multi-modal complex representation of the subject being observed, while at the same time we perceive a person based on abstract representations already familiar to us.

[12] Note that this presupposes that the observer has already encountered lions or similar predators, or had been taught about them, to be able to identify 'possible lion'. The initial observation would need much finer-grained detail found at the lower level.

[13] I am using something like the language of thought hypothesis (LOTH) here. On the LOTH, representations form the basic building blocks for thoughts and they are then arranged 'sentence-like' into thoughts which take a propositional form (Sterelny, 1990, pp. 23–32).

Both the FFP and RHT rely on complex informational processes. The FFP involves the building up of incoming information into complex representations of the world. Going back to §4.3.2, the incoming perceptions are thoughts about thoughts. In the RHT, the abstract representations consist of complex representational networks built from previous experiences. They are rapidly compared to the gist of the current perception. Again, perception is driven by thoughts about thoughts. While it is a trivial truth to say that perception relies on neural processes, the cognitive model adds something: it shows that getting a full and rich perception of the world involves processing of information. This perception relies on building up and integrating incoming information, as well as having existing relevant experiences. Cognition, thoughts about thoughts, is necessary for perception.

The role of information in identification and recognition of people, including one's self, shows that identity formation is a cognitive process, dependent upon the information an observer has about that person. When meeting a person, the observer will rely on the dual process schema. The FFP will be concerned with the fine-grained details of body shape, facial structures, voice tone and complex behavioural cues. The RHT will be concerned with identifying the person as someone new or previously met and will likely then be comparing novel behaviours with experience, attending to any noticeable differences in appearance, behaviour and so on. Identification of people, how the observer forms a representational experience of them, is ultimately a complex cognitive process involving a huge set of thoughts about thoughts. Starting with cognition, identity can be understood in informational terms.

4.4 EXPERIENCE: WHAT WE KNOW TELLS US WHAT WE WILL KNOW

This section presents evidence that background mental processes influence perception. The basic point is that our experience plays a major role in how we form identities for ourselves and others.

4.4.1 *Do You See What I See?*

The idea here is that a person's processing of observed sense data is heavily influenced by previous experience. That is, perception has a subjective element. Alan Chalmers notes that '[t]wo normal observers viewing the same object from the same place under the same physical circumstances do not necessarily have identical visual experiences, even though the images on their respective retinas may be virtually identical' (Chalmers, 1999). As Norwood Hanson stated 'there is more to seeing than meets the eyeball' (Hanson, 1958). Consider the figure below, a 'Necker Cube':

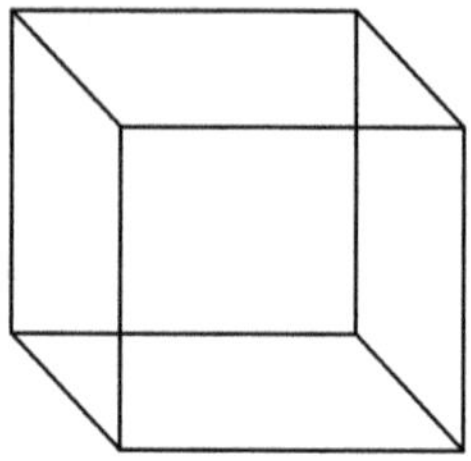

FIGURE 4.1 Necker Cube

The picture itself remains constant. That is, the information meeting the eyeballs of two observers will be the same, yet two observers can see two different images. Observer One may see the cube with the top left square as its front, while observer Two may see the cube with the bottom right square as the front. Importantly, this does not presume that one observer is correct while the other observer is confused or mistaken. They both receive the same information, both process it correctly but are both seeing something different.

To describe subjective perception from another angle, consider that twins John and Jim are each eating a slice of cake. Imagine that John and Jim have an exactly similar sense of taste – that is, both are the same age, with equivalent life experiences, the same cultural background and so on. The same cake is served to both John and Jim, yet both will experience the cake differently. John enjoys the cake but feels guilty as he is developing diabetes and promised his girlfriend that he would remain on a low-sugar and low-fat diet. Jim, however, is unaware that he is developing diabetes and the cake tastes similar to his wedding cake. For John, eating the cake produces sensations of flavour coupled with guilt, while for Jim, eating the cake produces sensations of flavour coupled with nostalgic happiness for his wedding day.

Brian Wansink describes a large set of experiments in which people's perception of food is influenced by things like colour, serving size and menu descriptions (Wansink, 2006).[14] Similarly, other research has shown that information as to the cost of wine can result in people tasting the same wine differently (Plassmann et al., 2008). The visual and flavour examples show that one thing with constant properties like the Necker Cube or, two things that are exactly similar, slices from the same cake, can be perceived differently by different observers. Further, as with

[14] In one particularly interesting example, two groups of diners were told that they are receiving a free bottle of wine, from different regions. Group A are told their wine is from a region known for making good wine, while Group B's wine is from a region not at all known for making good wine. However, despite being told differently, Group A and B receive the same wine and the same meals. Despite the wines and the meals being exactly the same, those people in Group A not only rated the taste of the wine higher than Group B, they ate more food, stayed longer and gave the food itself an overall better rating (Wansink, 2006).

the wine examples, differences in perception can even occur in the one observer, depending on what the observer is thinking. The particular point here is subjective experience, anticipation, expectation and prior knowledge heavily influence people's perceptions of the world.

4.4.2 *Existing Cognitive Networks and Dual Cognitive Processes*

The dual process model of perception can help[15] explain this differential model of perception. FFP involves the apprehension of fine-grained details about the world. In the RHT, the gist of the scene is presented to the observer in a top-down process. Importantly, 'a parsing decision is *first based* on the highest available level of ... representation' (Emphasis, Mine, Shamma, 2008, p. 1141). While FFP and the RHT both occur in perception,[16] the emphasis here is that the abstract representation often guides perception of the world.

Coming now to experience and identification, two areas of research offer evidence that the top-down processes of RHT guide perception of other people: inattentional blindness and content of experience. When we perceive things, we focus attention to things that matter and are 'blind' to other things. This is known as 'inattentional blindness'. Inattentional blindness is relevant to perception as it relates to what is actually 'picked up'. In experiments conducted in the late 1970s, by directing an observer's visual attention to one set of events, researchers showed that the observers were blind to another set of events (Neisser, 1979). The researchers had observers watch recorded footage of people passing a basketball amongst themselves, whilst counting the number of passes. At the same time as the basketball was being passed, a woman walked through the scene with an open umbrella. In the original experiments, only 21 per cent of the observers reported seeing the unexpected element, the woman with the umbrella. This was despite the fact that she was in plain view. More recently, this effect has been repeated using men in gorilla suits as the unexpected element (Simons and Chabris, 1999).[17] This can be explained via the dual process model of perception, in that the top-down representations are guiding the focus of attention. If Harry is looking for Sally in a crowd, the abstract representation for Sally guides Harry's attention, leaving him blind to other visual data.

However, the top-down representations do more than just guide data pick-up; they can also guide *how* a person is perceived. '[T]op-down processes coordinate and *bias local activity* across lower-level regions based on information derived from global, contextual and gist information' (Emphasis Mine, Kveraga, Ghuman and

[15] I say 'help' here as there are a host of different neurological processes occurring in perception, only some of which can be explained by the dual process model.

[16] A similar point about informational emergence and downward causation is made and elaborated in §5.8.

[17] Footage of the gorilla tests can be seen at www.youtube.com/watch?v=vJG698U2Mvo.

Bar, 2007, p. 148). For example, when Harry first met Sally, he took in a lot of fine-grained detail. But once he becomes familiar with her, the abstract representation of Sally will serve as the primary form of recognition.

> These [top-down] models ... generally posit that predictions based on prior experience are generated in higher-level areas and *projected to lower-level areas to guide the recognition process driven by sensory information*. Guidance is implemented by using these top-down predictions to sensitize bottom-up stimulus-driven processing. Therefore, top-down predictions facilitate the recognition process by reducing the number of candidate representations of an object that need to be considered.
>
> (Emphasis Mine, Kveraga, Ghuman and Bar, 2007, p. 149)

We have the abstract representation guiding the processing of fine detail. The higher level abstract representation of a person guides perception. Further to this, others propose that the observer's previous experiences will shape the perception of people:

> [T]his process is based on information that is extracted quickly ... whereby people ... link the new person with a familiar person in memory (e.g., "who does this person look like"), even if not explicitly. *Once a link is found, we automatically project information such as personality attributes to the new person based simply on this analogy*.
>
> (Emphasis Mine, Kveraga, Ghuman and Bar, 2007, p. 162)

Again, the RHT drives how others are perceived.

The basic point being made here is that an observer's perception of another person is heavily influenced by their experience: the observer's existing Cognitive Networks shape not only what the observer pays attention to, but how those things are perceived. The way in which another is experienced is the result of thoughts about thoughts. That is, identity formation is a cognitive process.

4.5 WHAT IS IDENTITY?[18]

So far identity remains unexplored. This section looks at different concepts of identity and raises them to a common level of abstraction in order to find a common element. My conclusion is that when one makes an identity claim, one is making some claim of 'relative equivalence', stemming from an evaluation that there is some equivalence (or sameness, similarity, commonality and so on) between two (or more) things. Finding a common element then allows a systemised discussion of identity – §4.5.

[18] Much of the discussion in this section is adapted from a paper published elsewhere (Henschke, 2010).

'What is identity?' The answer seems obvious – my identity is me, your identity is you, his identity is him and her identity is her. In its simplest terms, in making an identity claim, we are saying that 'Y = Y'. While this is true of strict identity,[19] in common use, identity can mean something different to the exact sameness of 'Y = Y'. In some uses, identity allows for some change between $Y_{\text{time } n}$ and $Y_{\text{time } n+1}$, while in other uses, identity means that Y has property *y* which is part of some set [A–Z]. There are at least four different concepts to which identity commonly tracks: Numeric Identity,[20] concerned with a person's persistence through time; Character Identity, the qualitative personality of an individual; Group Identity, socio-political communities; and Essentialised Identity, reduction of a person to a specific identifier.

This section does not seek to resolve what the content of a given concept *should* be.[21] The purpose here is to give enough clarity for each concept of identity to make it reasonably distinct from the other concepts, whilst seeing what they have in common. Second, while distinct, the concepts inform and impact each other; what one presumes about one concept can have an important relationship to another. Third, some disciplines may find the terms used are not the most common ones used for a particular area: I have adopted the given terms in order to make the differences between the concepts clearer. Fourth, the goal is to find a common element, not to reduce the concepts to a single definition:[22] the concepts are described with sufficient broadness such that the majority of common conceptions can fit within the descriptions offered. Finally, the taxonomy offered here is not the only way to carve up the concepts.[23] Again, my goal is to find some common element, such that I can show how identity is a morally relevant feature when considering Personal Information.

[19] I mean here to show that identity can commonly mean something different to the idea of strict identity such as in the sense covered by Leibniz's law, where identity means 'X and Y are *exactly* the same' (Olson, 2010). Following Bishop Butler (Butler, 2008, pp. 100–101) and Donald Baxter's distinction between strict and loose senses of identity (Baxter, 1988), I am using a looser sense of identity. I note that this possibly trades on identity as being relative, in which '[i]t is possible for objects *x* and *y* to be the same *F* and yet not the same *G*'(Deutsch, 2009). However, I cannot go into deeper discussions of the issues arising from a relative to identity approach here.

[20] Note here the capitalisation of Numeric Identity, Character Identity and so on. This is in line with the discussion of terminology from §1.5.2.

[21] For instance, Numeric Identity has a long history of people arguing about what it is (Perry, 2008b, pp. 3–30). I do not aim to resolve any of those arguments here.

[22] Often there are sound historical and practical reasons for the same word to track to different concepts (Griffiths and Stotz, 2006, pp. 500–501).

[23] Christine Hauskeller, for example, offers a different taxonomy, consisting of two different concepts: logical identity and psychological identity (Hauskeller, 2004). My taxonomy tracks to Hauskeller's, with my Numeric Identity and Essentialised Identity fitting mostly under her 'logical identity', while my Character Identity and Group Identity fit mostly under her 'psychological identity'. However, given the different goals of Hauskeller's paper and this book, the taxonomies are serving different purposes.

4.5.1 *Numeric Identity*

Discussions of Numeric Identity[24] are often concerned with what is needed for a thing to be the same as itself. If time passes, how do we judge that $Y_{\text{time n}}$ is the same thing as $Y_{\text{time n+1}}$? Sameness through time does not have to mean *exactly* the same. For instance, it seems reasonable to say the water in a river may change, whilst saying that the river remains the same (Perry, 1978, pp. 13–14, 22–25). But if we allow for change, how do we know that something or someone is the same as they were? The person who Sally was when she was young is vastly different in size, shape, knowledge, outlook and so on from who she is now. And if she lives to be eighty, future Sally will be different to who she is now. But despite these changes, most of us would say that Sally is the same person she was at ten years old, now and until she dies (and possibly beyond). That is, Sally's identity persists through time, despite the obvious fact that she has changed. How to explain this?[25]

John Locke offered memory as a way of explaining a persistent Numeric Identity for people through time.[26] Sally knows now that she is the same person she was when she was ten years old because she remembers that she was that person. Likewise, when she is eighty, she will remember who she is today. So we can say that she has the same identity through time, despite whatever changes have occurred.

But there are problems with the memory criterion – for instance, false memories (Levy, 2007, p. 159) and circular reasoning (Butler, 2008, p. 100). In response, the memory criterion has developed into that of 'psychological connectedness', whereby the criterion for Numeric Identity is that a person's psychological states *connect* through time. Psychological continuity requires overlapping chains of direct psychological relations (Parfit, 1971b, p. 20, 1987, pp. 204–209, 219–223). The person Sally is today is very similar to the person she was yesterday. The person she was yesterday is very similar to the person she was two days before and so on. So though she may not be similar now to the girl she was when she was ten years old, as long as

24 Use of the term *Numeric* Identity for this concept may be considered unorthodox as *Personal* Identity is typically used in philosophical discussions. Numeric Identity has been chosen as *Personal* Identity can immediately bring to mind the concept of a *personality*, a person's psychological or 'Character Identity' (§4.5.2). Use of 'Numeric Identity' is intended to make the concept distinct from Character Identity. Second, Personal Identity, while commonly used in philosophy to relate to persistence through time, is also conventionally used in other fields to relate to a person's psychological or Character Identity: Daniel Solove's book *The Digital Person* is one such example (Solove, 2004). I emphasise that Numeric Identity, as I describe it, can be considered equivalent to the philosophic conventional use of Personal Identity.

25 Though much more can be said about Numeric Identity, this overview is intended to give enough of an idea of the concept that it can be recognised in contrast to other identity concepts.

26 Note that Locke's Memory Criterion of Identity is often given as Locke's Memory Criterion of *Personal* Identity (Perry, 2008a). As mentioned, the term 'Personal Identity' is typically used in philosophical discussions of this sort.

there is a continuity of states that links the person she was then to the person she is now, an identity claim holds.

Others deny the *psychological* criterion of identity and instead propose that *physical* criteria are the proper criteria (DeGrazia, 2005, pp. 11–76). Eric Olson describes this as the 'somatic approach' (Olson, 2010). The reason for this, so the somatic theory goes, is that the correct criterion for identity is not psychological but the persistence of the physical body:[27] as long as Sally's body persists through time, she remains the same person.

4.5.2 *Character Identity*

The concept of *Character* Identity[28] is concerned with *characterising* a person. This concept relates to a question of the sort 'what am I like?' '[T]he *characterization* question [is a] question of which mental states and attitudes . . . belong to a person' (Emphasis Original, Levy, 2007, p. 158). Character Identity is heavily reliant upon memory.

> Our identities . . . are diachronic entities: I am the sum of my plans and policies; I work towards a goal and I understand myself in terms of my background – where I'm coming from, as we say, is where I come from . . . Memory links my past to my future self, *and makes me the person I am*".
>
> (Emphasis Mine, Levy, 2007, pp. 158–159)

Because of the role played by memory, confusion arises between Numeric Identity and Character Identity. Both concepts take into account a person existing through time and if one takes the psychological criterion of identity to be the proper location for identity persistence, then memory is an important part. Numeric Identity seeks to determine if Sally is the *same* person as she was yesterday, while Character Identity seeks to describe the *sort* of person she is: the first seeks answers to questions of logical identity, the second, questions of psychological identity (Hauskeller, 2004, pp. 286–287).

A person's character is liable to change through time and sometimes these changes can be profound. For example, consider that Sally was a lesbian anarchist vegan but is now in a heterosexual relationship, works as a corporate lawyer and eats meat daily. We are likely to agree when she says she is a different person, but we don't take that as meaning that her Numeric Identity has changed. Rather, we acknowledge that the traits, qualities and characteristics of her identity that we knew are now different: her *character* has changed. Her identity (Numeric) is the same, while her identity (Character) is different.

[27] Other examples of the somatic approach include Bernard Williams and David Mackie (Mackie, 1999; Williams, 1970).

[28] Note that Character Identity might also be called psychological identity, psycho-social or even personal identity, depending on the discipline and user.

4.5.3 *Group Identity*

Group Identity is concerned with the context and resulting content of a person's identity: the social environment that goes into forming a person's identity. While it is true that our identities, in the character sense, are psychological, it seems trivially true: if we don't know the origin of this identity we end up with a thin account of identity.

'The full definition of someone's identity thus usually involves not only his stand on moral and spiritual matters, but also some reference to a defining community' (Taylor, 1989, p. 37). Group Identity is concerned with acknowledging the social embeddedness[29] of our identities – our relations with others are essential to the development of our identities. '[P]ersons are fundamentally social beings who develop the competency for autonomy through social interaction with other persons' (Friedman, 2000, p. 40). A person's Character Identity is heavily influenced by the social groups that they identify with and the groups that others identify them with. 'One is a self only among other selves. A self can never be described without reference to those who surround it' (Taylor, 1989, p. 35). At the same time, these social groups are partially determined by the individuals that they are composed of and by those who compose the groups. 'I am part of their story, as they are part of mine. The narrative of any one life is part of an interlocking set of narratives' (MacIntyre, 2008, p. 218).

Group Identity becomes particularly important when discussing identity politics.

> [A] person or group of people can suffer real damage, real distortion, if the people or society around them mirror back to them a confining or demeaning or contemptible picture of themselves. Nonrecognition or misrecognition can inflict harm, can be a form of oppression, imprisoning someone in a false, distorted, and reduced mode of being.
>
> (Taylor, 1994b, p. 25)

Recognising the importance of Group Identity requires that when I describe Sally as 'a lesbian anarchist vegan', I am not simply listing a set of attributes associated with the person: I am acknowledging the vital role of society in formatting her identity and ascribing a set of values to that person. When I say 'she is an anarchist', I am not only saying that Sally's identity (Numeric) has always been an anarchist, nor am I saying that her identity (Character) is like an anarchist, but I am also

[29] For instance, this focus on social embeddedness seeks to make the self something more than the enlightenment ideal of the autonomous identity as something unencumbered and independent from its social context (Mackenzie and Stoljar, 2000, p. 11). However, this should not be taken to mean that we are the simple product of our social context, reflecting a given set of social values and ideas like a mirror. As Larry May has argued (May, 1996, pp. 14–18, 26–27), as people mature, they can develop the capacity to reflect upon their inherited values and can change those values through time, ultimately changing their identity through reflective repetition and willing identification. I talk about these issues and tensions in §6.3 and §6.4.

saying that the identity (Group) that I identify her with is that of the 'anarchist type', however that is conceptualised.

4.5.4 *Essentialised Identity*

Concerns about Group Identity occur when we reduce a person to a narrow set of Group Identity attributes. 'Lesbian anarchist vegan', for example, risks reducing Sally to *just* this set of attributes. The full richness of her character is reduced to an essence. To describe someone as simply 'a lesbian', 'an anarchist', 'a vegan' and so on can be morally problematic for a number of reasons. First, given the historical treatments of minorities, a reductionist description can recall and reinforce discrimination. Second, the individual ceases to be considered as a person and becomes simply that trait. Their human essence has been reduced to a single 'fact', a stereotype (Straub, 2002, p. 70).[30]

Essentialising can de-personalise an individual, or group of people, in a number of significant ways.[31] Distinct from the concept of Group Identity, it denies that the person is any more than the given attributes. Such a process can deny a person the right to wilfully create their own identity in their way. For instance, essentialising a person's identity can reduce their capacity to conceive of the values that are incorporated into their Character Identity (Mackenzie, 2000).

However, essentialising someone may not necessarily be morally problematic. Consider a biometric identifier like a fingerprint or retinal scan used to confirm that the person requesting access to a building or important file is Sally and she can legitimately access the building or file. For the purpose of access, Sally *is* reduced to a fingerprint or retinal scan. Identity Management is relevant to ICT (Information Communications Technology) and security, whereby the focus is on a given identifier.

Note also how something like personnel identity, mentioned in §2.2, comes almost full circle to Numeric Identity: a given identifier (Essential Identity) can be used to confirm that a person is who they say they are; it is used to confirm persistence through time.

4.5.5 A *Common Element*

What do these concepts have in common? The four concepts contain some judgement of relative equivalence. That is, they implicitly or explicitly make some comparison between two (or more) things and decide for whatever reason, that the two things are the same or relevantly similar, equivalent and so on. I suggest that a

30 Another way of characterising this problem is that essentialising a person consists in only appraising them in reference to a narrow set of traits and overlooks a requirement of recognition respect owed to all people in virtue of them being a person. Stephen Darwall differentiates between recognition respect and appraisal respect (Darwall, 1977), a point I return to in §8.5.

31 Further discussion of the moral importance of identity occurs throughout Chapters 7, 8 and 9.

common element across identity concepts is relative equivalence. That is, some judgement of equivalence is being made between Y and Z.

On this, Y and Z may be different things – a person changing through time. Y and Z may also be different types of things – a person and a particular characteristic of that person. Further, to say that Sally (thing Y) has a good sense of humour (thing Z) is not to say that that is *all* there is to Sally. Likewise, to say that Sally (person Y) is an anarchist (trait Z) is not to say that Sally is an anarchist and nothing more. In saying 'Y is equivalent to Z', that equivalence is *relative* to the given identity concept being used and the context of use.

4.6 A TAXONOMY OF IDENTITY ELEMENTS

This section builds from the discussion of cognition, perception, experience and relative equivalence to present a taxonomy of identity elements: Self-Regarding Identity, §4.6.1, Other-Regarding Identity, §4.6.2 and Other/Other-Regarding Identity, §4.6.3. A general account of identity is then presented as 'identity is who X perceives Y to be', written alternately as 'X perceives Y to be Z'. I spell out the different elements of the general account, §4.6.4. This general account works across the four identity concepts covered in §4.5. Depending on the identity concept being used, I could say for:

Numeric Identity that 'I perceive myself to be the same person I was yesterday',
Character Identity that 'I perceive myself to be a funny guy',
Group Identity that 'I perceive myself to be an anarchist', and
Essentialised Identity that 'I perceive myself to be employee #5425777'

The four identity concepts can be fitted to all three elements, Self-Regarding Identity, Other-Regarding Identity and Other/Other-Regarding Identity. These are considered as *elements*: they are all relevant to how an individual sees themselves and others.

4.6.1 *Self-Regarding Identity: I Am Who I Perceive Myself to Be*

If asked who they are, a person could reply 'I am me'. However, recall from §4.3 and §4.4 that perception constitutes processing of information about a particular object or thing and that perception is dependent in part on who is doing the perceiving. When considering the answer 'I am me', Self-Regarding Identity arises when a person has thoughts about the representations of their self.

First, this person may be consciously or unconsciously referring to any of the four identity concepts. They may be referring to:

(a) some set of persistence conditions in order to make a claim of Numeric Identity,

(b) some set of characteristics in order to make a claim of Character Identity,
(c) some particular group with which they strongly identify, Group Identity,
(d) some feature essential to who they are, Essentialised Identity, or,
(e) in common usage, most likely, some combination of any/all of the above.

When they are saying 'I am me', they are making a claim of relative equivalence between 'I' and 'me'. This leaves unexplained *how* they would come to make such a claim.

Recalling cognition, we have thoughts about thoughts. A person's Self-Regarding Identity refers to the cognitive frameworks that arise from those sets of things that the person identifies *as* belonging to them. Given the role of experience in perception §4.4 and the common element of a claim of relative equivalence §4.5, rather than 'I am me' a fuller answer is 'my identity is who I perceive myself to be'.

This raises a tension: that which is doing the perceiving is the same[32] as that which is perceived. Second, following the experience model of perception from §4.4, the capacity to perceive one's self changes the observer's experience set, which changes their cognitive framework, so produces changes in the things that the person perceives as their self.[33] So that which is doing the perceiving is different from the thing perceived.[34]

To resolve this tension, we start by differentiating between the thing doing the perceiving as the 'I' and the thing being perceived as the 'self'.[35] This idea has precedent:

> This I is the subjective sense of our existence. It is different from self-image, the body, passions, fears, social category – these are aspects of our person that we usually refer to when we speak of the self, but they do not refer to the core of our conscious being, they are not the origin of our sense of personal existence ... Thus, experience is dualistic, not the dualism of mind and matter but the dualism of awareness and the contents of awareness.
>
> (Deikman, 1996, pp. 350, 351)

[32] This is consistent with 'equivalence' from the common element of identity, relative equivalence, developed in §4.5.

[33] This is a complex claim and I spell it out in detail in Chapter 6.

[34] This is consistent with 'relative' from the common element of identity, relative equivalence, developed in §4.5.

[35] I point out that my use of the term 'self' is different to that of people like Daniel Dennett, whose use of self is more like my use of 'I'. He states: 'For some ... the self was a nonphysical soul, a ghost in the machine. For others ... , the self was nothing at all, a figment of metaphysically fevered imaginations ... for still others ... a self was in one way or another a sort of abstraction, something whose existence was not in the slightest impugned by its invisibility' (Dennett, 1991, p. 413). A more detailed description of this 'self' is given in §7.3. The purpose here is to focus on a difference between 'I' and 'self'.

To explain this 'I'/self distinction, Arthur Deikman asks us to

> [s]top for a moment and look inside. Try and sense the very origin of your most basic, most personal 'I', your core subjective experience. What is that root of the 'I' feeling? Try to find it . . . Every time you try to observe the 'I' it takes a jump back with you, remaining out of sight.
>
> (Deikman, 1996, p. 350)

This certainly seems[36] like Deikman is repeating David Hume's recognition that '[w]hen I enter most intimately into what I call *myself*, I always stumble on some particular perception or other . . . I never can catch *myself* at any time without a perception and can observe any thing but the perception' (Emphases Original, Hume, 1985, p. 300). In addition to Hume, the division between the 'I' as knower and 'self' as thing known presents the 'I' as similar to Immanuel Kant's noumenon, 'that is, of a thing which must be thought not as an object of sense, but as a thing in itself' (Kant, 1934, p. 213).

These two references to Hume and Kant give us pause. First, the concept of identity that Hume was speaking of was identity understood as persistence through time, the Numeric Identity concept: Hume himself used this inability to identify one's identity as an argument to the affect that there was no such thing as identity.

The quote from Kant shows that positing of a noumenal self within us can lead us towards a homuncular regress: Glover notes (Glover, 1988, p. 89) that Kant later refers to 'the being that thinks within us' (Kant, 1934, p. 304). The problem of homuncular regress is described by John Searle: he begins by highlighting the fact that people can shift their attention and begin actions at will. He asks '[w]ho does the shifting and initiating', then answers, '[i]t is very tempting to think that there is a little guy in my head who does my thinking, perceiving and acting. Of course, the homunculus fallacy is a fallacy, because it leads to an infinite regress' (Searle, 2008, p. 146). On the homuncular regress, if there is a little homunculus inside us watching and operating us like a driver of a car, the question that Searle raises is, where is the conscious controller in the driver? Talking of an 'I', I may fall into an infinite regress whereby a second 'I' sits in the first, a third in the second and so on. Splitting the 'I' and the self produces an infinite regress by dividing the identity of a person into both observer and subject and postulating a distinction between consciousness and the self.

However, there are three ways to read the 'I'/self division: strongly, moderately and weakly. In the strong reading, the 'I' and the self are actually two separate things. In the moderate reading, the 'I' and the self are the same thing, but refer to two different aspects of the same thing. Finally, in the weakest version, the 'I'/self division is merely a conceptual device, pointing to two different concepts. I think

[36] I say 'seems' here, as despite the strong similarity between Deikman's example and Hume, Deikman does not reference Hume in his paper.

that the homunculus regress presents a convincing argument against the strong reading.[37] I am agnostic whether the 'I' and the self are, in fact, two aspects of the same thing. The idea being pursued here stands on the weak reading: that any division between the 'I' and self is a conceptual division, that is, the two *concepts* can be divided, irrespective of whether there is such a division in reality.

This raises a question of why mention a division between the 'I'/self at all? On the weak reading, the 'I' and self are referring to two different concepts. Does this mean that that which is doing the perceiving changes itself as it perceives its self? In short, yes. By dividing the conceptual terrain up into the 'I' and self, 'I' as process of observation and the self as that which is observed, we can start to explain how identity comes about and why *an* identity can be so hard to pin down.

Taking the conscious 'I' as the starting point, the '"self" is simply the human person — as she appears to herself. And whatever thus appears, that is the self' (Brook, 1998, p. 584).[38] The cognitive account of identity explains this as a person's thoughts about their self telling them who they are: 'my identity is who I perceive *my self* to be'.

However, as most people typically[39] develop, the 'I' is not merely a passive observer. Similarly to Hegelian individuation, discussed in §3.4.3, the 'I' and the self are fundamentally related; what the 'I' identifies as self becomes integrated into that 'I' and in turn, informs how the 'I' perceives the world.[40] Recall from the perception discussion that previous experience influences what and how the world (including the self) is perceived. Through perception of the self, the 'I' changes. However, changing the 'I' changes how the observer perceives and so the perception of the self also changes: self changes 'I', as 'I' changes the self: This relation between 'I' and self is mutually causal. I spell out the particulars of mutually causal relations in Chapter 6.

To make this clear, consider this scenario: Thompson is an adult who has always believed that Julie was his sister and Amy was his mother. One day, however, Thompson finds out that Julie is in fact his mother and Amy is his grandmother.

[37] I am assuming consciousness here. It is beyond the scope of this book, which does not seek to offer any deep understandings of what consciousness is. And without having any leaning towards his view, as David Chalmers says, '[s]ome say that consciousness is an "illusion," but I have little idea what this could even mean. It seems to me that we are surer of the existence of conscious experience than we are of anything else in the world' (Chalmers, 1996 xii). It is thus not especially controversial to assume consciousness, whatever form it takes.

[38] This is a simplification of Andrew Brook's view. I talk more about this in §7.3.

[39] I say 'typically' here, as there are a number of people who do not fit this description.

[40] This deliberately mirrors Hegel's dialectic approach to individuation, introduced in §3.4. In Hegel's dialectic the 'mind has emerged as the Idea that has reached its being-for-self. The *object* of the Idea as well as the *subject is the concept* ... [T]he concept has, in this externalization, become identical with itself' (Emphasis Original, Hegel and Inwood, 2007 §381, p. 9). The object (self) and subject ('I') are both the same thing that become realised by an expression of the 'I' through the self, marking the self as something belonging to the 'I', in contrast to those things marked 'not-self', so identified as some 'other'.

Upon finding this out, Thompson's understanding of himself is bound to change, perhaps dramatically. He, as a cognitive being, who had perceived himself in one way, finds out this information about his relation to his biological mother, changing not only how he perceives Julie and Amy, but how he perceives himself. Following this change in how he perceives himself, it will likely affect how he perceives the world: this new information about his self changes Thompson's understanding of who he is; it changes his 'I', which changes how he perceives the world, ultimately changing his perception of his self. Past experiences change how humans think about the world. In terms of Self-Regarding Identity, the thoughts we have about our self will change how we perceive our self. By dividing this iterative process into 'I' and self, we can see how each aspect can influence each other. Put simply, the thoughts that the 'I' has about its self changes the thoughts that the 'I' has about its self.

Identity is a cognitive process in which a relation of equivalence is a set of thoughts about thoughts. Taking into account the role of past experience in perception, we see that identity not as a single stable thing, but a constantly evolving result of dynamic cognitive processes, arising from the dialogue between an 'I' that is perceiving the self and of the self as forming the epistemic foundations from which the 'I' perceives. This is close to a dialectic methodology,[41] like that of Georg Hegel.[42]

So, there is an 'I', a self and some relative equivalence between them, but the 'relative' part of the perceptual relation requires explanation. Like personhood and intimacy, discussed in §2.3, some things are going to be more important to self-development than others. To explain this, let us start with the idea that '[a] person's identity is constituted by a configuration of *central* traits' (Emphasis Mine, Rorty and Wong, 1990, p. 19). Amélie Rorty and David Wong clarify what they mean by central traits: 'We are focussing on traits that typically make a systematic difference to a person's life'. They then note the potential for variation in these traits, as '[t]he kinds of traits that form identity vary culturally, across class and gender lines and indeed, individually' (Rorty and Wong, 1990, pp. 19–20). This idea of central traits also plays a major role in Bernard Williams' discussions of identity,[43] where he states 'the idea that an individual person has a set of desires, concerns or, as I shall often call them, projects, which help to constitute a *character*' (Emphasis Original,

[41] In order to step around terms of art like a 'Hegelian Dialectic' or 'Kantian Dialectic', which carry with them a deep set of investigations and histories, I prefer to use the term 'dyadic relationship'. I spell out what I mean by a dyadic relationship in Chapter 6.

[42] Such dialectic methods were not wholly and solely Hegel's province. Kant, for example, had an 'implied dialectic' relevant to this 'I'/Self dialogue in which 'there can be no existing things, no factual reality, that is not constituted by the forms available to us; factual relating is mediated by these forms . . . Conversely, however, the forms are in their turn mediated by existing reality' (Adorno, 2001, p. 87).

[43] Williams first mentioned this as a problem for integrity in the face of utilitarianism (Williams, 1973, p. 118) and then developed in Persons, Character And Morality (Williams, 1981b).

Williams, 1981b, p. 5). A similar point is found in Jonathan Glover's statements on beliefs and identity:

> We define ourselves partly by our distinctive beliefs about the world and about how to live ... No matter how absurd, any belief *can* be preserved if you are prepared to make sufficient adjustments in the rest of the system ... Sometimes [these] beliefs are part of our identity in a quite explicit way.
>
> (Glover, 1988, pp. 154, 155, 157)

Mirroring the cognitive account of identity, Christine Korsgaard's 'practical identity' postulates that essential to human identity is not merely that we have these central projects and so on but that we reflectively endorse them (Korsgaard, 1996, pp. 100–102); in short, identity is not merely the traits, but our *thoughts about those traits*. This marks the importance of the identity processes to things like personhood and intimacy and fills out earlier discussions of privacy and ownership.

Yet, as was seen in the discussion of Numeric Identity, §4.5.1, our identities change through time (Perry, 2008a). In much the same way, our Character Identity can (and should) change through time. Alasdair MacIntyre's *After Virtue* developed a narrative account of identity where our identities are understood not as a set of independent facts but as a series of interlinked and dynamic stories about ourselves and our cultures (MacIntyre, 2008, pp. 204–225). Further to this, our identities do not only change with time, but within context; contexts like a social role are important to human identity (Rorty and Wong, 1990, pp. 22–23): the traits that I express as a lecturer teaching first year philosophy students might be quite different to the ones I express as an underperforming academic meeting with a job selection panel: in the first situation I might be authoritative and confident, deeply assured of my skill set and knowledge, while in the second situation, I may be anxious and passive, totally convinced of lack of skill as a philosopher and general failure as an academic. Yet which of these traits constitutes the *real* me? Or is it both of these sets? Or is it the 'ideal self' that I wish myself to be (Rorty and Wong, 1990, pp. 23–24)? The point of all of this is that reference to a set of central traits does not immediately get us closer to recognising the importance of identity.

Harry Frankfurt offered a wilful identification with particular traits as an indication of the person's Character Identity.

> Becoming responsible for one's character is not essentially a matter of *producing that character* but of *taking responsibility for it*. This happens when a person selectively identifies with certain of his own attitudes or dispositions ... In identifying with them, he incorporates them into himself and makes them his own.
>
> (Emphasis Original, Frankfurt, 2006, p. 7)

Similar to Hegel's right of individuation, Frankfurt considers that identity is the expression of the person's will, 'It is in securing the conformity of his will to his second-order volitions, then, that a person exercises freedom of will' (Frankfurt, 1971, p. 15).

Frankfurt's account is less concerned with a set of traits that makes us who we are, but rather how we identify with those traits: I might be totally dependent upon heroin, for example, but what separates me from a wanton addict is my desire to distance myself from that addiction (Frankfurt, 1971, pp. 11–13). Again, my identity is not shown merely or simply by particular traits, but by how I *identify* with and value those traits. As Korsgaard says, one's identity is best 'understood as a description under which you value yourself, a description under which you find your life to be worth living and your actions to be worth undertaking' (Korsgaard, 1996, p. 101).

Central traits are important to self-development, but to make greater sense of this, we need to see how the person responds to these traits, whether they identify with the traits or whether they reject them. It is how a person reacts to their self, their thoughts about thoughts, that we recognise their identity.

To summarise, a description of Self-Regarding Identity must be able to capture relations between the 'I' and the self, whilst allowing for changes in both the 'I' and the self and must be able to accommodate differences between central and non-central traits. Saying that Self-Regarding Identity is 'I am who I perceive myself to be' covers all these requirements. Putting this more generally, I hold that Self-Regarding Identity occurs when 'I perceive myself to be me'. To generalise, we replace 'I' with X, 'myself' with Y and 'me' with Z; we have a general form of Self-Regarding Identity as 'X perceives Y to be Z'.

4.6.2 *Other-Regarding Identity: You Are Who I Perceive You to Be*

The second aspect of identity is Other Regarding Identity, or 'who I perceive you to be'. Much of the discussion so far has been concerned with perception and the subjective components of identity that arise from each conscious person having a unique private experience of the world.

Taking a closer look at the two-way model of perception described in §4.3, the FFP and RHT involve two sorts of identifications. Recall that the FFP uses incoming information from sense modes like the eyes, ears and so on to get fine-grained detail of the subject of observation. The RHT process rapidly tracks the incoming information to the observer's existing cognitive frameworks, to access the generalised and abstracted concepts that are used as rapid generalised identifiers. I have so far only discussed the formation of identity as a first-person subjective experience: That is, that the identity constructed occurs only in the mind of the observer. Yet it must be obvious that the subject of observation has an identity that exists prior to and independent from, any observer.

In presenting identity as a cognitive construct, it may seem that I am presenting an 'identity of idealism', an idealism of the kind offered by Bishop Berkeley in which he sought to 'prove that there is no such thing as matter at all and the world consists of nothing but ideas' (Russell, 1912, pp. 12–13). Yet Berkeley's problem might have been that he confused 'the thing apprehended with the act of apprehension' (Russell, 1912,

p. 42). So, to get a fuller account of identity than an 'identity of idealism', I will look to the thing being apprehended by discussing the epistemic basis for identification and will then integrate this with the subjective account of identity.

'Epistemological questions about identity can be expressed by asking how identity judgments, or identity judgments about object of such and such a kind, are ... known' (Shoemaker, 1963, p. 3). Put another way, how does an observer make an identity judgement about a given subject? Upon what basis does the observer claim to know that a subject $Y = Y$? The answer is that the observer will have some belief or set of beliefs upon which they are basing their identity judgements. The basis for these beliefs can be found by tracking to facts in the external world,[44] and so are open to discussion – that is, when people disagree, the truth of a claim can be determined. 'Some statements can be known to be true or false independently of any prejudices or attitudes on the part of observers' (Searle, 1997, p. 113). This sort of statement reflects John Locke's 'primary qualities' of bodies,[45] when Locke says

> the *Ideas of primary Qualities* of Bodies, *are Resemblances* of them, and their Patterns do really exist in the Bodies themselves; but the *Ideas, produced* in us *by* these *Secondary Qualities, have no resemblance* of them at all ... what is Sweet, Blue or Warm in *Idea*, is but the certain Bulk, Figure, and Motion of the insensible Parts in the Bodies themselves, which we call so.
>
> (Locke, 1975, p. 15)

Searle makes a distinction between those things that are epistemically objective and those things that are ontologically subjective. 'Some entities, mountains for example, have an existence which is objective, in the sense that it does not depend on any subject. Others ... are subjective in that their existence depends on being felt by a subject' (Searle, 1997, pp. 113–114). Like the Necker Cube from §4.4.1, eye defects aside, two people may construct different identities for the mountain; it is uncontroversial to say that (a) the mountain exists and (b) the observers (or their eyes at least) receive the same visual information, but (c) the observers have different experiences of the mountain. No doubt what happens for each observer in the identity construction is going to be influenced by the two observer's perceptions of the mountain. But, as Searle points out, the mountain's existence is not dependent upon an observer. Entities that exist in the external world, mountains, rocks, puppies and people, exist prior to observation and these entities have properties that are potentially observable.

Returning to the earlier discussion on perception, the observer receives information about a given entity via their sense organs and this information is parsed into

[44] I am making epistemological claims about the truth of the world and how we get access to it. I give a more detailed account of how I use truth and knowledge in §5.6.

[45] This reference to Locke's resemblances should not be taken as an endorsement of the theory that he proposed. As Sterelny notes, the theory of resemblance to explain mind-world relations is problematic (Sterelny, 1990, p. 112).

sense data that is received at finer and finer detail, potentially down to the level of individual neurons – the FFP model of perception. On the FFP model, the observer will receive information about a given subject which then converges through neural hubs to produce an emergent identity in the mind[46] of the observer. When observing another person, the observer will likely receive information about the person's body, their face, their mood, their voice and other things.[47] At the same time, as the RHT explains, the observer has an existing set of information about the person being observed, an integrated information set formed from previous experiences.

For people as 'the thing apprehended', there are two main types of fact claim, with a loose distinction between the two – the physical and the historical. We identify people on both physical and historical accounts. Consider the identity of a close friend. How does an observer know that this person in front of them is in fact their friend? The answer is obvious: 'This person looks like my friend, they talk like my friend, they act like my friend.' That is, the physical properties like their face, body and voice are consistent with the observer's existing cognitive framework. In addition, how the friend acts and what they say needs to match what the observer knows of the friend:

> Our identity judgments about persons other than ourselves are most commonly based on similarity of bodily appearance . . . But there is no doubt that our grounds for making identity judgments about other persons sometimes involves psychological considerations. I might know that this twin is John, not Tom, because he is lively and good humoured. Better still, I might know that this is John because he remembers . . . events that happened yesterday while John was present and Tom was not.
>
> (Shoemaker, 1963, pp. 20–21)

Like the dynamic between the FFP and the RHT, the criteria that an observer uses to determine the identity of a subject will likely be physical first (FFP-like processes). As the friendship evolves, the observer's cognitive framework about the subject expands (RHT-like processes); behavioural cues and historical facts play a greater role in constructing and maintaining an identity for the friend. Such a claim of relative equivalence involves assumptions of Numeric Identity and Character Identity, influenced by Group Identity.

Note also that the historical facts do not necessarily have to be those facts of shared experiences. Essentialised Identities are central to human interactions. Consider how a subject can be identified by a stranger – that is, how does an observer identify a subject not familiar to them? The observer may use identity candidates of a

[46] Emergence is discussed in §5.8 and its relation to identity formation is discussed in Chapter 6.

[47] Note that I have not included any discussion about sensory inputs of smell, taste or touch. I do not wish to deny the importance of these inputs in an observer's construction of another's identity, or of self. Rather, it is that the discussion of these senses should suffice to flesh out the neuroanatomical basis for perception and in identity construction.

historical type like a name, birthdate, signature or PIN to access or verify the subject's identity. These candidates for identification are contingent historical facts that cumulatively produce a historical information set about the subject and are likely to be used extensively in identification of strangers. These contingent historical facts are, like the physical properties of a person, truth verifiable. That is, they provide the epistemic basis upon which observers base and build the identities of others.

This subsection began by pointing to a tension between claiming that 'a person's identity is who X perceives Y to be' and the idea that there are facts about a person. This tension is resolved by going back to the discussions of the two-way model of perception and the dialogical and dynamic nature of identity construction. First, following the FFP, the Other-Regarding Identity will initially be based upon those properties of a person that have an epistemically objective basis – we form an Other-Regarding Identity using a complex of the Numeric and Character Identity concepts, such as how the person looks, sounds and what their unique history is. As an observer builds up a knowledge set for a given subject, the RHT will produce more rapid identification via higher level abstractions than was initially used. Each time an observer meets their spouse of twenty years, they don't need to remember what their spouse looks like, or any contingent facts about them.

Second, we must recall that the higher level abstractions are always amenable to updating with new information: relations of relative equivalence can evolve. The relation between FFP and the RHT allows for new information to update or replace the old. The identity that an observer has for a given subject is an integrated one that is dynamic and responsive to epistemically verifiable objective considerations.

But what happens when the observer's existing cognitive framework and the incoming epistemically verifiable information don't match? Section 4.4 said that the two-way model of perception tells us that the FFP is re-engaged to gain more fine-grained details. But this does not solve the problem of how two conflicting facts are dealt with by the cognitive model of identity.

Recall Harry and his sister Sally from §4.4.2. Suppose that as they talk, she tells Harry that she has learned that she was adopted. Despite the simplicity of this fact, there is no doubt this will take a great deal of time and effort for Harry to process: While an abstracted set of ideas may easily take in the data that Sally has different parents to Harry, historical facts like this can have profound effects upon how Harry perceives Sally and most probably the ways that Harry perceives himself. Recall from §4.5.1 that the important aspects of Self-Regarding Identity are the 'configuration of central traits' (Rorty and Wong, 1990, p. 19). For a host of possible reasons,[48] one's genetic parents are often seen as one set of these central traits.

[48] Some of the issues surrounding genetic relatedness and parent-child relations are discussed in (Kolers, 2003; Kolers and Bayne, 2001).

The final point to be made is that epistemically verifiable claims are an essential element to the construction of any identity. It would be wrong to state that an observer perceives another in a purely subjective sense. The Other-Regarding Identity that is perceived by an observer is partially caused by and is reactive to, the external world. What I mean to capture by Other-Regarding Identity is to state that there is an objective *component* to how an observer constructs the identity of a subject. This is different from saying that the objective factors are *all* that happens in identity construction. On the cognitive account of identity, identity is influenced by the observer's thoughts, beliefs and experiences. Yet this does not clarify how these thoughts, beliefs and experiences come about or how they are valued and integrated. Other-Regarding Identity, particularly the truth verifiable aspects, go some way to filling in the objective processes, showing that identity is more than a Berkeley-like idealism.

With this in mind, when answering a question of who someone else is, an observer can sensibly claim a relation of relative equivalence by saying 'your identity is who I perceive you to be'. Note again that this general type of Other-Regarding Identity covers all four of the general identity concepts introduced in §4.5, whilst making the subject of such a claim different to the general account of Self-Regarding Identity, presented in §4.6.1.

4.6.3 *Other/Other-Regarding Identity: They Are Who I Perceive Others to Perceive Them to Be*

The final aspect of identity is what I call Other/Other-Regarding Identity. This is especially concerned with how a primary observer, X, perceives the construction of identity for a subject, made by a second observer, X*, given as 'X perceives another, X*, to perceive Y to be Z'. The basic point is that humans construct identities for others not simply based on their own personal experiences and not simply based on objective factors, but also on how they think *others* perceive the subject. Two simple ways of describing this are 'any friend of yours is a friend of mine' and 'the enemy of my enemy is my friend'. In short, an observer's *attitude* to Y is affected by what they think X*'s attitude to Y is. This section captures an important aspect of identity construction: that the relations of relative equivalence humans make for a given subject are impacted by how they think *others* think of that subject.

To explain, consider that humans are distinct from many other animals in that humans have a capacity not only to recognise others and form relations *with* them, but also that humans can also recognise the relations that exist *between* other people that do not involve the primary observer.

> Most mammals are sensitive only to the social relations second parties bear to them. They register the fact that they outrank, or are outranked by, another. They are sensitive to the fact that another animal is their mother, their sib, their offspring,

> unrelated, a stranger . . . But it does not include how others stand to one another. In contrast, primates register and respond to third-party relations.
>
> (Sterelny, 2003, pp. 51–52)

The basic point is that humans can recognise the relations that exist between other people. In contrast to an animal like a chicken in a pecking order or a dog in a pack, humans recognise social relations within a group even if they are not a part of that group.

The relevance of this is that humans have evolved to recognise not only individuals but how others relate to individuals. In fact, this ability to recognise the social position of others may be a central element of our social evolution. As Kim Sterelny argues, a 'cooperation explosion' within human social groups was essential to our rapid evolution (Sterelny, 2003, pp. 123–145). Similarly, when discussing the role of reciprocity and recognition in human evolution (Joyce, 2006, pp. 88–92), Richard Joyce argues that language may have originally developed in part to express judgement about others:

> Our ancestors didn't just want to *describe* the fact that someone failed to reciprocate; the purpose of their gossip was that others could be *criticized* . . . we come to the conclusion that an important evolutionary function of language is to convey certain types of social evaluative content.
>
> (Emphasis Original, Joyce, 2006, pp. 91–92)

So, we have recognition of individuals, not merely as individuals, 'this person in front of me is Quinn', but as individuals located in a social hierarchy, 'this person in front of me, Quinn, who others think is a bad person'.

The outcome of this is that humans can recognise how a group values an individual. The other/other element of identity takes into account not the objective facts about a person, discussed in section §4.6.2, but intersubjective or social assessments about that person. These intersubjective components of identity are less involved with epistemically objective facts and more involved with the inter-personal values that can come bundled or 'nested' with the objective facts.[49] As such, the other/other element of identity aligns, in part, with Group and Essentialised Identity. Importantly, this intersubjective value is from the observer's subjective view point: the intersubjective value that the primary observer, X, ascribes to Y is dependent on the primary observer's perception of how a secondary observer, X*, values Y, not necessarily how X* *actually* values Y.

Following from section §4.6.2, it is uncontroversial to state that objective facts like physical attributes of a person will play a major role in how people identify others and thus are involved in the process of identity construction. It should also be

[49] Fred Dretske talks about nested information, 'whenever s is F, t is Gm . . . then no signal can bear the message that s is F without also conveying the information that t is G' (Dretske, 1981, p. 71). I consider Other/Other Identity to involve this sort of composite information.

reasonably uncontroversial to state that objective facts can also carry with them other aspects that come into play when an observer forms an identity of a subject. Consider Jenny, when she meets Fred for the first time. No doubt Jenny will recognise that Fred is male. The fact of his sex/gender will be one of the objective facts about Fred that Jenny uses in constructing her identity of Fred. Yet her formation of Fred is not simply a composite of different objective facts; it is more complex than this: The objective information about Fred is not inert.

While a person's sex/gender may be largely objective,[50] there is often a host of social aspects that are strongly associated with sex\gender: intersubjective components derived from a perceived value about a given objective trait or set of traits. The observer may be more or less conscious of these associations. To support this claim, consider the studies that indicate that parents treat infants differently, based on the perceived gender of the infant (Lewis and Brooks-Gunn, 1979, pp. 267–269). This differential sex/gender treatment is one example that there is more included in identity construction than just the integration of objective information into an observer's cognitive frameworks. What is this additional component and where does this additional component of identity come from? Simply put, this is an intersubjective component that is formed through the interactions between people. I call this the Other/Other-Regarding Identity.

Consider again Jenny and Fred. Jenny meets Fred for the first time and as part of the strong human tendency to observe, identify and ultimately recognise,[51] Jenny observes a set of information about Fred. She observes that Fred is male. This recognition of another's sex/gender will likely have influence on Jenny's identity construction for Fred, evidenced[52] by differential treatment based on sex/gender. Though it may be slightly controversial to say *that* Jenny will treat Fred in a predictable way, based upon the epistemically verifiable fact of his being male, there is evidence to support the claim that sex/gender observation will alter how an observer treats a subject. Interestingly, these differences in treatment seem to be somewhat independent of the gender of the observer (Brennan, 2009, p. 143).

[50] I recognise here that sex/gender is highly complex, in that some people born physically male may be psychologically female and that binary distinctions between male and female overlook the blurred boundaries displayed by intersex people. Deterministic and coarse distinctions like male/female are examples of Essentialised Identity.

[51] This is perhaps a controversial claim, to say that there is a strong human tendency to observe, identify and recognise. However, given the strong neurological evidence that neonates and infants can recognise particular human physical traits (Cassia et al., 2009; Elsabbagh et al., 2009; Farroni et al., 2002; Meltzoff and Moore, 1997), it would seem that as recognition of other human's physical traits happens so early in individual development, that the tendency to observe, identify and recognise is strong.

[52] Samantha Brennan, for example, discusses gender-based differential treatment of individuals, with examples ranging from the time taken to get served in a coffee shop, to studies that show that 'having a female-gendered name on an academic curriculum vitae costs candidates in a process of peer evaluation, both for hiring and for promotion and tenure' (Brennan, 2009, p. 142).

What is more controversial is to predict *how* Jenny will treat Fred differently, say compared to his sister Freda – Jenny may treat Fred worse or better than Freda. The point being made here is that the recognition of a subject's sex/gender by an observer will typically have an effect upon the observer's treatment of that person.

Underpinning Other/Other Regarding Identity is a relatively uncontroversial claim: humans have the capacity for evaluation. This can be based on simple 'folk psychology', where we ascribe beliefs and desires to others in order to explain behaviours that seem similar to our own. Folk psychology is the process where

> [t]he average person is able to explain, and even predict, the behavior of other persons with a facility and success that is remarkable. Such explanations and predictions standardly make reference to the desires, beliefs . . . to which the agents are presumed subject.
>
> (Churchland, 1981, p. 68)[53]

The relation between having a capacity for evaluation and folk psychology is that folk psychology assumes that other people have beliefs and desires. From this we can say if someone has a thought about something like an ice-cream, that thought can take the form of a belief, 'I believe this is an ice-cream', or a desire 'I desire this ice-cream'. In both cases, belief or desire, the person is making an evaluation about the ice-cream: that it *is* an ice-cream or that the ice-cream *is* desired. 'It is part of the folk picture that thoughts have content. A preference is satisfied or not satisfied. A belief is true or false. A belief is about something' (Sterelny, 2003, p. 7).

These claims about evaluation do not mean that all beliefs and desires, much less all thoughts, are *necessarily* evaluative. Rather, that people have this capacity for evaluation. This is a basic upshot of the model of cognition proposed, thoughts about thoughts, where the primary thought is 'ice-cream' and the secondary thought is a belief or desire about ice-cream.[54]

Relating the Other/Other-Regarding aspect to evaluation, humans have the capacity to recognise (or at least presume) the status of an individual within a social group independently of whether that observer is part of the social group or not. The role that folk psychology plays here is that the observer of the social group ascribes a

[53] It should be noted that this quote from Paul Churchland is taken from a paper where he argues *against* folk psychology in favour of eliminative materialism; 'folk psychology is a radically inadequate account of our internal activities, too confused and too defective to win survival through intertheoretic reduction' (Churchland, 1981, p. 72). However, Churchland's arguments do not necessarily defeat folk psychology, a point argued by Frank Jackson and Philip Pettit (Jackson and Pettit, 2004), amongst others.

[54] Note that I am assuming something like the language of thought hypothesis, where the thoughts that I am interested in are typically propositional attitudes. 'Propositional attitudes are the thoughts described by such sentence forms as "S believes that P", "S hopes that P", "S desires that P" and so on, where "S" refers to the subject of the attitude, "P" is any sentence and "that P" refers to the proposition that is the object of the attitude' (Aydede, 2010).

particular social value to that individual based on how that observer perceives the individual's hierarchical location. As we saw, both Sterelny (Sterelny, 2003, pp. 123–145) and Joyce (Joyce, 2006, pp. 88–92) argued not only that we can recognise in-group dynamics, but that this is a central facet of human evolution and ultimately, one of the fundamental facts about our cognition that separates us from many other animals. The importance of evaluation is that not only can humans recognise the way group members treat each other, but as individuals, humans can and do form opinions about others. Putting these two observations together, it follows that the evaluations an observer makes about others influence the thoughts that the observer has about that individual. In short, Other/Other Regarding Identity is important for how people treat others. I return to this more in Chapters 8 and 9. On the cognitive account of identity, one of the key roles that the Other/Other Regarding element plays in identity construction is to have value-ascribing thoughts about an individual, with those values arising from the way in which a particular group values, or is perceived to value, that individual.

A more general point being also made is that the construction of a person's identity is neither psychologically nor socially inert: seemingly objective facts like a person's sex/gender can often carry with them a set of values or additional information that influences how the observer constructs the identity of the subject and those values have their origin in how society at large is seen to value that person or group. A way of stating this Other/Other-Regarding Identity is to say that 'identity is who I perceive others to perceive you to be'.

4.6.4 *Spelling Out the General Account of Identity:* X *Perceives* Y *to Be* Z

Following the discussion of the three components of a cognitive account of identity, I can now present a general account of identity: when making an identity claim, an observer, X, perceives a subject, Y, to be relatively equivalent to Z. Given that this is an identity claim, the reference to relative equivalence is redundant. So a general identity claim becomes 'X perceives Y to be Z'. Written differently, 'Identity (Z) is who[55] X perceives Y to be'. This section explains the general account and gives the reasons for developing this account of identity.

This general account has five elements; 'X', 'perceives', 'Y', 'to be' and 'Z'. I will explain my use of each in turn.

X – X refers to the observer making the identification. The cognitive states of the observer, X, can change.

Perceives – The issues of perception and experience have been discussed in §4.2 and §4.3. Identifications involve transformation of sensory inputs

[55] This general account could also be written as 'Identity (Z) is what X perceives Y to be'. However, given that the focus of this thesis is on people, 'Identity (Z) is who X perceives Y to be' has been chosen.

into something that the observer can use. This will likely be a complex process involving the dual processes of FFP and RHT.

Y – Any use of identity needs a subject of identification. Whether this is a person, or a thing like the Necker Cube, there needs to be something that is being identified.

To Be – The observer perceives a relative equivalence between two or more things. It is sensible to say 'I perceive Elvis *to be* the singer of "Hound Dog"'. The observer, X, is claiming Elvis, Y, *to be* relevantly equivalent to the singer of the song 'Hound Dog'. The reason for X making such a claim is that X perceives Y to be relevantly equivalent to Z. This '*to be*' is based upon the observer's existing cognitive framework. It presupposes that X has a relevant cognitive framework used to identify Y. This may be reduced to something as simple as 'Y is different from ¬Z'. For example, if John meets someone for the first time, he may identify the person as 'not anyone that I have ever met before'. That is Y (John's newly met person) is ¬Z (where Z is every person that John has met before). In the case where John already knows and meets Jim, we have an instance of John re-identifying Y as Jim, due to his previous knowledge of Jim.

Z – As a result of a set of mental processes, the observer, X, has some experience, either conscious or sub-personal, of Y. This experience is Z. Given the complexity of mental processes, this Z might be the result of FFP, some abstract mental representation as in the RHT, a combination of both, a memory of similar experiences and so on. Z is intended to capture the cognitive aspects of making claims of relative equivalence: Z emerges[56] from thoughts about thoughts arising from perceiving Y.[57]

Given these five aspects, the general formulation of identity is 'X perceives Y to be Z'.

To see how the general account relates to Self-Regarding, Other-Regarding and Other/Other-Regarding Identity, recall that when thinking about themselves, the observer can be understood as claiming that 'I (X) perceive myself (Y) to be me (Z)'. Likewise, to make a claim of Other-Regarding Identity, the observer can be understood as claiming that 'I (X) perceive you (Y) to be my sister (Z)'. In cases of Other/Other-Regarding Identity, the observer can be understood as claiming that 'I (X) perceive another (X*) to perceive you (Y) to be my sister (Z)'. The general formulation allows for the claim of relative equivalence to relate to any of the four identity concepts from §4.5:

56 Emergence is covered in §5.8.

57 Note that this Z can be a definite or indefinite claim. That is, consider an observer looking at a photo of Elvis Presley performing on stage. It is equally sensible to state 'X perceives Y to be Elvis Presley' or 'X perceives Y to be a rock singer' or even 'X perceives Y to be a white male human', where Z can equally refer to 'Elvis Presley', 'rock singer' or 'white male human'.

Numeric Identity: '*I* perceive *myself* to be *the same person I was yesterday*',
Character Identity: '*I* perceive *myself* to be *a funny guy*',
Group Identity: '*I* perceive *myself* to be *a Christian*',
Essentialised Identity: '*I* perceive *myself* to be *employee #5425777*'.

This can be converted to Other-Regarding Identity, with Numeric Identity being: '*I* perceive *you* to be *the same person as you were yesterday*' and so on. For Other/Other-Regarding Identity '*I* perceive *Brian* to perceive you to be *the same person you were yesterday*' and so on.

In summary, this section has discussed three different elements of identity, Self-Regarding, Other-Regarding and Other/Other-Regarding. A general account of identity was presented, 'X perceives Y to be Z'. These elements of identity, though described separately, bear upon each other. By developing a cognitive account of identity, as a *dynamic* set of thoughts about thoughts, not only does the cognitive account seek to explain that there are different aspects to identity, but this account also seeks to bring the different aspects together in a way such that each aspect is causally relevant to the others. We not only rely on the different aspects to construct identities, but in many situations, individuals may need all three aspects to form a stable identity. In short, a full identity is likely to be an integrated set of thoughts, constructed from the Self-Regarding, Other-Regarding and Other/Other-Regarding aspects of identity.

4.7 SALLY REVISITED: VIRTUAL IDENTITY

So, what does any of this discussion have to do with surveillance technologies? Given its fairly theoretical approach, the discussion of identity may seem obscure in a discussion about surveillance. In order make the discussion of identity relevant to surveillance a final identity concept is introduced: Virtual Identity.

A Virtual Identity, as I use it, refers to some information set in the world that calls to mind a person.[58] Virtual Identity refers to a particular type of information, which encourages the observer to experience the information as Personal Information. Information is discussed in detail in the next chapter,[59] so for now consider that Virtual Identity refers to an ordered data set, considered independent of the observer's experience of that ordered data set.[60] However, because of the way a set of data

58 As with previous discussions, I intend for this identity concept to hold to people and groups. But rather than saying 'people and groups' every time, I will simply refer to a single person, unless otherwise indicated.

59 In Chapter 5, I talk about two types of information – Thin Information, as simply ordered data and Thick Information, as ordered data that is meaningful and judged to be true.

60 However, in line with the discussions in this chapter, this information when observed is experienced by the given cognitive agent. As Floridi recognises, while we can describe some information as something independent of cognitive interpretation, in practice, any time a person encounters such data in the world, they will experience it as information that carries

is ordered, the social conventions associated with that ordering and the cognitive agent's existing Cognitive Networks, this data encourages or 'affords'[61] a particular type of experience: the observer will likely experience the information as an identity. That is, upon seeing the ordered data set such as a photograph of a celebrity, the observer will see that photo as the given celebrity. X perceives Y to be Z; the observer, X, perceives the photograph, Y, to be the celebrity, Z.

Virtual Identity fits with the discussions of the four identity concepts introduced in §4.5: Numeric Identity, Character Identity, Group Identity and Essentialised Identity. Recall that a basic quality that cut across all four of these identity concepts was that someone was making a claim of relative equivalence between something and a person or group. Virtual Identity, I suggest, also does this, but does it in an importantly different way.

For instance, when showing Sally a photograph of Elvis, the data is ordered in such a way that Sally will experience the photo as a human face. Presuming she knows what Elvis looked like, she will experience the photo as the face of Elvis. So, while the photo itself is just a set of coloured dots arranged in a particular way, because Sally is a human with a given set of experiences and knowledge about the world, her capacity to experience the photo of Elvis as anything but a photo of Elvis is heavily constrained. In this sense, the photo is a Virtual Identity of Elvis.

Given our neural processes and social conventions, the information will typically 'invite' the observer to experience a photo as a person's face, to experience a name as referring to some person and so on.[62] A Virtual Identity can refer to anything from a single name, a fingerprint, a genetic profile, to a photo of Elvis, to a very rich and detailed one, a biography like *The Identity of Elvis Presley*. Or an online profile like Sally's Facebook page.

I say that something like a photo of Elvis is a Virtual Identity, but given that the photo is some information in the world, ordered independent of a given observer's experience, Virtual Identity is different to the identity concepts and elements discussed thus far. Though an observer such as Sally establishes relative equivalence between a photo of Elvis and the person, Elvis, there is a different set of relations going on than those discussed in §4.5. I want to draw attention to the fact that in a Virtual Identity, the relations of equivalence that the observer is making between

with it meanings and truth judgements. I discuss this in Chapter 5. See also Floridi, (2011a, pp. 85–87).

[61] Affordances and their relation to information are described in §5.4. In advance of that discussion, I provide a brief description of affordances and information: '[d]ata are *constraining affordances*: they allow or invite certain constructs (they are *affordances* for the information agent that can take advantage of them) and resist or impede some others (they are *constraints* for the same agent), depending on the interaction with and the nature of, the information agent that processes them' (Emphases Original, Floridi, 2011a, p. 87).

[62] I note here that, given the multirealisability of information, to be discussed in detail in Chapters 5 and 6, there is variation in the ways that different people will experience a Virtual Identity. A major factor affecting this sort of variance is Other/Other Identity, discussed in §4.6.3.

something in the world and a given person are mediated by the informational entity that is the Virtual Identity. Again, thinking of the photo, were some of the properties of that photo to change, it would no longer call Elvis to mind. The discussion of identity as a cognitive process and information starts to link up: if information is mediating the way that people form identities and if – as argued throughout this book, particularly in Part III – those identities carry with them important moral values, then information is something that is morally relevant.

While something like a photo of Elvis most clearly brings about an Other-Regarding Identity, what of a photo of one's self? That is, how do Sally's experiences of the photo of Elvis and Elvis' experience of it differ? This shows the strength of the cognitive identity approach I have developed: if Sally looks at a photo of Elvis, she will likely perceive it differently than if Elvis (were he still alive) were to look at it. Sally, combining Other-Regarding and Other/Other-Regarding Identities, may see the photo as a cool rock icon, to be held in high esteem. As an experience of Self-Regarding Identity, however, Elvis may see it as a harsh indictment of his lifestyle and a depressing reminder of how fat and unhealthy he has become. Like a Necker Cube, despite its stability in the world, the photo is experienced differently by different cognitive agents, dependent upon their existing Cognitive Networks.

Further, the identity elements detailed in §4.6 – Self-Regarding Identity, Other-Regarding Identity and Other/Other-Regarding Identity – all refer to a cognitive agent's perceptual experience. On my account, Virtual Identity refers to information which stands prior to a cognitive agent's perception of the ordered data. The reason for focussing on Virtual Identity is that surveillance technologies order data – as covered in Chapter 3, the whole point of surveillance technologies is to produce information. The information that this book is concerned with is information about people, Personal Information. In short, the entire purpose of epistemic action of surveillance is to produce Virtual Identities.

The increasing importance of Virtual Identities in the age of surveillance is captured by Daniel Solove:

> Small details that were once captured in dim memories or fading scraps of paper are now preserved forever in the digital minds of computers, in vast databases with fertile fields of personal data. Our wallets are stuffed with ATM cards, calling cards, frequent shopper cards, and credit cards – all of which can be used to record where we are and what we do. Every day, rivulets of information stream into electric brains to be sifted, sorted, rearranged, and combined in hundreds of different ways. Digital technology enables the preservation of the minutia of our everyday comings and goings, of our likes and dislikes, of who were are and what we own. It is ever more possible to create an electronic collage that covers much of a person's life – a life captured in records, a *digital person composed in the collective computer networks of the world*.
>
> (Emphasis Mine, Solove, 2004, p. 1)

Solove refers to digital dossiers as a 'collection of detailed data about an individual', which he intimates are used 'in order to reach a judgment' about the subject of the dossier (Solove, 2004, pp. 1–2). These dossiers produce what he calls a 'digital person'.

Instead of a 'digital person', I refer to a Virtual Identity. The reason for this is that the term 'digital *person*' implies personhood, which can carry with it a lot of baggage, in particular, some cognitive agency. However, to mark this identity off from the other forms of identity used elsewhere in the book, I add the prefix 'Virtual'. The purpose of this prefix is to indicate that the identity being referred to is neither an actual person in the world, nor is it a particular agent's cognitive experience. Instead, a Virtual Identity refers to some information about a person. Further, contrasting Solove's use of 'digital' I have opted for 'virtual' to indicate that the identity is not necessarily located in some computer database, Virtual Identity can include things like photos, books and so on not obviously covered by the term 'digital'.

Sally's example is a case in point – she posts sets of information about herself online in a process of self creation through presentation of a Virtual Identity online. The information she posts is an expression of a set of aspects about her Self-Regarding Identity. When Harry sees photos of her, reads about her day and so on he is getting some set of information about her. In an Other-Regarding sense, the Virtual Identity (Z) informs Harry's (X) perception of Sally (Y). Finally, things such as the 'number of friends' and 'like' functions on Facebook give an explicit tool to denote how others see that person: they afford Other/Other Identities.

In the sea of information produced by surveillance technologies and propagated by our behaviours, Virtual Identities have an ever-increasing presence and power to impact our lives. What the world of information gives us is the capacity to produce, store, distribute and use Virtual Identities like no other time in history. Personal Information and its uses and abuses, has been essential to human evolution and our development as social animals. What's new is the role played by this intermediary informational entity, the Virtual Identity.

The final point is that, given the capacity for technologies to construct Virtual Identities from information, Virtual Identities matter. That is, if we care about identity, then we ought to care about things like Virtual Identities and how they are constructed. However, in order to properly understand what a Virtual Identity is and how they are constructed, information needs explanation and is the focus of the next chapter.

5

On Information

5.1 INFORMATION EVERYWHERE

Our Personal Information is everywhere and it's being used. The age of surveillance is marked by the fact that every tiny piece of Personal Information can be used and reused, in a multiplicity of ways that we are typically ignorant of and cannot predict in advance. The reason for this is that information is *reactive*: if you add it to other information it creates new information. And if you shift its context of use, it can change. Recall the example of the company Target using sets of Personal Information to produce a pregnancy score – the fact that you buy cocoa-butter is of little interest. The same if you buy a large purse, vitamin supplements or a rug. But combine these and – according to Target's algorithms – you have a pregnancy score of 87 per cent. Information is reactive; add it together and something new comes out.

Parallel to the capacity to make new information is that the context of information use matters. Contrast your doctor telling you that you have an 87 per cent chance of being pregnant with a whole family finding out your pregnancy status via some directed advertising. The medical context of use is fundamentally different from that of a teenager's parents finding out through targeted junk mail – you have consented, though perhaps implicitly, to receive unexpected medical information while at a doctor. Moreover, the doctor would likely deliver this information with some amount of professional care. Finally, you can keep this information confidential – all other things being equal, you have a reasonable degree of control over who learns about your pregnancy. None of these conditions are met when your pregnancy score is delivered via advertiser. Note, however, that the specific information remains constant; the specific information of an 87 per cent chance of pregnancy is the same. Information is not just reactive with other information, but with context.

We can explain this reactivity by seeing that information is 'multirealisable': what it is can change depending on a range of factors including what other information it is used with and the context in which it is used. This is important because, as discussed at the close of Chapter 4, Personal Information can be used to form Virtual Identities. These Virtual Identities can be constructed from innocuous information, things like shopping habits. Given that these Virtual Identities are reactive, are multirealisable, they can change depending on their content and context of use. Further, these Virtual Identities are morally important. When surveillance technologies constantly capture and communicate our Personal Information, the range of possible Virtual Identities and multiplicity of things they can be used for everywhere is vast and was inconceivable even a decade ago.

Recognition of the capacity to construct Virtual Identities from innocuous Personal Information and the multirealisability of that information helps us explain why the arguments about our involvement in publicising Personal Information and the innocuousness of tiny bits of information fail: even if we willingly put Personal Information 'out there' we have no idea who is using it or what it can be used for; and in its new constructions, aggregated information like a Virtual Identity is no longer innocuous. However, in order to properly explain these phenomena we need to see that there is such a thing as multirealisability. And in order to explain how information is multirealisable, we need an understanding of what information is. The following section uses an example of scientific information to show that multirealisability exists and subsequent sections detail what information is and how it can be multirealisable.

5.2 INFORMATION AS MORALLY REACTIVE: THE CASE OF THE AGGRESSION GENE[1]

In 1993, the journal *Science* published an article that displayed a link between a particular sequence of human DNA and increased 'impulsive aggression, arson, attempted rape and exhibitionism' (Brunner, et al., 1993). Particular individual males carrying a specific variant of the Monoamine Oxidase A (MAOA) gene were shown to be more aggressive and display greater anti-social tendencies than the average person and the MAOA gene was christened 'the aggression gene'. From 2006, a series of studies were published that linked the aggression gene with complex behaviours and the indigenous people of New Zealand, the Maoris. One article states that '[m]ale carriers of low MAOA activity alleles ... [are] at risk for becoming a gang member and, once a gang member ... at risk for using weapons in a fight' (Beaver et al., 2010, p. 130).

Unsurprisingly, publishing a connection between genes, specific ethnic groups and violent gang behaviour was controversial. One commentary on the research article describes '[t]he scientists ... as hiding behind a veneer of supposedly "objective" western science, using it to perpetuate "racist and oppressive discourses"'

[1] Note that this use of the MAOA example and the later treatment of different concepts of information have been published elsewhere (Henschke, 2010).

(Wensley and King, 2008, p. 507). The MAOA example shows that people can have multiple understandings of the same piece of information and that these multiple interpretations can be controversial; that is, some people say that the MAOA gene is merely some set of facts about the world, while others see it as racism coupled with genetic determinism.

At the core of the controversy is the information itself: a specific DNA sequence and the behaviour associated with it. More generally, the MAOA example shows us that information can be controversial: something as supposedly objective as scientific research, something so 'inert' as a genetic sequence can be the source not just of controversy but can potentially harm groups of people. Living in the age of surveillance, surrounded by increasing amounts of Personal Information, the potential for information to be used in ways that are morally problematic rises greatly. An attempt to understand the controversy and to prevent or avoid any moral problems arising from Personal Information will benefit from clarity of discussions around information itself – if we want to talk sensibly about Personal Information, we need to know what information is. However, as Fred Dretske writes, 'information' can refer to a number of different things:

> In thinking about information, one tends to think of something objective and quantifiable – the electrical pulses surging down a copper wire, for example – and at the same time, of something more abstract, of the news or message that these pulses carry – something not so clearly objective and quantifiable. For many purposes, this is a useful ambiguity.
>
> (Dretske, 1981, p. ix)

To have a sensible discussion about information, we need to be clear about what information is and how it is used. This chapter describes and uses three different but related approaches to information. First, there is a common approach which understands information by reference to data and knowledge, in which data builds into information and information then builds into knowledge – this can be referred to as the 'Data-Information-Knowledge' sequence (DIK sequence).[2] A second approach is that offered by Luciano Floridi,[3] where he develops and presents a 'General Definition of Information' (GDI) as 'ordered, meaningful and true data' (Floridi, 2004, 2011a, b, pp. 80–84). A third approach relates information to communication, in two complementary ways – the quantification of information, such as the 'Mathematical Theory of Communication' (Dretske, 1981, pp. 1–62) and the result of being informed arising from some communicative activity.

2 Chaim Zins gives a thorough description of how the data information and knowledge elements of the DIK sequence are understood differently by different people (Zins, 2007).

3 Floridi has written extensively about philosophy of information. His book *The Philosophy Of Information* (Floridi, 2011a) will be my primary and so on reference with relevant pages given for specific quotations. However, wherever possible I will supply references to other publications where he makes similar points.

5.3 DATA: THE PIECES OF THE PUZZLE

The DIK sequence is a very common way of understanding information: Chaim Zins conducted a survey of forty-five scholars from different fields relating to philosophy of information and between them they formulated about 130 definitions of data, information and knowledge. Despite this variation, Zins concludes that the DIK sequence is frequently used as a way of parsing the territory of discussion (Zins, 2007, p. 487). This section integrates the elements of Floridi's GDI within the DIK sequence, in order to avoid the variation and confusion that can arise in discussions of information. Later sections of this chapter then integrate the GDI into discussions about information and communication.

On both the DIK sequence and within Floridi's account, data are 'the atoms of information'; they are the smallest parts from which information is constructed. But what are data? Floridi notes that thinking of information as composed of data helps in understanding the concept of information, but acknowledges that the concept of data itself is not typically well-understood (Floridi, 2011b, a, pp. 85–86). A simple way to conceptualise a datum is a *relation of difference* between two things. Starting from the Greek word for difference, *diaphora*, Floridi proposes a 'diaphoric definition of data' where a 'datum is a putative fact regarding some difference or lack of uniformity within some context' (Floridi, 2011b, a, p. 85). While information is typically encountered as 'large clusters of well formed, codified data ... in its simplest form a datum can be reduced to *just a lack of uniformity*, that is, a difference between the presence and absence of' (Emphasis Mine, Floridi, 2005a, p. 356). Put in another way, a datum can be defined as: '$d = (x \neq y)$, where the x and the y are two uninterrupted variables' (Floridi, 2004, p. 43).

Floridi offers a simple description of a datum as a black dot on a white sheet of paper (Floridi, 2005a, p. 11, 2011a, pp. 85–87). In this example, there are two things – the black dot and the white paper and the lack of uniformity between the two produces the datum. This example brings out the importance of the relation between the black dot and white sheet as essential to the existence of a datum. The datum is not just the black dot, but the white background *and* the relation of non-uniformity or difference between them. The relation between the two things is core to understanding the datum, a 'datum is a relational entity' (Floridi, 2004, p. 43, 2011a, p. 87). The 'white sheet of paper is not just the necessary background condition for the occurrence of a black dot as a datum, it is a *constitutive* part of the datum itself, together with the fundamental relation of inequality that couple it with the dot' (Emphasis Mine, Floridi, 2004, p. 43). On the GDI account, a datum is neither the black dot nor the white paper, but the differential relation between them (Floridi, 2011a, pp. 86–87). To reiterate the point, the essential components of a datum are the difference between two things *and* a relation of difference between these two things.[4] While there is a further interesting discussion about what a datum is, particularly what the status of the black dot and the white paper are when considered independently of each other, that discussion is beyond the scope of this book to cover, much less resolve. What's relevant here is to focus on the idea of a datum as a relation of difference[5] between two things.

To make a simplistic comparison to basic chemistry, adding atoms to atoms produces molecules. Likewise, adding data to data gives us information. But simply adding data alone does not give us information. We need (at least) some order or syntax between these data.

5.4 SYNTAX: THE RULES OF THE GAME

The second necessary component for Floridi's general definition is that 'the data are *well formed*' (Emphasis Original, Floridi, 2011a, p. 84). It is syntax that gives form to the data. This syntactic requirement is minimal and broad and shouldn't be understood as limited to linguistic conventions; instead it ought to be understood 'as what determines the form, construction, composition or structuring of something . . . ' (Floridi, 2011b, p. 7, 2011a, p. 84). The basic claim here is that syntax is necessary for information. A handful of related differences are simply data if they are not ordered in some way or other; syntax is necessary for information. Simply stated, syntax refers to the rules by which the data are ordered.[6]

The ordering of data can impact on information in two different ways: if the order of the data is changed, we can have different information. Consider the numbers 04092011. Depending on the rules of the system, presenting them as 11029040 or 04092011 can give different information. Further, presuming we are interested in meaningful information, if the rules of the system change, again, the meaning of the information may change. That is, it is not the order alone, but the recognition of the rules that govern the order that change the information. Think again of the numbers 04092011. If this is written as '04/09/2011' it may refer to a date. However, for an Australian these numbers correspond to the date 4th of September, 2011, while for an American, these numbers correspond to the date 9th of March, 2011.[7] The data may remain constant but by changing the rules, the syntax, the information changes.

4 This idea of a datum as a difference relation between two things raises a question of whether the datum refers to the two things, the relation of difference or both. §5.7 looks at two different ways of understanding this.

5 As Floridi notes, many discussions of information and data focus on the importance of a relation of difference in understanding data (Floridi, 2011a, p. 85).

6 There is a considerable vagueness between syntax and meaning, in that it may be hard to make an explicit distinction between them. What is important here is to show the role that syntax and meaning play in information, rather than defining boundaries between them. Meaning, core to Floridi's GDI, is discussed in §5.5.

7 There is a question of whether the dates contain the meaning. §5.5 takes a line that, given particular conventions, the order of the data will encourage or afford the observer to assign a given meaning to the data set.

These changes can be quite important. Consider that Anne is travelling on a plane and asks the airline for the date of departure and they give her the information that 'Your plane departs on 04/09/2011'. For Anne to use this data,[8] it is important that she know rules governing the presentation of the data.

The discussion of information could end here, with information being simply data and syntax. This is a limited account of information, which I call 'Thin Information'. It is like a 'naturalist' approach to information in that it refers to the way that information might be found in the world, conceptualised as independent of an observer.[9] For instance, Dretske presents information in a 'naturalistic' way when he says that the accomplishments of intelligent life on earth rely on the 'raw material [of] information' (Dretske, 1981, p. vii). However, this Thin Information does not cover an element commonly spoken of in relation to information – meaning.[10]

5.5 SEMANTICS: WHAT IS THE MEANING OF THIS?

To introduce the idea of meaning, think again that data 04/09/2011 can provide two different tokens of information. One refers to the 4th of September 2011, while the other refers to the 9th of April 2011. An explanation for the different information is that the conventional uses correspond to Australian and US meanings. When I communicate with Australians, because I am assuming the Australian day/month/year convention, I assume that they *mean* the 4th of September, 2011. When I communicate with Americans, because I am assuming the American month/day/year convention, I assume that they *mean* the 9th of April, 2011. In this way, the assumed conventions point to an assumed meaning. While the reference to meaning may help explain why the information is different without some discussion of meaning, we don't actually know *how* the different information arises.

To begin explaining the 'how', we can refer to convention – the common practice for writing dates in Australia is day/month/year. The common practice in America is month/day/year. So convention is important. Yet convention alone does not give us all we want. The person who is the source of the information may be adhering to a particular convention, but how does convention explain meaning? A further element of explanation is needed. This element is the speaker's intention.

In his paper *Meaning*, Paul Grice proposed that meaning is tied to a speaker's[11] intention: '[W]e may say that "A meant . . . something by *x*" is roughly equivalent to

8 This point about use is made relevant in §5.5.

9 Floridi recognises this point when discussing environmental information (Floridi, 2011b, p. 18).

10 As with the comment in §5.3 about parsing the discussion into syntax and meaning, I recognise that there is overlap between syntax and meaning. However, it is beyond the scope of this thesis to explore this problem further. The key point is that syntax and meaning are *both* important conceptual elements in a thick account of information and need to be discussed.

11 Note that though Grice took pains to describe his account in terms of utterers and utterances, to keep a reasonably consistent style within this section of the book, 'speaker' is used instead of utterer.

"A uttered *x* with the intention of inducing a belief by means of the recognition of his [A's] intention"' (Grice, 1957, p. 384). On the Gricean account, the meaning is the intention of the speaker. 'What [the speaker] means by producing *x* on a given occasion is a function of what [the speaker] intends, in a complex way, to *get across* to his audience' (Emphasis Original, Neale, 1992, pp. 514–515). This account holds that meaning corresponds to the speaker intending that some utterance or speech act will produce a change or response in an audience by means of that utterance or speech act. For example, if Sam says 'the ball is red', the desired change is that the audience now believe that the ball is red – Sam's words have brought about a change in the belief states of the audience. The speaker, Sam, intends that the audience has new beliefs as the result of his speech act. When Anne asked the airline about the date of departure, the speaker responded with 04/09/2011, intending that Anne now has the belief that the plane is departing on 04/09/2011.

However, what of things like genetic codes, or other data sets that seem to have no speaker intention behind them? Rather than trying to resolve issues of the source or origin of the meaning,[12] I approach this problem of the meaning of Thin Information by focussing on how an agent uses that Thin Information. Stephen Neale holds that with Grice's account of meaning, '[i]t ought to be possible . . . to explicate the meaning of an expression (or any other sign) in terms of what users *do with it*, that is, in terms of what its users . . . mean by it on particular occasions of use' (Emphasis Original, Neale, 1992, pp. 514–515). This formulation bears a resemblance to Ludwig Wittgenstein's idea of 'meaning as use'. 'For a *large* class of cases of the employment of the word "meaning" – though not for *all* – this word can be explained in this way: the meaning of a word is its use in the language' (Emphases Original, Wittgenstein, Hacker and Schulte, 2009, §43, p. 25). If meaning is an essential element of information – as Floridi's GDI has it – and if differential use changes the meaning, then differential use can change information: information may change even if data and syntax remain constant.

To explain this point, consider again the numbers 04/09/2011. Now, consider that Anne must provide some password to access her boarding pass and decides to use 04/09/2011 as her password. Though the numbers and their order remain constant, the information is now different, as it is being used differently. Because Anne is using the numbers for a different use, the meaning shifts from the date of departure to a password. Bringing the discussion back to intention and information, Anne uses the same numbers with different intentions and so the information across different uses changes. By including semantic content as a necessary element of information, a 'thick' account of information results in information being dependent on how it used. §5.8 explores the relevance of this, in particular, the multirealisability of information.

[12] This goes to the discussion between Putnam, (1973, 1975) and others, that is, Devitt, (1990) and Grice, (1957) and Weckert, (1986). This discussion is, in part, about whether the reference of a term – its extension – determines the psychological state – its intension – or whether the psychological state determines the reference.

In addition to explaining the multirealisability of information, 'information as use' can help explain how some information has limits on its use. Simply stated, the data and syntax can function as affordances to what meanings can be ascribed to the data, ultimately affecting what information a person has access to. Here, the term 'affordance' 'refers to the perceived and actual properties of the thing, primarily, *those fundamental properties that determine just how the thing could possibly be used* ... Affordances provide strong clues to the operation of things' (Emphasis Mine, Norman, 2002, p. 9). Particular properties of a thing can influence how that thing is used. The properties of a big heavy rock afford using it as a doorstop and don't afford using it as an eating utensil. Properties act as constraints on possible use. This point about constraints is important – someone *could* use a big heavy rock as an eating utensil, but given its properties, all other things being equal, there is a very low chance of this use arising.

Affordances are relevant to information in that the data and syntax are affordances to particular meanings and against other particular meanings. This point about data as an affordance is recognised by Floridi:

> [d]ata are *constraining affordances*: they allow or invite certain constructs (they are *affordances* for the information agent that can take advantage of them) and resist or impede some others (they are *constraints* for the same agent), depending on the interaction with, and the nature of, the information agent that processes them.
>
> (Emphases Original, Floridi, 2011a, p. 87)[13]

While Floridi is correct in saying that data are constraining affordances, syntax acts similarly as an affordance. That is, a particular data set and a particular syntax will afford a particular use. For instance, consider natural information,[14] like a genetic sequence. The particular sequence of base pairs and the syntax will strongly affect what meanings are ascribed to that sequence. The given order and conventional syntax typically constrain the range of use that the genetic sequence can be put to. The introduction of affordances explains how information use can be constrained or encouraged by particular data and syntax, without needing to refer to an intentional agent *creating* the data.

Above and beyond the data and syntax, the way data are used is affected by the mental states of the user. For example, one person reading a sequence of DNA is simply going to be reading a string of As, Cs, Gs and Ts.[15] Yet for someone who is

[13] This point about affordances is repeated by Floridi elsewhere (Floridi, 2011b, p. 40).

[14] As mentioned earlier, natural information refers to the thin conception of information, which is concerned only with data and syntax. In the case of genetic information, I call it 'natural' as its origin is not human. But – to be clear – the focus on 'meaning as use' is engaged when we have a cognitive agent ascribing meaning to the Thin Information.

[15] A genetic sequence refers to the order of nucleic acid base pairs. There are four of these – Adenosine, Cytosine, Guanine and Thyamine, commonly notated as A, C, G and T, respectively. A genetic sequence might then be presented as ATAACGTTGTCACAGTC TGGCGTA.

competent in genetics and molecular biology, these strings of A, C, G and T will mean (a) that there are particular base pairs of DNA found in a particular order and that (b) given a host of other information,[16] these base pairs will produce a given protein built up from amino acids. Similar to affordances, the mental states can act as encouragements or constraints on how the information is used. An agent's background knowledge affects information.

5.6 KNOWLEDGE: FITTING INFORMATION TO TRUTH

This section looks at knowledge and information. The first subsection looks at the idea that information is necessary for producing knowledge. The second subsection describes how information produces knowledge and the third subsection examines the idea that knowledge affects information. The final subsection attends to some potential criticisms about talking about information and knowledge in relation to each other. Before progressing, I wish to point out that this section is not intended to be an exposition of the analysis of knowledge,[17] nor is this section intended to resolve sceptical issues in epistemology,[18] nor to provide an overview of the general issues in epistemology.[19] Finally, I recognise that certain informative statements such as 'that painting is beautiful' may not easily fit into a discussion of truth. Such statements are perhaps better considered as communicative actions, which are discussed in §5.7. The focus here is how concepts of knowledge impact our understanding of concepts of information.

5.6.1 *Knowledge, Truth and Information*

This subsection covers two different arguments about what role truth plays in information. To begin, consider that beliefs are concerned with how the world is.[20] Knowledge is a special kind of belief in that it both represents the way the world is and a non-accidentally caused belief. To this end, knowledge was commonly

16 For instance, there are various transcription elements of DNA, including when to start assigning base pairs to particular amino acids. Syntax for DNA translation to proteins is essential, as if you have a frameshift, the syntax changes and the proteins produced change.

17 For instance, various issues like those discussed by Matthias Steup, (2009).

18 Peter Klein points to the importance of scepticism in epistemology, saying '[m]uch of epistemology has arisen either in defense of, or in opposition to, various forms of skepticism. Indeed, one could classify various theories of knowledge by their responses to scepticism' (Klein, 2011). *Skepticism: A Contemporary Reader* covers many recent discussions and response to scepticism in epistemology.

19 The collection edited by Ernest Sosa, Jaegwon Kim and Matthew McGrath *Epistemology: An Anthology* (Sosa, Kim and McGrath, 2000) covers many key texts in epistemology.

20 This very basic premise is built from the Humean account of human psychology, in which beliefs and desires are contrasted. Beliefs are psychological 'states that purport to represent the way the world is . . . [O]n the other hand . . . [desires] represent how the world is to be' (Smith, 1994, p. 7).

described as 'justified true belief'. Traditionally, '[t]o know that *s* is *F* is to be fully justified in one's (true) belief that *s* is *F*' (Dretske, 1981, p. 85). However, as Edmund Gettier pointed out (Gettier, 1963), there are situations where a person has a true belief, that is justified, but we would not call this knowledge.[21]

Dretske describes knowledge as 'information-produced belief' (Dretske, 1981, p. 92). Saying that the account of knowledge as justified true belief 'remains seriously incomplete insofar as the concept of *justification* is left unanalysed' (Emphasis, Original, Dretske, 1981, p. 85), Dretske gives an information theoretic account of knowledge. He states that:

> [t]he idea of information causing (or causally sustaining) belief is intended to capture what is worth capturing in the doctrine that for a person's belief to qualify as knowledge, there must not only *be* evidence to support [the belief], the belief must be *based on* that evidence. Insofar as the information that *s* is *F* causes [a person's] belief that *s* is *F*, we can say that the belief is *based on* the information that *s* is *F*.
>
> (Emphases Original, Dretske, 1981, p. 91)

As such, Dretske's information theoretic analysis stresses the role that information plays in justifying a true belief. In relation to truth, if knowledge is information-produced belief and if knowledge is held to be true belief, then it follows that the information producing the knowledge must itself be true. 'Information is what is capable of yielding knowledge and *since knowledge requires truth, information requires it also*' (Dretske, 1981 Emphasis Mine, p. 45). As presented though, this argument does not make the claim that information *must* be true.[22]

Floridi posits a stronger claim that in order for an ordered and meaningful data set to be properly called information, it *must* be true. In his 'semantic' argument for the truth-necessity claim on information (Floridi, 2004, pp. 45–46, 2005a, pp. 359–364, 2011b, p. 39, 2011a, pp. 93–107), he reasons that if we allow false information to be information, then '[o]perators like 'not' lose their semantic power to corrupt information' (Floridi, 2011a, p. 104). This leads him to conclude that the idea of false information is 'utterly implausible, even if not logically impossible' (Floridi, 2011a, p. 104). In short, following Floridi, ordered, meaningful data that is not true is not information.

In addition to his 'semantic argument' Floridi develops a second line of reasoning about the truth-necessity claim on information. He does this by explaining that an adjective can be predicative or attributive. '[I]f an adjective in a compound is

[21] A relevant discussion on this point comes from the idea of epistemic luck; whether something would count as knowledge if an agent comes by knowledge largely as the result of lucky circumstances (Pritchard, 2004).

[22] What I mean by this is it seems sensible to talk about non-true information as long as it is not involved in knowledge. The argument described here does not say why *all* information *must* be true.

attributive, the [compound] cannot be split up without semantic loss' (Emphasis Original, Floridi, 2011a, p. 97). Consider a 'false banknote' or a 'false constable' (Floridi, 2005a, pp. 364–365, 2011a, p. 97). We can't split the compound – that is, 'false banknote' into 'false' and 'banknote' – without losing the meaning of the term 'false banknote'. Floridi then argues that a 'false banknote' is not actually a banknote, but a counterfeit. Likewise, a 'false constable' is not an officer of the law, but someone pretending to be. He reasons similarly, that 'false information' is not information.

However, a common-sense response to this sort of truth-necessity claim is to ask what is involved if the information is not true. Consider that Sam tells Donna 'the ball is red', when the ball is in fact green. Note that the sentence 'the ball is red' conforms to the three elements of information discussed so far – data, order and meaning. Donna receives something and if it is not information, then what is it? Floridi makes two points to this. First, he points to the difference between 'information as content' and 'information as process' (Floridi, 2011a, p. 96). The focus here will be on information as content, particularly, what ordered, meaningful data is if it isn't true; information as a communicative process is discussed in §5.7.

Floridi suggests we should instead consider false information as pseudoinformation. Within pseudoinformation, Floridi proposes two forms: misinformation and disinformation. Misinformation is well-ordered, meaningful data that is not true. However, if a source knows that they are communicating pseudoinformation, that is, consciously lying, then it is *dis*information (Floridi, 2011b, p. 46). Tracking to the 'information as use' account developed in §5.5, the speaker's intention is relevant to determining the status of meaningful, ordered data. A car's speedometer *mis*informs the driver if the speedometer registers '90 km h', when the car is in fact going 100 km h. The driver *dis*informs their passenger if they read the speedometer as '100 km h' but, despite this, say that the speedometer registers '90 km h'.

We can also include a further form to pseudoinformation – 'incomplete information'. On this form, well-ordered, meaningful data can count as pseudoinformation in particular contexts, even if the content is true. Incomplete information arises in a communicative context when a speaker presents true, well-ordered, meaningful data, but this communicative act either does not succeed in meeting the speaker's actual intention or the speaker's expressed intention is different to their actual intention.

Consider that Hans is buying a car that he wants to drive that day. Hans believes that it is $4,000. This is well-ordered, meaningful and true. However, the car requires new tyres before Hans can drive it. These will cost a further $300. In this sense, the total cost of the car is $4,300, so $4,000 is not true in a broader sense. Consider that Hans first talks with Amy, who tells him the car is $4,000. However, Amy says this, not knowing that the car needs new tires to drive and/or that Hans wants information about a drivable car. Consider that Hans also talks to Bill and Bill intentionally deceives Hans, stating the car is $4,000 instead of $4,300. Again, the car *itself* does only cost $4,000 but Bill knows that it will cost an extra $300 before it can be driven and that Hans wants a car that is drivable.

The issue of pseudoinformation arises from the fact that the intended meaning was unsuccessfully communicated to Hans because the data used was incomplete to meet the recognised intention of the communication. Despite the fact that Amy's intention was not to deceive Hans, Amy has given incomplete information to Hans. Bill gave Hans true, well-ordered, meaningful data. Importantly, this was limited in that it did not meet the implicit intention that Bill was giving Hans full knowledge about the price of the car. What can be called true information becomes slightly more subjective in a communicative context, expanding the scope of pseudoinformation. Having meaning and truth both as necessary elements of information results in the capacity for meaning to impact on the truth-aptness of information in particular communicative circumstances. The communicative aspect of information is discussed further in §5.7.

5.6.2 *Information as Knowledge*

Instead of thinking about truth as necessary for information, a second way of thinking about knowledge and information is to look at the conditions when the *agent* judges that their information is knowledge. This is a loose interpretation of 'knowledge' as it is not concerned with whether the beliefs the agent has are *actually* justified as being called true. Instead, I am focussing on the mental states that the agent has when they *feel* their beliefs to be justified to be true. This folk conception of knowledge may be looser than standard philosophic use of knowledge; however, it is relevant to a discussion of knowledge and information in that the agent considers themselves to be in a state of justified true belief with regard to some information.

For example, following the publication of Charles Darwin's *Origin of Species*, Samuel Wilberforce and Thomas Henry Huxley were part of a debate on Darwin's theories. Wilberforce believed that a Christian deity was the cause of different species, while Huxley believed that natural selection was the cause.[23] What's relevant in this example is that both Wilberforce and Huxley counted their beliefs as knowledge. This is despite the fact that at least one of the beliefs could not be true, so at least one of their beliefs would not be knowledge in the standard philosophic sense.

This brings us to the important point for this subsection – if Wilberforce and Huxley both have access to Darwin's work, counted here as potential information,[24] why would they both contend that they had knowledge? We can answer by saying that the potential information is judged against what the agent 'already

[23] Obviously, this is not intended to be much more than a caricature of the debate. It is described in detail in *Of Apes and Ancestors* (Hesketh, 2009).

[24] I am following Dretske and Floridi here, in that a well-ordered, meaningful data set is not yet information, as it needs to be assessed as true or false.

knows'.[25] The agent's set of antecedent beliefs bear upon whether an ordered data set is accepted or rejected by the agent. In short, when an agent judges the truth-aptness of a given ordered data set, the data set is judged in relation to the agent's existing Cognitive Networks.[26]

This claim comes from neuroscientific and cognitive psychological research. Consider 'Capgras delusion', in which the sufferers believe that their significant others have been replaced with robots, imposters or aliens (Ellis and Lewis, 2001). While different neurological causes for Capgras delusion have been postulated,[27] common to them is the idea that the sufferers do not have the standard affective response to seeing their loved ones. Despite the fact that the data received by the sufferer is standard, their emotional response to the loved one is 'wrong'. That is, when they encounter their loved one, they 'fail to experience normal feelings of familiarity ... It *looks like* mom, but it doesn't *feel* like her' (Emphases Original, Levy, 2007, p. 19). The information 'feels wrong' and as such, the sufferer rejects the truth of ordered and meaningful data. Perhaps the affective response can go some way to explaining why Wilberforce and Huxley had such different experiences of Darwin's work: given their background beliefs, it is likely that they had different affective responses to Darwin's work. For Wilberforce, Darwin's work felt wrong, whereas for Huxley, it felt correct. Given that many of these background beliefs and affective responses occur at sub-personal levels, both Wilberforce and Huxley may have been equally convinced of the truth of their position and the correctness of their knowledge.

If some ordered, meaningful data doesn't 'feel right' or 'doesn't make sense', the agent may reject it as being true. Knowledge, understood loosely as the agent's contention that their beliefs are true, has an important emotional component. Whether the agent accepts the ordered, meaningful data as true, then, is dependent on how the agent's Cognitive Networks are structured. On the full account of information as ordered, meaningful data that is (perceived as) true, the Cognitive Networks of the agent are essential. If we are to talk meaningfully about information in the full sense, we must take into account the agent's Cognitive Networks.

5.6.3 *Information and Integration*

The idea that knowledge influences information is presented here. §4.4 discussed how people's previous experiences influenced their current perceptions. In another example, a group of soldiers ate lemon-flavoured jelly and thought it tasted like

[25] 'Already knows' is put in scare quotes as the examples demonstrate belief states that would not count as knowledge. The ideas of antecedent beliefs and other existing cognitive states are covered in the next subsection.

[26] Recall from §4.4 that 'Cognitive Network' is used to refer to the set of neurological and mental networks of the agent, including both affective or emotional states, including states that we are conscious and not conscious of.

[27] Garry Young, (2008) and Haydn Ellis and Michael Lewis (Ellis and Lewis, 2001) present a series of different explanations for the aetiology of the delusion.

cherry, because the cook had run out of cherry-flavoured jelly and had coloured the lemon jelly red (Wansink, 2006, pp. 120–121). The previous experiences of the soldiers in which red jelly tasted like cherry had influenced their current perception and seemingly overridden the actual flavour of the jelly. Again, taking the loose use of knowledge as 'when a person *feels* that their beliefs are justified as true', information can be influenced by the person's knowledge.[28] This line of reasoning presents the justification of beliefs in a similar form to a coherentist account of beliefs like that presented by Laurence BonJour:

> [C]oherence is a matter of how well a body of beliefs "hangs together": how well its component beliefs fit together, agree or dovetail with each other, so as to produce an organized, tightly structured system of beliefs, rather than a helter-skelter collection or a set of conflicting subsystems.
>
> (BonJour, 1985, p. 93)

And while there are a host of different causal factors in why, how and when different mental stages interact, the relevant point here is that the person's knowledge changes information: new ordered, meaningful data will be accepted as true or not true depending on how it 'hangs together' with the agent's existing system of beliefs.

While coherence alone may not suffice as a proper *justification* for knowledge in the strong sense,[29] it does seem to indicate how people *actually* experience the world. To explain, consider that how an agent experiences the world is 'dependent upon the experience, knowledge and expectations of the observer' (Chalmers, 1999, p. 7). This sort of claim should not be controversial. The value-ladenness of theory has been a common element in philosophy of science, captured by Norwood Hanson's phrase 'there's more to seeing than meets the eyeball' (Hanson, 1958). Existing Cognitive Networks influence how an observer experiences the world. 'Two normal observers viewing the same object from the same place under the same physical circumstances do not necessarily have identical visual experiences ... It would seem that there is a sense in which what an observer sees is affected by his or her past experience' (Chalmers, 1999, pp. 5,7). We can explain value-ladenness[30] by looking at Dretske's idea that 'information is knowledge causing', in the opposite way: 'knowledge is information causing'.

[28] This point about the important causal role played by experience in information construction is further discussed in Chapter 6, especially in §6.4.

[29] For instance, as Michael Williams argues: 'Global justification depends on our checking our system of beliefs for how well it hangs together ... But it is not enough for me just to have (meta) beliefs about my (first) order beliefs. Those meta beliefs must themselves amount to knowledge, or at least be justified. If they are not justified, appealing to them will do nothing towards providing a global justification of my beliefs about the world' (Williams, 1991, p. 293).

[30] I do not mean to say that all value-ladenness of theories or of information can be explained by reference to knowledge. Instead, that the value-ladenness of many types of information can be explained by reference to existing knowledge.

The idea that knowledge causes information relies on the idea that information is constructed from the syntax, the meaning and assumed truth of a data set. Information – ordered, semantic, truthful data – is shaped by how it hangs together or coheres with the agent's existing body of beliefs. As displayed in §5.6, it is not only consciously held propositions about the world, or the agent's conscious memory that goes to producing information, but subpersonal cognitive mechanisms like affective judgements. Further, the available meanings and syntax that are at an agent's disposal to create the information are contingent on the agent's existing Cognitive Networks. The meanings that go with an ordered data set and the perceived truth-value of the ordered data set are dependent on the agent's mental states. Knowledge in the loose sense is a fundamental causal element in information construction.

5.6.4 *Why Information?*

Why talk about information at all? Given the reliance on truth and semantic content, isn't it better to simply talk of knowledge or meaning rather than information? I am agnostic, in that I am not seeking to argue for *why* it is correct that we consider information in terms of well-ordered, meaningful true data, or that what is presented is information rather than an information-theoretic account of meaning or knowledge. Instead, what is offered here is (a) a description of information *as* well-ordered, meaningful true data that (b) relates to meaning and knowledge. The value of this approach is twofold. Describing information as well-ordered, meaningful true data makes it clear what I am referring to when talking about information. Second, given that the focus of attention in this book are the ethical concerns arising from surveillance, this approach allows for a focus on the informational aspects of surveillance technologies, ultimately allowing for a pragmatic response to the concerns raised in the book's final chapter.

5.7 INFORMATION AND COMMUNICATION

As mentioned, Floridi parses pseudoinformation into misinformation and disinformation. §5.6.1 added incomplete information. The division of pseudoinformation into these three forms presumes some communication between multiple semantic agents. Communication is relevant to information in two ways. Communication theory has played an important historical role in the development of theories of information, via the development of the Mathematical Theory of Communication (MTC), described below. Second, in common use, information often refers not only to information as content – the ordered, semantic, truthful data – but also to the process of informing and being informed,[31] described in §5.7.2.

[31] This distinction is made by Floridi, via 'the principle of "exportation" . . . [going] from information as process to information as content' (Floridi, 2011a, p. 96).

5.7.1 *The Mathematical Theory of Communication*

The MTC is a large field of investigation into information, sometimes called information theory or communication theory (Shannon and Weaver, 1949). Evolving from electrical engineering, the MTC is concerned with Thin Information (that is non semantic, non–truth-apt) and has a focus on the *quantitative* transfer of information. The two driving interests in developing the theory were determining how small a message could be whilst still giving the same information and the speed of data transmission, given as entropy and channel capacity (Floridi, 2004, pp. 46–47, 2011b, pp. 46–52). Again, the primary focus of the MTC was quantification of information in a message:

> The mathematical theory of information, or communication theory ... provides a measure of how much information is to be associated with a given state of affairs and, in turn, a measure for how much of this information is transmitted to, and thus available at other points. The theory is purely quantitative. It deals with *amounts of information* – not, except indirectly and by implication, with the information that comes in those amounts.
>
> (Emphasis Original, Dretske, 1981, p. 3)

The relevance of the MTC comes from its focus on key elements in a general communication system – the source, transmitter, message, receiver, destination and channel.

> An *information source* ... produces a message or sequence of messages to be communicated to the receiving terminal ... [the] *transmitter* operates on the message in some way to produce a signal suitable for transmission over the channel ... The *channel* is merely the medium used to transmit the signal from transmitter to receiver ... The *receiver* ordinarily performs the inverse operation of that done by the transmitter ... The *destination* is the person (or thing) for whom the message is intended.
>
> (Emphases Original, Shannon and Weaver, 1949, pp. 4–6)

Treating the source and transmitter as a person and the receiver and destination as another, we can start to connect information as process to the discussions from §5.4–5.6.

5.7.2 *Information as a Communicative Process*

Consider people, two communicative agents, Source and Destination, Sam and Donna. When Sam says 'the ball is red', he intends for Donna to understand that he means that the ball is red. Sam's message is composed of four words, which have been ordered following standard English grammar. In a standard context of English speakers, whether as a spoken or written message, the meaning of the statement is reasonably straightforward. There is a ball and it is red in colour. However, following the 'meaning as use' concept from §5.5, 'the ball is red' might mean something completely different. Consider that Sam is a spy meeting a covert operative. 'The ball is red' might be code for 'we will go ahead with the assassination of the president. Proceed as per the initial plan.'

Conventional use of 'the ball is red' would assume that the speaker intends to produce in their audience the belief that the ball is red. In non-conventional use the speaker saying 'the ball is red' may intend to produce in their source the belief that they ought to go ahead with the assassination of the president. This shows the importance of recognising the syntax as the rules governing the communication and the intended meaning and the knowledge as the cognitive states of the agents involved. Dretske talks about nested information, where one set of ordered data can carry with it other information. If the destination knows that 'whenever s is F, t is G ... then no signal can bear the message that s is F without also conveying the information that t is G' (Dretske, 1981, p. 71). What is nested in the message is heavily dependent upon both the source and the knowledge that the destination has, a point made in §5.6.

Note, however, that in multi-agent communications, meaning as intention refers to the meaning that the source of communication has for a message. If Sam says 'the ball is red' to a new-born with no language skills, a foreigner with no knowledge of English, a person without the capacity to hear, a dog or an inanimate object, the meaning of the message seems to stay the same, because Sam's intention as speaker remains the same.

However, consider the spy example again. This time, Sam sits next to a person Norm, who is a normal member of the public. In this example, Sam thinks that Norm is the would-be assassin. While Sam intends the message 'the ball is red' to mean 'kill the president', Norm understands the message to mean that somewhere, there is a ball and it is red. The point here is that there can be a destination meaning that is independent of the source intention. What if Sam sits next to a stranger in a park and happens to say that the ball is red, but this stranger is an assassin waiting for a code? For the assassin, the meaning is independent from what Sam intended. This stranger might be a political assassin, awaiting orders, while Sam is just a friendly person talking about the colour of balls. The meaning for the assassin is different to Sam's intention. This event has been described as explicature – the meaning that the person receiving the information derives from the given message (Bach, 2006). Instead of jettisoning the idea of meaning as intention, we need to be clear about whether the meaning is referring to the source's intention or to the destination's cognitive states after receiving the message, a point discussed further in §5.9.

The red ball/green ball discussion also provides a good example of the information/pseudoinformation division. Consider that Sam is holding a red ball and Donna asks him to say what he sees. Sam replies 'the ball is red'. If Donna's eyes are open, this is information, probably trivial. If Donna's eyes are closed and Sam tells her that the ball is red, Sam has given her some information. Now, consider that

Sam is now holding a green ball and Donna asks Sam to say what he sees. Again, his reply is 'the ball is red'. Under strict truth conditions, Sam has given Donna no *direct* information about the ball; instead Sam gave her pseudoinformation. That is, either he lied or made a mistake.

As was discussed, this seems counterintuitive – surely Donna receives information, irrespective of the truth contained in Sam's message. However, this is dependent upon the specifics of what one is concerned with. If we are looking *strictly* at the message 'the ball is red', then Donna has no information, but instead has pseudoinformation. Yet, as Floridi rightly notes in passing, information is additive (Floridi, 2011a, p. 98). So if Donna knows that the ball is green and Sam says that 'the ball is red', then Donna has received information, just not about the colour of the ball. She might now have the information that Sam is a compulsive liar, or that he has red-green colour blindness. Adapting[32] Dretske, 'if Donna happens to know (on other grounds) that what Sam is saying is false, then she may nonetheless get information, information about *Sam* (he is lying) from what he says, but she will not get information corresponding to the conventional meaning of what he said' (Dretske, 1981, p. 44). We have now expanded our set of concerns from the meaning of the message to include knowledge about the speaker.

Consider again the message 'the ball is red'. Adapting another example from Dretske (Dretske, 1981, pp. 94–95), imagine that a game of chance is being played. It has ten balls of different colours and players cannot see the balls. The balls are removed at random, the announcer calls out the ball that has been removed and the players must guess the next ball that will come out. After all ten balls are removed, they go back into the pot. If a player guesses correctly, they win $100. Victor and Louisa are playing this game and both hear 'the ball is red'. Clearly both have received the same message, ostensibly containing the same information: that the ball that has been removed from the pot is red. Now, consider that Victor had been watching the game for eight rounds, such that he has the knowledge that there are only two balls remaining – a red and a green. By the announcer calling 'the ball is red' Victor now has the information that the remaining ball is green. Louisa, on the other hand, had not been watching the game and entered only as the announcer called 'the ball is red'. The only information that she has is that out of the remaining nine balls, none of them is red.

As argued in §5.6, a given ordered, meaningful data set produces different information in different receivers, given the pre-existing knowledge that the people have about the source.

[32] The original Dretske quotation is: 'If you happen to know (on other grounds) that what I am saying is false, then you may nonetheless get information, information about *me* (I am lying) from what I say, but you will not get information corresponding to the conventional meaning of what I say' (Emphasis Original, Dretske, 1981, p. 44).

> [T]he single observation ... carries the same information to both of us. The explanation for why I learned more from it than you ... is that *I knew more to begin with* ... The latter piece of information is ... nested in the former piece of information ... This constitutes a *relativization* of the information contained in a signal because *how much* information a signal contains, and hence *what* information it carries, depends on what the potential receiver already knows about the various possibilities that exist at the source.
>
> (Emphasis Original, Dretske, 1981, pp. 78–79)

This point is vital to emphasise. If Donna has knowledge in the form of an information set *x* and Sam provides her with one more piece of data, *y*, given her pre-existing information set of *x*, the addition of *y* may provide her with entirely new information.

We can now see why information is reactive and additive. It is reactive in that the information is constructed by the agent through reactions with data and the agent's knowledge. It is additive in that data received by a destination will add to the existing information that they have about the world, their knowledge set, to produce new information.

5.8 NEW INFORMATION

What is *new* information? To answer this, this section returns to a discussion of data, introduces four different types of emergence to show that information is a form of soft epistemic emergence and then says something about what has actually emerged.[33]

5.8.1 *Something from Something*

Recall that information is ordered, meaningful true data. So what is *new* information? On the 'information as use' line developed in §5.5, new information may simply be a novel use for existing data sets. However, information is additive (Floridi, 2011a, p. 98). That is, we get new information when one data set is integrated with another one.

The additive process can be described in terms of adding discrete units of information, which Floridi calls infons[34]. So, infon 1 + infon 2 = infon 3. But what is

[33] I recognise that the question of whether there are truly emergent properties is debatable. Rather than necessarily arguing that there are such things as emergent properties, this section can be read as part of the project to better make sense of information. In this way, my methodology is similar to that of Jaegwon Kim, 'I am not primarily concerned with the truth or tenability of emergentism or nonreductive materialism; rather, my main concern is with making sense of the idea of emergence – the idea that certain properties of complex systems are emergent while others are not' (Kim, 1999).

[34] An infon is the term used by Floridi for a 'discrete item of information' (Floridi, 2011a, p. 85). An infon is a particular ordered, meaningful and true data set. The term infon is used now to avoid repeating the discussion of meaning and information as use, as I wish to instead focus on the addition of different sets of information.

infon 3? Infon 3 is something *new* that has *emerged* from the integration of infon 1 and infon 2. This may leave some people a little worried: a criticism of emergence is that one is getting something from nothing. So a concerned reader might be thinking 'new information emerges from existing information? That sounds a little like one is getting something from nothing.' However, in the case of information this is not correct: it is not that we are getting something from nothing. Instead we are getting something from something. This is because information is, at its foundation, relational.

To explain, recall that the foundation of information is data. As was noted in §5.3, data itself is hard to pin down. Recall that 'the nature of data is not well-understood philosophically' (Floridi, 2011b, a, pp. 85–86). This lack of an ability to explain data may be in part because data is relational. Returning to Floridi's example of the black dot on white paper (Floridi, 2005a, p. 11, 2011a, pp. 85–87), 'a sheet of white paper is not just the necessary background condition for the occurrence of a black dot as a datum, but a *constitutive part of the black-dot-on-white-sheet datum itself*, together with *the fundamental relation of inequality* that couples it with the dot' (Emphases Mine, Floridi, 2011a, p. 87). A necessary element of the datum is the relation that arises from the difference *between* the white paper *and* the black dot.

Is this relation something? Avoiding a discussion of the ontology of data, if we count experience as something, then the answer is yes. That is, given that we as observers construct this relation, then a datum is something in a subjective phenomenological sense. These relations of difference are proposed to be an 'external anchor of our information ... their presence is empirically inferred from and *required by, experience*' (Floridi 2011a My Emphasis, pp. 85–86). As long as subjective experience is something, then data is also something. And if data is something, then adding something to something can generate something. In this manner, we can describe information generally as something, so the concern about getting something from nothing is not substantiated. When we add infon 1 and infon 2 we produce infon 3; we get something from something. In short, infon 3 emerges from the integration of infon 1 and infon 2.

5.8.2 *Four Types of Emergence*

New information emerges from the convergence of different subsets of existing information, the integration of infon 1 and infon 2 to produce infon 3. At first blush, this claim may be controversial. Part of the reason is that emergence feels like getting something from nothing.[35] However, as was shown in the previous section, 'something from nothing' is not a fair description, as data can be something. This

[35] One of the controversial aspects of emergence is that it seems to be getting something from nothing. As Mark Bedau writes, emergent phenomena 'raise the spectre of illegitimately getting something from nothing' (Bedau, 1997). However, I have shown that in the discussions of information, it is not a case of something from nothing, but something from something.

subsection presents four different types of emergence and presents new information as emerging from the integration that occurs when data converges with meaning and knowledge.

There is a long history of emergence, with the Greeks, to Locke and through the early twentieth century and 'British Emergentism' (O'Connor and Wong, 2009, pp. 2–14). Recently,[36] emergence has returned to philosophic debates (Kim, 1999), particularly in the fields of philosophy of mind and consciousness (Chalmers, 2006) and now in engineering and complex systems theory (Kroes, 2009, pp. 277–278). On one description, 'emergent entities (properties or substances) 'arise' out of more fundamental entities and yet *are "novel" or "irreducible" with respect to them*' (Emphasis Mine, O'Connor and Wong, 2009, p. 1). Another account is offered by Peter Kroes: 'Emergence is said to occur when certain properties appear in a system that are novel or unexpected and go beyond the properties of the parts of that system' (Kroes, 2009, p. 277). A further element, important to the current discussion, is that the emergent entity can then influence the parts that it is composed of, known as downward causation (Kim, 1999). §5.8.3 discusses the relevance of downward causation to this book. So, as a general description, emergence occurs when parts of a system are brought together to produce something new or novel that can then influence the more fundamental elements that it is composed of. Important for this discussion is the recognition that the novel thing cannot be immediately reduced to its component parts without losing an understanding of the whole (Kim, 2006; Mitchell, 2004, pp. 83–85).

Kroes holds that there are two essential aspects of emergence that need to be recognised, such that we better describe what type of emergence is being spoken of (Kroes, 2009). We need to determine if the emergence is ontological or epistemic and if it is strong or weak emergence. Following Kroes, when something new emerges, which is independent of observation, 'a real-world item', then it is ontologically emergent. If it is subjective, that is, 'in the sense that whether a property is emergent or not depends on a knowing subject or the knowledge base of a cognitive practice', then it is epistemically emergent (Kroes, 2009, pp. 280, 285). Second, following Kroes again, strong emergence is where, even with a perfect knowledge set, the emergent property is unpredictable or unexplainable, a point made about consciousness (Chalmers, 2006, pp. 129–130). Weak emergence occurs when the emergent property can be predicted or explained, if given a perfect knowledge set. Given the discussion about data being relational and following Kroes' distinctions, new information can be described as weak and epistemically emergent.[37]

[36] Kim states '[s]ince around 1990, the idea of emergence has been making a big comeback, from decades of general neglect and disdain on the part of mainstream analytic philosophers' (Kim, 2006, p. 547).

[37] I note that, for some, only strong emergence is true emergence, as weak emergence becomes trivial. For example, consciousness is held by Chalmers to be strongly emergent, while all other things are, given a perfect information set, weakly emergent (Chalmers, 2006).

To explain this, epistemic emergence means that it occurs subjectively and weak emergence means that the emergent entity can be explained. Now, consider an example where Catie sees John. John exists in the world and has a set of properties that Catie has sensory access to.[38] Catie looks at the shape in front of her and Catie's mind gets the information that John is standing in front of her from the meaningful and truthful data presented: his body shape, his facial structure, his eyes and so on.[39] The convergence of these different pieces of information, the different infons, provides the anchors for the experience of John *as a whole entity*. It is this whole entity experience of John that is emergent. This experience is emergent in that the different pieces of visual information have been brought together to produce something new or novel.

Importantly, the representation that Catie has of John, $John_R$, cannot be fully understood by reducing it simply to the isolated infons. To speak of Catie's representation of John as being 'body', 'face' or 'eyes' misses the whole informationally integrated picture of $John_R$. Consider prosopagnosia, a condition whereby individuals are unable to visually recognise faces despite having normal vision and visual information processing. A key element in many cases of prosopagnosia is the inability to perform holistic processing, the integration of 'facial features into a whole' and limits in second order relations, the 'encoding [of] spacing among facial features' (Le Grand et al., 2006, p. 142). That is, there is a limitation on recognition of the higher order relations between facial features. To properly understand the experience of a person's face, we need to see the face *as an emergent representation*. Catie's representation of John, $John_R$, is *epistemically* emergent in that it is a phenomenon that occurs in Catie's mind and is *weakly* emergent in that we can explain how it comes about from the integration of the different infons.

5.8.3 *What Has Emerged?*

In the case of Catie seeing John, it is the abstract representation of John in Catie's mind $John_R$, that has emerged. This is explained by showing the relevance of the emergent entity to the discussion of information. As mentioned in the discussion of Catie and John and previously discussed, humans perceive the world by converting direct sensory experience into something the human mind can use.[40] Recalling the discussion of identity, §4.3 and §4.4, sense organs, like the ears, the eyes and so on receive information about the world and through transducers and input systems transform the world into a format that the brain can use. '*[W]hat perception must do is to represent the world as to make it accessible to thought*' (Emphasis Original,

[38] For brevity sake, we will limit the sense modality here to Catie seeing John.

[39] As was discussed in §4.3 and §4.4, human visual recognition of other humans occurs via the recognition of different physical attributes that are abstracted and integrated.

[40] Dretske discusses the process underpinning the coding information from something perceptual to something cognitive, that is, something that can be used, in detail in chapter 6, particularly the 'Sensory vs. Cognitive Processes' section (Dretske, 1981, pp. 141–153).

Fodor, 1983, p. 40). Importantly for this subsection, the transformed data is then processed upwards, producing greater complexity of information. Smaller, discrete infons converge, are processed and integrated by neuroanatomical computational hubs (Rauschecker and Scott, 2009; Sporns, Honey and Kotter, 2007). Through these neuroanatomical hubs, the infons are fed forward and integrated to construct new abstract representational forms, objects and categories (Hochstein and Ahissar, 2002, p. 792). Catie's representation, $John_R$, is constructed via the integration of the different infons relevant to particular aspects of John.

Importantly, it is not the independent infons of his eyes, face shape, body shape and so on but the *integration* of these infons to form the abstract representation that is the unified entity $John_R$. Given that I am focussing here on Catie's experience of John, $John_R$ is *epistemically* emergent. Neuroscience[41] explains that $John_R$ is constructed from the different infons, so $John_R$ is *weakly* emergent, perhaps quite weakly. However, note that $John_R$ can only be properly understood as an integrated representation constructed from different infons. The reason for calling $John_R$ emergent is that we lose something important if we try to understand $John_R$ in terms of the isolated infons. The novel property is thus that unified representation $John_R$, which exists above and beyond 'face, eyes, nose and so on'.

Further, the emergent entity $John_R$ exhibits downward causation on its constituent elements: the emergent whole affects the constituent parts. Kim states that 'downward causation involves vertical directionality – an "upward" direction and a "downward" direction' (Kim, 1999, p. 19). Recall the dual process model of perception discussed in §4.3, where perception occurs in two directions, 'feedforward processing' (FFP) and 'reverse hierarchy theory' (RHT). 'Processing along the feedforward hierarchy of areas, leading to increasingly complex representations, is automatic and implicit, while conscious perception begins at the hierarchy's top, gradually returning downward as needed' (Hochstein and Ahissar, 2002, p. 791). The RHT 'postulates that a parsing decision is first based on the highest available level of ... representation (e.g., objects)' (Shamma, 2008). That is, the high level abstract representations influence when the fine-grained perceptual feedforward processes are engaged. In addition to affecting cognitive processes, these abstract representations substantially influence the perceptual processes as well, discussed in §4.4 and §5.6. This is what Kim calls the 'causal efficacy of the emergents'. 'What is distinctive about this form of downward causation appears to be this: Some activity or event involving a whole W is a cause of, or has a causal influence on, the events involving its *own* microconstituents' (Emphasis Original, Kim, 1999, p. 26). In a form of downward causation, the entity $John_R$ influences how Catie will perceive John.

Two related questions arise: why speak of the emergent entity in informational terms and is the new information actually emergent or predictably resultant?

[41] (Mishkin, Ungerleider and Macko, 1983; Rauschecker and Scott, 2009).

Answering the second question also offers an answer to the first. To explain, we need to look at the level of abstraction[42] at which infon 3 is experienced. 'Systems with a higher-level of complexity emerge from the coming together of lower-level entities in new structural configurations' (Kim, 1999, p. 20). While infon 3 may seem like it is occurring at the same level as infons 1 and 2, this is not correct. §4.3 described cognition as thoughts about thoughts, increasing levels of abstractions arising from increased integration of lower level representations. Infon 3 is a cognitive product that sits at a higher level of abstraction than infons 1 and 2. $John_R$ is the whole that emerges from the integration of the discrete infons. Mereologically, $John_R$ is a qualitatively different entity to the single entities of eyes, nose, mouth and so on.

Infon 3 is new and unpredictable because infon 3 cannot be properly understood until experienced as a whole. Catie can only understand $John_R$ as a singular entity through experiencing that entity. Infon 3 is a novel whole entity composed of its two subunits, infons 1 and 2. Importantly, if infon 3 has not been experienced before, then no description of infons 1 and 2 and their relation can capture infon 3. 'In cases where [the emergent property] E is a phenomenal property of experiences . . . we may have no idea what E is like before we experience it' (Kim, 1999, p. 8). Kim notes in footnote 12 (Kim, 1999, p. 34) that this is the point made by Frank Jackson in his paper 'What Mary Didn't Know' (Jackson, 1991). In this paper, Jackson argued that the neuroscientist Mary can have no proper understanding of the colour red until she experiences it – no amount of scientific research can accurately give Mary a full understanding of red; she must experience it.[43] This is important in that the unpredictability of emergent phenomena does not mean that its occurrence cannot be anticipated, rather that the specifics of experience cannot actually be predicted until experienced.

So, cashing out $John_R$ in terms of the unpredictability of experience may show that $John_R$ is an emergent entity. However, why speak of new information in terms of emergence? The reason is that $John_R$ is describable in informational terms. Catie's experience of John is the result of perceptual and cognitive processes, converting the world state of John into a form that is usable by Catie. $John_R$ is composed of infons, which themselves are constructed from perceptual data that have been cognitively processed such that they are ordered, meaningful and true. The larger point is that identity and information bear a strong relation to each other. This point is returned to in Chapter 6.

5.9 THE AGGRESSION GENE REVISITED: MULTIREALISABILITY

The opening case example of the MAOA gene was used to show how Personal Information can be controversial. On one hand, the identification of the MAOA

[42] Floridi provides an in-depth discussion of the method of levels of abstraction (Floridi, 2008, 2011a).

[43] I recognise that Jackson has amended his view about what conclusions can be drawn from 'What Mary Didn't Know', in particular, a shift from epiphenomenalism to indirection realism (Jackson, 2003). However, Kim's point about emergence as a novel experience should still hold.

gene represents scientific investigation, ideally an objective pursuit of knowledge about the world. On the other hand, the MAOA gene represents an instance of 'ethically charged' information, a case of where the information was seen to perpetuate and deepen racial prejudice. A central factor in the two positions is that information is multirealisable.[44] Scientific investigation presents reports on the MAOA gene as message information, thin and inert. It is simply ordered data and nothing more. Neither the source nor the destination is considered relevant to information.

However, as this chapter presents it, information can be understood beyond ordered data. Information is reactive and when different infons are integrated, new information emerges. When encountered by people, reports on the MAOA gene are interpreted and integrated into their Cognitive Networks. Reporting on the MAOA gene can become pseudoinformation, in the form of incomplete information. When we have simplified genetic explanations for complex behaviours, like the MAOA 'warrior gene' and genetic shortcuts for complex social relationships and phenomena like family and race, we reduce complex individuals to Essentialised Identities, 'aggressive warriors,' seemingly supported by the Virtual Identity constructed from scientific information. The explicit links noted by Alia-Klein et al. between MAOA and severe childhood stresses (Alia-Klein et al., 2008) get lost in the translation from scientific reporting to public communication. Suddenly a rich and complex individual and their particularly relevant personal history become reduced to 'warrior gene'.

Further, when the aggressive variant of the gene is correlated with character traits like aggression, gang membership and particular behaviours like weapon use, we have a larger range of data to interpret. For some, coupling the scientific source of the message with the existing social beliefs that certain ethnic groups are violent gang members, the ethnic message becomes knowledge. 'This group is scientifically shown to be aggressive.' For others, coupling the message to complex behaviours and the message is rejected. 'This is another example of Western science reinforcing prejudice.' This is because information is more than data and order; it is meaning and knowledge. And, as the receivers of that information have different personal histories and different understandings of the world, the MAOA gene is different information to different people. It is multirealisable. That is, the information changes depending on who is using it and how.

While this sort of controversy about use/misuse of scientific research is hardly novel – think of the ways that phrenology was used to justify and perpetuate racial prejudice – new surveillance technologies make the moral issue of informational multirealisability more obvious and more subtle at the same time. Basically, the capacity to construct Virtual Identities for people and groups is so great as to be inconceivable. While we know and understand that our Personal Information's 'out

[44] Elsewhere, I have identified a different factor, concept creep (Henschke, 2010).

there' and that 'they' are using it, at the same time, we have no grasp on who 'they' are, no idea what they're doing with our information, nor what uses they'll put that information to. Who would've anticipated that our mundane shopping habits could tell people about the likelihood of us being pregnant? As the case of the aggression gene illustrates, the products of surveillance have very different meanings for different people.

So what? Information may be multirealisable, understood and used differently by different people, this may be true. However, this is trivial. A hammer is also multirealisable – it can be used to nail nails or to kill a person, yet we are not in a state of moral panic about hammers. What is the relevance of talking about information in such a way? The answer is that certain types of information like Personal Information are more ethically important than others. The following chapters explain what I mean by Personal Information and why it matters in the age of surveillance.

6

On Identity and Information

6.1 IDENTITY AND INFORMATION: STEPPING INTO THE CIRCLE OF SURVEILLANCE

Instagram is a popular website where users put their photos online for others to look at, comment on them and so on. It's a paradigm example of how many experience their world in the age of surveillance – it both gives observers access to other people's lives and gives users the opportunity to make themselves the subjects of such observation. From late 2015 to early 2016, 'Instagram Star' Essena O'Neill updated her account and then quit Instagram altogether. 'She recaptioned nearly 100 photos to expose their "contrived perfection" to her more than 612,000 followers' (Hunt, 2016) and then deleted her account. She explained that this online persona was both unrealistic and harmful. 'I was getting more and more followers, thinner and thinner, better and more visually appealing pictures ... Online it looked like I had the perfect life ... yet I was so completely lonely and miserable inside ... I was lost, with serious problems so beautifully hidden' (Hunt, 2016). While the emotional vulnerabilities of being a teenager are hardly news, this case prompts the question – is online life good or bad for you?

Underneath this is a deeper question – what causes online life to be good or bad for you? One might say that vulnerable people like teenagers are too fragile to lead such public lives, or that the capacity to exhibit and control one's best points is a great way to strengthen one's self-esteem. In contrast, one might say that the high risks of cyberbullying and trolling online are inevitably going to cause even the most confident of people to feel bad about themselves, or that participation in groups of like-minded people having similar experiences can create a sense of community and belonging that we wouldn't once have had such easy access to. On this, one set of responders take it that the individual's *existing* psychological states drive the experience, while the other set take it that it is the way that their *Personal Information* is used and treated by others that drives the user's experience.

So which is it? Does a person's background psychological state drive their experience or does the way that the world responds to their Personal Information drive their experience? What's more important, the person's self-identity or the information that they're presenting to the world? The age of surveillance is particularly vexing for these questions as there is no obvious point of causal origin – identity and information both matter. And, as we can see with O'Neill's experience of posting photos to social media sites, it can be very hard to identify what is causing what. It is like being asked to point to the start of a circle. Where do you step into a circle?

Building from the conceptual work in Chapters 4 and 5, this chapter brings identity and information together. It explores the relation between identity and information to argue that identity and information are in a relation of mutual reciprocal causation; they both influence each other. Given that identity and information are mutually causal, I propose the idea of the 'Identity/Information Dyad'. This Identity/Information Dyad is introduced by reference to different responses that individuals have to Closed Circuit Television (CCTV) information. §6.3 presents the story that information forms identity and in §6.4, that identity forms information. §6.5 then discusses the general idea of a dyadic relation and §6.6 and §6.7 explicate the conceptual elements and processes of this particular dyadic relation between identity and information. The concept of explanatory priority is used in §6.8 to explain why people would favour identity over information to explain different phenomena and vice versa. The conclusion is that the Identity/Information Dyad is a useful tool for drawing attention to the importance of the relation between identity and information and for analysing how they impact on each other. The Identity/Information Dyad is a way of showing how the ethical values bear upon surveillance technologies and how these technologies play a role in our shifting moral practices in the age of surveillance.

This chapter argues against a strong reductionist approach to either identity or information as *the* causal element in the development of the other. The analysis of *both* identity and information *together* benefits us, as this dual analysis offers a better way understanding how people live and understand their worlds in the age of surveillance than we get by looking at identity or information independently. The integration of surveillance technologies into our lives and the increased role that information plays in how people live and understand their worlds motivate this investigation into the relation between identity and information. Part III of the book moves to the ethical importance of this relation between identity and information and draws attention to the impact that identity and Personal Information have on how individuals live and governments understand their worlds.

6.2 WHAT CAUSES WHAT? THE CASE OF WATCHING WATCHERS/CCTV OPERATORS

Consider again the operators of CCTV systems. As shown in Chapter 3, the operators play a key role in production of information. This information, as we saw in Chapter 5, was Thick Information – well-ordered data thought to be true and meaningful. The operators provide the semantic element; the meaningfulness of the information is provided by and reliant on the operators.

While CCTV and other large-scale surveillance programmes are typically cast as elaborate Orwellian panopticonic tools of an aggressive police state (Lyon, 1994, pp. 57–80), the variability of operators and the impacts of their job on their self-understanding are typically overlooked. When looking more closely at the experiences of being a 'surveillance expert' we see that such a job can both empower and traumatise those operators. The first thing to recall is that surveillance has information as its end product and in order for that information to be meaningful, humans are needed. 'A CCTV system is only as good as the people operating it – without them it is just a collection of mechanical and electrical components' (CCTV Manager 8, quoted in Smith, 2015, p .84). As covered in Chapter 5, because of the semantic and truth element, information is multirealisable. And if you have different people engaged in the same epistemic activity, you have variable outcomes. In his study of the experiences of CCTV operators, Gavin Smith writes that the operators 'imaginatively construct identities for the subjects they watch and furnish the unfolding action with a range of creative commentaries' (Smith, 2015, p. 114). The operators become story-tellers, if nothing else, to minimise the boredom of the job.

A further point to draw out is that the variability of the operators means both the multirealisability of the surveillance product and that the operators' experience of producing that information is variable. In addition to helping pass the time, the stories created around the subjects of attention both bear upon and display the operator's experiences of the world. This can be both empowering and traumatic. 'Camera operators perceive themselves as custodians of the vulnerable and guardians of the peace . . . Over time they become expert risk assessors and behavioural specialists. They are socialised and transfigured by what they see' (Smith, 2015, pp. 122, 123). A core part of the job of a CCTV operator is to bear witness to horrible things: drunken violence, suicides, fatal car accidents. 'Some of the things we see and have to deal with are horrendous. Really, quite traumatic. I've seen guys committing suicide right in front of my eyes and people being stabbed and beaten unconscious. It's just one of those jobs where you're always looking at the nastier sides of life' (Camera Operator 2, quoted in Smith, 2015, p. 130). Some operators feel empowered by this: 'It's nice safeguarding vulnerable persons, like lone females or drunk persons, at night, making sure they get home okay and keeping an eye on them. I like protecting the public' (Camera Operator 8, quoted in Smith, 2015, p. 144). However, for others, such exposure leads to long-term emotional problems: 'I worry that my family might fall victim to crime . . . I also worry if my husband is on a night out, as I know how easily trouble can break out' and 'Nowadays I don't go out at night in case I bump into the wrong person in a bar or taxi queue, 'cos I've seen what happen to unlucky people. You can get a beating from just being in the wrong place at the wrong time' (Camera Operators 3 and 5, quoted in Smith, 2015, p. 133).

Exposure to this incoming information can both empower and traumatise the CCTV operators. While the psychological motivations are undoubtedly broad, varied and complex, identity presents one useful way to frame differentiated responses to information.

First, observing the world and having the capacity to respond to it can be very empowering. 'Camera operators perceive themselves as custodians of the vulnerable and guardians of the peace' (Smith, 2015, p. 122). Feeling like they are part of a larger institution that protects and serves the public can give a CCTV operator a sense of agency, enabling them to see themselves as a force for good in the world and this can have a major impact on the person's Self-Regarding Identity; how a person views themselves in the future plays a major role in their present and how their character develops. Catriona Mackenzie argues that the ability to imagine different selves in the future is 'crucial' to self-understanding and self-development (Mackenzie, 2000). Knowing that they can help protect people and prevent bad things from occurring positions the CCTV operator as an important part of society. Information in this sense plays a central causal role in Self-Regarding Identity, through the effect it has on one's capacity to imagine the way they extend into the future.

However, being exposed to such information can also traumatise and disempower an operator. 'Over time they become expert risk assessors and behavioural specialists. They are socialised and transfigured by what they see' (Smith, 2015, p. 123). One issue is the problem of witnessing a terrible event about to occur, but being unable to stop it happening. 'As impotent bystanders they find themselves either implicated in explosive scenes of conflict or privy to profound moments of despair' (Smith, 2015). Second is that the operators are being asked to look for the risks, threats and dangers in common life. Both of these elements of the job can impact negatively on a person's belief that they are an autonomous agent.

As was argued in Chapter 5, information is multirealisable, in part because the *meaningfulness* of data varies from person to person. For some people, the CCTV information about the future may empower them, but for others, CCTV data about the risks of the world means something different. And this multirealisability arises because of the different personalities of the people processing the data. The Self-Regarding Identity, in particular a person's existing Cognitive Networks,[1] causes the information to be different as a result of the different meanings that different people attach to the same sets of data.

However, we now have a tension. The explanation why some CCTV operators feel empowered was that the information they work with gives them a sense of agency, while for others, that information undermines their belief that they can do anything about the world. The reason offered for feeling empowered is that information plays a major causal role in Self-Regarding Identity formation, while the reason offered for feeling disempowered is that Self-Regarding Identity plays a major

[1] Recall from §4.4 that I use 'Cognitive Network' to refer to the set of neurological and mental networks of the agent, including both affective or emotional states. This includes, states that we are conscious and not conscious of.

causal role in how the information is constructed. A similar set of tensions can be developed for Other-Regarding and Other/Other-Regarding Identity. So what is it – does information cause identity, or does identity cause information? My answer is both: each plays an important causal role in the other. In order to understand one, we need to understand the other and to recognise the relations between them.[2]

To contextualise this claim, consider discussions about the causal role of artefacts, from philosophy of technology. In those discussions, questions are asked such as '[d]o artifacts act? Should agency be assigned to them in account of social change? Or are the only social agents human beings and social structures like groups and organisations?' (Brey, 2005). A similar set of questions are being asked here: does information act? Should causal agency be assigned to information in account of the way it affects identity? Or is it only social agents like humans and their social structures that determine the way information is used? In *Artifacts as Social Agents*, Philip Brey proposes a model whereby artefacts and social constructs *both* play important roles in how people live and understand their worlds (Brey, 2005).

Bringing in a discussion from philosophy of technology serves two purposes. It shows that the idea of mutually causal relations has precedent. This point is relevant to the claims made here and the argument is strengthened with evidence that there is precedent for such an approach. Second, one of the key points of this book is to argue that, given its causal role in identity development, Personal Information is a morally relevant feature that requires analysis. However, perhaps the idea of a non-agent, non-real thing having some causal role may seem to miss the point of ethics: only agents like humans have choice, so we should focus our moral judgements only on such agents.[3] Discussions of agency of artefacts (albeit a highly constrained sense of agency) helps show that such an approach has precedent.

Further, the discussion of agency of artefacts is more than mere explanatory analogy. The problem that this chapter is addressing, at its core, is the same as the discussions of artefactual agency: what causal role does information play in bringing about particular identities and what causal role do identities play in forming information? My answer is equivalent to that of Brey: the Identity/Information Dyad demonstrates and explains that identity and information both play important *mutually causal roles* in how people live and understand their worlds. Philosophy of technology presents a comparable theoretic foundation to information in that technologies and information are not agents but have something like causal agency.

This chapter explains the claim of mutual causation by explicating the type of relation that occurs between identity and information. This is explained by

[2] This is a similar concept to the Hegelian dialectic, mentioned in §3.4. However, it is a particular form of dialectic, in that I am not saying that each element of the dialectic is revealed by the other, or that each creates the other, but that each continuously and mutually influence the other. I call this a dyadic relationship and explain it in detail in §6.5.

[3] This sort of discussion can be found in the attribution of moral autonomy to robots, see Heather Roff, (2013).

reference to the special type of relation that occurs between identity and information – a dyadic one. Providing the key elements within this dyadic relation and the details about the cognitive processes underpinning this relation, I conclude that the dyadic identity/information relation can explain a phenomenon like differential responses to CCTV footage.

Before beginning, recall that Chapter 4 presented a general account of identity as 'X perceives Y to be Z', written alternately as 'identity is who X perceives Y to be'. When a person thinks about themselves, they develop their 'Self-Regarding Identity', §4.6.1, from the combined information that they relate to their selves. When a person thinks about others, they form an 'Other-Regarding Identity', §4.6.2, from the combined information that they relate to the other person and that the values of a given society inform how a person views another, called 'Other/Other-Regarding Identity', §4.6.3. Chapter 5 presented an account of information as ordered, meaningful true data, §5.3–§5.6. When integrating different units of information, infons, new information emerges: §5.8 and §5.9. For particular types of information, the new information that emerges is experienced as an identity.

6.3 THE ROLE OF COGNITION: INFORMATION FORMS IDENTITY

This section is concerned with how information forms identity to detail the central role that information plays in the process of identity construction. For now, a strong view is presented where information plays the major role in causing identity.[4] This

> attribution of agency to the artifact alone is justified because the artifact functions as the *major independent variable*. That is, whereas the agency is dependent on other variables as well, that are found in the environment of the artifact, the artifact itself is most directly and specifically linked to the changes that occur.
>
> (Emphasis Original, Brey, 2005)

Parallel to this, an 'informational causation'[5] would hold that in the formation of identities, information is *the major independent variable* – as information is most directly and specifically linked to changes that occur in identity. That is, information forms identity.

In Chapter 4, identity was developed as the way an observer perceives the world, 'I am who I *perceive* myself to be, you are who I *perceive* you to be and so on.' The discussion here will be primarily concerned with the experience that the given

[4] A strong view that information 'causes' identity is presented here to focus on the causal role that information plays in identity construction. §6.4 develops a similar but oppositional position that identity 'causes' information. Referring to these processes as 'causes' may strike some as problematic, but this is exactly the point that I wish to bring out: that there is a tension between seeing information as the major causal factor in identity formation and seeing identity as the major causal factor in identity formation.

[5] See footnote above.

observer has of some thing or person in the world, such as Catie's experience of John as 'John$_R$', the emergent representation of John as discussed in §5.8. Building from the notion of cognition as thoughts about thoughts and insofar as phenomenology is the experience of something, Catie's experience of things in the world like John is here called a 'Phenomenological Identity'.[6]

6.3.1 *Epistemic Group Action*

Deriving Phenomenological Identity from the notion of cognition as thoughts about thoughts, we can develop a systematic understanding of identity arising from informational activities. We begin with the idea of an epistemic action – an action that is conducted to bring about information. Epistemic actions are '[a]ctions designed to change the input to an agent's information processing system. They are ways an agent has of modifying the external environment to provide crucial bits of information' (Kirsh and Maglio, 1994, pp. 541–542). Andy Clark marks the distinction between pragmatic actions and epistemic actions in which pragmatic actions 'are actions designed to bring one physically closer to a goal. Walking to the fridge to fetch a beer is a pragmatic action. Epistemic actions may or may not yield such physical advance. *Instead, they are designed to extract or uncover information*' (Emphasis Mine, Clark, 2008, p. 71). An epistemic action is thus defined by its purpose,[7] which is to bring about new information. The link to surveillance is clear – as developed in Chapter 3, surveillance is an explicitly epistemic action, conducted to produce new information about the world.

However, with complex surveillance systems like CCTV, there are typically a group of actors involved in the epistemic action. This is a form of group epistemic action. Seumas Miller describes a group action as 'actions involving a number of agents, performing independent actions to realize some common goal' (Miller, 2010b, p. 37). Epistemic *group* action, then, is action intended to bring about new information, conducted by *multiple* agents. It is a situation whereby a set of individuals work towards a common epistemic goal. Their actions include the collection, aggregation and integration of data with the common purpose of producing new information.

A paradigm example of an epistemic group action would be a police investigation, involving different investigative teams, with the common goal to identify a burglar. Group A collect and analyse evidence from the scene, Group B question witnesses, Group C compare the current crime to previous crimes and Group D question likely suspects. Following their epistemic actions, Group A deduce that the burglar

6 This notion of a Phenomenological Identity is considered in contrast to the pre-experienced identity of the Thing In The World, a 'Natural Identity'. These terms are explained in detail in §6.6, in particular, in Figure 6.1.

7 I have discussed elsewhere ways and reasons for understanding full actions by reference to their intended aims (Henschke, 2012).

acted alone, was tall and strong enough to climb the eight-foot fence and in through a window and probably a male. Group B hear from a neighbour that a red van was parked out the front of the house during the time of the burglary. Group C find out that a series of burglaries have occurred within the area, seven of which were similar houses, similar times and similar things stolen. Group D find out that there are five local suspects and of these, one was in jail, one was in hospital, one was visiting his mother, one was out of the country and one had no alibi. By bringing these four groups together – the description of the crime, the witness testimony, the previous crimes and the location of likely suspects, the group of investigators deduce that the most likely person to have committed the burglary is the final suspect. A fifth group of officers, Group E, go to the suspect's house and find a red van, a pile of stolen goods from the given crime and previous crimes. As a result of the epistemic group action, the suspect has been identified as the burglar and is charged with the crime.

Like other surveillance actions, the purpose of this epistemic group action has been to identify the culprit. That is, the burglar's identity was not known to the investigators before the investigation,[8] but through investigation and aggregation of information, the investigating teams come to know who the culprit is. Now that they have information as to who the culprit is, a claim of relative equivalence is being made between the crime and the culprit. The new set of knowledge, experienced by the investigators as relative equivalence between a given Phenomenological Identity and some Person In The World,[9] the product of the surveillance action is new information to the investigators. This Phenomenological Identity is new information in that it was not known to the investigators who the burglar was. As was discussed in §5.8 and §5.9, this is new emergent information.

When thinking of group actions aiming to produce identity of people for others to use, central to the production of the Phenomenological Identity is that the teams communicate with each other about what information they find and as a result of this communication, that the relevant information is aggregated. The importance of such intergroup communication was highlighted in the United States in May 2010. On the 1st of May, 2010, someone made an attempt to detonate a car bomb in Times Square in New York. The integration of small pieces of information led to the identification and subsequent arrest of Faisal Shahzad on the 3rd of May 2010 as he tried to leave the United States. Mr Shahzad was identified via the integration of a vehicle number, a phone number and Personal Information provided by Mr Shahzad to an airline company upon entry to the United States (Baker and Shane, 2010).

8 The identity was not known to the investigators, or the community at large. Presumably, the burglar knows that they are the burglar. I mean here to refer to the identity of the burglar being made known to the investigators due to the epistemic group action. This builds from the point made in §5.8 about new information.

9 'Person In The World' is a special category of the subject or target of surveillance. Its meaning is specified and discussed in §6.6, in particular, in Figure 6.1.

The point here is that Mr Shahzad was identified through the communication, integration and aggregation of information from different investigative teams. The relative equivalence between a set of knowledge and Mr Shahzad was produced as the result of an epistemic group action, facilitated by groups communicating what information they had.[10] As in the initial burglar case, the Phenomenological Identity of Mr Shahzad was produced as the result of epistemic group action. The culprit's identity emerged from the integration of information. The epistemic group action produced information which identified the attempted car bomber.[11] The epistemic action, in particular, the aggregation of information, produced an identity.

6.3.2 *Individual Epistemic Action and Identity*

Returning to the investigating team, instead of five investigative teams, A, B, C, D and E, consider now one lone officer investigating the burglary. Instead of the teams producing the information about the crime, the lone officer conducts tasks of A, B, C, D and E. Like the group investigation, the lone officer goes through the set of epistemic actions and ultimately identifies the culprit. The lone officer's investigation is functionally equivalent[12] to that of the group investigation, as the lone officer conducts a set of epistemic actions that are functionally equivalent to that of the group investigation, with the same outcome; the lone officer gets some knowledge from the emergent information that a given person is equivalent to the culprit. This emergent information is experienced by the lone officer as a Phenomenological Identity.

Now consider that the case is an old one that is being reopened. All the necessary information to solve the crime had been recorded and is accessed by the lone officer. The necessary files have been located; now the lone officer sits down to read them. All the relevant files are read and by integrating the relevant information, the Phenomenological Identity of the culprit emerges. Functional equivalence holds that we would consider the group investigation and the lone officer to be conducting a set of epistemic actions that are equivalent.

In a further example, consider that instead of the lone officer actively producing the information and instead of the lone officer merely reading the relevant files, a

10 In a contrasting case, the investigation of the Yorkshire Ripper, Peter Sutcliffe, was substantially delayed as a result of not integrating important facts of the case. See *Wicked Beyond Belief* for a description of the Yorkshire Ripper investigation (Bilton, 2003).

11 To reiterate a comment made at the end of §6.3, I recognise here, especially with regard to Phenomenological Identity, that the use of different senses of identity may be unclear. Figure 6.1 and the definitions that go with it should help explain this term. However, in order to show that there is a tension between identity and information, I have opted to use §6.3 and §6.4 to pose the problem before offering my solution.

12 This is a reference to functional equivalence. For more on this see Andy Clark and Jonathan Glover (Clark, 2008, pp. 196–217; Glover, 1988, pp. 85–87).

computer surveillance program has been developed, called SuperSnooper.[13] In this example, SuperSnooper conducts the necessary epistemic actions[14] to identify the culprit. All the relevant police officer has to do is read the identity from the screen. Note the similarities between the group investigation, the lone officer and the computer. If, in all situations, (a) all the incoming information is correct and (b) the culprit identified is in fact the perpetrator of the crime, we have functional equivalence between the investigating group, the lone officer and SuperSnooper. The relevance of the SuperSnooper program is that – as the Snowden revelations have shown – we can and do, use data aggregation programs to construct identities for people. That is, given the incredible amounts of personal data gathered by government surveillance programmes like 'BOUNDLESS INFORMANT' (Harding 2014, p. 266), some form of automated analysis is needed to create Virtual Identities in order for the information to be actually useful for operators.

Again, insofar as we are looking at how an investigation of a crime identifies the culprit, the identity is produced as a result of a set of epistemic actions. In each case, the Virtual Identity was produced as the result of multiple epistemic actions and ultimately experienced[15] as a Phenomenological Identity. In each case, information was central to producing the Phenomenological Identity of the culprit. In the case of Mr Shazhad, it is unlikely that any individual piece of information alone would have identified him. The relation of relative equivalence between him and the culprit was produced by the process of epistemic group action, necessarily dependent upon the *integration* and *aggregation* of different sets of information.

6.3.3 *Neurobureaucrats and Information*

Bringing this discussion back to the concept of cognition as thoughts about thoughts, consider now a form of epistemic group action where the entities within the group are not people, or a person considered through time, but neurons involved in the production of information. In the neurological construction of identity, many neurons are used to shuttle data around, in order to produce the

[13] This is not a mere hypothetical proposal: the UK's Home Office Large Major Enquiry System, HOLMES 2, is 'a single, computer-based information technology application for major investigations which is compatible with the information systems of all the UK police forces' (Miller and Gordon, 2014, p. 124). Consider also the US 'Total Information Awareness (TIA) Project', which 'sought to create a giant network of integrated computer technologies for intercepting, storing, searching, monitoring, reading and analysing all private, computerized records of 300 million Americans' (Cohen, 2010, p. 21).

[14] This might involve SuperSnooper analysing the existing police files for likely connections. However, the program could be more active in the world in that engages in internet searches, monitors CCTVs, sends drones and so on to collect the initial information about the crime scene, particular people's movements and so on (Cohen, 2010, p. 21).

[15] This claim is dependent upon the premise that conscious agents like humans experience things, while computers, as they do not (yet) have the capacity for conscious experience, cannot form a Phenomenological Identity. Perhaps in the SuperSnooper case, it would instead be a pre-Phenomenological, Virtual Identity.

integrated identity that people experience. On this 'neurobureaucrats' model, many neurons and neural populations act like bureaucrats. That is,

> many neurons and neuronal populations serve not as direct encodings of knowledge or information but as (dumb) middle managers routing and trafficking the internal flow of information between and within cortical areas. These "control neurons" serve to open and close channels of activity and allow for the creation of a kind of instantaneous, context sensitive modular cortical architecture.
>
> (Clark, 2008, p. 117)

Clark's account describes what was introduced in §4.3 as cognition, thoughts about thoughts. It is a process whereby many neurons and neuronal populations are not involved in the direct collection of data about the world, or responding to the resulting information. Rather, the neurons' role is in the transfer and communication of data to produce information: this cognition is epistemic group action at the neurological level. Like bureaucrats, neurons are engaged in group action, but rather than paper shuffling and human resource management, the neurons' and neuronal populations' role is the production of information. And like the police investigators described in §6.3.1 and §6.3.2, the end result of the epistemic group action is the production of an identity for a given object. Emergent information is produced as a result of cognitive activity.

§4.3 and §4.4 described the neural processes associated with Phenomenological Identity production and §5.8 recast identity production in informational terms. Catie's experience, $John_R$, of seeing John emerges from the integration of different data about the world. To produce an identity, we don't see eyes, nose, hair colour, head shape and so on – Catie experiences her friend as an integrated whole. Chapter 5 argued that this was an emergent entity, a cognitive experience arising from the integration of different sets of information to produce the experience of John. Following Clark's description of a neural bureaucracy, Catie's experience of her friend John, the emergent Phenomenal Identity $John_R$, is the product of epistemic action of groups of neurons, including the neurobureaucrats.

This informational foundation of Phenomenological Identity applies not just to the experience of others like John, a form of Other-Regarding Identity, but also to Self-Regarding Identity. Self-Regarding Identity arises as the result of neurobureaucratic processing of data: integrating data from different sources to produce a coherent and stable identity.[16]

Whether it is the production of Other-Regarding Identity or Self-Regarding Identity, the general claim is that Phenomenological Identities are produced through the processes of epistemic group action. And from this, we see how an informational approach can explain identity formation. Like a team investigating a crime, a person's neurons act in concert: ordering data, giving it meaning and

[16] Note the overlap here between the stability arising from time-locked multimodal sense data and the coherentist account of truth judgements offered in §5.6.

judging its truth against other data sources. If the information is to change, the Phenomenological Identity will change. In short, the experience of an identity for some person in the world emerges as the result of group actions that are epistemic in their function. That is, whether it is a group of police officers investigating a burglary or a collection of neurons shuttling information in cognitive processes, information forms identity.

6.4 IDENTITY FORMS INFORMATION

Contrasting the previous section, this section shows the important causal role that *identity* plays in *information* construction. We return to the three elements of identity introduced in §4.6, Self-Regarding Identity, Other-Regarding Identity and Other/Other-Regarding Identity. The argument here is that Identity, whether Self-Regarding, Other-Regarding or Other/Other-Regarding, plays a central role in the construction of information. The strongest interpretation of this claim sits alongside a strong[17] social constructivist line of reasoning where '[s]ocial representations are not just claimed to play a major role in the constitution of agency, they are claimed to fully determine it' (Brey, 2005). Likewise, to paraphrase Brey, 'identity forms are not just claimed to play a major role in the construction of information, they are claimed to fully determine it'. The subjective constraints posed by identity are the *major independent variables* in what and how data is ordered and made meaningful and truthful. That is, identity forms information. This is in direct contrast to §6.3, where information was presented as forming identity. Discussion of the two contrasting views is taken up in later sections of this chapter.

6.4.1 *Self-Regarding Identity and Information: On Expertise*

In *What Is This Thing Called Science*, Alan Chalmers describes a person looking through a microscope and seeing some biological material (Chalmers, 1999, pp. 7–9). Chalmers contrasts a novice and an experienced biologist looking at the same slide under a microscope but seeing different things:

> When a beginner looks at a slide prepared by an instructor through a microscope it is rare that the appropriate cell structures can be discerned, even though the instructor has no difficulty discerning them when looking at the same slide through the same microscope.
>
> (Chalmers, 1999, p. 7)

Chalmers explains this by reference to the different experience levels of the two observers. While the novice can only recognise basic shapes and outlines, the

[17] The strong view that identity causes information is presented here to focus on the causal role that identity plays in information formation. Later sections of this chapter develop a less deterministic approach.

experienced biologist can see what those shapes and outlines represent, can see which fine details are important cellular components and which are merely debris.

§4.4 argued that experience is central to how a person perceives the world. Chapter 5 presented a detailed philosophic account of Thick Information as data that is ordered, meaningful and judged as true.[18] By integrating the role that previous experience plays in perception with the thick account of information, we can explain how two people can experience the same thing differently.[19] If information, as people experience it, emerges from data, order, meaning and truth then varying the order, meanings and truth judgements about the given data set will vary the information. This was the point of informational multirealisability, argued in Chapter 5, particularly §5.9. The range of semantic possibilities of a given data set varies from person to person and has an impact on the information constructed:

> For a novice [chess] player who understands very little about chess, the arrangement of pieces on a board is not particularly *meaningful*, and the chess board is analogous to an array of letters or shapes. For an experienced chess player, however, piece arrangements are *meaningful* and are more analogous to scenes.
>
> (Emphases Mine, Brockmole et al., 2008, p. 1888)

The point is that due to experience changing the range of meanings and truth judgements used in information construction, experience, particularly expertise, changes how a person interacts with data to change what information is produced. Experience ultimately changes the Thick Information that a person constructs from a given data set; information is multirealisable. In a simple sense then, as prior experience is a key element in information formation, the identity of the observer causes the information constructed from a stable data set.

Given the role of prior experience in forming information, we can claim that 'Observer Identity' is a necessary element to understanding information. The particular meanings of this 'Observer Identity' are given in §6.6. Suffice to say here, Observer Identity refers to the existing Cognitive Networks of that person who is doing the perceiving, who we can describe as the observer. Observer Identity is the 'X' from the general form of identity, where 'identity is who X perceives Y to be', §4.6.4.

The cognitive processes arising from experience impact information beyond altering the range of meanings an observer has at their cognitive disposal. Individual *expertise* includes more than simply having an individuated range of meanings to

[18] Recall from §5.6 that 'truth' is used in a weak 'folk' sense. Rather than a strong epistemological claim that true information justifiably correlates with something in or from the real world, truth is used to refer to situations when a person *thinks* or *feels* that they are justified that some information correlates with something in or from the real world.

[19] This point was mentioned in §4.4 when talking about different experiences of the same wine and food.

scaffold onto data. An expert is often recognised by their ability to rapidly ascribe meaning to some observation.

This can be explained in part by a neurological model of expertise offered by Olav Krigolson, Lara Pierce, Clay Holroyd and James Tananka (Krigolson et al., 2008). In their model, a person is exposed to a certain set of stimuli and receives 'performance feedback' as to whether they correctly classify the stimuli. Through time, the feedback exhibits reinforcement mechanisms such that the observer develops an internal 'set of implicit rules needed to make subordinate level object classifications' (Krigolson et al., 2008, p. 1833). When exposed to the positive feedback, a person forms an internal set of representations which afford a faster capacity of recognition for the given stimuli. 'As learning progressed, participants who learned to correctly identify the [stimuli,] ... the high learners ... developed a representation that afforded the ability to internally evaluate the consequences of their behavioral responses' (Krigolson et al., 2008, p. 1839). Rather than relying on the external fine-grained and detailed data, in line with the Reverse Hypothesis Theory (RHT) discussed in §4.3.3, the expert uses the abstracted representations for a given input, affording rapid cognitive processes.[20]

Further, other work on expertise suggests that the *purpose* plays a central role in the development of expert skills. Contrasting expertise with performance and play, 'the key activity in the acquisition of expertise is *deliberate* practice, [defined] as appropriately challenging tasks that are chosen *with the goal of improving a particular skill*' (Emphaseis Mine, Charness et al., 2005, p. 152). On this line, to gain expertise, it is not enough that a person merely repeats an action, but that they must purposefully repeat the action with a particular goal in mind, altering their practice in pursuit of this goal. Conscious attentive repetition creates the expert and if the neurological model offered above by Krigolson and others is correct, a key element in expertise is the production of an internal set of representations available to the expert. Expertise correlates with the range of meanings available to the person and the capacity to quickly access internal representations produced via conscious efforts. Self-Regarding Identity, I am who *I* perceive *myself* to be, arises from the endorsement and rejection of particular traits: Those things that a person identifies strongly with are afforded a stronger place in Self-Regarding Identity than those that a person rejects. Likewise, in expertise, reinforcement of neural associations are utilised to make more rapid assessments of external stimuli via internal representations. Identification of a given input coupled with positive reinforcement creates experts. We have seen that experts see the world differently to novices. A commonly experienced data set becomes strongly associated with a given set of internal representations. Observer Identity causes information not only because the semantic possibilities for a given data set vary based on experience, but also because

[20] The relevance of the RHT to information construction is covered in more detail in §6.4.2.

the given Observer Identity makes certain semantic contents more rapidly accessible than others. Through exposure and repetition, Observer Identity causes information.

Importantly, the notion of expertise being considered is deliberately broad – I do not want to limit it to special cases like chess masters. As Smith details, those involved in the production of information in surveillance systems like CCTV are to be considered 'expert risk assesors' (Smith, 2015, pp. 121–123). The CCTV operator forms an identity for the given subjects.

6.4.2 *Other-Regarding Identity and Information: Define Yourself*

§6.4.1 discussed the idea that through exposure an internal representation for an observable can emerge through repeated exposure and feedback to the given observable. The claim was that Self-Regarding Identity causes information. Recall also from §4.6.2 that Other-Regarding Identity is 'who X perceives Y to be', where Y is another person; 'your identity is who *I* perceive *you* to be'. §4.3 introduced the dual process model of perception, whereby we interpret our world through two parallel perceptual systems, feedforward processing (FFP) and the RHT. Recall also inattentional blindness, from §4.4.2, whereby observers do not see things that are within their field of vision. Arien Mack states that the research on inattentional blindness 'conclusively demonstrates that, with rare exceptions, observers generally do not see what they are looking directly at when they are attending to something else … Under these conditions, observers often failed to perceive a clearly visible stimulus that was located exactly where they were looking' (Mack, 2003, p. 181). The point here is that if an observer's attention is focussed on one thing, that thing will often determine what data is attended to. By constraining the data picked up, attention ultimately acts as a limiting factor on what information a person forms. This can be explained via the dual process model of perception, in that the top-down representations are guiding the focus of attention. If Catie is looking for John,[21] the internal abstract representation $John_R$ guides Catie's attention, leaving her blind to other visual data. In this way, Other-Regarding Identity plays a central causal role in data pick-up.

However, the top-down representations do more than guide data pick-up, as they can also guide *how* information is constructed, §4.4. Again, we have the abstract representation guiding the processing of the fine-grained incoming information. This is what is referred to as global precedence, 'in which global information in an image is processed before the fine details and predominates perception' (Kveraga, Ghuman and Bar, 2007, p. 153). The higher level abstract representation of an observed person guides the data processing. The Other-Regarding Identity drives the observer's production of information.

[21] This was discussed in §5.8, where Catie sees John as an emergent visual representation.

Repeating a reference to Kestutis Kveraga, Avniel Ghuman and Moshe Bar from §4.4.2, the high-level abstractions do more than guide attention; previous experience and associations shape the perception of people.

> [P]eople use these global properties to link the new person with a familiar person in memory (e.g., "who does this person look like"), even if not explicitly. *Once a link is found, we automatically project information such as personality attributes to the new person based simply on this analogy.*
>
> (Emphasis Mine, Kveraga, Ghuman and Bar, 2007, p. 162)

Note that these 'global properties' track to the high-level abstract representations, such as Phenomenological Identities, discussed in §5.8. Again, the Other-Regarding Identity drives information formation.

Finally, the emotional responses that one has to an object will impact a person's perception of it. This can occur in two ways. First, the increased desire for another thing will change the apprehension of that object (Veltkamp, Aarts and Custers, 2008). The idea here is that the observer's perception of another person changes in relation to the observer's desire. Martijn Veltkamp, Henk Aarts and Ruud Custers' research looks at how goal motivation affects size perception in objects, concluding that motivation does affect size perception (Veltkamp, Aarts and Custers, 2008). On this model, the more motivated a person is towards achieving something, the larger that thing appears to the person.

The mechanism proposed by Veltkamp, Aarts and Custers is that given the limited cognitive capacities of people, the more important a given goal is, the more attention is given to it. Further, Veltkamp, Aarts and Custers propose that the mechanism involves top-down cognitive processes of RHT. 'In the light of this research, it could be the case that other processes in the service of motivation also rely on such a top-down process' (Veltkamp, Aarts and Custers, 2008, p. 723). Their work implies that the top-down processes are general mechanisms. As such, I propose that the observer's desire for another person will change the observer's perception of that person. Who the other person is and the way the observer has constructed a Phenomenological Identity for the other person guides the construction of information for that desired person. Again, we see that Other-Regarding Identity plays a central causal role in information construction.

Further to this is a common idea that emotions or affective responses change perception. Studies on the neuroscience of maternal and romantic love relations postulate that the hormone oxytocin[22] plays a key role in these love relations. Both maternal and romantic love relations suppress 'not only negative emotions but also affect the network involved in making social judgments about that person' (Bartels and Zeki, 2004, p. 1162). That is, 'both romantic and maternal love activate specific

[22] For an overview of studies on oxytocin, see Mauricio Delgado and on its behavioural implications, see H. K. Caldwell and W. S. Young (Delgado, 2008, Caldwell and Young, 2006).

regions in the reward system and lead to suppression of activity in the neural machineries associated with the *critical social assessment* of other people and with negative emotions' (Emphasis Mine, Bartels and Zeki, 2004, p. 1164). Emotions make us judge people and things differently. Maternal and romantic love relations both produce increased levels of oxytocin (Bartels and Zeki, 2004, p. 1162). Recalling the role of truth judgements in information construction, §5.6, the change in critical social assessment is relevant in that data will be processed differently for someone that a person loves than someone they don't love. Other-Regarding Identity drives information construction.[23]

As a risk expert, the CCTV operator's attention is implicitly guided towards those people and actions that present some form of risk. The potential targets for observation guide data pick-up and construction of the information that the observer experiences. So, we have Other-Regarding Identity guiding data pick-up, the meanings associated with a given data set and the truth judgement of a given meaningful data set. In short, Other-Regarding Identity drives information construction.

6.4.3 *Other/Other-Regarding Identity and Information: I Think What They Think*

The third element of identity introduced in §4.6.3 was Other/Other-Regarding Identity, described as 'who X perceives X* to perceive Y to be': 'my perception of others is strongly influenced by how *I* perceive *you* to perceive those *other* people'. Other/Other-Regarding Identity is relevant to information in that the social foundation for many of the meanings associated with others provides the background frames of reference that a Phenomenological Identity is built from and thus is the basis for many truth-regarding judgements of others.

Consider the prevalence of implicit racial prejudice in those who do not consciously hold racially prejudiced views.[24] If a given group is commonly devalued by society, an observer will often implicitly value them similarly, even if the observer

[23] Further evidence can be found in experiments that showed that maternal and romantic love can both be stimulated by photos of the loved one (Sharpley and Bitsika, 2010). That is, visualising the loved other releases oxytocin. Oxytocin has many effects on biology and cognition. For instance, oxytocin increases the attractiveness of others (Theodoridou et al., 2009) and as discussed, increases trust (Baumgartner et al., 2008). The hormone changes the perception of incoming data via its influence on semantic content and truth ascriptions. Loving someone produces changes in how we perceive them and how we respond to them. The differential experience of loved others as 'positive illusions' has been long established (Murray, Holmes and Griffin, 1996), producing what is sometimes called the 'love-is-blind' bias (Swami and Furnham, 2008). The information constructed from a given data set changes depending on who that person is. And, given that hormones like oxytocin are released by recognition of the other person, we can say that Other-Regarding Identity causes information formation.

[24] Evidence for this implicit bias has been long established (Devine, 1989; Payne et al., 2005; Payne, 2005, 2001; Wittenbrink, Judd and Park, 1997). Jan Lauwereyns looks at the neural underpinnings of cognitive biases generally (Lauwereyns, 2010).

consciously views the marginalised group as equals. For instance, Jennifer Eberhardt, Atiba Goff, Valerie Purdie and Paul Davies investigated how perception of race, in particular black faces, can influence an individual's response to people with black/dark skin. First, they discuss a large body of research that shows that '[m]erely thinking about Blacks can lead people to evaluate ambiguous behavior as aggressive, to miscategorise harmless objects as weapons, or to shoot quickly and, at times, inappropriately' (Eberhardt et al., 2004, p. 876). Their research goes further by arguing that 'just as Black faces and Black bodies can trigger thoughts of crime, thinking of crime can trigger thoughts of Black people – that is, some associations between social groups and concepts are bidirectional' (Eberhardt et al., 2004, p. 876). In short, the values that one perceives as part of Other/Other-Regarding Identity can influence the behaviour of individuals towards particular individuals and groups, to the point where a given social concept like criminality can then produce thoughts of particular groups.[25] The association of a given group with a particular socialised value is more likely to occur with less-frequently encountered groups.[26]

The Other/Other-Regarding Identity informs what meanings and judgements are used in the experience of the other person. Bringing the discussion back to information, as encultured values become tightly coupled to particular data,[27] a particular set of meanings is more rapidly associated with a given group. An explanation in line with the cognitive discussion of identity is as follows: the top-down representation is more likely to be used for an other-race face, than same-race faces. So, other-race faces are processed quickly and implicitly, often carrying with them the implicit judgements associated with the other-race group.[28] Building on the availability of given meanings and social valuing, Other/Other-Regarding Identity is central to judgements made about data such as 'this person is black'. Again, we find that Phenomenological Identity causes information. Such racial profiling and the associated prejudice and moral concern are typical worries in surveillance; whether it is the particular focus of police on black youths driving cars in the United States[29]

[25] Note also that the prejudice against a given group may be held by members of the marginalised group itself (Brennan, 2009).

[26] As Roberto Caldara, Bruno Rossion, Pierre Bovert and Claude-Alain Hauert show, 'other-race' face classifications occur faster than 'same-race' faces (Caldara et al., 2004). One explanation offered for this is that the abstract representations for other-race faces are less complex than same-race faces (Feng et al., 2011; Gosling and Eimer, 2011).

[27] This is a similar point to the nesting of information, discussed in §5.7.2.

[28] One way of explaining the background causes for this is by reference to enculturation. '[E]ach of us has the values we do as the result of a process of enculturation; that is, as a result of having been brought up in a particular society, in a particular manner' (Levy, 2002, p. 32).

[29] This police attention directed to minorities is a particular expression of the problem of Essentialised Identities, §4.5.4, where a person is stopped and searched not because of any particular suspicion or explicit anti-social behaviour, but because of their membership of a particular group of people. Given the context of racial discrimination and criminal justice, it is highly controversial (Bowling and Phillips, 2007; Gelman, Fagan and Kiss, 2007; Miller, 2010a; Waddington, Stenson and Don, 2004; Wortley and Owusu-Bempah, 2011).

or the special attention paid by New York law enforcement to black youths online (Hackman, 2015), implicit and explicit social biases play a substantial role in surveillance. Other/Other-Regarding Identity drives information production.

The overall claim being made in this section is that identity causes information. A person's self-perception is fundamental to how they experience the world and causes the data that is attended to, the meanings ascribed to it and the truth judgements made about that data. Likewise, the abstract representations for another person play a major role in determining how that person is perceived. The emergent identity for another bears down on what data is picked up, the meanings ascribed to it and the truth judgements made about that data. Finally, the social values commonly associated with others strongly influence how an observer perceives those others. The meanings ascribed to others and the truth judgements made about them are dependent upon the way we think others think about that. In all cases, identity is a *major independent variable* in information construction.

6.5 DYADIC RELATIONS AND MUTUAL CAUSATION

Two deliberately contradictory claims have been presented: §6.3 showed that an experience of identity emerges from group epistemic actions performed by neural cells and processes to explain the claim that identity was caused by information. §6.4 presented evidence that information is constructed from the experiences of Self-Regarding, Other-Regarding and Other/Other-Regarding Identity to claim that information is caused by identity. Obviously, there is a tension here.

One explanation of the tension is the use of the term 'cause'. 'Cause' was used to draw attention to the tension between the two views. Underpinning the tension is the question of what plays *the* causal role: is identity *the* cause of the information that a person forms about the world, or is it information that causes *the* formation of identity?[30] An answer to this is both: identity and information play a major role in the formation of the other. They are mutually causal.

This claim about mutual causation is founded on the particular type of relation that occurs between identity and information.[31] Identity and information share a 'dyadic relationship', in which each is an element that influences the other. This parallels a view of Brey's 'differentiated constructivism'. Brey posits that the agency of an artefact is found both in the design of artefacts and in the social processes (Brey, 2005). On my view, identity and information both play important causal roles

[30] Given that I am making a more general claim about the relations between identity and information, for the remainder of this section I will not specify Phenomenological Identity, Self-Regarding Identity and so on. Again, the relations between the different types of identity are explicated in detail in §6.6 and 6.7.

[31] Chapter 7 points out that this claim holds more or less, depending in part on the type of information considered. The focus of Chapter 7 is that *Personal Information* is a type of information that is especially relevant to the Identity/Information Dyad.

in how people live in and understand their worlds. This novel concept of what I call 'the Identity/Information Dyad' shows the causal roles that each plays in the other.

This dyadic interpretation of identity and information has two premises. First, that a relation holds between identity and information. Second, that this relation is dyadic in form. On premise one, §6.3 and §6.4 showed that there is a relation between identity and information. The two sections presented this relation as a causal one, in that information is one of the key causal elements in identity formation, §6.3 and that identity is one of the key causal elements in information formation, §6.4.

So, given the mutual causal relations between identity and information, a *dyadic* relation exists between the two. The Oxford Dictionaries define a dyad as 'something that consists of two elements or parts' and it is precisely this dual element of the relation that the dyadic relationship highlights.[32] Central to the concept of a dyadic relationship, as it is presented here, is the idea of mutual causation. There is a particular 'whole' which consists in two elements, each of which stands in a causal relation to the other.

Andy Clark discusses reciprocal causation,[33] in which analysis of a system with multiple components fails if we look at each component independently of and insulated from, the other components of that system (Clark, 1997a, p. 163). Clark argues that we should consider continuous reciprocal causation when

> the target phenomena is an emergent property of the coupling of the two ... components, and should not be "assigned" to either alone ... Thus, to the extent that brain, body and world can at times be joint participants in episodes of dense reciprocal causal influence, we will confront *behavioral unfoldings that resist explanation* in terms of inputs to and outputs from a supposedly insulated cognitive engine.
>
> (Emphasis Mine, Clark, 1997a, pp. 164–165)

Clark's concern, that a person and the world are not mutually isolated from each other and so need be understood in relation to each other,[34] is different to mine. However, the same reasoning holds here – the behaviour that we are attempting to explain is concerned with how an agent recognises and responds to other agents and ultimately

[32] As §3.6 noted, the term 'dyadic relationship' has been chosen, rather than use a term like a 'dialectic relation'. The reason for this is that the term 'dialectic' is a particular term of philosophic art, which carries with it a huge range of different meanings, views and arguments. To clear the discussion space, I am introducing this new term of a 'dyadic relation' to focus specifically on what I see of relevance to this book: two elements in a relation of mutual causation.

[33] Note that Clark discusses reciprocal causation in a series of different publications. The concept was first introduced and discussed in *Being There* (Clark, 1997b, a, 2008).

[34] A point Clark has substantially developed into what is often referred to as the extended mind theory (Clark, 2008; Clark and Chalmers, 1998).

how people live in and understand their worlds. In order to explain this relation, we need to recognise a dyadic relationship between identity and information.[35]

To describe the dynamics of a dyadic relationship, consider first that the elements in a dyadic relationship do not need to *consciously* communicate with each other. Allelomimesis is the term given to group behaviour, whereby one individual's actions impact the actions of others in the group and vice versa, 'if I do as others and others do as I . . . we all end up doing the same thing' (Deneubourg and Goss, 1989, p. 297). This allelomimesis can produce highly complex group behaviours in individuals through very simple processes: an ant will lay a trail pheromone that influences other termites to follow this trail,[36] thereby communicating to the other ants the presence of food (Deneubourg and Goss, 1989, p. 297). Similarly, many flocks of birds and schools of fish seem to move as one, without any need for communication between individuals. In flocks of birds and schools of fish, each individual orientates themselves in relation to where the other individuals are. '[P]ositional preference is formulated as a preferred distance to one or more nearest neighbour' (Parrish, Viscido and Grunbaum, 2002, p. 299). These are all simple examples in which the actions of one element in a group impact on the actions of another and vice versa: mutual causation.

Consider now a paradigm example of a dyadic relationship: two members of a band 'jamming', that is, not playing a fully pre-structured song. The guitarist plays a particular melody, which causes the drummer to play a particular beat, which in turn causes the guitarist to play a different melody and so on. 'Each member's playing is continually responsive to the others' and at the same time exerts its own modulatory force' (Clark, 1997a, p. 165). In these sorts of relations, the individuals in the group mutually influence each other. Importantly, due to this mutual influence we cannot identify one element as *the* causal element. While it is easy to understand the concept of a guitarist changing their melody and a drummer changing their beat, when thinking about the band, we cannot identify 'the' causal member. There is no band leader, as each member leads the other. Further, to properly explain the behaviour of the band, we need to understand that *both* guitarist and drummer are causally relevant. They are dyads, two elements, engaged in mutual reciprocal causation. Instead of physical elements like individual birds or fish, or a guitarist and drummer, the monads (the constitutive elements) of the whole being considered in this book are identity and information.

[35] A counter argument that may arise here is that if this dyadic relation between identity and information is so important, why has not such a relation been discussed before? The later chapters expand the argument that given the changes in how we produce, access, communicate and use information, the relation between identity and information is much more important now than it has been.

[36] The basic process is that as more foragers find food in a given sector, more pheromones are laid down, increasing the numbers of ants in that sector. As food runs out in the given sector, fewer ants go there, so there is less pheromone laid down, thus fewer ants (Deneubourg and Goss, 1989, pp. 300–301).

To summarise, the term 'dyadic relation' refers to two key points. First, that the elements in the relation are mutually causal. Second, that the understanding of the whole and the elements in that whole, requires recognition of the mutually causal relation. When I talk of the 'Identity/Information Dyad' it is exactly these two points that I wish to highlight. Identity and information play important causal roles in the formation, development and construction of each other. Further, if we are to understand identity development, information formation and how people live and understand the information-rich worlds offered in the age of surveillance, we benefit greatly by recognising this dyadic relation between identity and information. In the age of surveillance the recognition of this dyadic relation is becoming much more important due to the increasing role that information plays in our lives, the point first raised in Chapter 1.

6.6 EXPLICATING THE ELEMENTS OF THE IDENTITY/INFORMATION DYAD

Simply stating that there is a relation of mutual causation between identity and information does not tell us much about this relation, nor explain why it is morally important. This section introduces key types of identity and information that are central to the dyadic relation from previous discussions and §6.7 gives a detailed description of how these different types interact. Different people will be seeking to understand different things, so different forms of identity and different types of information will take precedence in different people's analysis, a point covered in §6.8.

If we encounter something in the world, a dog for example, we may be interested in this as a particular dog, or as a brown, hairy, mammal with two eyes, a snout, teeth and so on. Think of Michael playing with his pet dog Rupert and a veterinarian, Michelle, who has been asked to treat Rupert. For Michael, he is interested in the dog as a specific entity: Rupert. For Michelle, in order to treat the animal she may only be interested in what breed of dog it is, what size it is, what it has eaten and so on. The two observers are attending differently to the same thing.

Chapter 4 described identity as a relation of relative equivalence between two or more things.[37] Chapter 5 described data as difference.[38] Central to understanding and using the Identity/Information Dyad, we must first decide whether we are concerned with the relations of relative equivalence or relations of difference. In short, we must ascertain whether we are talking about identity or information. So, when encountering something in the world, an observer like Michael may be focusing on a given thing's relations of relative equivalence, or like Michelle, another observer may be focusing on a given thing's relations of difference. While both are concerned with a dog's health, Michael is attending to Rupert *as* Rupert, so

[37] §4.5.5. [38] §5.3.

Explanatory Priority	**Thing In The World**	**Thing As Perceived**	**Thing Perceiving**
Identity	Natural Identity	Phenomenological Identity	Observer Identity
Information	Thin Information	Semantic Information	Cognitive Network

FIGURE 6.1 Conceptual types in the Identity/Information Dyad

is focused on the dog's identity. Michelle is attending to Rupert as a patient, so is focused on information about Rupert.

This is not to say that Michael *only* experiences Rupert's identity and that Michelle *only* experiences the information about Rupert – both processes occur simultaneously. Rather, the point is that some observers will be more concerned with identity and others with information. This is what Clark refers to as 'explanatory priority' (Clark, 1997b, pp. 476–477), where one set of people is more interested in one set of analytic tools to explain something, while others will be more interested in another.

The two types of analysis can be further discussed at three different levels, the 'Thing In The World', the 'Thing As Perceived' and the 'Thing Perceiving'. The terms are set out in Figure 6.1 and the particular meanings used to describe the dyadic process follow.

Explanatory Priority

Explanatory Priority: 'Explanatory Priority' introduced above, is about what an observer is primarily concerned with. The two types of attention of interest here are identity and information. Depending on what is of interest – relative equivalence or difference – we have two ways of conceptualising what is being discussed, conceptualised here as identity or information, respectively.

Depending on what is being attended to, a person may be more interested in the relative equivalence of a thing with something else and the difference of the thing. When considering the 'Thing In The World' (see below), the subject of attention stands independent of whichever classification – relative equivalence or difference – is of concern. Following this, it is reasonable to say that The Thing In The World can be understood in reference to both identity and information. For instance, if an observer sees a dog, then the observer may attend to the fact that this is a dog, that is, the same as a 'dog type', or that this dog is Rupert who has a particular character. However, the observer may attend to the eyes, snout, fur colour and so on, that is, the qualitative differences within the dog itself, information about the dog. This goes to the different explanatory priorities of Michael and Michelle. Michael is focussed on Rupert because he is Rupert, whereas Michelle is focussed on Rupert because he has some abnormality that is making him unwell. The implications of having different explanatory priorities are discussed in §6.8.

Thing In The World

The Thing In The World is the subject of attention that exists independently of an observer: Rupert exists independently of whether Michael or Michelle are attending to him. His 'pre-observation state' can be conceptualised in reference to either identity or information.

Natural Identity: 'Natural Identity' refers to the conditions of Numeric and Character Identity, considered when independent of/prior to any observer/observation. Think here of a stone at the bottom of a cave, on a planet in some universe without life. The stone is never encountered by any agent with any capacity for observation (however described). This stone, however, has an identity: it is the same as itself and has a set of properties that mark it as unique to other stones. The basic claim here is that things have an identity independent of any observer. In the case of Rupert, he exists, independent of any observation. He is the same as himself and relevantly similar to other dogs: this is his Natural Identity.

Thin Information: 'Thin Information' is data and order, independent of/prior to an observer's ascriptions of meaning or truth. There is a particular set of data about Rupert, what he has done, what his physical states are and so on. This is Thin Information about Rupert.

Thing As Perceived

Rupert, however, is being understood here in reference to the perception of a cognitive agent.

Phenomenological Identity: 'Phenomenological Identity' is a cognitive agent's experience of the thing. Consider now that the thing is observed by a cognitive agent: Michael sees his dog. The Phenomenological Identity is the experience that the Michael has of his dog Rupert. It is different to the Natural Identity in that it is limited by and responsive to, the capacities and experiences of the cognitive agent.

Semantic Information: 'Semantic Information' is the thick concept of information as data, order, meaning and truth judgements. Michelle looks at the dog and gets information about Rupert's state of health, different from the information that Michael gets when he sees Rupert. It is different to Thin Information in that each observer is using their experience, their pre-existing Cognitive Networks, to assign meanings to the biological data about Rupert. For instance,

Michelle checks the incoming information against what she knows about biology, dogs and Rupert.

Thing Perceiving

In addition to understanding Rupert as the cognitive agent experiences him, we also need to understand that cognitive agent, the 'Thing Perceiving'.

Observer Identity: The 'Observer Identity' refers to the set of relevant qualities that we use to talk about the cognitive agent who is doing the observing. This is the 'X' of 'identity is who X perceives Y to be', §4.6.4. Michael's unique relationship with Rupert is one relevant element of Michael's Observer Identity. Michelle's interest in assessing Rupert is one relevant element of a different person's Observer Identity.

Cognitive Network: 'Cognitive Network' refers to the complex information connections underpinned by neurological and mental networks that the cognitive agent uses in their perception. This goes to both perception, §4.4 and knowledge, §5.6. The Cognitive Networks would be neurological processes such as those involved in Michael's compassion towards Rupert and Michelle's assessment of Rupert's health.

6.7 THE IDENTITY/INFORMATION DYAD: HOW ONE SHAPES THE OTHER

To describe the Identity/Information Dyad in action, consider a cognitive agent with some background knowledge about the world. They have a set of perceptual capacities allowing them to observe the world and to reflect upon those observations. They have the capacity to discriminate between different things in the world and they have semantic content to fit to the things that they're observing. As this description of the identity and information interaction develops, the background mental states, earlier described as Cognitive Networks, §4.4.2 and §5.6, become particularly relevant.

Consider a Thing In The World and an observer, a common human adult. The Thing In The World is a dog and the observer is Michael. For simplicity, the discussion focusses on a single sense modality, visual experience.[39] The dog is a Thing In The World as described in §6.6: it has a Natural Identity and a set of Thin Information. Assuming that Michael has a Cognitive Network such that he can discriminate different things in the world, Michael observes this thing and comes to believe that he is looking at a dog. How?

[39] As the discussion of auditory and taste modalities from Chapter 4 show, these processes should hold equally for sight, sound, taste, smell and touch. Further, a full Phenomenological Identity will likely emerge as a combination of multiple sense modalities, as stated in §5.8.

First, Michael accesses visual data (Sterelny, 1990, pp. 62–80). Following Jerry Fodor, this data is some basic cognitively impermeable representation[40] of the world: that is, a shape, colours and fine detail. Michael constructs a representation of the dog from the Thin Information. This involves recognition of the particular ordering of the data relations – fur here, eyes here, colours here, overall shape and so on. As the relations between different visual data are established, an 'infon'[41] emerges as relevantly equivalent to (a) itself, (b) a general dog concept and (c) Rupert. This is important for two reasons. Michael is now having a 'meaningful experience' of the dog: he has made a connection between this particular experience and the general concept of 'dog' and his knowledge that this set of data correlates with his idea of Rupert. Second, presuming that Michael has no reason to distrust his senses, he now has connected semantic content to the data; the dog is now experienced as *Semantic* Information.

Michael now has Semantic Information and is experiencing an identity of the dog, in particular, Rupert. That is, Michael is making a relation of relative equivalence between the shape in front of him and his knowledge of what Rupert looks like. Following the general description of identity as 'X perceives Y to be Z', §4.6.4, '*Michael* perceives *The Thing In The World* to be *Rupert*'. Michael's experience is not just Semantic Information; The Thing As Perceived is now experienced as a particular Phenomenological Identity, Rupert. The information from the visual experience that Michael is having is coupled with Michael's Cognitive Network to produce a Phenomenological Identity for what Michael is experiencing visually. As §5.8 and §6.3 argued, Semantic Information forms the foundation for an emergent Phenomenological Identity.

The next step concerns the integration of this new experience into Michael's Cognitive Network. This information 'there is a dog' is related to Michael in that he is now thinking that 'I am experiencing that there is a dog'.[42] The identity of this particular dog is integrated into Michael's Cognitive Network. For instance, if this Thing In The World looked the same as Rupert, but Rupert had died a year before, Michael would either reject the idea that he was seeing Rupert, or would question whether Rupert was actually dead. In short, the Phenomenological Identity of the dog informs and changes Michael's Cognitive Network.

[40] Or as Jerry Fodor puts it, at this stage of perception, the data is informationally encapsulated (Fodor, 1983, pp. 64–86).

[41] Recall from §5.8.1 that an infon is the term used by Floridi to refer to a 'discrete item of information' (Floridi, 2011a, p. 83).

[42] This is perhaps similar to a Kantian approach to self-knowledge, in which we have two types of mutually dependent types of self-knowledge, 'inner sense' and 'pure apperception', discussed by Richard Moran and expanded by Matthew Boyle (Boyle, 2009; Moran, 2001). While this view is controversial, it is beyond the scope of the book to discuss it further. What is important is the division between what we actively judge about our senses, the 'pure apperception' and the knowledge of our sensations, the 'inner sense'. This view is complementary to the model of cognition presented in §4.5 and the truth assessments made about data, from §5.6.

The integration of the Phenomenological Identity into Michael's Cognitive Network produces a new information set (Michael's new Cognitive Network). As argued in §6.3, this impacts on who Michael is: if Michael is seeing Rupert, but Rupert had died a year before, he will either have to change his mind about what he is seeing, change his mind about Rupert being dead or perhaps change his mind about the capacity of dogs to have ghosts. When a person's Cognitive Networks change, we would say that the Observer Identity has changed. While most of these changes are likely to be imperceptible and/or trivial, some types of information are extremely important to a person's identity. For instance, Michael seeing a dog that looks like his dead pet may invoke some memory of that pet. Consider now that rather than Rupert being a dog, he is a loved human who Michael thought had died. This Phenomenological Identity would likely produce strong emotions in Michael and if he confronted this person and found out that it *is* the loved one Rupert and he had faked his own death, it seems fair to say that this would produce major changes in Michael's personality. His Observer Identity would change as the result of the integration of new Semantic Information into his Cognitive Networks.[43]

Given that the changes in Michael's Cognitive Network have changed Michael's identity, Michael's capacity as an observer has also changed. Michael will now experience the world differently. Importantly, as argued in §6.4.1, who the observer is changes what information is attended to and what concepts are used as part of developing Semantic Information for new experiences.

To summarise – incoming Thin Information coupled with existing information (in the form of the agent's existing Cognitive Network) forms the basis of the construction of Semantic Information, experienced as Phenomenological Identities of things observed, which in turn change the observer's Cognitive Network, which change the Observer Identity, which change how the observer understands new and existing information.

§6.3 and §6.4 showed that identity and information impact each other. Change the identity and you fundamentally change the information, in terms of the Thin Information that is picked up, but also in terms of the Semantic Information and the observer's Cognitive Network. Change the information and you fundamentally change the identity; not only the Phenomenological Identity but also the Observer Identity.

As presented here, this is a highly simplified *model* of actual perception and cognition.[44] This model suggests a set of cognitive events separated through time. While new brain imaging technologies like fMRIs seem to indicate temporal

[43] The larger point about particular types of information having a major impact on identity is discussed in Chapter 7.

[44] However, this model is informed by discussions from the natural sciences, as evidenced in this chapter by §6.4 and the discussions of the roles of cognition, perception and experience in identity, §4.3 and 4.4.

differences between different mental events, in practice, we don't experience this temporal spacing between these different events.[45] Likewise, we are typically not going to recognise shifts from Semantic Information to Phenomenological Identity and the integration of this information into our Cognitive Networks. Further, this is a simplification of the brain itself. 'A typical brain contains 100 billion neurons, each of which makes electrical connections, or synapses, with up to 10,000 other neurons . . . about the number of people on 150,000 Earths' (Carlato, 2008). The brain is an amazingly complex organ and as we learn more about it, we are beginning to realise how complex it actually is and how complex its processes are.

The basic aim is to show how identity and information interact, by modelling how the Identity/Information Dyad applies to cognitive processes. The key steps involve the observer encountering The Thing In The World, the conversion of data into Semantic Information, the emergence of a Phenomenological Identity for The Thing In The World, the integration of this experienced identity into the observer's Cognitive Network and the resulting changes to the Observer Identity arising from the changes in the observer's Cognitive Networks.

6.8 DYADIC RELATIONS, PERSONAL INFORMATION AND SURVEILLANCE

The purpose of this chapter has been to illustrate the dyadic relation between identity and information. Though quite technical the key point is that identity and information stand in this relation of mutual causation. Insofar as we are to understand the ways that information impacts our lives, we need to see that information impacts identity. Yet, in order to do this, we need to see that identity impacts information.

Thin Information can arise from a whole set of sources – it might be information arising from the actions of a loved one, a pet, a car or a tree falling in the woods. And on the Identity/Information Dyad account so presented, any such information has the potential to impact identity of the observer. However, it would be odd to say that the Thin Information about one's self or a loved one is equivalent to Thin Information about a tree falling in the woods. Moreover, it is a banal truth that certain sorts of information are likely to be more important to people than others. Bearing those points in mind, one particular set of information that is sure to have a particular salience for the Identity/Information Dyad is Personal Information. That is, information that relates to people has a particular salience for the Identity/Information Dyad.

[45] This point about neurological actions occurring before we are aware of them is commonly discussed and often given some relevance to philosophic discussions, such as arguments about moral psychology (Haidt, 2001; Kennett and Fine, 2009).

Surveillance, insofar as we're considering it in relation to people, is therefore of critical importance to the Identity/Information Dyad – surveillance generally impacts the Identity/Information Dyad as its purpose is the production of Personal Information, information about people. And insofar as we are concerned with identity, then we ought to be especially concerned about Personal Information that surveillance produces, more so than other sorts of information. The Identity/Information Dyad thus presents a particularly useful explanatory tool to see how surveillance impacts our world and given the moral importance of identity, the Identity/Information Dyad further offers a way of morally assessing that surveillance.

6.9 CCTV OPERATORS REVISITED: EXPLANATORY PRIORITY

§6.3 proposed that information causes identity. This can be explained as the result of explanatory priority going to the informational elements of the Identity/Information Dyad: if it is information that is the explanatory priority, then the analysis will focus on the role of Thin Information, the Semantic Information and/or the Cognitive Network. §6.4 proposed that identity causes information. This can be explained by a focus on the identity elements of the Identity/Information Dyad: if it is identity that is the explanatory priority, then the analysis will focus on the role of Natural Identity, Phenomenological Identity and/or the Observer Identity.

We need to recognise that identity and information play important mutually causal roles in the development of the other. For instance, it is hard to properly explain Semantic Information without recognising the role that the Observer Identity plays in forming the Semantic Information. It is hard to properly explain how information is integrated into a person's Cognitive Network without recognising the role that Phenomenological Identity plays in informational integration. Likewise, it is hard to talk about Phenomenological Identity without recognising the role that Semantic Information plays in producing the particular identity. And it is hard to talk sensibly about Observer Identity without reference to the informational processes of the agent's Cognitive Network.

§6.2 began with a description of different responses to CCTV footage. The discussion was framed by reference to identity which led to a tension between the causal roles of identity and information. The question was asked, 'does information determine identity, or does identity determine information?' The answer was both: each plays an important role in the other. We can now see why such an answer is sensible. For those whose explanatory priority is identity, identity plays the important causal role in their analysis of the psychology of the CCTV operators. The Identity/Information Dyad can explain the different responses.

Consider that two CCTV operators have a different set of experiences in that one operator, Mark, places a high value on efforts to protect strangers. Another CCTV operator, Fiona, places a high value on risk minimisation; she is particularly risk averse. In this sense, the Thing Perceiving differs as Mark and Fiona have different Observer Identities. However, both Mark and Fiona are confronted with the same Thing In The World: they both have access to the same CCTV footage, a fact about whether a particular person is at risk or not. In the case of Mark, the Semantic Information is informed by his Observer Identity: he wants to be active in the world, to change it in a positive way. If he is observing a potentially risky event on CCTV, he is inspired to act, to change the world for the better and so sees this as an opportunity to reinforce that he has that capacity to change the world. The information about the world integrates with his Cognitive Network to confirm an established Self-Regarding Identity as a force for good. In the case of Fiona, the Semantic Information is informed by her Observer Identity: she is highly risk averse. If she is observing a potentially risky event on CCTV, she is reminded that the world is dangerous, so sees this as an event that reinforces that she lives in a dangerous place. The information about the world integrates with her Cognitive Network to confirm an established Self-Regarding Identity that she ought to avoid risk and danger. Both Mark and Fiona see the same events on the CCTV and both may superficially respond in the same way. But their experience of it is different and insofar as we are thinking of the information as thick and meaningful, they see the world differently.

While overly simplified, there are three related points to be drawn from this. First, changing explanatory priority will change which element is seen as most important in analysis of the observer's behaviour. If the focus is identity, then identity becomes the chief causal factor in determining how people react to information. If the focus is information, then information becomes the chief causal factor in determining how people's identity develops.

Second, analysis that is strictly reduced to either identity or information loses usefulness. Brey writes that description of differentiated constructivism can 'specifically point to the relative contributions of artifacts, social representations and other structures and processes' (Brey, 2005). The utility of recognising the dual roles of artefacts and social constructivism is that such a model can offer a detailed explanation of the causal importance of each element, without collapsing one into the other or being so general as to lose sight of the relations. Likewise the model offered here, the Identity/Information Dyad, shows that both elements contribute causally to the development of the other. Such a model offers a tool for analysis that recognises the role of each element, without reducing one element to the other, but without sacrificing the explanatory power that each element offers.

Third, this model points to the importance of recognising the relations between identity and information. The upshot of recognising the Identity/Information Dyad is that we can now see that if by substantially changing one element, the other element may substantially change. This is why the question 'is online life good or bad for you?' is both easy and hard to answer. It is easy if one element of the Identity/Information Dyad has explanatory priority. But it is hard if you attempt to find the start of that circle, because each element impacts and is impacted by the other. The identity of a person posting things to Instagram is as important as the information put online and each changes the other. The Identity/Information Dyad is a tool that can explicate how these changes come about and what it means if you substantially change one of the elements. Chapter 7 explores this in detail by focussing on changes to information. In particular, one type of information – Personal Information – and the moral importance of changes to Personal Information.

PART III

Ethical Importance of Information

7

On Importance

7.1 SURVEILLANCE TECHNOLOGIES AND MORAL IMPORTANCE: PERSONALISING INFORMATION

This book's fundamental point is that the age of surveillance is morally important because of the relations between identity and Personal Information. Surveillance technologies afford particular epistemic actions – they enable information to be linked to people. This happens in two ways: where a person is the source of the information and where a person is the target of information. With the addition of a semantic element provided by people such as CCTV operators, surveillance technologies produce meaningful information about people. In short, surveillance technologies are about personalising information. Surveillance technologies allow identity relations to be created and recognised between people in the world and an informational representation of a person, the Virtual Identity. These identity relations are constructed through aggregation of information.

Information is aggregated to make that information practically useful. This aggregation not only changes the usefulness of that information; it also changes the moral importance of that information. Chapter 4 introduced the concept of a Virtual Identity – by aggregating disparate sets of information that relate to people in the world, Virtual Identities emerge. As Chapter 5 showed, by aggregating information sets together, new information emerges. And, as Chapter 6 has argued, given the Identity/Information Dyad, aggregation of information to produce a Virtual Identity not only changes the information's practical use, but makes it morally important.

This chapter begins with an analysis of metadata to illuminate the deeper moral issue about aggregation of information and starts to resolve the motivating problem of this book – why should we care about the information that surveillance technologies produce about us? On its own, much of that information is useless and innocuous. Put it together and it's useful, but it is now of a different moral reactivity.

These functional and moral changes can be explained by reference to identity. That is, the aggregated information is now about identity – it is personalised information. Metadata demonstrates this point exceptionally well – by and large, very few people care about what time an email is sent, or what time a phone call is made. Such a single data point is as innocuous as it comes. But bring those data points together, add them with other information and you've got something new and this new information is of great moral importance.

This chapter's aim is to make clear why we are morally required to give moral weight to Personal Information, that is, to give reasons *why* we should treat innocuous Personal Information as important. This claim follows Chapter 6 in stating that identity and information are mutually causal. Clearly a range of things still need to be argued for this claim. First, what information is problematic here? As presented in Chapter 5 and discussed in Chapter 6, information is data that is ordered, meaningful and judged to be true. Information that meets these conditions alone does not necessarily have any impact on identity. The key factor that relates identity to information is that the information be *about* a person, in some way or another: the explanatory focus is Personal Information. Following the discussion of metadata, §7.3 talks about the need to set limits on what counts in identity and §7.4 and §7.5 give us clarity about what information is relevant. §7.6 brings the discussion back to metadata. The book's final chapters close out the discussion with a detailed ethical analysis of the age of surveillance.

7.2 PERSONAL INFORMATION IN PIECES: THE BENIGN AND POWERFUL ROLE OF METADATA

Prior to the release of information by Edward Snowden, discussions of metadata were largely the province of technical specialists and the odd academic. However, with the public recognition that state agencies were using this metadata as a key plank of their surveillance programmes, a wider public discussion about metadata, its use and usefulness evolved (Branch, Daley and Henschke, 2015; Henschke, 2014; Henschke, 2015c, e). Unfortunately, much of that public discussion has been confused and obscured as people are unclear about just what metadata is and why we should care about it.

At its most basic, 'metadata' is information about other information. Luciano Floridi says metadata is descriptions of the nature of the primary data, 'such as location, format ... availability ... and so forth' (Floridi, 2011b). If you send an email, the primary information is what's in the email *itself*: the *content* of the message. Metadata, in contrast, is information *about* the email: who sent the email, who they sent it to, what time and where from. For a phone call, it's not what you talk about, but who you're talking to, what time you called them, how long the call goes on for.

As public discussion of metadata has continued, there has been a rise in confusion about what metadata is[1] and what its moral status is. Debates about metadata are confused in large part because public discussions often portrayed metadata as something normal and familiar, *totally benign*, whilst simultaneously being *powerful* and fundamental to the future of law enforcement and national security. More than mere inconsistency, these multiple characterisations of metadata are internally contradictory – we are told that we needn't worry about the state use of metadata, while at the same time being told that metadata is absolutely necessary for our individual and national security. Take, for example, a former Australian Prime Minister's comments about why the government was seeking mandatory retention of metadata:

> We're talking here about metadata . . . It's just the data that the system generates . . . To use an old fashioned metaphor if you like, if you look at a letter, you've got the address, you've got the sender, you've got the date stamp, where it was posted and what time it was posted. [Metadata is] the electronic version of what is on the front of the letter that we want to keep. The contents of the letter, well people can only get access to that with a warrant.
>
> (Abbott, 2015)

On this, metadata is benign, the same as information that you'd find on a letter. Something so normal and familiar that its use doesn't bother us in the slightest. Like the reductionist arguments introduced in Chapter 1, metadata is presented as morally innocuous. However, the Prime Minister's 'old fashioned metaphor' was preceded by this: '[i]f we want to combat crime, we need this legislation and if we don't get it, it will be a form of unilateral disarmament in the face of criminals and the price of that is very, very high indeed' (Abbott, 2015). Now metadata is a powerful weapon, absolutely essential in the fight against crime. Metadata is so powerful that without it we'll be disarming ourselves, leaving ourselves vulnerable to criminal attack. In this description, metadata is vitally useful because of its power. Chapter 5 explained how such contradictions arise by showing that information is emergent and multirealisable. What's confusing is that in public representations like that just described, metadata is presented as something *both* benign and powerful, nothing to worry about and a powerful weapon.

Such contradictions go to the rhetorical motivations of the speaker. They want the audience to be both nonplussed by the retention and use of metadata as well as deeply concerned about not having it. It is practically the same as an ordinary envelope but without it we're weaponless in the face of implacable enemies. In short, we should accept the changes because they're both benign and powerful. Robert Sparrow describes these as rhetorical contradictions: new technologies are often sold as both familiar and revolutionary, both benign and powerful. We needn't worry about new technologies because they're just doing the same thing as

[1] For example, while seeking to have new legislation passed about metadata retention, the Australian Attorney General, George Brandis, could not actually say what metadata was (Dingle, 2014).

technologies we're familiar with, while at the same time being awed by their revolutionary capacity (Sparrow, 2007). Likewise, metadata is both familiar and revolutionary, simultaneously benign and powerful.

Having detailed what information is and how new information emerges from the old, we are now in a better position to understand the mechanisms that underpin claims displaying these rhetorical contradictions. Further, with the conceptual tools of multirealisability and explanatory priorities, we can point to specific descriptive explanations to detail how the rhetorical contradictions arise. Multirealisability tells us how information changes. The force of the rhetorical contradictions can be dissolved by pointing out the shifts in the explanatory priorities. The descriptions of metadata move between a narrow descriptive account, information on a letter, to a broad use-based account, a tool against cyber-criminals. Depending on the explanatory priority, metadata is both benign and powerful.

That said, what's left is the moral element – why should we *care* about these changes to information? The answer is simple – the Identity/Information Dyad. Metadata is both practically useful and morally important because it is used to construct Virtual Identities. It is, quite simply, used as the building blocks for highly detailed Personal Information. And, given the relations between identity and information, these Virtual Identities that emerge from detailed Personal Information are morally important. However, for the Identity/Information Dyad to be a useful tool, we must have some instruction as to its use. Part II of this book has been a detailed analysis of the relations between identity and Personal Information to tell us why we ought to care about things like metadata. However, it is not enough to say that identity and information are morally important. We need to set limits on what counts in identity and we need clarity about what information is relevant.

7.3 SETTING LIMITS ON IDENTITY

Before entering into the discussions of wrongs, harms and fairness arising from the production and use of Virtual Identities, there is a potential problem with locating the source of moral importance of Virtual Identities in Personal Information. As I have constructed it in Chapter 4, identity is to be considered in terms of cognitive processes – thoughts about thoughts. The problem here is that this seems to allow identity to become a practically useless term. Christine Korsgaard says

> [T]here is no *you* prior to your choices and actions because your identity is in a quite literal way *constituted* by your choices and actions . . . When you deliberately decide what sorts of effects you will bring into the world, you are also deliberately deciding what sort of cause you will be. And that means you are deciding who you are.
>
> (Emphases Original, Korsgaard, 2009, p. 19)

Conceptualising identity as 'I am who I perceive myself to be' (§4.6) invites a concern stemming from self-constitution, namely, where does this self end? This discussion of the end of the self is essential for the conceptual and moral analysis to have any practical use because we need to set limits on identity.

7.3.1 *Where Does the Self End?*

When considering identity as a cognitive process, a person's boundaries cease to be simply physical. If what counts as a person is not simply their physical limits, then other things should be included in the self. This of course raises the question of where to draw the line on what counts as being part of a person? We can build from §1.5 that the answer of where to draw a line on a person is by reference to reasons including, but not limited to, basic respect, harms and equality.

What is important in identity are not just the bare facts about a person, but how they identify with them. On Harry Frankfurt's account, a person's identity develops through how the person *endorses* facts and attributes about their self:

> Becoming responsible for one's character is not essentially a matter of *producing that character but of taking responsibility for it.* This happens when a person selectively identifies with certain of his own attitudes or dispositions . . . In identifying with them, he incorporates them into himself and makes them his own.
>
> (Emphases Original, Frankfurt, 2006, p. 7)

When she talks about 'practical identity', Korsgaard says that we constitute ourselves through our endorsed actions (Korsgaard, 2009, pp. 41–44). §4.3 suggested a set of cognitive processes[2] that bring Self-Regarding Identity about: thoughts about thoughts building from prior experience.

Taking identity to be the result of cognitive processes means that identity is not set by a person's physical boundaries. This may seem counter-intuitive; the 'bodily frontier' of a person seems to be a reasonable and objective boundary of a person's identity (Glover, 1988, p. 82). However, there are examples that challenge the idea of the physical boundary of a person being the necessary boundary of their identity. Consider the 'rubber hand illusion'. Experimental subjects who 'view stimulation of a rubber hand while feeling congruent stimulation of their own hand . . . may come to feel that the rubber hand is part of their own body' (Costantini and Haggard, 2007, p. 229). The experimental subjects identify with an external

[2] By focusing on the cognitive processes of endorsement and self-recognition, this brings the focus of discussion closer to Character Identity than Numeric Identity. I recognise here that I am building assumptions about Numeric Identity into the general discussion of identity – where the primary ethical concern is not whether persistence through time is biological or psychological, but what matters is survival of a stable identity through time. This should chime with those sympathetic to Parfit's approach, that what matters in questions of Numeric Identity is survival (Parfit, 1971a, 1987, pp. 260–266).

element, the rubber hand, so much so that they can actually feel physical pain when viewing a pin stabbing the rubber hand. Strong identification with external objects can result in the person having an experience of physical suffering: the cognitive process account explains why a person's identity can extend *beyond* their physical boundaries.

Similarly, a person's identity can contract *within* their physical boundaries. Consider Body Identity Integrity Disorder (BIID), a condition where an individual feels that a particular physical part of their body, like an arm or a leg, does not belong to them. 'People suffering from body integrity identity disorder report that a particular limb does not belong to them and that they feel "over complete"' (Muller, 2009, p. 36). This lack of identification with the limb is so strong that a number of people have attempted to self-amputate the particular limb without medical support (Bayne and Levy, 2005). While there are a number of candidate reasons for BIID, one study (First, 2005) proposed that BIID (or many forms of it at least) was a dysfunction of anatomical identity, arising from an inability to identify the given body part as 'self'. While BIID likely has a neurological basis (Muller, 2009, pp. 38–39), the relevance is that forms of BIID support a cognitive process approach to identity. 'BIID stems from a mismatch between the agent's body and their experience of their body, what we might call their *subjective body*' (Emphasis Original, Levy, 2007, p. 3). In cases like BIID, the cognitive processes can override the physical boundaries that are normally associated with the body. The rubber hand illusion and BIID challenge the claim to limit identity to physical boundaries, suggesting that Self-Regarding Identity is not limited to the bodily frontier.

The cognitive process approach also makes discussions of Group Identity (§4.5.3) meaningful. The basic idea of Group Identity is that ethnic groups, cultural groups, nations, particular personal relationships, even sporting teams are legitimate elements of a person's identity. Constructing an identity through identification with a parochial sporting team may be irrational, but it is surely hard to deny that individuals who identify strongly with particular sports teams develop a strong sense of self as a result of this identification. The point is that identity is not limited to physical boundaries. So too, cognitive processes can effectively explain how conceptual things, like groups, are legitimate aspects of a Self-Regarding Identity.

The relevance is that if something like a weak ethical parity principle[3] is employed between one's body and the things one identifies with, absurd conclusions can result. Take John Stuart Mill's view that '[o]ver himself, over his own body

[3] I mean here to refer to Levy's weak ethical parity principle which 'asks us to examine the (rational) reasons we find some interventions into or alterations of the (narrowly construed) mind ethically impermissible or problematic. If we can find that these reasons apply equally strongly to actual or possible interventions into the environmental scaffolding that supports the mind, then we ought to hold that internal and external interventions are (*ceteris paribus*) equally problematic ... Unless we can identify *ethically relevant* differences between internal and external interventions and alterations, we ought to treat them on a par' (Emphasis Original, Levy, 2007, p. 62).

and mind, the individual is sovereign' (Mill, 1971, p. 135). If Jenny identifies with something, the cognitive process approach considers that thing is part of her identity, is morally equivalent to her body. So what happens if Jenny really strongly identifies with Dan's wallet? What if she identifies more strongly with it than Dan? Does Jenny now have a stronger claim to the wallet than Dan? Likewise, it may seem legitimate for Jenny to claim special privileges or treatment due to her identification with a particular cultural group. But what if that group advocates something morally reprehensible like genocide? The cognitive process approach seems to allow for a range of absurdities. We need some way of limiting what is included in a person's identity.

Ethical reasons can limit identity claims. That is, if a person is making a moral claim that Y *should* be considered part of their identity, they need to offer some sound justifications for *why* Y should be considered part of their identity. Three factors need to be considered: how strongly does the given thing figure in their Self-Regarding Identity? How will the person be harmed by not having this thing recognised as part of their Self-Regarding Identity? Finally, how does recognition of the person's Self-Regarding Identity impact on other people? These questions are answered in Chapters 8 (§8.5) and 9 (§9.3).

7.3.2 *Setting Reasonable Limits on Identity*

In anticipation of the following chapters, they connect this discussion about the need to set *reasonable* limits on identity with the core moral values of autonomy/liberty, utility/efficiency and equality/justice. In order for such discussions to be distinctive, there are two explanatory priorities – when people are the source of Personal Information and when people are the target. Chapter 8 focuses on 'Person As Source' to see if an individual has legitimate claims against others using Personal Information. In keeping with this individual focus, rights expressed as claims feature heavily in the language that is used. To maintain the focus on the Person As Source, 'wrongs' is used to indicate when some individual's legitimate rights claim has been overlooked or violated. However, in line with the discussion of methodology, §1.5, this is not to say that this section is necessarily deontological in its foundation – a sophisticated consequentialist theory can include rights either as part of its theory or as part of a pluralistic conception of the good. Moreover, in line with a threshold deontology, there may be situations where a source person is wronged by the production and use of Personal Information, but this production and use is justified. Rather than rights as trumps, the rights claims presented should be understood as *pro tanto* claims that can be overridden. However, overriding these claims requires justification. In order for the discussion to be reason-giving and justificatory, each type of claim will explain how the identity/information dyad figures in such claims.

Chapter 9 then focusses on moral issues arising when the explanatory focus is the 'Person As Target'. It identifies moral issues that arise when a given set of

Personal Information targets an individual or group. Like Chapter 8, it adopts a particular terminology to keep the attention focussed on the Person As Target: this chapter is concerned with informational harms. This is roughly consequentialist in approach, in that it focuses attention on the harms that arise as some consequence of the use of a particular set of Personal Information. While the explanatory focus here is given in rough consequentialist terms, this should not be understood as inimical to deontological interests. First, the harms described in terms of consequences are likely to overlap with many of the rights concerns described in Chapter 8: a person might be both the source of and the target of Personal Information. Second, the moral foundation for the harm might be deontological – if Steve suffers because of Φ, a deontologist can say that Φing is wrong, not (just) because it causes Steve pain, but because causing pain is a violation of a duty to respect him. The concerns described in this section are relevant to deontologists as much as consequentialists.

A third set of moral concerns derives from Virtual Identities and distribution. This concern can be understood in relation to access to resources, how Personal Information itself is distributed and how the harms and benefits arising from Personal Information are distributed. Chapter 9 closes out by adding existing discussions of equality and justice by explicating the roles that Virtual Identity play in differential treatment of people.

7.4 WHAT IS PERSONAL INFORMATION?

In order to make the discussion of the moral importance of Personal Information in the age of surveillance useful, we need clarity on what is meant by Personal Information. Personal Information is information that relates to a person or group of people[4] in some way. The 'relation to a person' can be considered from two different explanatory[5] priorities. The first explanatory priority considers the relation when a person is the source of information. The second explanatory priority considers the relation when a person is the target of information. I call these 'Person As Source' and 'Person As Target', respectively.

7.4.1 *When A Person Is the Data Source*

§6.6 presented a list of different elements in the identity/information dyad. One of these elements was the Thing In The World – something that exists independently

[4] For ease of use, I will simply refer to a single person unless otherwise stated. However, all that is said about an individual person here is applicable to groups of people.

[5] This a reference to a general form of explanatory priority, from §6.6, as discussed by Clarke (Clark, 1997b, p. 477), where one set of people are more interested in one set of analytic tools to explain something, while others will be more interested in another. This is different to the particular Explanatory Priorities of identity and information introduced in Figure 6.1.

of a cognitive agent's experience of it. In 'Person As Source', the Thing In The World is a person. Their Natural Identity provides the initial Thin Information to the observer. From this Thin Information, Semantic Information is formed and experienced by an observer as a Phenomenological Identity.[6]

To illustrate what is meant by Person As Source, think of Ben, the subject of a surveillance programme. Ben is under round the clock surveillance: his movements, who he talks to, what he says and what they say to him are observed and recorded by those watching him. Ben is the *source* of the Thin Information that is then processed as part of an epistemic group action aimed at producing knowledge about what he's doing. If Ben were not under surveillance, then that Thin Information would not have been produced. In this sense the data is *source dependent*.

Source dependency can be understood as strong or weak. For *strong* source dependency, consider that without Ben the particular Semantic Information would not exist. Ben plays a central role in a criminal organisation and by following him, those watching him learn that a large drug deal is going to occur at the docks on the following night at 10pm. The information is strongly source dependent; if Ben were not under surveillance, the breakthrough in this case would not have been made. If the Semantic Information is unique, the source dependency is strong and the links between the Person As Source and the Semantic Information are stronger.[7]

In *weak* source dependency, a person is the source of Thin Information, but the Semantic Information produced has been or could have been equally formed from another source. Think now of Barry, who is also part of a surveillance programme: a massive international effort using advanced technologies that gathers information on hundreds of millions of people. Barry is one of many millions of people under surveillance and if he wasn't producing the relevant data, the programme could continue without him. It is an example of *weak* source dependency as the Semantic Information is still dependent upon Barry but only very weakly.[8]

Both sorts of source-dependent information have moral importance but they are of different kinds. Given the direct connections to the individual source person, strongly source-dependent information is of particular concern to issues of privacy and property. Chapters 2 and 3 both established the notion of a rule of thumb where – insofar as we're concerned about privacy or property claims – the person who is most connected to the Personal Information has a particular moral

6 §7.4.2, gives a description of the process of relating information to a target person.

7 This grants the source person a stronger *pro tanto* claim to the Semantic Information produced from the Thin Information. *Pro tanto* is used to signify that a person has a legitimate claim, but one that can be justifiably overridden.

8 Differences between strong and weak source dependency are a matter of degree. That is, Semantic Information can be more or less dependent upon the source, with no clear boundary between strong and weakly source-dependent information. This raises issues of vagueness, which I cannot discuss in depth here. For a discussion on vagueness problems in philosophy see (Sorensen, 2009). Simply, the more source-dependent, the more there is a *prima facie* moral concern about that information.

importance. In the case of weakly dependent source information, it might seem that it has negligible moral value. However, the information produced from Barry as the source is of a different type of importance to the strongly source-dependent Semantic Information produced in a situation like Ben's. In Barry's case, there are privacy and property claims, but these are derived from group claims following aggregation of the information. This point is returned to in Chapter 9.

7.4.2 *When a Person Is the Target of Information*

In 'Person As Target', instead of explaining why we should be concerned about Personal Information based on the *source* of the Thin Information, we are now looking at situations where an observer has Semantic Information that *targets* a person or group of people.[9] Recalling the different elements of the Identity/Information Dyad, §6.6, target means that an observer has some Semantic Information in mind, which they *relate*[10] to a person or group in the world.[11] The Semantic Information has a target of intentional thought and the targets I am interested in here are people.

This focus on people[12] is similar to how the European Union regulations on data protection define personal data. They stipulate personal data to be:

> any information relating to an identified or identifiable natural person hereinafter referred to as 'data subject'; an identifiable person is one who can be identified, directly or indirectly, in particular by reference to an identification number or to one or more factors specific to his or her physical, physiological, mental, economic, cultural or social identity.
>
> (Article 2(a) European Data Protection Supervisor, 2001)

Like the EU focus, the explanatory priority is given to situations where Semantic Information is used *to identify* a natural person, some human who has been, is, or will be in the world. Person As Target makes the focus of interest in ethical analysis the object of a mental process involving Semantic Information. Referring back to the Observer Identity from §6.6, Person As Target also considers how Personal

9 As with the rest of the book, for ease of reading, unless otherwise stated, reference will be made to a single person. However, all that is said about an individual person here is applicable to groups of people.

10 This can be an active or passive mental process. For the current discussion, it does not matter whether the observer is actively relating Semantic Information to a target person or if the relation comes about through some sub-personal neurological processes.

11 In philosophy of mind terms, a person or group of people is an intentional object, 'in so far as it is an object for some thinker or some subject' (Crane, 2001, p. 342).

12 The term 'natural person' is taken from the European Union regulation on Data Protection. It is understood to differentiate human people who have been, are or will be in the world, as opposed to legal persons like corporations. This differentiation, I suggest, is an important point when considering things like ownership claims, as a real person is substantially different from a legal person such as a corporation. I discuss the relevance of this distinction more in §7.5.2.

Information changes the observer using the Semantic Information: Semantic Information provides the basis for some change in the observer's Cognitive Networks. This should enter into ethical analysis when the observer acts in morally objectionable ways towards the Target Person as a result of some use of the Personal Information.[13]

To illustrate this, let us expand on an example introduced in §4.7, where Jane is looking at a biography, *The Identity of Elvis Presley*, about the deceased[14] pop star Elvis Presley. The book has a photo of him on the cover that will likely give her some visual experience of Elvis Presley: the book's cover, a Thing In The World, provides an ordered data set that will likely produce in Jane the experience of seeing a photo of someone, a Phenomenological Identity. Presuming that Jane's Cognitive Network is such that she knows about Elvis, including an idea of what he looked like, this photo is Personal Information. Further, it involves a Person As Target in that the Thin Information causes[15] her to think of a particular person in the world, Elvis. Likewise, each time she reads the name 'Elvis', Jane has some mental processes involving Elvis as the target. In this sense, written information calls to Jane's mind a particular person.[16] A set of ordered data brings about some set of mental processes in which Jane thinks about a person in the world – Elvis is the Person As Target.

Consider now that Jane is reading in the book that Elvis was addicted to prescription drugs. The coupling of the identifier, 'Elvis', with some character description like addiction to drugs introduces new Personal Information about Elvis to Jane. However, in this second case, the information does more than identify the person, it characterises him.[17] The coupling of Thin Information such as the photo on the book's cover, Elvis' name, descriptions of his character and so on, are involved in a set of mental processes that have him as a target.

As Jane continues to read her book, she reads that Elvis first met Lisa-Marie Presley when she was fourteen and he was twenty-four. The book's author implies that Elvis had sex with the fourteen-year-old girl.[18] Confronted with this, Jane thinks

[13] In Chapters 4 and 6, I described ways in which identity and behaviour are shaped by information.

[14] I recognise that Elvis is dead, so is no longer in the world. However, that should not change the purposes of this description.

[15] I realise here that saying something of the form 'X causes mental process Y' is fraught with problems. However, it is beyond the scope of this book to discuss issues of mental causation. For an overview of these issues see (Robb and Heil, 2009).

[16] I note here that the use of the name 'Elvis' produces a Phenomenological Identity of a form that mostly relates to Numeric Identity concepts. However, Jane's Phenomenological Identity relates character attributes to the target. As such, the identity concepts I discuss in these paragraphs deliberately shift from Numeric Identity concepts to Character Identity concepts. These were discussed in more detail in §4.5 and elsewhere (Henschke, 2010).

[17] Like the discussion from §4.6.2, this sort of Thin Information relates to Other-Regarding Identity.

[18] I don't want to imply here that Elvis did have sex with Lisa-Marie when she was fourteen. Rather, I use this example to show how people can use facts to make conclusions about people that can then lead to particular behaviours. The book's implication and Jane's reaction arise

'I didn't know that. I tell you – if I had've met him then, I would've smacked him in the face.' In this example, the description of Elvis' relations with Lisa-Marie produces some change of attitude in Jane, targeted towards Elvis.[19] Elvis is now the target of identification, characterisation and a particular characterisation that Jane feels morally warrants some particular response. The book identifies Elvis, a person in the world. With the addition of more Thin Information, he becomes the target for some particular set of actions. As Jane integrates these descriptions, a thicker Phenomenological Identity of Elvis emerges in her mind. Importantly for this section, Elvis, a person, is the target of Semantic Information. Further, Jane's experiences are responses to a highly structured and convention-dependent set of Thin Information – a book about a person.

The target can also be narrow or broad. For instance, the book about Elvis is focused on one individual – Elvis. As such, we can say that the book has a *narrow* target.[20] Consider in contrast a news article that says that one in ten people in English-speaking countries have a copy of *The Identity of Elvis Presley*. In this example, the Thin Information is Personal Information about a group of people. This target is very broad: it refers to the whole population of a country. The more focused on a particular person or people, the narrower the target information is and the more people captured by a given data set, the broader the target information is. Like the strong and weakly source-dependent information discussed above, narrow and broadly targeted information vary by degree. And like the strong and weak source dependency, the narrow/broad variation can produce different moral problems.[21]

7.5 PERSONAL INFORMATION AND VIRTUAL IDENTITY

Revisiting the concept of Virtual Identity, §4.9, we begin to see how the identity/information dyad can be used to assess the role that technology plays in impacting our lives. Virtual Identity refers to a particular type of Thin Information, which affords experiencing ordered data as Personal Information, information that relates to a person or group of people in some way. Virtual Identity refers to a set of ordered data and, given social conventions and the Cognitive Networks of the observer, that observer is likely to experience the ordered data as an Other-Regarding Identity. In the book about Elvis, he was the subject of the book, a source person.[22] When Jane

from the use of incomplete information, discussed in §5.6.1, with potentially harmful results had Jane met Elvis when he was alive. I discuss the moral problems that can arise from incomplete information and harms in §9.3.3.

19 Note how this is an example of how Semantic Information can lead to changes in Observer Identity, as discussed in Chapter 6.

20 That said, given that it also discusses his wife and others, it is not totally focused to one person. However, the focus is very narrow.

21 These are covered in §7.6.

22 I recognise here that the author is also a source of the data and so ought to be described as a source person. To keep the discussion narrow, I have focused only on Elvis. §7.5.2 covers the

sees the cover photo, she thinks of Elvis. Upon reading about him, she ascribes particular character traits to Elvis and changes her attitude towards him. These changes are the result of her exposure to a Virtual Identity. Given that the Virtual Identity is based on a single person, it is strongly source dependent.[23] Likewise, given that the Virtual Identity is focused on a particular person, it is narrowly targeted Personal Information.

Depending on explanatory priority, we may be concerned with the source of the Virtual Identity, or its targets. In some cases, the source and target refer to the same person or people in the world, while in others the source and targets may be different. The question arises – so what? The following chapters point to a set of justificatory reasons as to how Virtual Identities bear upon people in such a way as to be relevant to concerns of autonomy/liberty, utility/efficiency and/or equality/justice. In short, they set out the foundational elements for a justificatory explanation of how Virtual Identities can impact on how people see themselves and others, by making explicit the moral importance of these impacts. Underpinning all of these claims is the identity/information dyad, as explicated in Chapter 6.

7.6 METADATA REVISITED: THE MORAL IMPORTANCE OF VIRTUAL IDENTITIES

This chapter was motivated by confusion arising from our treatment of metadata, in particular, the contradictions about its moral importance and whether it is benign or powerful. However, such contradictions should no longer be puzzling. Having engaged in analyses of identity, information and their relations, we are now in a better place to understand how such contractions can arise. Taking information as the explanatory priority and reducing information to a narrowly described set of Thin Information, metadata is indeed morally benign. Stating that metadata is something familiar, like a name and address on an envelope, is descriptively accurate, but this is a form of incomplete information.[24] The reason is that those seeking to access, produce and use metadata are not telling the whole story. The metadata is not being left as Thin Information. It was collected with the intent to aggregate it with other metadata. It is added to other information, it is analysed and it is spread beyond the initial point of acquisition. As we can now see, metadata is sought after because such information is potentially meaningful and multirealisable. And, insofar as we're concerned with metadata that is part of surveillance practices,

point that in many cases simply referring to a single person as *the* source of a Virtual Identity is misleading. Further, multiple sources create complications when considering how we ought to treat particular Virtual Identities. The issues arising from this are covered in §7.5.2 and §7.5.3.

[23] Had Elvis lived a different life, the content of the book would be different. However, if the data set was drawn from thousands of people around the world, then the Virtual Identity is weakly source dependent.

[24] See §5.6.1 for the discussion on incomplete information.

the usefulness, the power and moral importance can be explained by reference to metadata's capacity to produce Virtual Identities. The underlying reason why governments, companies and individuals are interested in metadata is that it can produce highly revealing and powerful Personal Information.

The deeper point here is not that metadata is necessarily good or bad, nor that we should outright reject or simply accept its retention and use. Nor is it even to find fault with politicians and others for having rhetorical contradictions in their language. Rather, as Sparrow argues with new technologies, '[a]n increased awareness of these rhetorical contradictions may allow us to better assess the likely impact and future of … technology' (Sparrow, 2007, p. 57). The Identity/Information Dyad, with its exposition of the construction of Virtual Identities, is a vital step in outlining the mechanisms that underpin the importance of Personal Information in the age of surveillance. This chapter has also mapped out the moral foundations necessary for a full assessment of the impacts and future of surveillance technologies. Chapters 8 and 9 build directly from those foundations, adding fine-grained detail into the analyses of the basic rights claims, consequences and issues of access and distribution in the age of surveillance. What we need to do is identify the specific points of moral relevance – let us move onto Chapters 8 and 9.

8

On Individuals

8.1 INDIVIDUALS AS WILLING INFORMATIONAL AGENTS

One of the biggest challenges for ethics in an age of surveillance is that people are, by-and-large, willing informational agents – we either consent to our information being used by others and institutions, or we actively offer that Personal Information up to the world ourselves. And this seems to make any concerns about personal rights moot. If I willingly and actively give $100 to someone else, I can hardly complain when it's gone. Likewise, basic common sense says that if I keep my PIN next to my credit card and I give my wallet away, it is my fault if $100 is taken from my bank account. So too, the reasoning would suggest that in the age of surveillance if I willingly and actively put my Personal Information 'out there', I hardly have a moral basis to claim that others shouldn't use it. In fact, to hold others to account would patronisingly deny me agency. So, on a cursory analysis, insofar as we can be implicated as a willing and active source in the production of Personal Information, then we cannot make claims about privacy or property violations.

The Identity/Information Dyad can now be used to challenge that line of reasoning, showing that even if an individual is an 'active' source of information, it does not necessarily follow that they give up certain rights claims with regard to that information. This chapter returns to one of the book's core themes, that we ought to treat innocuous information with due moral care. Having provided the theory for information's multirealisability in Chapter 5, Chapter 7 showed how rhetorical contradictions can arise depending on the explanatory focus given to information. The Identity/Information Dyad provides us with the justificatory apparatus for why we ought to see Personal Information in its aggregated form as a Virtual Identity, rather than as isolated data points. However, in order for the explanation to be properly explanatory, this chapter focuses on the individual to present three justificatory reasons why we should care about Personal Information.

Three sorts of individual rights claims are presented such that a Person As Source can legitimately advance in regards to Personal Information: privacy claims, ownership claims and basic respect claims. The individual takes explanatory priority; Person As Source is focused on, to see if they have legitimate claims against others using Personal Information. In keeping with this individualistic focus, rights expressed as claims feature heavily in the language that is used here. To maintain the focus on the Person As Source, 'wrongs' is used to indicate when some individual's legitimate rights claim has been overlooked or violated.[1] However, in line with the discussion of methodology, §1.5, this is not to say that this section is necessarily deontological in its foundation – a sophisticated consequentialist theory can include rights either as part of its theory, or as part of a pluralistic conception of the good.[2] Further, in line with a threshold deontology,[3] there will be situations where a source person is wronged by the production and use of Personal Information, but this production and use is justified. Rather than rights as trumps, the rights claims presented should be understood as *pro tanto*[4] claims that can be overridden. However, as is discussed throughout, overriding these claims requires justification.

[1] Parallel to this, in Chapter 9 'moral harms' is used to identify when a Person As Target suffers as a result of some use of Personal Information that relates to them. Talk of moral wrongs coming from rights claims and moral harms coming from suffering, is meant simply as a rough taxonomic guide such that attention is given to Person As Source and Person As Target, respectively. I do not mean to take any stronger philosophic position about wrongs and harms than that.

[2] Philip Pettit is one such example (Pettit, 1988). Such theories can do so by presenting a pluralistic conception of the good that extends beyond the welfarism of utilitarianism. For instance, a 'pluralistic theory of the good – one that acknowledges other factors besides well-being having a role in determining the goodness of outcomes . . . Such a theory will admittedly no longer be *utilitarian*, but it will still be consequentialist' (Emphasis Original, Kagan, 1998a, p. 62).

[3] To repeat from §1.5, a sophisticated deontological theory will be concerned with consequences. 'Deontological theories are defined as non-teleological ones, not as views that characterize the rightness of institutions and acts independently from their consequences. All ethical doctrines worth our attention take consequences into account in judging rightness. One which did not would simply be irrational, crazy' (Rawls, 1971, 30). In some situations if a threshold is breached, large goods/harms can justifiably take precedence over individual rights. But one would have to offer some justificatory explanation for the threshold's location and why it is overridden in the specific case.

[4] By *pro tanto* here, I mean to show that in some situations, we may override a claim, given sufficient justification. Like William (W. D.) Ross' *prima facie* duties, 'almost all moralists except Kant are agreed . . . it is sometimes right to tell a lie or to break a promise . . . [When we do] we do not for a moment cease to recognise a *prima facie* duty to keep our promise . . . we recognise, further, that it is our duty to make up somehow to the promisee for the breaking of the promise' (Ross, 1930, p. 28). Ross' point is important in that even if we do override the claim, we owe the claimant some recompense. Following Shelly Kagan, *pro tanto* is used instead of *prima facie*, where a *pro tanto* reason has genuine weight but can be overridden, while a *prima facie* reason only *appears* to have genuine weight (Kagan, 1989, p. 17).

8.2 PERSONAL INFORMATION FOR ALL: THE CASE OF WEARABLE HEALTH TECHNOLOGIES

Consider jogging: a series of surveillance technologies and related websites exist[5] enabling people to collect, store and share Personal Information about their jogging habits. The site www.endomondo.com offers this description of their services:

> Bring your mobile or Garmin device whenever you run, walk, bike or do any other outdoor sport across a distance. While you are out there, your route is automatically tracked together with your distance, end time, average speed, split time, calories burned, and more. If you use a GPS phone, you will be informed about your speed for each kilometer or mile and your effort is tracked in real time sparing you for synchronizing with your computer manually … Users can choose to create a profile on Endomondo.com, which will then host their personal training diary and enable them to challenge their friends … Live tracking also enables your personal fans to follow you live and to send you pep talk messages that will be read out loud to you while you exercise. Users can integrate their Endomondo profile with Twitter and Facebook to auto-post their activities.
>
> (Endomondo.com 2012)

§6 of the Endomondo Terms And Conditions state:

> You allow Endomondo to anonymise your personal data and then copy, process, use, public display and distribute such anonymised data. *Such anonymised data is, when anonymised, no longer considered "personal data".*
>
> You give your explicit consent that Endomondo may transfer and make public the content, including personal data, you automatically upload to the Site by using the Endomondo services, unless you restrict such data processing by changing your privacy settings on the Site. *Hence, your data will by default be published and made publicly available on the internet from any country in the world upon upload.* Notwithstanding the above your e-mail, password to the Site and phone number will not be made public unless you decide to do so.
>
> (Emphases Mine, Endomondo, 2011)

This technology presents a paradigm example of the way in which convergent technologies afford the production, collection, aggregation, analysis and distribution of Personal Information. Recalling Chapter 3, surveillance technologies produce Thick Information about things and people. Also, these surveillance technologies are actively designed with the capacity to share this Personal Information. The Endomondo website is a prime example of this: a series of different technologies, converging through their capacity to produce, integrate, communicate and store information.

Importantly and in line with the discussion in §1.4, much of this data seems inert in a moral sense. The production, aggregation and communication of data about someone's running practices seems totally innocuous: beyond a limited set of

[5] For instance, runkeeper.com, dailymile.com, endomondo.com.

scenarios,[6] someone intentionally uploading jogging information seems to be of little moral concern as it presents little in the way of either problems for rights, harms or discrimination.[7] When viewed independently, in isolation from other information and prior to integration with other information, jogging information seems 'morally insignificant'.[8] However, such data is not morally inert.

The reasons underpinning this claim should be a little clearer now: First, jogging information is not simply data. When data is ordered and coupled with meanings and judged to be true, it becomes information and information can be revealing and powerful. Given the multirealisability[9] of information, even jogging information has the potential for (at least) three situations of moral concern. First, when integrated with other information, it can be highly revealing of a given individual or group. Second, when integrated with other information, it can cause suffering in individuals or groups. Third, it can lead to unequal treatment of people. On all accounts, we have incidents which are of serious moral concern: potential rights violations, morally significant harms and unjust discrimination.[10] This chapter focuses on the first set of concerns, explaining the potential rights violations as underpinned by the Identity/Information Dyad. Harms and discrimination are the focus of Chapter 9.

8.3 PRIVACY CLAIMS

The explanatory focus here rests on privacy claims,[11] and shows what role the Identity/Information Dyad can play in appealing to them. Recall that Chapter 2

6 This information about someone's jogging patterns can present some serious risks. For instance, given its public nature, it can potentially be abused by a stalker to track and locate their victim. However, the moral concern about this sort of example is relatively easy to point to and I won't discuss the example further here.

7 Recalling §1.5, the three foundations for common morality for this book are autonomy/liberty, utility/efficiency and equality/justice.

8 Recall §1.4 and Jonathan Glover and Derek Parfit's arguments about assessing the moral weight of certain things. Glover presented an 'argument from insignificant difference', in which if each individual action or event is morally innocuous, then it would seem to follow that the assessment of the actor or the action as a whole is also morally innocuous. An individual transgression of autonomy is so innocuous that it doesn't deserve to be included in moral calculations. Or, looking at consequences, the difference that each individual consequence makes is insignificant, so the total consequences must also be insignificant. As pointed out in §1.4.1, both Glover and Parfit take issue with these conclusions (Glover, 1986; Parfit, 1987).

9 §5.9.

10 While Thin Information may be morally problematic for a number of reasons, the focus here is on moral problems that arise when considering a special type of Semantic Information, Personal Information. I recognise that there are other information types and uses that are morally concerning. For instance, the dangers arising from the publication of potentially dangerous scientific research (Miller and Selgelid, 2006). However, the focus of this book is on a particular set of moral concerns that arise from production and use of personal data.

11 Rather than argue for the moral importance of privacy, in this subsection I show that if one already holds that privacy (or something like it – data protection, e.g.) is a good justificatory reason to do or not do something, treating like-cases alike, one ought to care about how Personal Information is produced, distributed and used.

argued that accounts like maximising social good, §2.5.1, context relative informational norms, §2.5.2 and data protection, §2.5.3 would be extended by explicating what was wrong with innocuous information. The Identity/Information Dyad adds to discussion of privacy in two ways. First, the dyad explains why innocuous Personal Information is a relevant focus of a privacy claim. Second, the dyad gives some rough quantifier about how much weight we should give to the source person's claims.

On the issue of innocuous Personal Information, recall the jogger: a person willingly posts information about themselves to a publicly accessible website. For the sake of argument, let us say that these posts in-and-of-themselves are morally innocuous. That is, given that the jogger willingly and actively posts their jogging data themselves and that the individual posts are extremely unlikely to bring any harm to the source, a privacy claim about this information seems to be on very weak footing.

Surveillance technologies actively seek to produce information by aggregating personal data. Aggregated data about a person produces a Virtual Identity, new information.[12] When the individual posts are brought together they can reveal a great deal about the jogger: following aggregation and analysis, a Virtual Identity can be produced that reveals the source's weight, age, gender, physical location and general health. Given a deeper analysis,[13] the Virtual Identity can reveal things like the jogger's buying habits – how often they buy running shoes, their personal relationships with others – who accesses their profile and who the jogger engages with online regularly. Further, the data could be used to make predictions[14] about the jogger's cognitive decline and emotional states. What were innocuous data become intimately personal. As more of a person is revealed by aggregating and analysing Personal Information, a rich and complex Virtual Identity emerges. As a general rule of thumb, the more revealing the Virtual Identity is of the source person, the greater the chances of that information being central to the person's Self-Regarding Identity, so more care needs to be taken in aggregating, protecting and distributing that information.[15] This general rule of thumb holds that as the amount of intimate Personal Information revealed by the Virtual Identity increases, other things being equal, there ought to be a parallel increase in the importance of the source person's privacy claim. For instance, most people would treat a revealing

[12] These arguments are found in §4.7 and §5.8.

[13] Stephen Baker discusses a host of different forms of data analysis that reveal a great deal of Personal Information about someone (Baker, 2007).

[14] §1.2 and §2.2 gave examples of predicting cognitive decline from walking patterns and predicting emotional states from keystroke patterns, respectively. The idea here is that *if* patterns of repeated physical activity can predict cognitive decline and emotional states, then the jogging data would also be able to reveal the jogger's decline and emotions. I say *if* because such predictive analysis needs to be properly verified. However, a privacy claim would still seem to hold if someone is trying to find these things out, even if their conclusions are wrong.

[15] This point is further elaborated in Chapter 9.

nude photo of a person as warranting a greater privacy claim than a photo of the person's left index finger.

By establishing the dyadic relation between identity and information, we now have a tool that explains how such innocuous personal data can be quite revealing. Sophisticated data analysis can produce a Virtual Identity that reveals much more than simple jogging information; this new information is revealing and intimate. Despite willingly posting their jogging data, it remains to be seen if the jogger has consented to a creation of *this* new information. In line with privacy being about some controls or limited access to intimate information, the privacy claim is now much more substantive. The dyad captures the weight of this claim by explaining why we should view personal data in aggregate.

Second, Self-Regarding Identity is concerned with who a person perceives themselves to be. A series of accounts[16] propose that those things that are strongly identified with are central to one's Self-Regarding identity. The basic position here is that the more central a given property is to a person, the more careful others should be with that. This is borne out by a Rawlsian idea that we ought to recognise other citizens as 'self-authenticating sources of valid claims' (Rawls, 2001, p. 23).[17] The basic point brought out by Rawls is not simply that we form a moral identity through conscious recognition of core projects, values and relations, but that recognition of this moral identity is a necessary element of a good democratic society. It follows that in a good democratic society, other things being equal,[18] the more central a given thing is to a person, the more that it ought to be treated with care.

Think of a person who attaches importance to a set of love letters they wrote to an old flame. These love letters have gained some intrinsic value[19] by virtue of the fact that the author identifies so strongly with the love letters. All other things being equal, if we hold that a person's interests or preferences are important, then we ought to treat those love letters with more care than a note that person wrote to

[16] As raised in Chapter 4, some of the people who have covered the importance of self-identification to identity are Harry Frankfurt (Frankfurt, 1988), Bernard Williams (Williams, 1981a), Christine Korsgaard (Korsgaard, 1996, 2009), Jonathan Glover (Glover, 1988) and Samuel Scheffler (Scheffler, 1993).

[17] While Rawls may seem like an odd point of authority, consider that he says that a person 'may regard it as simply unthinkable to view themselves apart from certain religious, philosophical and moral convictions, or from certain enduring attachments and loyalties' (Rawls, 2001, p. 22). For many different philosophers, the centrality of traits to a person is a fundamental aspect of how we ought to treat them. Obviously, I consider that Personal Information is important to add to this discussion.

[18] This 'other things being equal' proviso is important. In Chapter 10 a substantial claim is made that strong identification with a given trait needs to be understood in reference to the justificatory claims for why that trait is strongly identified with and how acting on such a claim interacts with other people.

[19] On this point, insofar as we see that things can have intrinsic value, I follow Kagan that certain things can gain intrinsic value by virtue of the way that people relate to them (Kagan, 1998b).

themselves as a reminder that the car registration has been paid. The reason is that though the letters and note are both source data, the love letters would typically figure more centrally to the person's Self-Regarding Identity than the note about car registration. As such, like the love letters, we ought to treat Personal Information with care and the more important that information is to the person, the more care others should take when accessing and using that information.

Aggregation, analysis and use of Personal Information require an increase in the justification needed to override the privacy claim. The justification for this basic rule of thumb is explained by the Identity/Information Dyad: as information aggregation increases, so too will the breadth and depth of the Virtual Identity and so too there is an increase in the Personal Information revealed. The Virtual Identity affords a richer Semantic Identity, producing a more detailed Phenomenological Identity for observers of the source data.

So, if one already holds that privacy is, or points to, something of moral value, then one ought also to hold that aggregated source data can produce legitimate privacy claims. Increasing the amount revealed and increasing the importance of the given Personal Information, there is an increase in the need to justify others' use of this information. However, as this is a *pro tanto* claim, it can be overridden, as covered in Chapters 9 and 10.

8.4 OWNERSHIP CLAIMS

This section focuses on individual claims to ownership over Personal Information.[20] Recall from §3.3 that there are three commonly held legitimating reasons for recognising an individual's claims to ownership: Lockean rights claims founded in labour investment, §3.3.3, Hegelian rights claims founded in psychological individuation, §3.3.4 and the overall good §3.3.5.[21] The labour investment was the weakest justification as we cannot properly identify how a person 'mixes their labour' with things, §3.3.3. Instead, §3.3.4 showed that Hegel's location of ownership claims in psychological individuation presented the strongest foundation for a rights claim. Also, recall from §3.5 and §3.6 that individual ownership claims are *pro tanto* and can be outweighed by other interests.

§3.6 and §7.3 said that the Personal Information which is in most need of ethical oversight are those sets of information about a person or people which have the most impact on how a person feels about themselves and/or is most strongly identified

[20] Like §8.3 this subsection does not argue directly for the moral importance of ownership. Rather, it shows that if one holds that individuals do have legitimate ownership claims, then one ought also to recognise that a source person has some legitimate claim of ownership over Personal Information.

[21] Recall that §3.6 showed that such social good foundations must take into account the harms that arise from the ownership and use of Personal Information. These harms are returned to in §9.3.

with that person or people. In order to justify claims of ownership over Personal Information we must seek to identify who will be most affected by that information and who is most strongly identified with that information. The more revealing a Virtual Identity is of a person, the stronger the source dependency and the more important that the revealed Personal Information is to that source. Relating this back to Hegel, other things being equal, the source person is the most affected and the most strongly identified by Personal Information. So it follows that Virtual Identities formed from aggregated information give the source person stronger claims of ownership over the information the more it relates to them.

Similarly, a non-source individual's claim to ownership over Personal Information will be less than that of the source person. This is especially important for corporate ownership claims. As Peter Drahos and John Braithwaite note with intellectual property, the original creator is often not the owner of the patent or copyright (Drahos and Braithwaite, 2002, pp. 48, 166, 176). Often, patents on human information like genes or databases of Personal Information will not be owned by an individual, but by a 'corporate person' – a legal but not a moral entity. Given that a source person *is actually a person*, while a corporation is a fiction brought about by legal convention, on Hegelian accounts, the Person As Source has a far stronger ownership claim over information that relates to them than a corporation. As a result, we either recognise that the source person has a legitimate claim of ownership that outweighs non-source claims, or we refute any moral claims about a natural right of ownership and instead must go by some other justification such as ownership of that given set of information increases the overall good and has no significant bad consequences[22] arising from production, analysis, use or distribution.

As with the privacy discussion above, a general rule of thumb is that as source dependency increases and as the amount revealed by Virtual Identity increases, so too should the source person's claims of ownership. Further, recalling that given either Hegelian or social good foundation, individual ownership claims are *pro tanto* claims, with suitable justifications, they can be overridden.[23]

In line with the privacy claims, as source dependency increases and as the amount revealed increases, so too should the weight of reasons needed to override the ownership claims increase. For instance, consider a jogger's uploaded information. This is strongly source-dependent data and when aggregated and analysed, it produces a revealing Virtual Identity. Consider a non-source person who produced that Virtual Identity in order to make money out of selling the source person's profile to a medical insurance company. Compare this creator with a different non-source person who wants access to the jogger's information as part of a research programme aimed at developing a response to an outbreak of a highly infectious

[22] Harms are discussed in §9.3.

[23] While this is expressed here as a Hegelian justification, as per the discussion of §3.3, for those still committed to a Lockean labour investment type of approach, the same claim holds.

virus,[24] in which accessing the personal data is an extremely important factor in tracing the epidemiology of the breakout, needed to bring about a rapid response to a developing pandemic. A common sense morality[25] and our discussion of the moral foundations of property claims in Hegelian individuation and promotion of the social good suggest that one individual's desire to make money is of lesser moral importance than reducing the risks of a killer pandemic outbreak.

As presented, the creators of Virtual Identities need to be included in ownership claims. So far, attention has been on the Person As Source. However, given the discussion of Chapters 3 and 5, surveillance technologies rely on humans to provide the semantic layer to information as information is not simply random data but ordered data, afforded particular meanings. Surveillance necessarily involves people. Virtual Identities may be created directly through the collection and arrangement of the data, indirectly through the programming and development of the technologies that collect and arrange the data, through support of those producing the Virtual Identities or some combination of these. The people necessary to the creation of the Virtual Identity also have some claim to that Virtual Identity. For instance, imagine a person in a photo and the photographer. The person in the photo is the source of the data, but the Virtual Identity is similarly dependent upon the photographer to create that given image. Likewise, on Hegelian reasoning, a medical researcher who collects and aggregates and analyses data surely has some legitimate 'creator's claim' to that Virtual Identity. Similarly, a person who designs a set of programs that harvest and aggregate data from the internet has also helped create the Virtual Identities. How do we balance competing ownership claims between the Person As Source and the Person As Creator?

Like source claims, a creator's claims are *pro tanto* claims, in that the claims are limited and can be overridden. Bearing this in mind, the Identity/Information Dyad shows that Personal Information is important to the source person. And if the creator is grounding their claims within a Hegelian system, as shown in Chapter 3, then any claim the creator makes must also take into account the source person and any wrongs or harms that might arise from their creation and use of Virtual Identity. Thus, a creator's rights need to factor in all the moral concerns discussed in this chapter.

Further, an epistemic action necessarily has some intended goal.[26] Chapter 10 holds that the telos of epistemic actions provides a principled way of assessing the moral importance of different pursuits. And, as mentioned, a common-sense morality would hold that some set of epistemic group actions intended at saving millions of

[24] A recent example would be the creation of a form of highly infectious, highly lethal bird flu. (Kwek, 2011; Garrett, 2012). At some points, it was feared this could result in the deaths of up to 3 billion people worldwide, though these mortality figures were later seen to be problematic (Evans, 2012).

[25] §1.5 described a common morality as one that recognises the importance of plural values. A common-sense morality would then take these plural values into account when assessing a given problem. This decision procedure features in §10.2.

[26] Epistemic actions were introduced in §6.3 and I have discussed this point in more detail elsewhere (Henschke, 2012).

lives would outweigh an individual source person's claim. Likewise, such an epistemic action which saves millions of lives would outweigh an individual creator's claim. On the weight of things, the artistic goals of a photographer or the desire to make money are of less importance than saving millions of people's lives, so the artist or businessperson's claims are less than that of the medical researchers. Further, given the limits of ownership claims, the creator must make significant efforts to respect the privacy of any source people, must go to lengths to gain informed consent from the source people[27] *and* there ought to be no significant harms that arise from public release of such a photo or its trade to another group, discussed in chapter 9.

Finally, extending from Hegel, the ownership claims are not wholly transitive: that is, if the creator sells the Virtual Identity onwards to a third party, that third party has an even more limited set of ownership claims than the creator. A creator, given that they have attended to the source and target people, might be permitted to sell the Virtual Identity on to a third party. However, that third party is constrained in what they can do with that Personal Information. Chapter 10 raises the point that the third party is justified in using the Personal Information for a given set of purposes and should the third party intend to use the Personal Information in a different way, they need to justify this new use. All other things being equal, the third party would need to take into account any source and target people, as well as the creator's interests.

Like the privacy discussion, the point is not to repeat arguments for ownership as a foundation for moral claims. Rather, the point is to appeal to those who either believe that property is a morally valuable thing and/or those who seek to locate their own use of and access to Personal Information in individualised property claims. Building from this, if one thinks that property is something of moral value, particularly when considering it in an individualised rights form, then, given the Identity/Information Dyad, one ought to also think that Personal Information is something of moral value. The greater the source dependency and the greater the amount revealed by a Virtual Identity, the stronger the claims of the source person and stronger the justification must be to override the source claims. The claims made about a source person gain legitimacy through the explanation offered by the Identity/Information Dyad: it makes clear how and why Personal Information figures in a property claim.

8.5 BASIC RECOGNITION CLAIMS

The explanatory focus here rests on basic recognition claims.[28] Simply stated, we ought to treat Personal Information with care, because of the information's importance to the source person. For this claim to be viewed as reasonable, three points

[27] The justifications for this point about informed consent are located in the basic recognition claim, presented in §8.5.

[28] Rather than argue for the moral basis of recognition, in this subsection, I show that if one sees recognition as a good justificatory reason to do or not do something, then one ought to care about how Personal Information is produced, distributed and used. It is beyond this book to argue the general claim of why people ought to receive respect, specifically recognition respect.

must be made. First, that people deserve recognition respect. Second, that recognition and Personal Information have some relevant relation. Finally, that Personal Information should and can, be treated differentially. As with privacy and ownership, basic recognition claims correspond to a *pro tanto* right, in that they can be overridden but when doing so there must be some justificatory reason. Importantly, even if there is some justificatory reason to override the recognition claim, the claim holder is still deserving of some substantive respect: as we will see, it is this basic recognition that underpins the persistence of the claim holder's interests in the face of other overriding claims.

The first point, that people deserve recognition respect, builds from a distinction proposed by Stephen Darwall (Darwall, 1977). Darwall argues that respect ought to be considered as two forms of attitude: recognition and appraisal. Recognition respect is something that all people deserve in virtue of the fact that they are people, while appraisal respect is something that a person deserves in virtue of the fact that some trait deserves to be appraised as good.[29]

> To say that persons as such are entitled to [recognition] respect is to say that *they are entitled to have other persons take seriously and weigh appropriately the fact that they are persons in deliberating about what to do* ... The crucial point is that to conceive of all persons as entitled to respect is to have some conception of what sort of consideration the fact of being a person requires ... Unlike recognition respect, [appraisal respect's] exclusive objects are persons or features which are held to manifest their excellence as persons or as engaged in some specific pursuit ... Such [appraisal] respect, then, consists in an attitude of positive appraisal of that person either as a person or as engaged in some particular pursuit.
>
> (Emphasis Mine, Darwall, 1977, p. 38)

A claim about recognition respect is common to the individualist strands of human rights dialogue, where '[i]n their typical expression, rights are attractive because they express the great moral significance of every individual human being' (Campbell, 2006, p. 3).

The connection between recognition respect and Personal Information is as follows. First, the way that an individual constructs a Self-Regarding Identity is influenced by Other-Regarding and Other/Other-Regarding Identity: how an individual sees themselves is influenced by how others see them and how they imagine others seeing them.[30] '[M]y discovering my own identity doesn't mean that I work it out in isolation, but that I negotiate it through dialogue, partly overt, partly internal with others ... My own identity crucially depends on my dialogical relations with

I assume the position that people are important in virtue of being people and as such we generally hold recognition to be morally important. The purpose of this subsection is to show how information figures in such a claim.

[29] Appraisal respect and its moral relevance to Personal Information are covered later in §8.5.

[30] This point was made in §4.6 and through Chapter 6.

others' (Taylor, 1994a, p. 34). Darwall writes that '[o]thers may or may not respond appropriately to the presented self. *To fail to take seriously the person as the presented self* in one's responses to the person is to fail to give the person recognition respect *as that presented self* or in that role' (Emphases Mine, Darwall, 1977, p. 38). Darwall's claims about a presented self align with a source person and Virtual Identity; a Virtual Identity is one way a person presents themselves and one way that others can form their perception of the person. Following Darwall, key to responding appropriately to a person is to take presentations of their Virtual Identity *seriously* and to *weigh them appropriately*.

What does 'weigh appropriately' consist in? This brings us to the third point, that Personal Information ought to be treated differentially. Following the thread of this chapter, the basic rule of thumb is that the more important a given trait is to a person's Self-Regarding Identity, the more it ought to weigh in our considerations. Consider that a person, Malcolm, can be identified with both trait X and trait Y. Malcolm strongly identifies as a member of ethnic group X*, which typically correlates with the trait, skin colour X.[31] Trait X is central to Malcolm's identity, for him it is one of the prime information sets through which he forms his Self-Regarding Identity. In contrast, Y is Malcolm's job; he is a labourer.[32] However, differently to trait X, as Malcolm does not care about his job, Y bears very little importance to his Self-Regarding Identity.

In Malcolm's case, recognition respect would have us weigh X and Y differently.[33] We ought to weigh that X is central to Malcolm's identity when acting in some way that involves trait X, whereas we need not consider trait Y as carefully. One way that trait X is more important to Malcolm than trait Y is that X cannot be changed, while Y is variable: it is no accident that stable traits like race, ethnicity and gender are central to the discussion in Charles Taylor's influential essay *The Politics of Recognition* (Taylor, 1994a); race, ethnicity and gender are often central to a person's self-understanding and figure heavily in discussions of recognition.

> One of the most important determinants in this differential importance or value is the nature of the decision and subsequent action in question . . . Other things being equal, the more central and far reaching the impact of a particular decision on an individual's life, the more substantial a person's self determination interest in making it.
>
> (Buchanan et al., 2000, p. 216)

31 The point here is that skin colour and ethnicity are correlations; variability in skin pigmentation does not 'cause' a person to be a specific ethnicity. For more on this see (Haslanger, 2000; Ossorio, 2006; Smedley and Smedley, 2005; Stevens, 2003).

32 The job of labourer was chosen deliberately. For some people, labouring may be some mere means to an end, a way to get paid. However, for others, labouring is a valuable job worthy of respect, as evidenced by the 'working class' and 'labour movements'. The point is that a variable trait like one's job can be valued differently by different people.

33 Note that this also tracks to the basic intuition of treating like-cases alike and reasonably treating unlike-cases differently, raised in §1.5.

Likewise, other things being equal, the more central and far reaching the trait is to a person's Self-Regarding Identity, the more substantial their self determination interest in that trait and the greater corresponding care that ought to be shown to treatment of that trait.[34]

However, presenting the importance of identity by reference to the strength of self-identification risks making a mistake that there is some 'authentic self' to be discovered.[35] This sort of thinking holds that '[t]here is a certain way of being human that is *my* way. I am called upon to live my life my life in this way and not in imitation of anyone else's life ... Being true to myself means being true to my own originality, which is something only I can articulate and discover' (Emphasis Original, Taylor, 1994a, pp. 30, 31). As Taylor subsequently notes (Taylor, 1994a, pp. 32–33), such a view of an 'authentic self' is a misnomer, as our identities are not fully formed awaiting discovery, but developed in dialogue with others.[36]

Further, an uncritical commitment to certain traits can lead to practical and moral concerns. If we are to take people *seriously*, as Darwall's account of recognition respect has it, then I suggest we need to do more than simply identify a person's central traits: we should also be able to critically reflect on those traits and what they mean for the individual and others.[37] To explain this point, contrast Malcolm with Michael and Martin. Central to Michael's Self-Regarding Identity is trait V, that he is a vampire and central to Martin's Self-Regarding Identity is trait VR, that he is a violent rapist. Here, trait V is factually unfounded while trait VR is morally repugnant. Assuming that Malcolm, Michael and Martin all consider X, V and VR as equally important, does recognition require us to treat X, V and VR equally? Taking people seriously means we attend not only to the strength of their identification with X, V or VR, but also attend to the reasons they have for identifying with the given trait and such identification with that trait impacts on others.[38] The justificatory reasons for such self-identification matter.

[34] This also corresponds to Griffin's account of Human Rights, particularly the roles played by autonomy and liberty in personal development (Griffin, 2008, pp. 142–179).

[35] Recall also the discussion of Chapter 7, about where the self ends.

[36] Taylor's account pays special attention to the dialogic nature of self-development (Taylor, 1994a, p. 31). In a similar vein, Dean Cocking and Jeanette Kennett offer a mutually dialogic account of self-development which they call the 'drawing view of friendship' (Cocking and Kennett, 1998).

[37] As James Sterba notes, when considering how to deal with conflict cases between self-interested and altruistic reasons for actions 'a certain amount of self-regard is morally required or at least morally acceptable. Where this is the case, high-ranking self interested reasons have priority over low-ranking altruistic reasons, *other things being equal*' (Emphasis Mine, Sterba, 2005, p. 20). I equate taking recognition respect seriously with attending to the reasons that one has for acting and considering how those actions will impact on others. Other things are not equal when those actions are likely to impact others and/or substantially interfere with them.

[38] As stated in §1.5, I consider this is the point of ethics, to give sensible reasons for why something ought to be/not be done. Importantly, ethics is about expressing these reasons in such a way as to be publicly understandable.

The cognitive account of identity presented in Chapter 4 helps us respond differentially to X, V and VR: people have a capacity to have thoughts about thoughts and have a capacity to give reasons for acting in certain ways. Christine Korsgaard says that

> self-consciousness makes it necessary to *take control* of our beliefs and actions, but we must then work out how to do that: we must find normative principles, laws, to govern what we believe and do. The distinctive feature of humans, reason, is therefore the capacity for normative self government.
>
> (Emphasis Original, Korsgaard, 2009, p. xi)

Likewise, Larry May argues that we form stable and coherent Self-Regarding Identities through time by not taking on our social values and leaving it at that, but *reflecting* on our central values and accepting some while rejecting others. '[M]oral integrity is best seen as a form of maturation in which reflection on a plurality of values provides a critical coherence to one's experiences ... The self's "core," in terms of which values are accepted or rejected, is itself, formed through a process of socialization' (May, 1996, p. 26).[39] That is, strong identification with a trait *alone* is not enough to warrant serious recognition respect. A person must be able to give reasons for *why* a particular trait is important or not.[40] In short, a person must be able to give public reasons why identification with a given trait is to be respected.

Revisiting the three traits X, V and VR, let us begin with X, skin colour. First, we must recognise that X is something that Malcolm cannot change; we have a principled reason for endorsing his claim that X is central to his self-identity. The burden of proof shifts to the reasons that others have for negatively or positively valuing X. There seem no justifiable reasons to hold that X is something that ought *not* to figure in Self-Regarding Identity; skin colour[41] is a morally irrelevant feature to judge the value of another person by: we cannot simply say that a person shouldn't identify with skin colour without substantial qualification.[42] As such, we have no principled reason for *rejecting* the centrality of X to *Malcolm*'s self-identity. Hence,

[39] I recognise here James Sterba's point that, depending on the individual's particular socialisation and nature, there are individual variations in how effectively different people can actually do this (Sterba, 2005, p. 26).

[40] Without entering into a further discussion here, this aligns with common ideas in political philosophy, whereby publicly available reasons and public dialogue are necessary elements of pluralistic societies. Such discussions can be found in (Habermas, 1995; Rawls, 1985, 1999b; Scanlon, 2000).

[41] As mentioned, it is beyond the scope of this book to go into a substantive philosophic and ethical discussion of what race is or isn't, particularly about correlations between skin colour and race. I simply point to other discussions of race, biology and ethnicity (Kitcher, 2007; Smedley and Smedley, 2005; Stevens, 2003).

[42] Consider here a racial supremacist, who ties their skin colour with substantive claims about their superiority over people of different skin colour. The problem is not that they identify with their skin colour, but the particular *way* that they value it. In this case, the problem is that they presume that substantive moral and political rights follow directly from their skin colour. Later in this section, I discuss how such presumptions stand up to taking recognition claims seriously.

other things being equal, we ought to recognise X as central to Malcolm and weigh X appropriately.

Now to the case of V, the factually unfounded trait. Perhaps we ought to reject Michael's claims that trait V is central, on the grounds that the trait cannot be supported by any appeals to truth: vampires do not exist, so Michael is wrong to identify with V. However, consider that religious beliefs, as well as many other key self-identificatory traits, do not rest on factual claims. An appeal to truth alone does not give a reason to reject Michael's claims to V. A 'radical realist' might object to this and say that if a central trait is not 'real', then identification with this unfounded trait can constitute a harm to self.[43] Yet without some further explanation of what truth is, how truth and identity interact and why truth is morally relevant an appeal to the factual validity of a trait *alone* does not give us a principled moral reason to reject Michael's strong identification with V.

A different line of argument is that we ought to reject V, not because of some objective moral value of truth, but because of an inconsistency within Michael's core beliefs: some of his traits are 'true' while others are 'fantasies'. Such an inconsistency may produce instability in Michael's character, which may lead to some diminishment in Michael's autonomy or some suffering. Hence identification with V is morally undesirable. Inconsistency alone does not seem to constitute a threat to autonomy or a harm to self. Instead, insofar as some form of paternalism is justified, what should concern us is not inconsistency but fundamental identity instability brought about by psychological dissonance.[44] As May argues, psychological integrity is less about the substance of one's core beliefs, but how these beliefs allow us adapt to our environment; 'it is important that a person can find resources within himself or herself in a way that he or she can live with'. Commitment to one's central traits typically involves 'conflicting value orientations . . . within a single self' (May, 1996, p. 25). If the fundamental instability does not occur, then we have no principled reason for rejecting Michael's claims to identify with V.

A further aspect to consider about Michael's claim is whether his actions relating to V violate another's rights or harm others. If he believes that he is a vampire *and* must therefore drink other people's blood, here is a reason to override *how* Michael

43 Whether or not he counts as a 'radical realist', a quote from Richard Dawkins fits this idea: 'As a scientist, I am hostile to fundamentalist religion because it actively debauches the scientific enterprise. It teaches us not to change our minds and not to want to know exciting things that are available to be known. It subverts science and saps the intellect . . . Fundamentalist religion is hell-bent on ruining the scientific education of countless thousands of innocent, well meaning, eager young minds. Non-fundamentalism . . . [makes] the world safe for fundamentalism by teaching children, from their earliest years, that unquestioning faith is a virtue' (Dawkins, 2006, pp. 284, 286).

44 A similar point about identity formation and religion is made by Philip Kitcher, where he argues that what is important is not the factual accuracy of the claim or simple psychological consistency but reflective stability: a trait is '*reflectively stable* when it survives detailed scrutiny of one's life and the lives of others; when it can be upheld as a worthy choice for the direction of one's transient existence' (Emphasis Original, Kitcher, 2011).

expresses trait V: Michael's identification causes him to violate another's rights and/or to harm them. However, note that it does not necessarily follow that Michael give up identification with trait V. Rather, he cannot act upon certain elements of this trait: we can respect Michael *qua* person, whilst not wholly and unreflectively endorsing his pursuit of V.

By allowing that rights violations, harms to others and discrimination can justifiably limit a trait's expression, we also find a principled way of dealing with Martin, who strongly self-identifies with trait VR, being a violent rapist. Clearly, acting upon this trait constitutes serious rights violations, harms to others and/or injustices. Short of an extreme form of egotistical hedonism, any moral system will argue against Martin having a legitimate claim to violently rape others.[45] Further, all moral systems will strongly negatively value such a trait. As such, Martin cannot offer any substantial justificatory reason for his positive endorsement of trait VR.

This sits with the cognitive model of identity from Chapter 4, which holds that identity is thoughts about who a person is: identity is not merely the trait but the thoughts that people have about those traits. On all moral accounts, Martin ought to negatively *value* violent rape as a personality trait. However, like Michael, this does not mean that Martin should attempt to believe that he does not have this trait. Rather, the point is that he has no justificatory reason for positively endorsing his identification with the trait, much less acting upon it. Finally, taking recognition seriously, we also have a principled foundation for rejecting groups that would publicly advocate morally repugnant traits like VR. Something like a 'pro-rape' webpage (Pollard, 2009) is clearly unjustified.[46]

In summary, the basic recognition claim requires that in order to offer recognition respect to people, we ought to take *seriously* the traits that they self-identify with: we should neither reject their claims to a given trait nor unreflectively endorse the trait. *Weighing appropriately* holds with the general rule of thumb that the more deeply the source person identifies with a given trait, the more care should be taken in how we practically recognise that trait. A limiting factor is the justificatory reasons offered for endorsing the trait. Like many other aspects of interpersonal relations, such traits, how they are valued and how they are expressed by the individuals ought to be open to moral criticism. Paraphrasing from Darwall's recognition respect claim from above, we ought to 'take seriously and weigh appropriately the fact that such traits are important in deliberating about how to care about and respond to traits'.

[45] Two things are meant here. First, by any *moral* system, I wish to exclude a strong form of moral nihilism from this claim. Second, to state the obvious, different ethical systems would differ as to *why* violent rape is morally prohibited. However, insofar as violent rape is a paradigm example of a moral wrong, the disagreements about why violent rape should not distract us from the universal agreement that violent rapes are morally wrong.

[46] Limiting the production and dissemination of particular morally problematic Virtual Identities may be considered interference in freedom of speech. However, there exists a body of literature that rejects simple claims about the primacy of freedom of speech over other values or rights (Alexander, 2005; Waldron, 2006, 2009; West, 2012).

The question is, how does this relate to surveillance technologies? It is redundant to say that the age of surveillance offers an unparalleled capacity to construct, distribute and publicise Virtual Identities of source people. What the basic recognition claim does is tell us *why* we should care about the construction, distribution and publicising of these Virtual Identities. Connecting the motivation to take such presentations seriously and weigh them appropriately with the Identity/Information Dyad, we now have a rough guide on *how* to take care with these Virtual Identities.

Consider the three traits X, V and VR. Basic recognition underpins the premise that, other things being equal, Malcolm, Michael and Martin all have a *pro tanto* claim to identify with X, V and VR. As we have seen, Malcolm ought to be able to produce Virtual Identities in a public way that is in line with the importance of trait X to him. In parallel, other things being equal, others are limited in producing demeaning Virtual Identities of Malcolm in virtue of X. By weighing X in regards to Malcolm's Self-Regarding Identity, we ought to permit Malcolm to produce a 'MalcolmX' website, whilst maintaining that a 'Hate MalcolmX Because He Is X' website is impermissible. Michael ought to be able to produce a website outlining his identification with vampires. However, in taking V seriously, Michael cannot advocate the drinking of other's blood on this website. Similarly, Martin's VR website is impermissible, given the rights violations and harms that are essential to Martin's identification with VR. Weighing traits appropriately means that we take into account the strength of identification with the trait; taking traits seriously means that we look to the reasons why *that* trait is central to a person's identity and contrast their reasons with other reasons why such a trait is morally reasonable. The dyad explains how this basic recognition plays out in the face of new technology.

8.6 WEARABLE HEALTH TECHNOLOGIES REVISITED: TRACKING THE STEPS

This chapter was introduced with surveillance technologies that produced innocuous information: websites for sporting enthusiasts. The goals of this chapter have been to make two critical points. In line with the Identity/Information Dyad explicated in Chapter 6, that the information put out into the public, such as on a jogging website, produces something more than and qualitatively different to, the innocuous information as it was originally publicised. Second, that such information is morally important.

Recall from §1.4 and §1.5 that the goal of this book is to give a detailed set of explanations as to how certain novel technologies tracked to key moral foundations. The moral foundation of this chapter is that people are due respect in virtue of them being people, simply put as rights claims. This chapter has explicated how a novel set of surveillance technologies produce and use information in such a way as to relate to those moral foundations. A set of rights and their relation to Personal Information have been made explicit.

To bring this back to the jogging data, it should now be clear that a given jogger can be a source of Personal Information on the relevant website: they may originally provide Thin Information to the website. While this example may be banal, consider the privacy, ownership and recognition rights that such a service might infringe: if a user has created a Virtual Identity such that their age, sex, weight, heart-rate, diet, km's run per day/week/month, social networks and attitudes on a given day are integrated we now have a situation of considerable moral importance. This information, once aggregated, is morally equivalent to a person's medical records. Assuming that privacy is a substantial right in medical practice, we should also consider the user's Virtual Identity as affording similar rights to privacy. Likewise, given the tight connection between the user-as-source and the Virtual Identity, the user might have a legitimate property claim over that Virtual Identity. Further, as with the case of medical histories, that Virtual Identity tracks closely to central traits, so basic recognition holds that that Personal Information ought to be weighed appropriately and treated seriously.

The core point is that surveillance technologies direct a shift towards aggregation of Personal Information. In the age of surveillance, innocuous information like jogging data needs to be recognised as potentially something more than simply that – Virtual Identities represent a qualitative shift in the information, from something morally innocuous to something morally important. The Identity/Information Dyad provides the necessary explanatory tool to detail how this qualitative shift occurs. However, it should be noted that the recognition that innocuous information is morally important does not get us all the way to how we ought to respond. Chapter 10 closes out the discussion by looking at the role that the Identity/Information Dyad can play in the value-sensitive design of surveillance technologies. But first we must look at informational harms and problems of distribution.

9

On Institutions

9.1 INFORMATION AND INSTITUTIONS

The age of surveillance presents special challenges to liberal democratic governments. On the one hand, following a series of increasingly high profile exposures of state-based surveillance programmes, citizens are often found to be protesting against this surveillance. On the other, with increased fear of terrorist attacks, the growth of cyber-crime and rising cyber-interference of foreign governments in domestic affairs, citizens are equally calling for increased government protection. We see a similar species of ambivalence to that about surveillance; we simultaneously criticise governments who have us under surveillance, whilst holding governments to account if they fail to protect us from bad people.

When thinking of Virtual Identities, this raises problems at an institutional level – institutions use Personal Information and use it in ways where people are its targets. While there are serious moral concerns about the production of Personal Information when people are the source, parallel to this are equally serious moral concerns about the ways that this Personal Information is used. We ought to care when Semantic Information targets a person or group of people. For some, the individualist arguments may not have much bite: it is not that a government agency or private company are collecting information on people. To take seriously non–rights-based moral concerns about surveillance, this chapter looks at the concerns that arise with the ways that Personal Information is used.

This chapter focuses on ways that institutions use Personal Information. This is of special moral importance as institutions have power that individuals lack. They have technical power in that they can aggregate, distribute and use information in ways that an individual can't. They also have semantic power in that, with certain institutions, the context of application of information has a power that is of special concern. For instance, given the multirealisability of information, application of Personal Information in a criminal justice context can have severe impacts on the human targets of that information in a way that is morally different from the way that an individual uses information. An investigation into the moral importance of Virtual Identities must look at institutions as informational actors.

This chapter is concerned with institutional use of information. In particular, the moral concerns arising when government institutions apply and use Personal Information with people as targets. The explanatory priority is now Person As Target. This includes direct impacts – the harmful consequences of use harms. It also looks at indirect outcomes of use – moral issues arising out of fairness and distribution of Personal Information.

9.2 THEY ARE WATCHING US: THE CASE OF EDWARD SNOWDEN

On the 5th of June, 2013, *The Guardian* newspaper published an article titled 'NSA Collecting Phone Records of Millions of Verizon Customers Daily'. On the 9th of June, they published the story 'Edward Snowden: The Whistleblower behind the NSA Surveillance Revelations', revealing that the source of the information was Edward Snowden, a contractor to the US National Security Agency (NSA) who was in Hong Kong at the time the stories were released. This began an unravelling of the biggest informational breach in the history of Western intelligence institutions (Greenwald, 2014; Harding, 2014). Starting with the NSA, documents that Snowden had given to the international press rapidly encompassed the US intelligence community, the United Kingdom, other 'Five Eyes'[1] countries and the world's largest technical companies. It sparked international diplomatic incidents such as the revelation that the United States was conducting surveillance on allies like the Vice Chancellor of Germany and companies like Brazil's Petrobras (Greenwald, 2014, pp. 141, 134–135). Following on from high-profile leaks of government information via sites like Wikileaks, Snowden's revelations confirmed that surveillance had truly come of age: the idea that governments around the world had us under surveillance was no longer the province of conspiracy theory. Moreover, given the involvement of companies like Google, Facebook and Apple in these surveillance programmes, our willing embrace of information technologies makes us all targets of surveillance.

Unsurprisingly, the Snowden revelations initiated extensive public discussion about institutional use of Personal Information. For some, this was confirmation that the intelligence institutions of liberal democratic governments were running amok. 'This wholesale invasion of Americans' and foreign citizens' privacy does not contribute to our security; it puts in danger the very liberties we're trying to protect' (Ellsberg, 2013). For others, even those familiar with government surveillance

[1] The 'Five Eyes' countries are the United States, the United Kingdom, Australia, Canada and New Zealand. They have a formal set of agreements about sharing of information and intelligence.

programmes, it came as a surprise that such comprehensive surveillance programmes existed at all (Greenwald, 2014, p. 90). And for some in the intelligence communities, there was frustration, anger and confusion. Frustration that Snowden's releases had caused massive historic damage to America's security agencies (Simeone, 2014). Anger that one of their own had 'violated his oath to safeguard the national security secrets entrusted to him' (Bolton, 2013). Confusion that people were surprised at all: talking to people working in the national security community, I recall a number of them saying words to the effect of 'but we all spy on each other and we all know that we're doing it. This is an open secret. How is this even a surprise?'[2] To say that there was a wide set of beliefs and opinions about surveillance following Snowden's revelations is an understatement. To say that the revelations prompted and demanded moral criticism and reflection is so true that it is trivial.

A sustained and comprehensive moral analysis of the role of institutions in the age of surveillance and of Snowden's revelations requires understanding – in order to make a proper moral appraisal of these events we need to have some understanding of the different elements involved (Henschke, 2012). Taking Snowden's revelations as a starting point, we have at least three elements for moral analysis. First, we have the character of the person who revealed the information. Second, we can ask if the person was correct in releasing that information.[3] The final line of enquiry is whether the various institutions were justified in having that information in the first place. Note that the answer to the third question is independent of the first and second: Snowden might be a bad guy or a hero and could be wrong or right for releasing that information about what intelligence institutions were doing. However, independent of Snowden's character or the way in which information about the surveillance programmes was released, we can still ask if these institutions ought to have collected, produced and used that Personal Information in the first place. That final question is the focus here.[4]

[2] This notion of the open secret of intelligence agencies and surveillance had been around long before Edward Snowden's revelations. Consider this discussion around the Watergate scandal: 'Not everyone was shocked. In 1973, Britain's Prime Minister Edward Heath, made a visit to China. Mao Tse-tung asked him, "what is all this Nixon nonsense about?" Heath asked him what he meant by "nonsense". Mao replied: "Well, they say he bugged his opponents, don't they? But we all bug our opponents, don't we and everybody knows it? So what's all this fuss about?"' (Aldrich, 2010, p. 4).

[3] A parallel set of questions involves whether such surveillance and intelligence programmes should stay secret. As Genevieve Lester discusses, there are many reasons for state secrets to remain secret (Lester, 2016). In contrast, Ross Bellaby proposes a more open approach to intelligence services (Bellaby, 2014).

[4] There are large and comprehensive accounts of Snowden's motivations (Greenwald, 2014; Harding, 2014) and criticisms of him as a person (Bolton, 2013; Simeone, 2014) and a large literature on the ethics of secrets (Bok, 1989) and ethics of whistleblowing (Delmas, 2015; Sieber, 1998; Vandekerckhove, 2006; Vandekerckhove and Lewis, 2012). While they are of interest, it is not my purpose to rehash them here. The point is, instead, to see this event of

We could answer no to this question – institutions generally and governments in particular should not collect, have access to or use Personal Information. Chapters 2, 3 and 8 presented a series of arguments about the importance of individual rights in relation to Personal Information which support such a position. The approach taken in this book, however, is that such rights are *pro tanto*: while individuals do have legitimate rights claims to Personal Information, these rights can be overridden in particular exceptional circumstances. That said, justifications have to be given for overriding them.

We could also simply answer yes – governments have a moral responsibility to access Personal Information; the world is dangerous and complex and governments need our Personal Information to protect us and do their job. 'The world of national security and intelligence takes a strongly rationalist stance based on the assumption that more information will lead to less ignorance, thus better informed decisions can be taken that have a higher chance of being favourable and hence can lead to better outcomes' (Omand, 2010, p. 23). Yet, liberal democracies balk at the idea that a government can do whatever it wants. A state that collects comprehensive information on its citizens without substantial justification or effective oversight is typically considered a police state, the antithesis of the liberal democratic model. 'Obviously, the United States is not now a police state. But given the extent of this invasion of people's privacy, we do have the full electronic and legislative infrastructure of such a state' (Ellsberg, 2013). In a liberal democratic society, any production of and access to, Personal Information must be justified and receive oversight.[5] The point here is that though surveillance by government institutions is permissible and in fact may be required, it needs to be justified. Looking at what Snowden revealed, we need to explore the limits and uses of government surveillance.

This chapter's focus on government institutions as informational actors may strike some as too narrow: the infrastructure of the age of surveillance is developed, provided and maintained in large part by private enterprise. Nine[6] of the top information technology companies had been exposed by Snowden as working with the US government, albeit unwillingly at times.[7] So why not focus on private or corporate institutions? First – many of the moral arguments about corporate production and use of Personal Information are covered by the discussions of privacy

revelation in the context of the age of surveillance and the role of institutions in shaping that, rather than a close exploration of Edward Snowden's moral character and actions.

5 As Lester points out, such oversight is complex and more oversight does not necessarily entail better practices (Lester, 2016).

6 One of the NSA programmes that Snowden revealed, PRISM, stated that the NSA has access to the Personal Information produced by Microsoft, Google, Yahoo!, Facebook, PalTalk, YouTube, Skype, AOL and Apple (Greenwald, 2014, pp 108–116).

7 Apple's legal battle about granting a federal judge access to a person's iPhone during a criminal trial shows the lack of cooperation between some companies and government agencies (Kharpal, 2016).

and property. The moral issues of property, the ownership of Personal Information by third parties, have been discussed in Chapters 3 and 8. Second, for those who hold that there are moral arguments about corporate production and use of Personal Information that extend beyond property rights, then the following arguments about government use will apply equally. As such, the core moral issues about governments as institutional informational actors can be applied to non-government institutions.

There are, however, considerable reasons to devote attention to government institutions and surveillance. Despite the fact that private companies like Google, Microsoft, Apple and the like wield immense power, they differ from governments in two fundamental ways. Governments have a monopoly of force and they have moral responsibilities to their citizens that non-government institutions lack. As citizens, we give up certain rights and responsibilities to the state, however this is construed.[8] In return, the state offers protection to us. This means that the state stands in a special relationship to people. There are special powers that the state has – it alone commands the police and military and it formally decides upon and enforces the laws of the land. And, insofar as its citizens are within the state's jurisdiction, then they are vulnerable to particular decisions that the state makes. In response to citizens forgoing certain rights, the state bears particular responsibilities to protect its citizens. There is a 'relationship between sovereign and subject in terms of a "mutual bond and obligation," under which the subject owed allegiance or obedience, while the sovereign was bound "to govern and protect his subjects ..."' or, as John Farnworthy put it, '[t]he first duty of the Government is to afford protection to its citizens' (Quoted in Heyman, 1991, pp. 513, 508). Citizens are simultaneously vulnerable to and protected by, the state.

This creates a tension for states:[9] they have the scope to interfere with the rights of their citizens while at the same time are charged with protecting and respecting those same rights.

> Since there is no absolute security to be had at an acceptable financial or moral cost in this world, at every stage a balance must be maintained within the framework of human rights based on the time-honoured principles of proportionality and necessity ... Central to sound strategy is having a clear statement of principles and values to inform the inevitable trade-offs and to highlight what cannot be compromised: the importance of human rights, including the absolute ban on torture, justice and the rule of law, legitimate and accountable government, and the maintenance of freedoms of assembly and speech.
>
> (Omand, 2010, p. 19)

8 This position implies a social contract between individuals and the state. For more on the social contract and arguments around its legitimacy, see (Cudd, 2013; D'Agostino, Gaus and Thrasher, 2014).

9 Or at least for liberal democratic states.

And nowhere is this more apparent than in issues of surveillance. The state has a duty to protect its citizens and so it has a moral responsibility to ensure that malicious actors are prevented from visiting harm upon citizens. Surveillance technologies provide an ideal tool for this. 'If every problem looks like a security issue then ministers will be conditioned to see the response in terms of seeking more security ... threatening further restrictions domestically on individual liberty and privacy. Care is thus needed that a subliminal message does not become reinforced that Good Government is just about security' (Omand, 2010, p. 20). They must be restrained in the ways that they use surveillance technologies. When it came out that the NSA had the German Chancellor under surveillance, she raised comparisons with the pervasive surveillance conducted by the East German secret police, the Stasi (Traynor and Lewis, 2013).

One of the key things that marks liberal democratic states out from totalitarian ones are the checks and balances put on the reach of the state. As Glen Greenwald puts it, '[w]hile the government, via surveillance, knows more and more about what its citizens are doing, its citizens know less and less about what their government is doing ... Democracy requires accountability and consent of the governed, which is only possible if citizens know what is done in their name' (Greenwald, 2014, pp. 208–209). This accountability to and consent by, the governed is a final distinction between government and non-government institutions – by and large, government surveillance programmes in liberal democratic states are subject to oversight and constraint that non-government surveillance programmes are not (Lester, 2016, pp. 1–28).

Issues around the responsibilities and limits of states are core issues of political philosophy and I make no attempt to resolve them here. Instead, what follows is a continuation of the discussion about Personal Information and surveillance. In particular, the moral issues that state institutions need to take into account when using Personal Information. However, this is of significance to political philosophy as the discussion is about the way that the responsibilities and limits of states are expressed and changed in the age of surveillance.

9.3 A TAXONOMY OF HARMS

The claims that will be developed in this section are phrased in terms of vulnerability:[10] the contention is that Personal Information makes people, particularly target people, vulnerable to the actions of others, particularly institutions. In *Protecting the Vulnerable*, Robert Goodin's[11] central thesis is that 'we bear special

[10] Daniel Solove makes a similar point about information and vulnerability (Solove, 2004, pp. 107–108).

[11] Note that Robert Goodin argues that 'the consequentialistic considerations implicit in the principle I am advocating are broadly consistent with the nonconsequentialistic constraints that characterize standard Kantian-style moralities' (Goodin, 1985, p. 15). His point is that though he

responsibilities for protecting those who are particularly vulnerable to us' (Goodin, 1985, p. 109). The special responsibilities generate duties that amount 'to an injunction to prevent harms from befalling people. Conceptually, "vulnerability" is essentially a matter of being *under threat of harm*; therefore, protecting the vulnerable is *primarily a matter of forestalling harms*' (Emphases Mine, Goodin, 1985, p. 110). This set of harms are drawn from the taxonomy of identity elements, outlined in the earlier discussion of identity, specifically in §4.6. In particular, this section will be looking at people's vulnerabilities to the harms that arise from Other-Regarding Identity, the way that Personal Information shapes who I perceive you to be and how that Other-Regarding Identity in the dyadic relationship with Personal Information guides my actions.

A key reason for focusing on vulnerability and its relation to Personal Information is to show that we have a duty to prevent or minimise as far as possible harms that *may arise*. When thinking of surveillance and government institutions, this responsibility to forestall harms is especially pertinent: they must both use Personal Information to protect their citizens against accident, disaster and malicious agents and restrain their collection and use, such that they themselves do not harm their citizens.

In order to show that Personal Information makes people vulnerable, I need to show the harms that can likely arise and that *Personal Information* warrants sustained attention. The following subsections present five types of information harms and show what role the Identity/Information Dyad plays in explaining these harms: Deliberate Information Harms, Negligent Information Harms, Incomplete Information Harms, Limited Opportunity Harms and Closed Identity Harms. The upshot of this is that surveillance technologies with a potential to construct Virtual Identities ought to be designed[12] and used in such a way as to minimise the probability and magnitude of information harms. This discussion of harms and Person As Target is in deliberate contrast to Chapter 8, with its focus on individuals and rights. Following this focus on the harmful consequences arising from the use of Personal Information, Section 9.4 then looks at moral concerns of information's distribution. Both Sections 9.3 and 9.4 take the Person As Target as the explanatory priority.

9.3.1 *Deliberate Information Harms*

Personal Information fits with deliberate harms quite simply: people can use Personal Information to harm others. A set of examples referring to broadly targeted and narrowly targeted information will bring this point out. Perhaps the most obvious misuse is identity theft: using Personal Information access to another's bank

is focused on consequences, an ethical theory founded in vulnerability is consistent with standard deontological theories. This is clearly along the same lines as my own position about functional equivalence of sophisticated deontological and consequentialist theories.

[12] This point of designing in values is covered in Chapter 10.

details in order to steal money from them. However, such deliberate harms extend beyond the economic sphere.

In an example of broad information targets, consider the activities of the Nazis in occupied Europe: the Nazis used information to target groups like Jews, Roma, communists, anarchists and so on, for deliberately harmful action.[13] One instance is the Nazi invasion of The Netherlands in 1940. After gaining access to Dutch census information, the Nazis easily and rapidly identified many Jewish members of the Dutch population, increasing the Nazi's efficiency in harming many people (van den Hoven, 2008). Contrast this with the Italians, whose bureaucratic inefficiency has been said to have reduced the effectiveness of the Nazi's policy to identify and target the Jewish populations there (Glover, 2000, pp. 389–390). The point here is that information made the Dutch targets more vulnerable to harms than the Italian targets.

In examples of narrow targets, consider that Fred is violently opposed to gay people.[14] Fred finds out that that Ellen is gay and given his hatred of gays, he finds out where Ellen lives and physically assaults her.[15] In a third example, consider that Ned is also violently opposed to gay people. Fred makes Ellen's sexual preferences and home address public and Ned then physically assaults Ellen. Holding Fred partially responsible for Ned's actions because of information that Fred has put online has legal precedent in Australia. A person was fined AU$150,000 after posting information that people convicted of sex-crimes were encouraged to stay at a specific motel after leaving jail, causing considerable economic and psychological harm to the motel's owners and staff (Partridge, 2016).[16]

In each of the cases, while the harms themselves are economic or physical, they come about because of Personal Information. Even in the case where Ellen suffers harm from the result of Ned's physical assault, Fred's posting of Ellen's Personal Information is an essential aspect in explaining how the harm came about.[17]

[13] The harms here certainly extend beyond informational analysis: I don't want to draw too much attention away from the moral catastrophe that was the Nazi genocide. Instead, I want to draw attention to the part that Personal Information played in making the Nazi programmes more efficient.

[14] This is a deliberate allusion to Fred Phelps, a real person, who was fundamentally and very publicly opposed to gay people. As part of his opposition to gay people he and members of his church (The Westboro Baptist Church) run websites like godhatesfags.com. They also regularly picket the funerals of recently killed US soldiers thanking God for the soldier's death, as they believe that the US government is in favour of gay lifestyles. According to the Westboro Baptist Church, the dead soldiers represent God's wrath against gays generally and the US government in particular.

[15] Fred Phelps, the real person, did not to my knowledge physically assault anyone.

[16] In the example cited, the claims that the motel housed people convicted of sex-crimes were false, so this would be an example of a negligent informational harm. The specific point being made here, however, is that use of identity-relating information has been deemed to be a sufficient causal connection to legally hold individuals responsible for harms that others commit.

[17] In this third example, some of the causal responsibility for Ellen's harm arises from Fred's actions and as such it is reasonable to assign moral responsibility to Fred also. Given space

Whether it is information that broadly or narrowly targets people, Personal Information is an essential part of people deliberately bringing the given harms about. Personal Information has made the targets more vulnerable to harms.

These examples draw attention to the important causal role of information in an action that harms another. That is, the bad agent uses Personal Information to deliberately harm people. Generally, unjustified harms are prohibited by any ethical system – even more so with deliberate harms. So what is being said here that is new in the age of surveillance? First, that more information is available for use and abuse. Second, the Virtual Identities increase the target's vulnerability to deliberate information harms.

It should be uncontroversial for me to say that in the age of surveillance, it is easier to produce and get access to Personal Information. However, this alone does not mean that the risk of information harms has necessarily risen. More relevant is the rise of surveillance technologies, increasing the capacity for targeting information to particular individuals and groups. As one study has shown, it is possible to predict a person's Social Security number from publicly available information with reasonable certainty (Acquisti and Gross, 2009). Other technologies can be used to identify individuals: RFIDs can be placed in clothing to locate and track individuals (Albrecht and Mcintyre, 2005; Lockton and Rosenberg, 2005), typing patterns can identify individuals (Peacock, Xian and Wilkerson, 2004) and various biometric technologies are being developed and used to identify individuals and groups (National Institute Of Standards And Technology, 2009; Alterman, 2003). This capacity to develop comprehensive Virtual Identities about people was the driving force behind the NSA surveillance programme. In one of the official documents released by Snowden, the NSA's strategy was given as *Know it All, Collect it All, Process it All, Exploit it All* (Greenwald, 2014, p. 97). In short, given access to the technology, it is relatively easy to identify people using informational technologies.[18]

Second, as these sorts of information can be combined to produce revealing Virtual Identities, the actual harms that can be committed can become worse in kind and are much easier to commit. Helen Nissenbaum describes this as problems arising from the ease of information aggregation and production of further

constraints we cannot go into discussion of why we should hold Fred morally responsible for Ellen's harms here. However, cases like complicity in the Rwanda genocide, as discussed by Larry May and hate speech and security, as discussed by Jeremy Waldron, give reasons as to why a person like Fred should be morally responsible for harms that arise from his publication of Personal Information targeting Ellen (May, 2010; Waldron, 2009).

18 Helen Nissenbaum notes that the 'democratization of database technologies' and 'information mobility' are pivotal transformations, brought about by cheap computer memory (Nissenbaum, 2009, pp. 38–40, 36). Consider the ease with which people can now identity targets and perform analysis on data to identify particular individual's traits, when contrasted with the former East Germany, who needed a pervasive police state to collect, store, aggregate and communicate Personal Information.

information and knowledge from existing databases (Nissenbaum, 2009, pp. 41–45).[19] As an example of how easy it is to post intimate Personal Information to cause harm, consider so called revenge pornography. This typically[20] concerns 'online pornography that includes amateur images or videos that were self-produced or manufactured with the consent of those depicted, but then later distributed without their consent' (Salter and Crofts, 2015, p. 233). Such revenge pornography is afforded by the ubiquity of recording technology and the ease with which recordings can be made public through posting on the internet. In this case, highly revealing information is put in a very public place, linked to a host of personal identifiers, in a way that is very easy for an irate ex-partner to do. Likewise, the aggregation of large swathes of Personal Information in a database presents an ideal location for hackers to access detailed Virtual Identities.[21] The hacking and subsequent release of Personal Information about users of the 'infidelity' website Ashley Madison shows how intimate Personal Information presents an ideal target for hackers. Moreover, a number of suicides were linked to the public release of user information, again showing the potential harms to release of Personal Information.[22] The publication of nude photos of a person by an irate ex-partner would typically be considered worse than the irate ex-partner speaking ill of them to a small circle of friends because the magnitudes of harms can be great either in the types of harms or the amount of harms enabled by surveillance technologies.

The basic point here is that the capacity for surveillance technologies to easily produce and distribute Virtual Identities exposes many people to risks of deliberate harms. Our vulnerability to such harms is increased by the aggregation of personal data. Insofar as harms are bad and that we ought to work to reduce people's vulnerability, then living in the age of surveillance essentially has increased people's vulnerability to deliberate information harms. Yet, as with the discussion of the wrongs to source people, it is hard to properly explain how significant harms can come about when considering innocuous information. The Identity/Information

[19] A similar conclusion is drawn by Floridi, when he says that information communication technologies can impact privacy concerns by making it easier for information to be used for unwanted purposes: what he calls ontological friction. 'The more the ontological friction in the infosphere decreases, the swifter these detached labels can flow around and the easier it becomes to grab and steal them and use them for illegal purposes' (Floridi, 2005b, p. 198).

[20] I say typically here, but there are many cases of images or photos being made without the knowledge or consent of one of the parties. These sorts of cases represent an even greater violation of the person's dignity, as the initial creation of the images did not take any of their interests into account.

[21] A host of tools are currently in use that claim that personal data can be used to characterise people. For instance, publicly available records may be used to predict a person's voting habits, (Baker, 2007, pp. 67–95; Scherer, 2012), personal prescriptions are sold to private firms (Freudenheim, 2009), a person's movements in a shopping centre can be tracked by their mobile phone (Morris, 2012) or via the GPS in their car (Ramli, 2011).

[22] There is considerable ethical complexity around the Ashley Madison hacks; a point I briefly cover elsewhere (Henschke, 2015a, b).

Dyad is a tool that can explain how the aggregation of innocuous information forms Virtual Identities which increase people's vulnerability to deliberate information harms. And, whether in the need to take considerable care with the collection of Personal Information, or how they apply that information to people, government institutions must take deliberate information harms very seriously.

9.3.2 *Negligent Information Harms*

Negligent Information Harms arise when a Virtual Identity is constructed that targets an individual or group, but the data is not accurate.[23] However, as the Virtual Identity is used in some decision procedures, the target person is harmed by unjustified or inappropriate actions of another, as a direct result of the inaccuracy. As before, the target can be broad or narrow, depending on how many people are identified by the Virtual Identity.

The targeting of individuals based on racial profiling presents a broad-based negligent information harm. One example of this involves the combination of racial profiling and police activities, where police selectively 'target sections of the population, especially ethnic minorities' (Waddington, Stenson and Don, 2004, p. 889) in order to stop and search or frisk them. This sort of racial/ethnic profiling in a criminal justice context is problematic as part of law enforcement strategies,[24] and can result in increased institutional discrimination of given ethnic groups (Ossorio, 2006; Ossorio and Duster, 2005). As a broad negligent information harm, the problem has three elements. First is the reduction of individuals to a single identifier, the issue of 'Essentialised Identity' raised in §4.5.4. Second is when this is done in a context of historical discrimination – the targeting of minority groups who have suffered a legacy of active discrimination. Third is that this is done in a criminal justice context. The combination of Essentialised Identity, historical discrimination and institutional context is particularly problematic.

The role of technology and Virtual Identities here cannot be understated. Consider the example where contestants with dark skin were selected against in a beauty contest judged by artificial intelligence (Levin, 2016). While we can assume that no one actively programmed in a racist component to the algorithm, the outcome is problematic and offensive. Now consider this occurring in a context of police surveillance of crowds. And make no mistake, information technologies are increasingly applied in a criminal justice context – some US jurisdictions are introducing algorithms to help set bail (Dewan, 2015). This is in part to help reduce costs, but in part to reduce racial and other biases of the human judges; 'the assessment tool could combat implicit bias, the invisible set of assumptions based on race, class and

[23] While some of the data is true, some of it is not. In Floridi's terms, such a Virtual Identity would be 'pseudoinformational', as this data is not true and this would not count as information. See §5.6.

[24] See, for example Guzik, (2009).

other factors that can come into play' (Dewan, 2015). The concern is that this can only be assured if and when the technological decision-making is understood by those applying the decisions and know when and how to apply human discretion to the automated decision-making processes. Surveillance technologies become of particular concern because Essentialised Identity and historical discrimination can become subtly combined to form a Virtual Identity which targets individuals in a way that seems scientific, technical and objective; thus normal concerns we would have about discrimination are overlooked. The Identity/Information Dyad is a useful device to draw our attention to this problem in surveillance technologies.

In an example of a narrow target, in an Australian case, Mohamed Haneef was said to have been involved in terrorist activity:

> Dr Haneef, an Indian national, was arrested on suspicion that he was guilty of supporting terrorism through a connection [to an] attack at Glasgow International Airport on 1 July 2007. He was taken into custody for questioning on 2 July and held for twelve days before being charged. He was granted bail two days later but remained in detention following the [Australian Immigration] Minister's immediate cancellation of his visa amid much talk of information that could not be released to the public but which implied that Haneef was meaningfully connected to terrorism. The criminal charges were withdrawn on 27 July 2007. The visa cancellation was overturned by the courts on 21 December 2007.
>
> (McNamara, 2009, footnote 6)

One of the key connections between Haneef and the Glasgow terrorists was they were found to have a phone SIM card that was thought to have originally belonged to Haneef. Though some of the information about Haneef was accurate, other information was not.[25]

While the particulars of the Haneef case are complex,[26] what is important for this example is that the Australian Immigration Minister at the time, Kevin Andrews, 'invoked the *character test* of the Migration Act in order to cancel Haneef's work visa and keep in him in detention even though he had been granted bail' (Emphasis Mine, Rix, 2011, p. 293). A Virtual Identity was constructed for Haneef that characterised him as a terrorist and following construction of this Virtual Identity, Haneef was held in custody, lost his job and suffered significant reputational costs. The reason why this is relevant is that these harms to Haneef would have likely been reduced or may not have come about had the Virtual Identity been accurate.

An important element to both broad and narrow examples of negligent information harms is the context of use. Both examples occurred when particular

[25] For instance, two of the key pieces of evidence used to charge Haneef were found to be incorrect – that he had lived with the Glasgow bombers and that a SIM card originally owned by Haneef was found at the scene of the bombing (See Endnote 9, Rix, 2011, p. 295).

[26] The Australian Government's enquiry into the case can be found at http://nla.gov.au/nla.arc-84427. Mark Rix and Lawrence McNamara offer analysis focusing on certain legal and media aspects of the case (McNamara, 2009; Rix, 2011).

government institutions used Virtual Identities as part of their decision procedures. Use of Personal Information in contexts like criminal justice raises significant moral concerns due to the magnitude of harms that can occur. Given the multirealisability of information, §5.8 and §5.9, a Virtual Identity can change given the contexts that it is used in. For a mobile phone salesperson, that Haneef lived with someone else and may have left them with a SIM card could result in Haneef receiving junk email about new rates to friends on the same mobile phone plan. That same Thin Information in the context of decision-making for law enforcement agencies resulted in far greater consequences for Haneef than receiving junk email.

Importantly, in both the broad and narrow cases described, the institutional actors may operate without any intention to deliberately harm the target people. However, given the vulnerability of minority groups or Haneef to the decisions of law enforcement agencies, the institutional actors were negligent in not ensuring a higher quality Virtual Identity prior to acting. The harms to the minority group and Haneef were of a criminal justice nature; however, the construction of the inaccurate Virtual Identity was a central element to bringing these harms about.

A counter argument can be raised here that, given the magnitude of harms of terrorist activity, such individual harms are a cost that must be borne to make society at large more secure. Similar to the case of Faisal Shahzad described in §6.3.1, potential terrorists can be identified through the construction of Virtual Identities. So though the law enforcement agencies described above got it wrong, aren't a few false positives a fair price to pay for making all our lives more secure?[27] Moreover, as was discussed at the opening of this chapter, the government has a responsibility to protect its citizens and a small number of false positives might be the price we have to pay for security.

In response to this, the general point that I am making is about *negligent* information harms; using statistical profiles of particular ethnic groups to determine law enforcement strategies is an instance of criminal profiling through the Essentialised Identities introduced in §4.5.4. The *negligence* arises in using *inaccurate* Virtual Identities to decide institutional activity. The purpose of this section is to demonstrate that harms *do* arise from negligent use of Personal Information. Second, drawing attention to the potential harms that arise from negligent information has a normative element; I am making a statement that due care needs to be taken in both avoiding the creation of inaccurate Virtual Identities and in the use of Virtual Identities. Third, given the context of use, the amount of care relies on a particular form of epistemic contextualism where the greater the harms of acting in a given way,[28] the greater the need for care in making decisions (Guerrero, 2007). Making

[27] Elliot Cohen discusses issues of harms and false positives and false negatives as part of the US Total Information Awareness (TIA) Project (Cohen, 2010, pp. 24–28).

[28] Vague language 'acting in a given way' is being used deliberately here. The decision procedures, particularly those in a criminal justice context, would typically involve more options than simply act/not act. In the Haneef case, for example, perhaps it was justified to arrest him in

decisions about how to treat a person if you are a law enforcement officer obviously involves increased standards of care compared to someone selling a mobile phone. Finally, there is an issue of fairness around the distribution of harms and benefits and vulnerabilities of particular individuals and groups arising from negligent information harms. Following sections return to this point.

9.3.3 *Incomplete Information Harms*

Information can be harmful to individuals but the harms do not need to be deliberate or a result of incorrect information. Instead of negligently using a Virtual Identity constructed from factually inaccurate data, harms can arise when the Virtual Identities are decontextualised and lose their intended meaning. Recall Incomplete Information from §5.6.1: incomplete Information arises when a speaker presents true, well-ordered, meaningful data, but this data either does not succeed in meeting the speaker's actual intention or the speaker's expressed intention is different to their actual intention. The reason for this lost meaning is that there is not enough additional contextual information to effectively afford that the destination's meaning corresponds to the source's intended meaning. Virtual Identities can produce Incomplete Information harms by being decontextualised and subsequently recontextualised.

Consider the reporting of scientific research without the necessary context. In the example of the MAOA gene from Chapter 5, one of the key controversial aspects was that the scientific research was communicated in a way that decoupled the genetic information from socio-economic factors, whilst claiming a link between genetic information and complex anti-social behaviours. 'The [MAOA] "warrior gene" controversy has shown how failing to emphasise the complexity of gene-environment interactions and their influence on behavioural differences between groups can plunge research into disrepute and fuel harmful discriminatory attitudes in society' (Wensley and King, 2008, p. 509).

The harms in the MAOA case arose from (at least) two complementary factors. First, genetic information was coupled with complex social behaviours, producing a Virtual Identity with a broad target – the indigenous population of New Zealand. In essence, a simplified reading of the research put forward the idea that Maoris are genetically predetermined to be anti-social. Second, like many minority ethnic groups, the Maori population in New Zealand is already subject to discrimination. Coupling a simplified Virtual Identity with a social context of discrimination, individual Maoris were at increased risk of further discrimination.

order to question him, but the cancellation of his visa by Minister Andrews on 'character grounds' was unjustified. In short, there is typically a plurality of options available, some combination of which is likely to be better than others. This sort of point is made by Michael Selgelid and Christian Enemark in a context of public health and security (Selgelid, 2009; Selgelid and Enemark, 2008).

And assuming that such unjustified discrimination is harmful, we have a situation of incomplete information harms.

Important for this example is that this sort of harm can come about without any deliberate intention to harm by either the researchers or any other people. And this lack of a deliberate will-to-harm can make it harder to identify such harms and harder to explain why we should care. By introducing the Identity/Information Dyad, we can now see how a Virtual Identity can form the basis for an Other/ Other-Regarding Identity, resulting in increased risk of vulnerable groups to discrimination. Given the multirealisability of information, these Virtual Identities can arise independently of the intentions of the individuals who produced the scientific information. As is the case with other race-based discrimination, the harmful practices can occur at a sub-personal level, where the agent neither intends nor knows that they are acting in a discriminatory fashion (Blair, Judd and Fallman, 2004). But until we show how identity and information interact, it may not be obvious how such incomplete information can be harmful.

A further element increasing vulnerability of targets to Incomplete Information Harms is, again, the institutional environment that the Virtual Identity is used in. Institutional practices often rely on Virtual Identities as central planks in decision procedures guiding the treatment of target individuals. However, if the base data from which Virtual Identities are constructed are not accurate: either because they are incorrect or incomplete, this can establish and entrench discriminatory practices. As with Negligent Information Harms, though no individual within the given institution is seeking to harm the target individuals, substantial harms can arise through a conjunction of negligent and incomplete informational practices.

One example of this is the increased discrimination faced by certain populations following the increased security measures adopted in response to terrorist activity in Western countries. Recent discussions of institutionalised profiling of Muslims falling under increased scrutiny and discrimination bear this out, what some are calling the danger of 'flying while Muslim': 'the tongue-in-cheek term for the discrimination many Muslim passengers feel they have faced at airports since 9/11. It can range from extra questions from airport staff, to formal searches by police, to secondary security screenings and visa problems when visiting America' (Khaleeli and BST, 2016). For instance, Faizah Shaheen was 'on her way back from her honeymoon when she was detained and questioned by police under schedule 7 of the Terrorism Act. Cabin crew on her outbound flight said they had spotted her reading a book about Syria. Shaheen said she was left in tears by the experience. Thomson airlines said: "Our crew are trained to report any concerns they may have as a precaution"' (Khaleeli and BST, 2016). The overall point is that Virtual Identities can produce Incomplete Information Harms by being decontextualised and subsequently recontextualised. Moreover, the institutional context of the recontexutualisation is an essential part in the severity of the impacts. The concern if Google's monitoring of your web-history incorrectly targets you for a particular advertisement due to negligent or incomplete information is much less than if people in a government security agency consider you a terrorist and seek to deport you, based on negligent or incomplete information.

9.3.4 *Limited Opportunity Harms*

Limited Opportunity Harms arise when a certain Virtual Identity is used to limit the range of opportunity that an individual might have. Norman Daniels argues that '[w]hile opportunity is a good enjoyed by individuals, protecting the space of exercisable opportunities is a societal obligation that creates a public good enjoyed by a population' (Daniels, 2008, pp. 2–3). The basic point here is that Virtual Identities can limit, sometimes quite substantially, the range of opportunities available to a person. Insofar as living a good life is contingent on a person having a reasonable range of opportunity, then limiting a person's opportunities is a harm.[29] Opportunity can be restricted in a number of ways; the target person can be broadly or narrowly targeted and the harms can be 'standard-harms' or 'micro-harms'.[30] A standard-harm is one which is an easily recognisable harm; a micro-harm is a harm that arises through the accumulation and/or aggregation of many small harms. An example of each is given and the role of Virtual Identity in these harms is brought out.

A Broad Standard Information Harm would be where a particular set of information is used to deny a *group* of people opportunity to access key social roles because they are of a certain group. For instance, denying people equality of access to particular social institutional roles based on the given gender, ethnicity, religious persuasion and so on. I call these standard-harms as it is standard that the outcome of such institutional roles is harmful: assuming that the group's particular Virtual Identity is irrelevant to the given discrimination, this is clearly against the standard accounts of equality and individual rights.[31] Further, this account holds that such decisions would lead to an overall worse state of affairs than without such limits on opportunity.

A Narrow Standard Information harm would arise when a particular set of information is used to deny opportunity to an *individual*. For instance, consider a case of

[29] The language of 'opportunity' here is deliberately Rawlsian: 'A second respect in which citizens view themselves as free is that they regard themselves as self-authenticating sources of valid claims. That is, they regard themselves as being entitled to make claims on their institutions so as to advance their conceptions of the good' (Rawls, 2001, p. 23). However, note that this tracks consequentialist concerns too. For instance, John Stewart Mill states: '[i]t is desirable, in short, that in things which do not primarily concern others, individuality should assert itself. Where, not the person's own character, but the traditions or customs of other people are the rule of conduct, there is wanting one of the principle ingredients of human happiness and quite the chief ingredient of individual and social progress' (Mill, 1971, p. 185). A similar set of points is made by James Griffin (Griffin, 1986, pp. 235–242).

[30] I take this terminology of 'micro-harms' from Samantha Brennan's work on 'micro-inequities', see Brennan, (2013).

[31] The idea of equal opportunity of access to offices and positions is a particularly Rawlsian account, appealing directly to his Second Principle of Justice (Rawls, 1971, p. 302).

a male on a sex offender registry: when he was fourteen, he sent naked photos of himself to his then fifteen-year-old girlfriend via his mobile phone. Some legal jurisdictions count this as producing and distributing child pornography and so he was put in a sex-offender registry list. At age twenty-four, he is still on this list and as a result of this information, has his opportunity limited. The capacity for him to move beyond his youthful action may be severely limited: certain jobs will be denied to him, personal relationships may suffer or not materialise and his own physical security may be under threat. In short, his range of opportunities is limited by a Virtual Identity. Note that this Virtual Identity, while accurate in a sense, is incomplete if the situation of his 'production and distribution of child pornography' is not part of his description on the sex offender registry: that he was fourteen and his girlfriend fifteen seems to be particularly relevant here. Additionally, the focus in this section is on harms beyond any particular reprisals – his opportunity to be an equal member of society is severely limited.

A Broad Micro-Harm would be a case where individuals of a certain group are limited in their opportunities by the constant and persistent use of a Virtual Identity. What makes this example distinct from the Broad Standard Harm is that the harms only materialise through accumulation and/or aggregation of many very small harms (Brennan, 2013). For instance, consider the many small inequalities faced by women in much of the developed world. Compared with men, 'women pay more for haircuts, dry cleaning and cars. More seriously, [women] also earn less, are less well represented in our political institutions, do more than our fair share of household work, enjoy less personal security on city streets and have less leisure time than do our male counterparts' (Brennan, 2009, p. 141). Each of these events alone may constitute a minimal harm. However, if practices such as this are repeated every day, an accumulation of harms develops. Second, summing across the harm types, we have an aggregation of harm types too – having to pay more for goods and services may only be a slightly bad thing, but if you are paid less and have little political opportunity to change things, then we have a more serious set of harms.

Samantha Brennan describes these sorts of harms as 'lumpy'. A lump is good or bad whose value qualitatively changes when considered in increments or in aggregate. 'Five minutes of a babysitter's time does me very little good. It's not equivalent to 1/12 the amount of a good an hour of his time would give me' (Brennan, 2006, p. 260). Being treated differently because of one's gender can produce a host of micro-harms that are only morally relevant when considered in lumps. This is exactly the core point recognised by the Identity/Information Dyad; we cannot properly recognise the moral importance of micro-harms when they are disaggregated. Virtual Identities can play a central role in this limiting opportunity as Deliberate, Negligent or Incomplete Information Harms. If institutional decision-making is based on the Virtual Identity for a given person and the particular aspect of the Virtual Identity is irrelevant to the decision-making, then a host of invisible micro-harms can propagate discrimination at an institutional level.

Narrow Micro-Harms operate in the same way as Broad Micro-Harms. However, rather than the informational target being a broad group, the target person is a particular individual. For instance, consider the phenomenon of cyber-bullying. Calling Adam 'fatty' once, while unpleasant and unkind, is unlikely to result in any serious harm to Adam. However, consider that Adam is called 'fatty' repeatedly, by a large group of his peers. Further, consider that this is done with the aid of an almost omnipresent internet-based social media: Adam has few places to escape to, to avoid being called Fatty. Now, consider that Adam is a fourteen-year-old school boy, especially vulnerable to the attitudes of his peers and heavily dependent on social media as a central part of his social life. The aggregation of micro-harms to Adam by being called 'fatty' should now be understood as morally substantive. The informational technologies enable a persistent and repetitive reinforcement of Adam's inferior social status, in a subtle but pervasive way.

In each of the situations so described, a particular Virtual Identity is ascribed to the individual, which limits their capacity to develop their own sense of the good as their range of opportunity is limited. This may obviously count as a harm – when being black or a registered sex offender limits the jobs that one can take and the places that one can live. Or it may be micro-harms – institutional discrimination and school-bullying both present the potential for certain groups or particular individuals to be excluded from important social activities. The Identity/Information Dyad operates to expose just how such harms come about, with a particular capacity to explain such harms arising from innocuous Personal Information.

9.3.5 *Closed Identity Harms*

For the opportunity harms described – broad/narrow and/or standard/micro – a parallel set of harms can also arise, often in tandem with the Limited Opportunity Harms. Rather than equality of opportunity, the explanatory priority here is focused on how such devalued Virtual Identities can negatively impact the target person's identity development. Situations like those described above can also involve harms of misrecognition. Charles Taylor writes:

> The demand for recognition ... is given urgency by the supposed links between recognition and identity, where this latter term designates something like a person's understanding of who they are, of their fundamental defining characteristics as a human being. The thesis is that our identity is partly shaped by recognition or its absence, often by the *mis*recognition of others, and so a person or group of people can suffer real damage, real distortion, if the people or society around them mirror back to them a confining or demeaning or contemptible picture of themselves. Nonrecognition or misrecognition can inflict harm, can be a form of oppression, imprisoning someone in a false, distorted, and reduced mode of being.
>
> (Emphasis Original, Taylor, 1994a, p. 25)

This is Self-Regarding Identity, filtered through a devalued Other/Other Identity. As argued, information forms identity, §6.3 and identity forms information, §6.4. If Adam is constantly called 'fatty' this promotes and reinforces to him that he is fat *and* that people think less of him *because* he is fat. Likewise, institutionalised omission of minorities from popular media or repeatedly promoting demeaning caricatures of already marginalised groups are likely to have negative impacts on their Self-Regarding Identity. As Catriona Mackenzie has argued (Mackenzie, 2000), the capacity to imagine oneself outside of a given social position is highly important in developing a person's capacity to develop a healthy Self-Regarding Identity.

Further, limiting people's capacity to imagine themselves into new social positions can have a bootstrapping effect on limiting opportunity: 'Even in a context of formal legal equality of opportunity, social reform has limited power to reshape people's lives and opportunities if the cultural imaginary is predominantly phallocentric' (Mackenzie, 2000, p. 125). Offering formal equality of opportunity, such that no-one is actively prevented from taking on an important office or position, may not be enough. Those who have not traditionally held such roles must know that they can actually have that role and can perform well in it.

Limiting identity development by treating people as less valued than others is harmful. The role that information plays in this is that the magnitude of harms can be made worse by technology. Such Closed Identity Harms are likely to already exist as a background set of social conditions. Adam is called 'fatty' because our society typically devalues the overweight and because school children can be unthinking in their actions. What informational technologies do is afford such demeaning Virtual Identities to be created and perpetuated with ease. Likewise, in cases like race-based institutional discrimination, building incomplete information into the basic decision-making procedures can afford particular existing discriminations to persist and extend their harms.

> If the designers of computer systems for forensic genetic profiling are guided by the idea that race is a scientifically valid categorization and integrate this assumption into the system, the result can be systematic and unfair discrimination between individuals or groups of individuals. The use of race within a criminal and forensic context, especially when based upon genetic information, creates the potential for conflation of race, criminality and genetics and poses concerns for social justice.
>
> (Weckert and Henschke, 2009)

Reducing the scope for opportunity can occur through institutional decision-making that relies on negligent and incomplete Virtual Identities. This reduced set of opportunities perpetuates the Broad Micro-Harms, continually devaluing Self-Regarding Identity, leading to a reduced scope for opportunity. Particular groups can become marginalised and suffer significant harms to their identity development, despite the fact the no individual is necessarily deliberately harming them.

In fact, given the lack of a deliberate will-to-harm, micro-harms arising from negligent and incomplete Virtual Identities can be very hard to recognise, explain and deal with. This is where the Identity/Information Dyad is especially useful: by drawing out the dyadic relation between identity and information it offers a way of explaining why such micro-harms are morally relevant. Second, it can readily explain how surveillance technologies can play an important causal role in harming target people. Considering that many of these harms are unintentional and invisible, such an explanatory tool is needed.

9.4 INFORMATIONAL ACCESS

Rather than looking at harms qua the vulnerability of individuals or groups to suffering brought about by problematic use of Personal Information, this section's moral foundation is built on the value of fairness. Fairness here covers three areas of discussion: the ways that Personal Information, through Virtual Identities, can restrict people's access to services; the ways that shifting the context of application and use Personal Information is itself an injustice; and inequalities in the ways that costs and benefits of Personal Information are distributed.

Like §9.3, the explanatory focus is harm to the Person As Target. In contrast to the direct information harms described above, however, the concern here derives its moral importance from the *interpersonal* impacts of the use of Virtual Identities. That is, this set of harms are also drawn from the taxonomy of identity elements, §4.6. But in contrast to §9.3, this section will be looking at people's vulnerabilities, to the harms that arise from Other/Other-Regarding Identity. The claim here is that Personal Information is also shaped by the interpersonal understanding of how I perceive you and that the Other/Other-Regarding Identity, in its dyadic relationship with Personal Information, guides my actions in morally relevant ways.

9.4.1 *Fair Distribution of Access*

Jeroen van den Hoven and Emma Rooksby have argued that 'information is necessary . . . for rational life planning and for making rational choices in carrying out a plan' (van den Hoven and Rooksby, 2008). Given this, they argue, 'access to information can be construed as a Rawlsian primary good' (van den Hoven and Rooksby, 2008). In short, on this account, access to information is a necessary condition of living a good life in the modern developed world.

A general claim about information being a primary good may hold, but something else needs to be added – we need to be able to say why that set of information is necessary to make an informed choice. For instance, having access to a rich and detailed Virtual Identity about one's self is likely to be extremely useful for making informed decisions about one's own life. In addition to the privacy and ownership claims described in Chapter 8, a parallel claim can be made that, insofar as a Virtual

Identity would be useful to informing a person's life-plan, they should have some access claims to it.[32]

Van den Hoven has also argued that information can be used to deny access unequally. The concern here derives from the modern technological developments that require people to give Personal Information to others in pursuit of good or service X, '[A]lthough a market mechanism for trading personal data seems to be kicking in on a global scale, not all individual consumers are aware of their economic opportunities and if they are, they are not always in a position to trade their data or pursue their interests in a *transparent* and *fair market* environment so as to get a fair price for them' (Emphasis Mine, van den Hoven, 2008, p. 312). Van den Hoven's claim has two elements: transparency and a fair market.

Though a user may be willing to enter such a transaction, if the transaction is not transparent it may not meet the basic conditions of properly *informed* consent.[33] This point is recognised by Daniel Solove (Solove, 2004) and Helen Nissenbaum (Nissenbaum, 2009). This lack of informed consent arises if we don't properly know who we are giving our Personal Information to, or what they plan on doing with it.[34] This may not be of great concern when considering that the good or service being pursued is without great value – the potential user can decide that giving access to their Personal Information is not worth the benefits of the given service – rejecting a 'cookie' and thus not being able to access a free entertainment website is unlikely to have any serious impact on a person's quality of life.

However, what if the good or service is of great value or is necessary to gain access to core human needs? Think here of government programmes that determine access to the given programme via provision of Personal Information. If these programmes are of special importance – access to food, healthcare, education and so on – then the user cannot simply choose not to use or reject the service. As before, it is government institutions that provide basic services for people that are of special concern here.

These situations will require Personal Information from the user to either prove the user is justified in gaining access to the given good or service, or to actualise the good or the service. Operating in a fair market would require fair trade of Personal Information for the given service. Consider that the user is buying a hat on the internet; it is reasonable to provide some set of Personal Information to verify that the user is who they say they are. However, we would consider it unreasonable if the

[32] Recall from §1.2 that this basic right of access to one's own information is seen by the UK Government as central to their Open Governance and Open Health Initiatives (§1.2, U.K. Government, 2012).

[33] In line with the discussion in §1.3, I am taking an account of informed consent like that proposed by Tom Beauchamp and James Childress (Beauchamp and Childress, 2001b, pp. 77–98). I do, however, note that there are problems with this approach to informed consent and informed consent more generally (Clayton, 2005; Manson and O'Neill, 2007; Netzer and Biller-Andorno, 2004; Skene and Milkwood, 1997).

[34] This sort of problem with informed consent has been discussed in relation to human data biobanks (Clayton, 2005).

Personal Information was unconnected to the good or service being requested: giving credit card verification details in order to buy a hat seems reasonable, providing nude photographs would not be.[35] Furthermore, while we would consider that credit card details may be needed for purchasing a hat online and giving personal medical data is needed for healthcare purposes, giving personal medical information to purchase a hat online is unreasonable. These points presume that the information being sought is in line with the goal of the access. This point is returned to in Chapter 10.

Taking van den Hoven and Rooksby's point that access to information may be a primary good, especially so in the case of Personal Information and van den Hoven's point that limiting access to necessary goods or services may promote inequality, we have a dual problem of access. The claim is that we may need access to our own Personal Information in order to make informed decisions about our own lives. Second, we should be able to access other primary goods without *needlessly* trading *unnecessary* Personal Information.

Virtual Identities can result in people and institutions treating like-cases differently and without justification. What my analysis offers is the explication of this discrimination. Given §8.4, it is potentially an infringement of property claims. Further, following, §8.5, such requirements may display a lack of due recognition for individuals, by inappropriately weighting the importance of the information. Finally, the institutions need to focus on minimising the sorts of harms outlined in §9.3 resulting from the way the Virtual Identity is used. The dyad adds to the discussion an explication of just *how* such discriminatory inequalities come about by showing the mechanisms operating between identity and information. Importantly, by requiring us to consider information in aggregate, the dyad shows that such inequalities can occur when accessing and using *innocuous* Personal Information.

The upshot of the access concern is that people should have access to Virtual Identities that relates to them, either as a source or target person. In order to make this claim reasonable, it needs to take three things into account. First, the Virtual Identity needs to actually be relevant to the person's life plans. That is, they must be able to provide reasons as to how that Virtual Identity is likely to be useful in their pursuit of their conception of the good. Second, they need to be able to show that their access to the Virtual Identity is not likely to result in any of the harms described in §9.3. Finally, as mentioned, some Personal Information may be required to access other primary goods. This chapter and Chapter 8 have both been extended discussions of why Virtual Identities ought to be treated with care: I have argued the general claims that the more revealing of the source person the Virtual Identity is and/or the more vulnerable it makes the target person, the more care should be taken with this Personal Information. This is relevant in that while a Virtual Identity

[35] Predatory loan sharks, for example, have demanded that nude photos are included with loan applications (Coonan, 2016).

may be necessary for access to a given good or service, the justification needed for that Virtual Identity increases as the amount revealed and the vulnerability of source and target increase. The conclusions here are that the need for the Virtual Identity should track to the purpose of the good or service and that those handling the Personal Information have a greater responsibility to treat it with care. These points are revisited in Chapter 10.

9.4.2 *Fair Distribution across Contexts*

In addition to informational *equality*, van den Hoven has also argued that we ought to care about informational *injustices*.[36] This starts from Michael Walzer's *Spheres of Justice*:

> Social goods have social meanings, and we find our way to distributive justice through an interpretation of those meanings. We search for principles internal to each distributive sphere ... the disregard of these principles is tyranny. To convert one good into another, when there is no *intrinsic connection* between the two, is to invade the sphere where another company of men and women properly rules.
>
> (Emphasis Mine, Walzer, 1983, p. 19)

Van den Hoven takes Walzer's spheres of justice concept and argues that information used in context A should not be used in context B (van den Hoven, 2008; van den Hoven and Rooksby, 2008). A paradigm example is that Personal Information given to a medical professional should be used only in a health care context. Medical information given in a health care context should not shift to a criminal justice context.[37] An informational injustice has occurred by using the Personal Information in a new context.

Walzer's basic premise is derived from the way that context changes the meaning of things (Walzer, 1983, p. 19). This goes to the multirealisability of information, as discussed in previous chapters, a point mirrored by van den Hoven. 'The meaning and value of information is local and allocative schemes and local practices that distribute access to information are also associated with specific spheres' (van den Hoven and Rooksby, 2008). A patient ascribes a certain meaning to their Personal Information and that meaning may carry with it a level of importance for the patient. Changing contexts changes the information. This qualitative change is accurately described by the emergence of Virtual Identities from aggregated information. The dyad offers the explanatory apparatus to show just how the information has actually changed.

36 Informational injustices were introduced in §2.5.3.

37 This claim has an important caveat – Medical information given in a health care context should not shift to a criminal justice context, *unless there is a justifying reason* to use it in that criminal justice context. That is, there will be circumstances where Personal Information given in a context of health care can be used in a criminal justice context, but further justification is needed. This point is touched on below and covered in Chapter 10.

Perhaps the greater intuitive force of a Walzerian approach to informational injustice arises from the expectation of how the information will be used. The intuition is that Personal Information given in context A was needed to provide a good or service also located in context A. This seems in part to track to a promissory obligation whereby the promise, in this case using Personal Information in context A only, arises due to the damages arising from the breach of contract, whether it is due to the increased vulnerability of the one or more parties to the contract, or importance of the institution that the contract has been conducted in.[38] As I understand it, van den Hoven's informational injustice holds that the source person has been wronged by not having their privacy, ownership and/or basic claims respected. Again, the dyad captures this promissory breach by explaining how aggregated information has become different from its original form.

Yet this does not mean that Personal Information should only stay in the particular sphere in which it originally arose. For instance, consider a parent and young child both present to a family doctor with the same sexually transmitted disease. In this case, the doctor should alert the relevant institutional actors such that the potential sexual abuse of the child is properly investigated. While medical information may have been transferred from the medical context to the criminal justice context, given the potential rights violation and/or harms to the child, this transfer from one context to another has justificatory reasons. Similarly, consider an example where a person arrives at an airport with a set of symptoms tracking to an emerging pandemic outbreak. In this example, Personal Information gathered in a transport context may have been transferred to a context of public health. Again, however, given the potentially massive rights violations and harms that could occur from an unchecked pandemic, the transfer of information from one context to another has a justificatory reason. This point is covered in more detail in Chapter 10.

As mentioned in §2.5.3, the Identity/Information Dyad adds explanatory force to van den Hoven's account of informational injustice by showing how information changes. Importantly, the dyad adds three explicatory steps between information and injustice. It argues that we need to see information in aggregate. It shows that information in aggregate is of a different form to non-aggregated information – what was once a set of innocuous information is now a revealing and powerful Virtual Identity. Finally, extending from the discussions of chapters 7, 8 and 9, the dyad has given us the tools to explain just *why* the changes in information from innocuous to Virtual Identity are morally important.

[38] This idea of promises making some parties to the promise vulnerable and the importance of the given social institution in which the promise was made, is taken from Goodin (Goodin, 1985, pp. 50–52).

9.4.3 *Fair Distribution Of Returns*

A final issue is concerned with the distribution of resources arising from Personal Information. This operates on the premise that that some people or groups should not profit unreasonably from the use of Personal Information and/or that some people or groups should not be unreasonably burdened with harms arising from the use of Personal Information. The basic idea here is that any harms and benefits arising from Personal Information use should be distributed in line with good reasons.[39]

To begin, consider the World Medical Association's *Ethical Principles for Medical Research Involving Human Subjects* (World Medical Association, 1964), which states that '[i]n medical practice and in medical research, most interventions involve risks and burdens' and that '[m]edical research is subject to ethical standards that promote respect for all human subjects and protect their health and rights' (Paragraphs 8 and 9 World Medical Association, 1964). There are risks and burdens in medical research and those who are subjects of research are entitled to care and respect. These are the points made about information harms, above and about the rights of source people, Chapter 8.

Clauses 19 and 30 are of particular interest here. Clause 19 was introduced in 2000 and addressed the concern of whether research would actually benefit the target communities or not and

> explicitly requires that research should only be done on a particular population *if the fruits of that research could realistically be expected to benefit that particular population*. According to the requirement, it would be ethically unacceptable to test a new treatment, for example, on an impoverished population unless there is reason to believe that the treatment will be affordable and *will actually become available to that population if the treatment is shown to be effective*.
>
> (Emphases Mine, Selgelid, 2005, p. 66)

Clause 30, introduced in 2004, deals with *continuing* standards of care that patients should receive after trials have ceased, requiring that '[i]f a new treatment is shown to be superior to the control arm therapy against which it is tested, for example, *then all subject-patients should be guaranteed access to the new treatment afterwards*' (Emphases Mine, Selgelid, 2005, p. 67). The motivations behind clauses 19 and 30 were to ensure that, given the basic rights that patients and medical research subjects are commonly held to have and given the vulnerability of individuals and groups to harms arising from interventions and research, they are entitled to some part of the

[39] In talking of 'good reasons' here, I am tying 'good reasons' to fair distribution. This tracks to the Rawlsian idea of operating within a veil of ignorance such that we would accept a given distribution in a way that did not unnecessarily burden the least well off and in a mutually reciprocal way in line with public reason. See Rawls, (1971, pp. 12, 136–142, 1999b, pp. 129–180, 1999a).

benefits arising from the research. As above, consider the various arguments introduced in §1.5 and developed in Chapter 8. Generally, holding like-cases alike, if we care that the harms and benefits arising from medical procedures are distributed fairly, we should care similarly about *all* similarly intimate Personal Information.

What the dyad adds to this discussion is a tool to explain just how benefits and harms can arise from information. While it may be a trivial truth to say that 'information is power', as has been argued throughout, this may not seem obviously true when applied to innocuous information. The dyad gives us such a way to recognise the benefits and harms of information, in a way that captures innocuous information. Importantly, by urging a focus on source and target people and spelling out the particular rights and harms that Personal Information can be involved in, the dyad gives a structure such that we can better recognise when benefits or harms are being distributed unfairly.

The discussion of distribution of medical benefits is instructive for government surveillance. First, Clause 19 makes a general point that the costs or harms of informational use should not be borne unfairly by particular individuals or groups in the population. Second, Clause 30 tells us that those who have taken on certain risks are entitled to continuing care. Consider surveillance for terrorism. Specific people and groups ought not unfairly bear the costs. And those who have helped with a surveillance programme are entitled to continuing care. That is, particular individuals ought not suffer the costs of surveillance programmes in a way that lacks justification. Further, care needs to be taken and benefits shared, as part of engagement with particular target communities.

9.5 WHERE TO NOW?

Even if the arguments have held so far, a much harder problem arises: so what do we do when different values are in conflict? For instance, I have raised a host of arguments about the limits of surveillance, with a particular focus on government surveillance programmes. I opened the chapter with the problem of government – they must be limited in their surveillance, but they cannot do nothing; they have a responsibility to act in ways that protect their own citizens and, arguably, cooperate with other governments to protect people irrespective of national ties. While rights, harms and fairness are important and surveillance programmes should be limited, what if there is a possible supreme emergency, like an international disease pandemic that could kill hundreds of millions and a global pandemic surveillance programme is needed to prevent this from occurring? It seems that the surveillance is justified and the potential or actual wrongs, harms and unfairness are trumped by the incoming global catastrophe.

This trades on the idea of hundreds of millions dead vs. the loss of one individual's rights/harms to an individual. The discussion can be justifiably criticised as being overly simplistic: in part, because I myself called for the use of sophisticated ethical theories over simplistic ones in §1.4 and in part because this is simplistic: I have reduced the decision-making to two options – hundreds of millions lives vs. one person's rights. In practice, very few cases are likely to meet this millions of lives at risk figure. And even in the case of pandemics, it is likely that many more millions of people will be under surveillance. A core concern about the surveillance programmes revealed by Snowden was the sheer amount of information gathered and the number of people under surveillance (Greenwald, 2014, pp. 90–169). As Snowden has shown, in the age of surveillance, the reality is that international surveillance networks do engage in frequent and repeated infringements of basic liberties. In short, is too much being made from the hundreds of millions dead vs. one person's rights example?

My response is twofold: one of the major points of this chapter and the book is to draw attention to the role that Personal Information plays in people's lives and the important mutual relation between identity and Personal Information. At its most basic, this book's aim is to convince people that they ought to consider Personal Information in dealing with people: that Personal Information is something that is of special moral concern. Second, this analysis is not expected to solve every issue concerning Personal Information. However, I can offer a basic answer: we need to take a moderate pluralist approach that is context sensitive:

> A moderate pluralist approach ... would start with the aim to promote utility, liberty and equality as independent legitimate social goals, and ... aim to strike a balance or make trade-offs between them in cases of conflict, without giving absolute priority to any one of these goals in particular (or taking any one of them to be the "default value") ... Perhaps the importance, priority or weight that should be given to the promotion of any one of these goals should not be fixed but, rather, context dependent. The importance of equality, for example, should arguably depend not only on the magnitude or degree of inequality, but should also depend on the nature of the inequalities in question.
>
> (Selgelid, 2009, pp. 199, 200)

This methodology is admittedly complex and must, by necessity, vary from case to case. However, a general methodology can be proposed.

Working from a principle of treating like-cases alike, we should, in fact, treat like-cases alike and different cases differently. As a general rule of thumb, the more alike cases are, the more they should be treated alike. However, underpinning this is the necessity to ensure that the particulars of each case are thoroughly described and the relevant ethical aspects of each case given, with principled justifications as to why aspects count as ethically relevant. For instance, in situations involving Personal Information, the relation between identity and Personal Information would need to be included, with reasons as to why privacy, ownership and recognition claims are legitimate/outweighed/not relevant, to show that harms have been minimised/outweighed/not relevant and people are treated equally and fairly.

Like the uses of cases in law and medicine (Jonsen and Toulmin, 1988, p. 42–46), a complex set of cases would develop through time, to allow a functioning principled methodology to emerge. Like legal case law, the judgements on cases will come with detailed reasoning as to why a given case received a particular decision (DeMarco and Ford, 2006, p. 490). This goes directly to the role of reason-giving in ethics, that passing judgement is not sufficient; justificatory reasons must be given. In addition, as Joseph DeMarco notes, a major limitation with the casuistic method is 'its inability to specify the proper role of principles and rules' (DeMarco, 1994, p. 61). Instead of relying on cases alone, the practice needs to be dynamic, actively developed through mutually causal process between abstract principles and practice. 'Principles take meaning and specificity ... from practice and rules, while practices and rules are judged by principles' (DeMarco, 1997, p. 297). Ideally, this would promote a stable reflective equilibrium.[40] 'Reflective equilibrium is the state of one's beliefs ... when "principles and judgments coincide." When a person's beliefs are in reflective equilibrium, the structure of those beliefs, from the particular to the most general, cohere' (Ebertz, 1993, p. 194). Through time, a publicly justified system would develop that not only offers normative guidance as to new cases, but can give explicit justificatory reasoning as to why a given case should be judged in a given way.

As should be clear, an approach such as this that seeks to take into account individual rights, harms and fairness is destined to encounter conflict between values.

> What we really need, then, is a ... framework of political philosophy that provides a principled way for striking a balance between them in cases of conflict ... no well-developed theory for striking such a balance appears to be on offer in mainstream political philosophy ... Until such a theory is developed, the approach of applied ethics [mentioned] – i.e., the application of existing theories to concrete cases – should not be considered all that promising, if, as I surmise, a large proportion of ethical questions arise because of conflicting values.
>
> (Selgelid, 2009, p. 199)

While there are ways of resolving some of these value conflicts,[41] such resolutions are likely to be unconvincing in cases of serious ethical dilemmas. This is a serious

40 There is not the space to enter into a discussion of reflective equilibrium here. However, the model that I am thinking of is that of a wide reflective equilibrium proposed by Rawls (particularly section 2.5 of *Outline of a Decision Procedure for Ethics*) and developed by Norman Daniels. (Daniels, 1979, 1980; Rawls, 1971, pp. 46–50, 1951. See especially §2.5 and Rawls' discussion of defining the class of considered judgements, pp. 181–183).

41 For instance, James Sterba argues that high ranking self-interested reasons take priority over low ranking altruistic reasons and vice versa (Sterba, 2005, p. 20). Similarly, DeMarco argues that '[c]onflict among parts of a system are inevitable. For example, it may be that we can only gain freedom when welfare is reduced. These trade-offs are unfortunate, perhaps even tragic, but in dynamic coherence, neither is given general priority. Instead, we expect circumstances to dominate. A serious loss of freedom is unacceptable given a small gain in welfare, especially under conditions of abundance' (DeMarco, 1997, p. 296).

challenge for any 'common-sense' morality that tries to develop a principled and guiding moral pluralism. The concluding chapter shows that the technological focus of the book, coupled to the Identity/Information Dyad, provides some way of stepping around this problem.

9.6 SNOWDEN REVISITED: HARMS, BENEFITS AND DISTRIBUTION

This chapter set up the problem of surveillance with reference to Snowden's leaks and the special power of institutions. In particular, the core problem posed was one of political philosophy – what are the rights and responsibilities of the states and how ought these play out in reference to the state's intelligence institutions in the age of surveillance? It is my contention that a focus on the character of Snowden is of little relevance to a moral assessment of institutions and surveillance – the question of whether those institutions should have Personal Information in the first place is independent of how it became publicly known that they have that Personal Information.

Just as the rights of an individual can be overridden in conditions of countervailing reasons, so too the claims of an institution can be overridden if there are justifying reasons. In this case, there are two relevant and serious institutional claims. First is the claim that an institution needs Personal Information in order to achieve its institutional ends. Second is a claim to secrecy: that certain things, such as government surveillance programmes, must remain secret in order to operate effectively. But again, this second claim about secrecy is derived from the first claim – it is only if that programme is morally justified in the first place that the claims to secrecy stand up. Further to this, the question about institutional access to Personal Information is logically prior to questions about public release of information about government surveillance programmes – Snowden couldn't release the information about the programmes if the programmes did not exist in the first place. So again, a comprehensive analysis of what Snowden revealed must include some engagement with the question of *why* those surveillance programmes were being conducted. Questions of a whistleblower's character are morally interesting, but they are not the point here.

So, we now turn to the question of justification. On Seumas Miller's account, a social institution derives its moral legitimacy from the collective good that it produces, where the collective good is 'a jointly produced good that is and ought to be, produced and made available to the whole community because it is a desirable good and one to which the members of the community have a joint moral right' (Miller, 2010b, p. 7). However, parallel with the permissions and responsibilities accorded to a given institution, 'there ought to be moral constraints on institutional activities, for example, human rights constraints' (Miller, 2010b, p. 64). So, in order to see if the state surveillance programmes are justified, we must identify the collective good that such institutions produce, whether the particular institutions actually meet that end and what the moral constraints should be.

On the issue of the justification of surveillance, the collective good is collective security. Lifting the discussion from the basic claim that 'the first duty of the state is to the security of its citizens', as former UK Security and Intelligence Coordinator David Omand puts it: 'The justification for secret intelligence is in the end an empirical one: it reduces the risks from decisions that governments decide have to be taken in the national interest' (Omand, 2010, p. 7). And in this, intelligence institutions are vital. So, we now have a justifying end for state surveillance and thus have a *potential* justification for the overriding of individual rights. This should be uncontroversial – when considering police surveillance of a criminal, for example, if there is sufficient concern about that criminal, surveillance can be justified even though it overrides the criminal's claims about a right to privacy.

However, in liberal democratic societies, this does not give carte blanche to the police; the conditions of proportionality, discrimination and necessity must be met.[42] Proportionality means that the criminal's actions or future actions pose sufficient risk to society that they outweigh the right of privacy – placing a known litterbug under surveillance is disproportional, while doing the same to a possible serial rapist is proportional.[43] Discrimination means that there must be sufficient cause to justify the surveillance – an individual can't be targeted for surveillance 'just because'; there has to be some justifying cause of suspicion in the first place. Necessity means that less intrusive methods than covert surveillance must be tried first.

So what of large-scale surveillance programmes? In Australia, the Parliamentary Joint Committee on Intelligence and Surveillance (PJCIS) review of the laws around metadata retention recommended that 'the authorised officer making the authorisation must be satisfied on reasonable grounds that any interference with the privacy of any person or persons that may result from the disclosure or use is justifiable and proportionate ... [regarding] the gravity of the conduct being investigated' (Parliamentary Joint Committee on Intelligence and Surveillance, 2015). The PJCIS report recognises that with Personal Information like metadata, proportionality is absolutely core to any justified use of that information.

42 These three conditions are taken from the literature on justified use of lethal violence in self-defence. In this literature, if proportionality, discrimination and necessity are met, then one can use lethal violence against the relevant target. I consider here that if meeting proportionality, discrimination and necessity can justify killing someone, then they would typically justify overriding other rights like privacy and property too. Such discussions are controversial and nuanced and cannot be covered in detail here, but for more exceptionalism, see (Allhoff, 2012; Fiala, 2006) and for more on rights forfeiture and lethal violence see (Fletcher and Ohlin, 2008; Uniacke, 1996).

43 Proportionality, while it seems simple, is complex. As Thomas Hurka notes when discussing proportionality in war, actual proportionality calculations are extremely complex (Hurka, 2005).

This chapter's discussion of information harms is fundamental to any proportionality calculation – the five harm types outlined must be recognised and calculated against the *likely* goods that would come from surveillance. That is, for a proportionality calculation to have moral legitimacy one must do more than simply refer to 'community security' or some other general collective good. The specific contribution of *this* particular surveillance effort must be specified. Moreover, note the way the Identity/Information Dyad keeps the scales balanced. As more weight is placed on the *collective* good of surveillance – the justifying cause emerges from the aggregation of the goods of surveillance; one must place a corresponding weight in the aggregated harm of surveillance – the rights violations and potential harm types must also be aggregated. Thus, an appeal to justify the collective good of surveillance must also include the emergent information harms from surveillance. And for the surveillance programmes revealed by Snowden, those aggregated rights violations and potential information harms are immense: for example, one unit of the NSA, in a thirty-day period, collected data on '97 billion emails and 124 billion phone calls from around the world' (Greenwald, 2014, p. 92).

In terms of surveillance, discrimination refers to the capacity to target people who are deserving of being targets. Even one of the harshest critics of the NSA's surveillance programme, Greenwald, recognises this distinction. 'Defenders of suspicionless mass surveillance often insist, for example, that some spying is always necessary. But this is a strawman proposition; nobody disagrees with that. The alternative to mass surveillance is not the complete elimination of surveillance. It is, instead, targeted surveillance, aimed only at those for whom there is substantial evidence to believe that they are engaged in real wrongdoing' (Greenwald, 2014, p. 251). Greenwald's point is that surveillance of specific targets is permissible, but there must be some justification to warrant that surveillance in the first place.

This point about discrimination concerns the willingness of citizens to give up basic rights like privacy in order to feel secure. 'The perception that invasive surveillance is confined only to a marginalized and deserving group of those doing wrong . . . ensures that the majority acquiesces to the abuse of power or even cheers it on' (Greenwald, 2014, 182). That we may feel comfortable about certain national security-oriented programmes indicates a sense of certainty and trust that our institutions are acting fairly. But this can be a cognitive bias, specifically, the 'just world belief',[44] where 'people operate under the assumption that the world is a just place, commonly expressed in the psychological literature as "people get what they deserve and deserve what they get" (Kasperbauer, 2015, p. 218). If I am not negatively

[44] The 'just world belief' was first researched by Melvin Lerner, outlined in his *The Belief in a Just World: A Fundamental Delusion* (Lerner, 1980) and has undergone a number of recent conceptual developments (Poon and Chen, 2014; Scott, 2008; Stroebe et al., 2015; Sutton and Winnard, 2007). However, the basic idea of the just world belief, that if the subject benefits from a given system, then the system's institutions are felt to be operating justly, is what is relevant here.

impacted or benefit from the way that a given institution operates, I have the sense that this institution must be fair. But the actual fairness of a given institution is something distinct from my sense that it is fair. That is, if we are to assess the fairness of a given system, we have to do more than take note of people's subjective experiences of that system.

As indicated in §9.4, the Identity/Information Dyad can offer useful granularity to questions of fairness and its relation to discrimination. That is, we need to ask, do those targeted by a surveillance programme deserve to be targets? Second, do those who benefit from surveillance targets bear the cost? For instance, is it justified for those who look Muslim to be targeted for increased suspicion at airports? Given the background concerns about terrorism, one might be inclined to say yes. However, in a working justice system in a liberal democratic society there must be some justifying reason why this person deserves close scrutiny beyond some classification within an Essentialised Identity. Moreover, as a Royal United Services Institute report pointed out, there are at least equal terrorism threats posed from nationalist terrorists (Royal United Services Institute, 2016). Thus, the indiscriminate targeting of Muslims runs counter to liberal democratic theories of justice and is not supported by the facts around actual terrorist threats.

Again, however, given the fear around terrorism, many citizens of liberal-democratic countries are willing to allow violations to their right to privacy in order to increase community security. So perhaps the majority of citizens are actually bearing the costs of the given surveillance programmes? However, this position needs to take into account who is actually bearing the heavy costs of such surveillance programmes. As a typical Caucasian on an Australian passport, I only suffer minor inconveniences when passing through airport security; I do not bear the costs of increased suspicion in the way that a dark-skinned bearded man from Yemen or a dark-skinned woman in a headscarf does. So on this, again untargeted surveillance fails the criteria discrimination, this time in relation to fairness as burden sharing.

Incorporating issues of fairness of burden sharing with the actual economic costs of surveillance programmes leads us to the criterion of necessity – do these large-scale and untargeted surveillance programmes actually work? In addition to the costs to individual citizens, these programmes are extremely costly.[45] Given the moral and

[45] Interestingly, one of the justifications that Edward Snowden offered for his public release was how he saw previous NSA whistleblowers treated by the US government (Harding, 2014, p. 50). In particular, Thomas Drake was indicted because he went public about the excessive cost of the surveillance architecture that ultimately led to the PRISM programmes that Snowden reacted to (Greenberg, 2012, pp. 220–225). There are serious questions about cost/benefit assessments and prioritisation of terrorism/counterterrorism operations over many other government policies (Mueller and Stewart, 2011, 2016). The point here is that the surveillance programmes are often very expensive and resource intensive. And, if the actual practice of closed circuit televisual (CCTV) surveillance is anything to go by, the costs of running and maintaining comprehensive and effective surveillance programmes through time are often far greater than anticipated (Smith, 2015, pp. 89–95).

economic costs, are such programmes needed? Again, the basic justification refers back to the institutional purpose – securing the community against risk and threat. But on the necessity criterion, given that such actions have costs, are there other ways of achieving equivalent outcomes or is large-scale surveillance the only option? As before, this is not a question of total surveillance versus no surveillance at all. Rather, the necessity question asks can we achieve similar outcomes using different less invasive or less costly means?

To answer this, we can take instructions from the proportionality and discrimination criteria. On proportionality, we ask, is the cost worth the outcome? Basically, has broad untargeted surveillance been a necessary part of counter-terrorism operations? While the secretive and classified nature of counter-terrorism operations makes it hard to have an authoritative position on this, there does seem to be a weight of evidence against the broad surveillance programmes being necessary for counter-terrorist programmes: Between 2006–2009, the PATRIOT act's 'license to exercise a search warrant without immediately informing the target ... was used in 1,618 drug-related cases, 122 cases connected with fraud and just 15 that involved terrorism' (Greenwald, 2014, p. 200). Further, the US President's Review Group on Intelligence and Communications Technologies concluded that the metadata programme 'was not essential to preventing attacks and could have readily been obtained in a timely manner using conventional [court] orders' (Review Group on Intelligence and Communications Technologies, 2013). To reiterate, the point here is not that surveillance programmes ought to be abandoned. Rather, it is that the costs of the large-scale programmes are extensive and require evidence of their efficacy. And this evidence is patchy at best.

Which leads us back to discrimination; framing it in relation to necessity, the question becomes whether surveillance programmes should be broadly or narrowly targeted. That is, can the open-ended dragnet strategies employed by the NSA be justified? Here, it seems to be that traditional investigative methods are as, if not far more, useful than dragnet surveillance. Commenting on the cost/benefit ratios of the NSA programmes following Snowden, John Mueller and Mark Stewart state '[t]housands of people are at work, gathering unbelievable quantities of information, or hay, simply because it has become technologically possible to do so in a process that has netted scarcely any terrorists' (Mueller and Stewart, 2016, p. 197). Instead, we should be directing resources at targeted surveillance towards known suspects, where there is existing evidence and justification for suspicion. That is, where discrimination is justified. Adding further weight to this claim is that there is a limited pool of economic and experiential resources for governments to support surveillance programmes. And for every dollar spent on untargeted surveillance programmes, that is one less dollar that could be spent on targeted traditional investigative methods. Moreover, when thinking of the threat posed by domestic terrorism, a necessary element is effective community policing. If a particular community feels that they are under constant and pervasive surveillance, they may be less inclined to trust the government institutions, which then makes community policing all the less effective.

So, on the weight of things, it seems that the state institutions were not justified in their broad-based surveillance programmes. Whether by proportionality, discrimination or necessity, the open-ended and untargeted surveillance programmes were unjustified. This is in part supported by the law – the 2nd U.S. Circuit Court of Appeals in Manhattan ruled that the NSA's collection of phone records was illegal (Stempel, 2015).

Finally, we can return to the institutional justification – the duty to secure the community against significant threats. In the United States at least, the Fourth Amendment places individual security as a counterweight to community security, enshrining '[t]he right of the people to be secure in their persons, houses, papers and effects, against *unreasonable* searches and seizures, shall not be violated and no warrants shall issue, *but on probable cause*, supported by oath or affirmation and particularly describing the place to be searched and the person or things to be seized' (Emphasis Mine, US Government, 1792). Individual security is thus contrasted with community security and in line with the discussion here, there is an assumption that individual security is the default position and any deviation from this requires substantial justifying reasons.

As a final note on this, this is not to say that we as citizens are free of any moral responsibilities around the collection of Personal Information and the state provision of security. First, given the widespread knowledge that there are surveillance technologies in constant use around us, we ought to take some care with how easy we make it for Personal Information to be collected and used against us. Second, insofar as we want to retain our basic rights, minimise the information harms from surveillance programmes and maximise their fairness, we must accept some costs. That is, it is incumbent on us as citizens to recognise this and accept some costs of terrorist and criminal activity. It is a simple fact that we cannot prevent all terrorist acts, 'unless (perhaps even if) we're prepared to accept massive intrusion by security agencies into every aspect of our daily lives . . . that means we have a choice; learn to live with a higher background threat or decide how much freedom we're prepared to trade for security against it' (Kilcullen, 2016, p. 203). My point is that the access to and use of seemingly innocuous Personal Information can come at a much higher price than is often recognised.

Furthermore, there must be some trust placed in the government institutions tasked with pursuing community security. However, that trust requires a greater openness and engagement from government.

> On balance, the public interest lies in encouraging government and its security authorities to feel confident that they can take calculated risks in order to uncover and neutralize the threats to public security. In the end, however, the public has to have confidence in the security authorities' ability to make those risk judgments.

> Government therefore has to explain through the media the rationale for the strategy it is following and convey a sense of where and why it is balancing the benefits from additional security with all the costs of providing it. Government has as a result to provide sufficient background information about its intelligence and security organizations and the kinds of people involved in them to engender the needed trust in operational security decisions.
>
> (Omand, 2010, p. 18)

This final point bring us back to the opening problem, about the relation between citizen and state and the ways that surveillance can impact those relations. Government institutions that are engaged in surveillance, particularly those engaged in security-orientated intelligence, rely on the trust of citizens. Situations where surveillance programmes or operations must be kept secret by definition require citizens to trust in government institutions to do their job not only well but to do it carefully. For this to occur there must be greater engagement from the intelligence institutions in setting out what the justifications for surveillance operations are and how such operations are constrained and overseen. Such explanations are to be given at a general level so need not compromise any operational integrity. The age of surveillance requires greater openness about institutions and, hard as this may be, it may require a fundamental shift in institutional cultures.

10

In Conclusion

10.1 SURVEILLANCE IS GOOD

This book's central goal has been to establish that innocuous information is morally important, so morally important that it is something we ought to care about. But focusing on the need to limit surveillance technologies because of the rights of individuals and responsibilities of institutions tends to obscure an important point – surveillance can be good. In fact, going back to the book's opening where I pointed to our ambivalence about surveillance technologies, we miss a fundamental part of the age of surveillance if we overlook the goods that these technologies bring.

People's ambivalence about surveillance technologies arises in part because these technologies are beneficial. They can be useful – an integrated and automated transport system, underpinned by surveillance technologies can make people's lives easier:

> By 2019, residents of Columbus [Ohio, US] could see autonomous shuttles cruising the Easton commercial district, motion-sensitive LED streetlights that also provide free Wi-Fi internet to the residential neighborhood of Linden, and 175 smart traffic signals that aim to ease traffic jams and speed first-responders' paths through the city. Residents will also be able to use one app to plan and pay for trips that require multiple types of public transportation.
>
> (Wheeland, 2016)

Surveillance technologies can be helpful – A smart house where appliances, services and remote and automated care are integrated in a network of communications and sensors can give the elderly and infirm the option of remaining at home rather than moving into assisted care. While there are a huge amount of ethical complexities around such technologies,[1] they do offer benefit to those wishing to maintain their autonomy

[1] For instance, there are issues of justice in the research and development of 'complex medical machines' (Henschke, 2015d) and there are issues about the layers of ethical concern in the 'internet of things' (Henschke, 2017).

and remain living at home. Finally, surveillance technologies can be an essential element in protecting innocent people and promoting justice – surveillance technologies and the collection, aggregation and analysis of innocuous information can enable international paedophile rings to be infiltrated by police, its members identified and subsequently arrested. In one example, this was achieved through the aggregation and analysis of pieces of information like the use of the greeting 'hiya', metadata in photographs that identified the make and model of the camera and cross-referencing with normal social media leading to the identification of specific individuals (Safi, 2016).

In short, there are many different ways that surveillance technologies make our lives easier, better and safer. So, while there are a host of reasons to be concerned about these technologies and their uses, we should not be throwing the baby out with the bathwater. Ideally, if we can fix the rules this does not have to be a zero-sum game; perhaps it is possible to take a path that pursues many of the goods of surveillance technologies whilst avoiding their undesirable elements. However, in order to do this, we need to know the goods and bads and have some idea of how those come about. This closing chapter embraces this challenge and proposes that the Identity/Information Dyad can offer the basis for a technological response, where good design seeks to maximise the goods brought about by the age of surveillance, whilst avoiding many of the concerns highlighted throughout the preceding chapters.

10.2 JUSTIFYING THE USE OF PERSONAL INFORMATION: WHAT'S THE POINT?

To see the goods of surveillance technologies, let us revisit a highly infective, highly lethal strain of bird flu (Garrett, 2012; Kwek, 2011). In a worst case scenario, a particular strain of bird flu had been thought to have the potential to kill approximately 60 per cent of the world's human population.[2] Central to any preparedness for such a pandemic is an international disease surveillance system, integrated with an effective public health network.[3] This book has argued that individuals have important rights and should not be harmed by use of Personal Information. At the same time, very few would disagree that that we ought to do a great deal to avoid the deaths of three billion people. If an internationally integrated pandemic surveillance network is needed to prevent such a catastrophe, then it would seem that the rights claims[4] of individuals

2 To repeat a previous point, such a high mortality rate was speculative and subsequently was scaled down (Evans, 2012). However, the point remains that such a strain of bird flu was feared to be able to kill hundreds of millions of people, a catastrophe in anyone's language.

3 See: Barnett and Sorenson, 2011; Bell et al., 2009; Garrett, 1996, 2001; Louie et al., 2009; Oshitani, Kamigaki and Suzuki, 2008.

4 A similar sort of concern arises in cases of a right to medical confidentiality and threats raised by potential acts of violence (Beauchamp and Childress, 2001a, pp. 415–418), or HIV-positive status (Ainslie, 2002).

would be overridden in this case: if it is needed, their Personal Information should be part of surveillance and response measures.[5]

This book has advanced a series of moral arguments as to why we should care about Personal Information, especially innocuous Personal Information. It may be because of a source person having a justified rights claim, that target people are especially vulnerable to Personal Information or the importance of fair access to primary goods and a fair distribution of the harms and benefits of Personal Information. However, each of these arguments came with an 'other things being equal' clause. That is, in each situation, there may be some competing values or purposes that override the individual rights, individual harms or equality concerns. Three billion people's deaths would be such an overriding condition. This section looks at how and when something can override a commitment to individual rights, harms or fairness – the purpose of information's access and use is a vital determinant in whether such access and use are justified.

10.2.1 *The Point So Far*

When thinking of surveillance as part of pandemic surveillance programmes, it may seem that the previous discussions have no substantive moral point: we merely pay lip service to individual rights claims or individual harms, but in the end, all we're doing is a cost benefit analysis. That is, while the rights of individuals are spoken of in deontological terms and fairness is presented as an issue, in the final analysis we are all consequentialists, as much in the age of surveillance as any other issue. However, this claim overlooks four key points. First, if one is inclined to take a simplistic utilitarian calculus to individual cases, as outlaid in Chapter 9, we need to include informational harms to individuals in the calculations. Second, on a more sophisticated consequentialist reasoning, we need to include the values underpinning the individual rights claims, individual harms and equality considerations into the calculation of the good that we are pursuing. Third, recall that the rights claims as described in Chapter 8 were *pro tanto* claims: it is possible for them to be outweighed, but those claims do not become invalid for any or all uses of Personal Information.[6] Finally, there must be some compelling justificatory reasons to override the *pro tanto* claims.

On the first point, a great deal has been written about the limits of applying a simplistic utilitarian calculus to all moral decisions[7]. In short, such discussions about simplistic calculations hold that in order to meet the challenges from rights theorists,

[5] Fritz Allhoff raises a similar problem, should we torture someone to prevent a ticking time bomb going off in a crowded city. He argues that we are justified in overriding a person's right not to be tortured by reference to a large number of other people's right not to be killed by the time bomb (Allhoff, 2012).

[6] This point was made originally in §1.5 when discussing the notion of rights as *pro tanto*.

[7] One such collection is *Utilitarianism and Its Critics* (Glover, 1990).

a utilitarian would need to follow John Stuart Mill in making 'the good' a suitably complex thing that includes more than a simple pleasure/pain balance sheet.[8] The simplistic calculation is just that – too simplistic to be practically useful. Instead, '[t]he consequentialist who claims to recognise a right must not just behave appropriately. He must behave appropriately, because he reasons appropriately' (Pettit, 1988, p. 48). In the language of recognition respect, §8.5, the sophisticated consequentialist must weigh the person's interests appropriately and take those interests seriously. This process is far more complex than simply maximising pleasure or welfare. This is all in line with what I have been arguing: a sophisticated consequentialist should take the individual's interests into account when dealing with Personal Information. When using Personal Information, both the consequentialist and deontologist will conclude that the individual rights and fairness, as well as the complex set of informational harms need to be included in a moral assessment of surveillance technologies, though for different reasons.

If we are committed to taking rights seriously, even when an individual's rights can be overridden, on the *pro tanto* approach discussed, the individual still retains the basic rights. Further, the person's right can only be overridden *as long as it is justified*. Consider what is at stake in preventing the spread of killer pathogens:

> Conflicting values are commonplace in the context of public health, and the context of infectious disease in particular. In the case of epidemic diseases, for example, the measures required for the protection of public health may include surveillance; mandatory vaccination, testing or treatment; and/or social distancing measures such as isolation and quarantine.
>
> (Selgelid, 2009, p. 196)

When focussing on Personal Information, I assume that most would consider that, despite the potential privacy infringement, some surveillance is justified to monitor the spread of particularly risky infections. In some situations, this Personal Information can lead to Deliberate Information Harms: for instance, the isolation and quarantine of infectious people.[9] This does not mean, however, that any and all rights violations are now justified. We would likely consider it an unjustified privacy violation if all their medical records were made publicly available. Likewise, we would consider it totally unreasonable for those under surveillance to be forced to engage in sexually explicit photo-shoots,[10] or to be enrolled into forced labour camps as a result of being infected. The way in which the Personal Information is used, who has access to it and for how long need to be in line with the reasons for

[8] I mean here to refer to Mill's idea that 'It is better to be a human being dissatisfied than a pig satisfied, better to be Socrates dissatisfied than a fool satisfied' (Mill, 1987, p. 301).

[9] Note that isolation and quarantine align with my description of Deliberate Information Harms, §9.3.1: Personal Information has been used in a way that directly and deliberately results in harm to a target individual.

[10] The rights abuses in Abu Ghraib are examples of failures to respect the basic qualities of prisoners.

outweighing the *pro tanto* rights and in such a way that the 'least restrictive alternative should be used to achieve *the public health goal* in question' (Emphasis Mine, Selgelid, 2009, p. 195).[11] The justification for overriding the rights of individuals is absolutely central to how the rights are infringed upon and for how long.

10.2.2 *Personal Information: Purpose Matters*

This brings us to the justificatory element: in order to override individual rights and justify the harms, we need to know why that Personal Information is being used. §1.5 stated that ethics is reason giving: some justificatory reason or reasons are needed as to why we should or should not do a particular action. In the case of extreme pandemics, the reason is clear: Personal Information is needed to limit the deaths of billions of people. However, even in a fairly clean-cut case like this, basic recognition respect holds that the person whose rights are infringed is owed some justificatory reason as to why their right to privacy or liberty has been outweighed.[12]

Second, the rights infringement is justified by reference to particular public health goals:[13] if it turns out that the person in quarantine does not have the infectious strain of the virus, or if it turns out that the virus is nowhere near as likely to cause a pandemic, we lose the justification to keep the person in quarantine. Likewise, their Personal Information – the medical data collected as part of pandemic surveillance – may no longer be needed for the stated purpose. As such, that Virtual Identity should be deleted or destroyed. The basic rule here is that if the justificatory goal ceases to be active, the action ceases to be justified.

As mentioned in §9.4.2, there may be situations where information collected in one context can legitimately change to another context, but a new justification is needed. Consider that as part of pandemic surveillance Gary's Personal Information is accessed and integrated. It comes to light that he has previously been convicted in England for paedophilia; he goes to South East Asia every six months to visit children's schools and on return always has medical checks for HIV and other sexually transmitted diseases. In this situation, it might be justified to pass this information on to relevant criminal justice authorities. The thing to draw out here is that because the purpose of surveillance has changed, a new justification is needed to move Gary's Personal Information into another context. Preventing

[11] I note here that Selgelid argues that rather than always going for the least restrictive option, other methods such as redistributive taxation may be a better option, all things considered (Selgelid, 2009). I cannot enter into a sustained discussion of his point here, but I think it does not detract from the general point about *pro tanto* claims that I am making here.

[12] Note that giving them reasons is also likely to promote good consequences: simply locking someone up is likely to make them very angry and/or very unhappy. Give them a justificatory reason and while they will still be angry or unhappy, most reasonable people would be more likely to be more responsive while in quarantine.

[13] I have spoken elsewhere on the importance of recognising an institution's goals and matching practice to those goals, specifically, the institution of the military (Henschke and Evans, 2012).

pandemics and punishing paedophilia are each part of justificatory stories about how, when and why Personal Information can be accessed, analysed and applied, but they are different stories and qua informational injustice, §9.5, the shift from the context of pandemic prevention to punishment of paedophiles must be justified. Moreover, this must be done with the requisite amount of care given to who has access to Gary's information and why.

The overall point to recognise here is that justifications matter. Having established that Personal Information, including innocuous information, is of moral concern, we ought to treat such information with care. Whether it is because one is convinced by the rights-based arguments of Chapter 8, or the harms and fairness issues raised in Chapter 9, Personal Information matters. From this it means that though certain conditions such as pandemics or paedophilia might permit access to or use of Personal Information, we must recognise the moral justifications that underpin such permissions. Recognition of the moral mechanics that justify the permissions are important as they not only explain *why* certain treatment of Personal Information is permitted, they also act to limit such uses.

10.3 FROM POTENTIAL CHALLENGES TO DISAGGREGATION

In contrast to the challenge that this is all just consequentialist cost/benefit reasoning, another challenge to the concern about innocuous information arises. Chapter 9, for instance, traded on the notion of vulnerability, that we ought to be concerned about harms and fairness because of the *potential* ways that Personal Information can be aggregated and used. However, this is an argument from potential; because of some potential future scenario, we ought to stop some act in the present.

These 'potential challenges' rely on a 'generic sense of potentiality, "if X has an active potentiality for giving rise to Y and Y has an active potentiality for giving rise to Z, then it must follow that X itself has an active potentiality for giving rise to Z", ... so that in the end everything is potentially something else' (Reichlin, 1997, p. 4). The challenge comes in two forms: metaphysical and epistemological. On the metaphysical[14] challenge, the problem is that we treat all innocuous information as a potentially revealing, harmful and/or powerful Virtual Identity, when it is, simply, still mere innocuous information. Second is what I will call the epistemological[15] challenge – that we should forgo the *known* goods that surveillance

[14] I refer to this as the 'metaphysical challenge' as the basis and history of it derives from Aristotle's *Metaphysics*. 'Aristotelian metaphysics appears here because it provided the origins of the potentiality principle, a foundational argument of enduring importance', (Morgan, 2013, p. S15). 'This corresponds to the general sense of potentiality as possibility which was also set out by Aristotle in *Metaphysics*' (Reichlin, 1997, p. 4).

[15] I refer to this as the 'epistemic challenge', as it is premised on issues around knowledge and certainty, which for some produces a 'strange account of moral epistemology' (Strawser, 2010, p. 359).

technologies can bring *now* because of the mere possibility of future misuse seems wrong. Both directions of the potential challenge are concerned to draw out that a potential future scenario should not morally count in the same way as the present. I briefly[16] address each challenge in turn.

On the metaphysical challenge, consider that 'it is often the case that a potential X does not have the rights of an actual X: Prince Charles is presently a potential king, but this does not now give him the rights of an actual king' (Perrett, 2000, p. 187). The problem here is the demand that we assign the same moral value to a thing now as some future variant of it. 'This is because transitivity fails for subjunctive conditionals: from A > B and B > C, we cannot infer A > C (where the conditional connective is symbolized by ">")' (Perrett, 2000, p. 188). Innocuous information is simply that and the fact that it could potentially be part of a revealing, harmful or powerful Virtual Identity does not give us reason to treat all innocuous information in the same way as a Virtual Identity.

On the epistemological challenge, consider the idea that police ought not use surveillance technologies to track down and convict paedophiles *now* just in case someone else misuses these technologies in the future to cause some informational harm.

> If that holds, we have a strange account of moral epistemology at work, to say the least. We should forego taking presently morally correct action A in order to help restrain our future selves from the likelihood of committing morally wrong action B. In other words, we should do something wrong now in order to (hopefully) better stop ourselves from doing something wrong in the future.
>
> (Strawser, 2010, p. 359)

As I understand it, the problem here is one of moral epistemology: we know at the present what the correct thing to do is, but because of some future scenario, which is unknowable, we forego the current, known situation. As Bradley Strawser puts it, this is, indeed, some strange moral epistemology.

Underneath both potential challenges sits a concern that I am overreaching. These challenges recognise that seeing all innocuous information as potentially morally reactive or morally important is true, but this then becomes trivial. If all innocuous information can potentially be used as part of a Virtual Identity, then every datum that could possibly be related to a source or target person in some way or another becomes equivalently morally concerning. And, as per the reductio, this takes us into a world where we are either prohibited from using any data at all, or all data is morally equivalent, so why not just use it all? Moreover, this seems to be a

[16] What follows are very brief treatments of the metaphysical and epistemological challenges. The literature on potential, specifically as it relates to metaphysics and epistemology, is deep and broad and I will not be able to do them justice here. Instead, I give a quick description of them as they relate to the Identity/Information Dyad and specifically focus on their illumination of my own reasoning.

similar problem that I identified with the data security where I said that when we talk of privacy concerns just as a moral problem of harm, inequality, injustice or as an autonomy violation, we risk making informational misuses and transgressions true but trivially so.[17] Further, these transgressions become lost amongst the world's other wrongs, harms and unfairnesses.

Am I making the same mistake that I had earlier identified with other approaches to privacy? Not exactly – the problem there was that those arguments needed more details, some way of specifying when informational transgressions and misuses were occurring and some way of clarifying how concerned we ought to be about such misuses and transgressions. Parts II and III of this book have developed the Identity/Information Dyad, which provides the specification of when informational transgressions and misuses are occurring and clarifies how morally concerned we ought to be in such circumstances. In this detail lies the response to the potential challenges.

To step back and summarise the book, the moral concerns proposed stem from the idea of identity: Identity and Personal Information are in a mutually causal dyadic relation. Because of this dyadic relation, insofar as identity is something that ought to figure in our moral landscape, then so too should Personal Information. However, as specified in Chapter 7, that information must relate to a person or group of people in some way. This relation to a person can be considered from two different explanatory priorities: when a person is the source of information and when a person is the target of information. And linking this whole story together is the notion of Virtual Identities.

The Virtual Identity specifies and clarifies when we ought to be concerned about Personal Information and how concerned we ought to be: it is not 'potential Personal Information' that we ought to be worried about per se; it is when Virtual Identities can be constructed, how easily they can be constructed, who is constructing them, for what reason, coupled with a thoroughgoing effort to recognise the centrality of identity to the rights that are violated in such constructions, the full range of informational harms involved and the ways that such constructions impact people within a society. The book presented a taxonomy of identity types, Self-Regarding, Other-Regarding and Other/Other-RegardingOther-Regarding identity that underpinned these three clusters of moral concern.

Returning to the potential challenges, the metaphysical challenge is met as the Identity/Information Dyad specifies the conditions under which merely innocuous information becomes morally concerning. Having identified the locus of moral concern – Virtual Identities – and having developed the Identity/Information Dyad, I have spelled out in great detail the conceptual and moral mechanics of how and why Virtual Identities are of moral concern. In this way, we have

[17] See §2.4.

something akin to a formal set of procedures that specify how and when particular data ought to figure in our moral compass and how much.

In this way, a better analogy than the potential king and king is a president elect. In a fair liberal democratic system, any citizen has the opportunity to become president, we are all potential presidents. However, there are a set of processes that must be met in order for a particular individual to become president. Even having elected a particular person, in some democracies such as the United States, there is a lag period where that person is 'president elect'. While the president elect does not have the rights and responsibilities of the actual president, they are surely and justifiably treated differently from when they were a citizen. All data that could potentially be related to a person is like the citizen in a democracy: potentially president but trivially so. Recalling the transitivity issue noted above, we are mistaken to infer that A>C from A>B and B>C. Instead, I propose that the president elect or certain data ought to be considered not as A or C, but B. Moreover, the status of B does involve morally relevant features.

Much as we ought to treat a president elect with particular concerns distinct from both the normal citizen and the president, information that is obviously and clearly on its way to being a Virtual Identity ought to be treated like the president elect – not *yet* a Virtual Identity but clearly not just innocuous information. Virtual Identity is like the president elect: not quite president, but afforded concerns quite distinct from a citizen in virtue of how close they are to becoming the thing in question. That is, while their metaphysical status is still 'potential', the president elect's metaphysical status is a very similar one to that of a citizen. Likewise, while a cluster of data that is personally attributable but not yet aggregated has the metaphysical status of potential Virtual Identity, the conditions about the ease at which the data can shift to actual Virtual Identity tell us how far off it is from simply data.

The epistemological challenge is met as the Identity/Information Dyad means we're no longer simply waving generally at information and the merely possible. Rather than comparing some known present good with some merely possible potential bad, if we know the present good and the probable future bad, we can make a decision between the two that is not dependent on some strange moral epistemology. If I was to push an innocent person to the ground to stop a malicious actor setting off a bomb, there is no strangeness in assessing that though pushing the innocent person to the ground is undeniably bad, a bomb going off in the future is far worse. Moreover, while I might have wronged the innocent person by pushing them over, it is a lesser wrong than letting them die in the explosion. Likewise, the cases we are concerned with are not, if a possible datum could perhaps one day be related to a possible individual. Instead, it is when those data are likely to produce a Virtual Identity that impacts a person's self-understanding at some core level and/or are likely to cause informational harms to a person or group and/or are likely to impact people in a way that is unfair. The Identity/Information Dyad tells us the story of moral concern and how far into that story we are.

Thus, both forms of the potential challenge are met – Virtual Identities are symptoms of the moral problem. And in identifying Virtual Identities as the symptom, we can treat the underlying problem: the solution is to disaggregate Personal Information.

10.4 PRACTICAL RESPONSES: VALUE-SENSITIVE DESIGN AND VIRTUAL IDENTITIES

Sections 10.2 and 10.3 have highlighted the need to recognise a complex chain of reasoning which includes identifying the purpose of use that offers the justifications for creation and use of Virtual Identities. When we combine this purposive reasoning with the realisation that it is the aggregation of Personal Information that gives moral weight to innocuous information, we are now pointing in the direction of a solution. If, as I have argued, it is the construction of Virtual Identities that causes the rights violations, the informational harms and the unfairness, then this diagnosis can also tell us how to respond: if informational aggregation is the problem and requires justification, then we either prevent aggregation in situations where there is no justification and/or we disaggregate when the justification ceases.

As this book has argued, information gains its moral value when it is Thick Information, particularly when it becomes meaningful. The specific construction considered here is when Personal Information becomes a Virtual Identity. The reason for aggregating the information, for constructing the Virtual Identity, is that it is valuable – a Virtual Identity is more revealing, more impactful and more discriminatory than mere data and this is why such constructions occur. This new valuation is what makes the Personal Information morally relevant.

To avoid the pitfalls identified by the potential challenges, however, we must pay special attention to the fact that, on this analysis, it is Thick Information, Semantic Information, that becomes actually problematic, rather than merely potentially concerning. On this, it is only semantic agents who pose the moral hazard – it is only when Virtual Identities are experienced by a human that the moral concerns become live. In this sense, perhaps the moral importance is only in the mind of the observer. From this, it would seem to follow that automated surveillance is free from this moral worry. In part, this is accurate – if it's Semantic Information that is of worry, then it would only be Semantic Information that we need to respond to.

Again, the dyad adds a conceptual sophistication to this analysis. As per Chapter 6, technologies afford certain behaviours and beliefs. When thinking of data analytics, there are affordances in the way that algorithms construct semantically reactive Virtual Identities. Consider how automated news algorithms can create bizarre and offensive constructions due to either absurd or socially insensitive semantics: A 'fully automated Facebook trending module pushed out a false story about Fox News host Megyn Kelly, a controversial piece about a comedian's four-letter word attack on rightwing pundit Ann Coulter and links to an article about a video of a man masturbating with a McDonald's chicken sandwich' (Thielman, 2016). It does not take a semantic agent like a human to construct information that affords semantically problematic information. The point here is that, given that these informational analytics are conducted in a social context, they are not semantically neutral.

This recognition draws out the need to have an existing justification to collect Personal Information *prior* to aggregation. However, in line with the recognition that this is not yet Thick Information, this justificatory apparatus may not be as stringent as the fully formed and experienced Thick Information. This comes from the recognition that rights, harms and injustices become instantiated when aggregated and experienced. However, we still need to recognise that the processes of collection and development of surveillance programmes *prior to* aggregation are intended for aggregation and are thus of moral concern.

Paying attention to the chain of reasoning here presents a solution to many (though not all) of the problems arising from the production and use of Personal Information – we can hope to avoid many of the problems identified through the smart design of the surveillance technologies. In order to demonstrate the ethical relevance of innocuous Personal Information, I have focused on the relations between identity and information. I have diagnosed a chief moral concern in the creation of Virtual Identities. However, instead of resolving extremely complicated value conflicts that arise *ex post* Virtual Identity creation and use, we can instead aim to design certain information technologies such that they take identity into account *before* the problems arise. If – as this analysis suggests – many moral problems occur as a result of aggregating Personal Information, the solution is to design technologies such that they either limit the creation of Virtual Identities from innocuous Personal Information and/or the technologies disaggregate the Virtual Identity after it has served its justifiable purpose. This is, quite simply, recognition of the interaction between ethics and design.

To begin, consider the 'mutuality principle' which 'guides us to *minimise or eliminate conflict over moral values* ... for example, we can attempt to *change practices, institutions and approaches* to moral development that stand as obstacles to the mutual achievement of moral value. Many moral conflicts ... are not natural but arise owing to the construction of variable aspects of social life' (Emphasis Mine DeMarco, 1997, 297). If we change practices, institutions and approaches, we can substantially limit conflict cases. Significant value conflicts, while intractable, might be able to be limited by changing the likelihood of such conflicts actually arising.

The point is that if we can design a system or institution in such a way to prevent dilemmas from occurring, this removes the need for us to choose between differing values. This goes directly to the idea of value-sensitive design, (VSD), in which engineers and designers actively design particular features into the technologies that we use.

> If our moral and political discourse on user autonomy, patient centred-ness and citizen centred-ness, our privacy, security is to be more than an empty promise, these values will have to be expressed in the design, architecture and specifications of systems. If we want our information technology – and the use that is made of it – to be just, fair and safe, we must see to it that it inherits our good intentions.
>
> (van den Hoven, 2007a, 69)

VSD can be understood in a number of ways: one key element of VSD is to show that particular designs import various values into the technology (Friedman, Kahn and Borning, 2002; Friedman and Nissenbaum, 2007). However, another element is to design technologies such that the moral conflicts are avoided or minimised. We can 'front-load ethics' 'by means of the pro-active integration of ethical reflection in the stage of design of architectures, requirements, specifications, standards, protocols, incentive structures and institutional arrangements' (van den Hoven, 2007a, 70).

This book has focussed on the relation between identity and information to argue that Personal Information ought to be considered a morally relevant feature of our practices. The Identity/Information Dyad offers guidance as to *how* to prevent these rights infringements, potential harms and inequalities from arising: if there are serious moral problems arising from the creation of Virtual Identities, then we should limit the occasions when such Virtual Identities are created. Integrating this idea with VSD, the idea is that technologies that handle Personal Information should be designed in such a way as to disincentivise the ease at which Virtual Identities can be created. In cases where it is justified that a Virtual Identity be created – such as in the pandemic surveillance described above – if the use is no longer justified, then the Virtual Identity should be destroyed by informational disaggregation.[18] For instance, we are told by our banks not to keep our ATM card and its PIN together. The reason is that the aggregation of the data on the card with our PIN authenticates access to our bank account via confirmation of a Virtual Identity. Likewise, institutions like banks should not co-locate Personal Information such that Virtual Identities are easily formed or accessed.

Technologies that handle Personal Information should be designed in such a way as to make it as hard as possible to aggregate Personal Information when third party use of that information is not justified. In cases where the use by third parties is justified, the technologies should be designed with identity in mind, such that the Virtual Identity is disaggregated immediately following its justified use. Further, the technologies need to be designed such that only those who are authorised to access the information in aggregate can do so. This sort of design has been a central element in partially anonymised medical databases.[19] Given the amount that can

[18] I thank Malcolm Crompton for giving me the original idea that users of Personal Information should disaggregate Personal Information after it has served its justified purpose (Crompton, 2011).

[19] For instance, double-coded databases assign unique codes to a person's entry, with two different keys linking the code and the individual keys stored separately (Council for International

be revealed by aggregated Personal Information this should be incorporated wherever possible in non-medical databases.

The U.K. National DNA Database uses DNA samples and profiles to assist in identifying criminals. The indefinite retention of profiles and samples has been recognised as a substantial privacy concern (U.K. Government, 2006). Similarly, the European Commission have introduced the idea of a 'right to be forgotten', which is a 'right of individuals to have their data no longer processed and deleted when they are no longer needed for legitimate purposes'(European Commission, 2010).[20] These actions to disaggregate Personal Information and delete Virtual Identities show that there is some practical potential to design in the concerns raised here, such that many of the value conflicts are minimised.

The social media service Snapchat is a further example of how this can operate in practice. Snapchat's primary feature is that it deletes a file such as a photo within a time frame specified by the sender. Basically, it allows a user to send a photo, have the receiver see the photo and then have it self-delete within ten seconds. Thus, intimate or other private information can be communicated without the fear of that information becoming permanent. This is disaggregation in practice, supported by technology specifically designed to disaggregate Virtual Identities. It shows that there is both a desire for such technologies and the capacity to create them.

Obviously, much more needs to be said on VSD and Virtual Identities. The devil truly is in the details. However, those devils need to be identified in the future. The goal of this project was to show why we ought to care about Personal Information and give suggestions about how we ought to respond. The next step is to bring those suggestions into practice.

10.5 REFLECTIONS ON ETHICS IN THE AGE OF SURVEILLANCE

As a final reflection, we can close off by considering the impacts that this age of surveillance has on our ethical principles. Rather than thinking that we ought simply to apply principles to the specific cases, the approach taken here has to recognise that 'we have various moral principles and various judgments regarding particular cases. Neither the principles nor the judgments enjoys any sort of privileged role. Rather, they engage each other in a process of mutual revision' (Allhoff, 2011, p. 4). This approach is modelled on establishing a 'wide reflective equilibrium' between our principles and intuitions where 'we advance philosophical arguments intended to bring out the relative strengths and weaknesses of the alternative sets of principles (or competing moral conceptions)' (Daniels, 1979, p. 258). In this

Organizations of Medical Sciences, 2005). That way, if *justified*, the right person can access an individual's entry in a safe, secure and reversible way.

20 This right to be forgotten is both controversial and complex (Ausloos, 2012; Rees and Heywood, 2014). However, it goes to the point of disaggregation of Virtual Identities after the information has served its justified purpose.

instance, it is not just that our ethical principles impact on the development, use and application of surveillance technologies, but that these new realities of surveillance ought to reflect back onto our principles.

Consider how the recognition of elements of the age of surveillance impacts the different concepts discussed here. Privacy, rather than being a dead and outdated concept is seen to be very much alive. Moreover, the proposal advanced in Chapter 2 is that the rise of widespread surveillance technologies puts pressure on individualised and monistic accounts of privacy. Instead, privacy ought to be considered as a complex pluralistic concept. Likewise, the exploration of ownership's descriptions and justifications found that existing conventions were limited in their capacity to respond to information when that information was viewed as disconnected from the people to whom it relates. Recognition of the impacts of surveillance technologies draws out the deep relation between identity and property.

Unsurprisingly, the age of surveillance gives us cause to reconsider notions of identity. Here, drawing from the new context of a world swamped with information, I have proposed a cognitive approach to identity. Understanding identity as a claim of relative equivalence allows us to see a range of different identity concepts: Numeric; Character; Group; and Essentialised and to embrace the novel concept of Virtual Identity. From the lens of cognitive identity the taxonomy of identity elements: Self-Regarding; Other-Regarding; and other/Other-Regarding comes into focus, attending to the individual, recognition of others and the social context in which identities are formed. Following from this, the need to better understand information leads us to appreciate that information in both its thin and thick forms. The thick form of information explains its moral reactivity by detailing the relation between the semantic element and its multirealisability. Bringing identity and information together, the notion of a dyadic relation surfaced. This dyadic relation is built on the explication of a series of mutually causal relations, in which identity plays a major causal role in information construction, while at the same time information plays a major causal role in identity formation.

The dyadic relation ultimately brought us to the moral elements, giving detail on our responsibilities as individuals and the moral expectations we have on institutions. The detailed engagement with identity and information framed the concerns on a Person As A Source and a Person As A Target of information. Having set these relations out, the discussion of just how the age of surveillance tracks to the three moral foundations originally identified in Chapter 1 – respect for people, not causing harm and treating people fairly. The book closed off in this chapter by discussing the problem of value conflicts and trade-offs and how smart technological design can hope to side-step many of the moral concerns brought up.

The main conclusion of this book is that Personal Information matters. There are real moral concerns arising from the ways in which new technologies produce, use and communicate information that relates to people. The reason why Personal Information matters is the relation between identity and information. Riding on top of these conclusions is the outcome that recognition of such mutually causal relations between identity and information not only speaks to the moral importance of Personal Information, but also spells out why and how such information becomes morally important. If we can limit the construction of Virtual Identities, we might be able to limit the moral concerns of the Personal Information.

The book opened by posing a problem of the age of surveillance: that we are ambivalent about these technologies. On the one hand we are happy to have a smart phone monitor our sleep, while on the other we rail against intrusive government surveillance programmes. In order to make sense of this ambivalence, we needed some deep, sustained and principled analysis of the reasons why such technologies were morally problematic. The Identity/Information Dyad tells us both how and why developing and using a pregnancy score for consumers is so morally problematic, while recognising the innocuousness of purchases of cocoa-butter lotion, a large purse, vitamin supplements (zinc and magnesium) and a bright blue rug. Moreover, the dyad offers some path out of this, where we can reap the benefits of the age of surveillance while minimising as many of the moral concerns as possible. Though it is true that we are all targets in the age of surveillance, we need not be passive in this age.

APPENDIX 1

Glossary of Terms

Basic Recognition Claim: That we ought to treat personal information with care, because of the information's importance to the source person, §8.5

Cognitive Network: A cognitive network is the set of integrated and interactive thoughts that a person has about the world, §4.4.2

Dyadic Relationship: Built on the idea of mutual causation. There is a particular 'whole' which consists in two elements, each of which stands in a causal relation to the other, §6.5

Explanatory Priority: Where one set of people is more interested in one set of analytic tools to explain something, while others will be more interested in another, §6.6

Harm, Broad Micro-: Where a certain group is limited in their opportunities by the constant and persistent use of information, §9.3.4

Harm, Broad Standard: Where a certain group are limited in their opportunities by the constant and persistent use of information, §9.3.4

Harm, Closed Identity: Where devalued Virtual Identities negatively impact the target person's identity development, §9.3.5

Harm, Deliberate Informational: When people use personal information to deliberately harm others, §9.3.1

Harm, Incomplete Informational: When information is decontextualised and the loss of the intended meaning results in harm to a person, §9.3.3

Harm, Limited Opportunity: When a specific set of information is used to limit the range of opportunity that an individual might have, §9.3.4.

Harm, Narrow Micro-Harm: Where an individual is limited in their opportunities by the constant and persistent use of information, §9.3.4

Harm, Narrow Standard: Where an individual is limited in their opportunities by the constant and persistent use of information, §9.3.4

Harm, Negligent Informational: When information is constructed that targets an individual or group, but the data is not accurate, resulting in harm to a person, §9.3.2

Identity, Character: Concerned with *characterising* a person, relates to a question of the sort 'what am I like?', §4.5.2

Identity, Essentialised: When a person is reduced to a narrow set of identity attributes, §4.5.4

Identity, General: 'X perceives Y to be Z', written alternately as 'Identity is who X perceives Y to be', §4.6.4

Identity, Group: Concerned with the context and resulting content of a person's identity, the social environment that goes into forming a person's identity, §4.5.3

Identity, Natural: Conditions of Numeric and Character Identity, considered when independent of/prior to any observer/observation, §6.6

Identity, Numeric: What is needed for a thing to be the same as itself, §4.5.1

Identity, Observer: The set of relevant qualities that we use to talk about the cognitive agent who is doing the observing. This is the 'X' of 'identity is who X perceives Y to be', §6.6

Identity, Other-Regarding: Arises when a person has thoughts about the representations of another, given as 'You are who I perceive you to be', §4.6.2

Identity, Other/Other-Regarding: Concerned with how a primary observer, X perceives the construction of identity for a subject, made by a second observer, X* given as 'You are who I perceive another to perceive you to be', §4.6.3

Identity, Phenomenological: A cognitive agent's experience of the Thing In The World, §6.6

Identity, Self-Regarding: Arises when a person has thoughts about the representations of their self, given as 'I am who I perceive myself to be', §4.6.1

Identity, Virtual: some information set in the world that calls to mind a person, §4.7, §7.5

Identity/Information Dyad: The products and process that arise from the relations between identity and information, §6.7

Information, Disinformation: Deliberate act of providing people with untruthful information, §5.6.1

Information, Incomplete: When a speaker presents true, well-ordered, meaningful data, but this data either does not succeed in meeting the speaker's actual intention or the speaker's expressed intention is different to their actual intention, §5.6.1

Information, Misinformation: Accidental act of providing people with untruthful information, §5.6.1

Information, Pseudo: Ordered, meaningful data that is not true, §5.6.1

Information, Personal: Information that relates to a person or group of people in some way, §7.4

Information, Semantic: The thick concept of information as data, order, meaning and truth judgements, §6.6

Information, Strong Source Dependent: When semantic information is strongly dependent on and responsive to a single person or a narrow set of people, §7.4.1

Information, Thin: data and order, independent of/prior to an observer's ascriptions of meaning or truth, §6.6

Information, Weak Source Dependent: When semantic information is weakly dependent on and responsive to a single person or a narrow set of people, §7.3.1

Legitimate Claim: When a person's (or people's) claim correctly tracks to a relevant moral foundation, §1.5, §2.7, §3.6.

Ownership Claim: When a person (or people) make(s) a claim that they have a right to use and limit other's use of a given tangible or intangible thing, §3.3

Person As Source: When a person, as Thing In The World, provides the initial Thin Information to the observer and from this Thin Information, Semantic Information is formed and experienced as a Phenomenological Identity, §7.3.1

Person As Target: Where an observer has Semantic Information that *targets* a person or group of people. The more focused on a particular person or people, the narrower the target information is and the more people captured by a given data set, the broader the target information is, §7.4.2

Privacy Claim: Some claim over a space – physical or informational – in which an individual is typically recognised as seeking to exclude others, §2.4

Relation of Relative Equivalence: An evaluation that there is some equivalence (or sameness, similarity, commonality and so on.) between two (or more) things, common element of different identity concepts, §4.5.5, §6.6

Relation of Difference: An evaluation that there is some relevant difference between two (or more) things, common element of data, §5.3, §6.6

Thing In The World: Something that exists independently of an observer, can be understood in terms of identity or information, §6.6

Thing As Perceived: An observer's experience of the Thing In The World, §6.6

Thing Perceiving: An observer experiencing, or capable of experiencing, something in the world, §6.6

Value-Sensitive Design: The design methodology that seeks to recognise and design for, a given set of values, §10.4

References

Aaronovitch, David. 2009. "The Strange Case of the Surveillance Cameras." *The Times* March 3. www.timesonline.co.uk/tol/comment/columnists/david_aaronovitch/article5834725.ece.

Abbott, Tony. 2015. Prime Minister: Joint Doorstop Interview. Office of the Prime Minister.

Acquisti, Alessandro, and Ralph Gross. 2009. "Predicting Social Security Numbers from Public Data." *Proceedings of the National Academy of Sciences* 106 (27):10975–10980. doi: 10.1073/pnas.0904891106.

Adorno, Theodor W. 2001. *Kant's Critique of Pure Reason*. Translated by Rodney Livingstone. Edited by Rolf Tiedemann. Stanford, California: Stanford University Press.

Ahmed, Ahmed Awad E., and Issa Traore. 2008. "Employee Surveillance Based on Free Text Detection of Keystroke Dynamics." In *Handbook of Research on Social and Organizational Liabilities in Information Security* edited by Manish Gupta and Raj Sharman. Hershey: Information Science Reference.

Ainslie, Donald C. 2002. "AIDS and Sex: Is Warning a Moral Obligation?" *Health Care Analysis* 10 (1):49–66.

Albrecht, Katherine, and Liz Mcintyre. 2005. *Spychips*. Nashville: Nelson Current.

Aldrich, Richard. 2010. *GCHQ: The Uncensored History of Britain's Most Secret Intelligence Agency*. New York: Harper Press.

Alexander, Larry. 2008. "Scalar Properties, Binary Judgments." *Journal of Applied Philosophy* 25 (2):85–104. doi: 10.1111/j.1468–5930.2008.00401.x.

Alexander, Lawrence. 2005. *Is There a Right to Freedom of Expression*. Cambridge: Cambridge University Press.

Alexandra, Andrew, and Seumas Miller. 1996. "Needs, Moral Self-Consciousness, and Professional Roles." *Professional Ethics* 5 (1&2):43–61.

Alexandra, Andrew, and Seumas Miller. 2009. *Ethics in Practice: Moral Theory and the Professions*. Sydney: UNSW Press.

Alia-Klein, Nelly, Rita Z. Goldstein, Aarti Kriplani, Jean Logan, Dardo Tomasi, Benjamin Williams, Frank Telang, Elena Shumay, Anat Biegon, Ian W. Craig, Fritz Henn, Gene-Jack Wang, Nora D. Volkow, and Joanna S. Fowler. 2008. "Brain Monoamine Oxidase a Activity Predicts Trait Aggression." *Journal of Neuroscience* 28 (19):5099–5104. doi: 10.1523/jneurosci.0925-08.2008.

Allen, Anita L. 1988. *Uneasy Access: Privacy for Women in a Free Society, New Feminist Perspectives*. Totowa, NJ: Rowman & Littlefield.

Allhoff, Fritz. 2011. "What Are Applied Ethics." *Science and Engineering Ethics* 17:1–19.

Allhoff, Fritz. 2012. *Terrorism, Ticking Time-Bombs, and Torture*. Chicago: The University of Chicago Press.

Alterman, Anton. 2003. "'A Piece of Yourself': Ethical Issues in Biometric Identification." *Ethics and Information Technology* 5 (3):139.

Andrews, Lori. 2006. "Who Owns Your Body? A Patient's Perspective on Washington University v. Catalona." *The Journal of Law, Medicine & Ethics* 34 (2):398–407. doi: 10.1111/j.1748–720X.2006.00046.x.

Andrews, Lori B. 2005. "Harnessing the Benefits of Biobanks." *The Journal of Law, Medicine & Ethics* 33 (1):22–30. doi: 10.1111/j.1748–720X.2005.tb00207.x.

Appiah, Kwame Anthony. 1994. "Identity, Authenticity, Survival: Multicultural Societies and Social Reproduction." In *Multiculturalism: Examining the Politics of Recognition*, edited by Amy Gutman, 149–163. Princeton, NJ: Princeton University Press.

Arendt, Hannah. 1958. *The Human Condition, Charles R. Walgreen Foundation Lectures*. Chicago: University of Chicago Press.

Arthur, Charles. 2010. "New Facebook Privacy Settings Are 'a Red Herring', Say Activists." *The Guardian*, 27 May.

Association, American Management. 17 November 2014. "The Latest on Workplace Monitoring and Surveillance." American Management Association, accessed 04/02/2016. www.amanet.org/training/articles/the-latest-on-workplace-monitoring-and-surveillance.aspx.

Ausloos, Jef. 2012. "The 'Right To Be Forgotten' – Worth Remembering?" *Computer Law & Security Review* 28 (2):143–152. doi: http://dx.doi.org/10.1016/j.clsr.2012.01.006.

Australian Government. 2010. *Healthcare Identifiers Act*. Department of Health and Aging. Canberra: Australian Government. www.legislation.gov.au/Details/C2010C00440

Aydede, Murat. 2010. "The Language of Thought Hypothesis." accessed 24/11/2010. http://plato.stanford.edu/archives/fall2010/entries/language-thought/.

Bach, Kent. 2006. "The Top Ten Misconceptions about Implicature." In *A Festschrift for Larry Horn*, edited by B. Birner and G. Ward. Amsterdam: John Benjamins.

Baker, Peter, and Scott Shane. 2010. "Suspect Was Tracked through Phone Numbers." *The New York Times*, May 5.

Baker, Stephen. 2007. *The Numerati*. New York: Mariner Books.

Bambrough, Renford. 1968. "Universals and Family Resemblances." In *Wittgenstein: The Philosophical Investigations*, edited by George Pitcher, 186–204. London: Macmillan.

Barnett, Tony, and Corinna Sorenson. 2011. "Infectious Disease Surveillance in the United States and the United Kingdom: From Public Goods to the Challenges of New Technologies." *Journal of Health Politics, Policy and Law* 36 (1):165–185. doi: 10.1215/03616878–1191144.

Bartels, Andreas, and Semir Zeki. 2004. "The Neural Correlates of Maternal and Romantic Love." *NeuroImage* 21 (3):1155–1166.

Baumgartner, T., M. Heinrichs, A. Vonlanthen, U. Fischbacher, and E. Fehr. 2008. "Oxytocin Shapes the Neural Circuitry of Trust and Trust Adaptation in Humans." *Neuron* 58 (4):639–650.

Baxter, Donald L. M. 1988. "Identity in the Loose and Popular Sense." *Mind* XCVII (388):575–582. doi: 10.1093/mind/XCVII.388.575.

Bayne, Tim, and Neil Levy. 2005. "Amputees by Choice: Body Integrity Identity Disorder and the Ethics of Amputation." *Journal of Applied Philosophy* 22 (1):75–86.

Beauchamp, Tom L., and James F. Childress. 2001a. "Appendix: Cases in Biomedical Ethics." In *Principles of Biomedical Ethics*, 415–431. Oxford: Oxford University Press.

Beauchamp, Tom L., and James F. Childress. 2001b. *Principles of Biomedical Ethics*. Fifth edn. Oxford: Oxford University Press.

Beauchamp, Tom L., and LeRoy Walters. 1994. "The Management of Medical Information." In *Contemporary Issues in Bioethics*, edited by Tom L. Beauchamp and LeRoy Walters, 123–130. Belmont: Wadsworth Publishing Company.

Beaver, Kevin M., Matt DeLisi, Michael G. Vaughn, and J. C. Barnes. 2010. "Monoamine Oxidase A Genotype Is Associated with Gang Membership and Weapon Use." *Comprehensive Psychiatry* 51 (2):130–134.

Bedau, Mark A. 1997. "Weak Emergence." In *Philosophical Perspectives: Mind, Causation, and World*, edited by James Tomberlin, 375–399. Hoboken: Wiley-Blackwell.

Bell, D. M., I. B. Weisfuse, M. Hernandez-Avila, C. del Rio, X. Bustamante, and G. Rodier. 2009. "Pandemic Influenza as a 21st Century Urban Public Health Crisis." *Emerging Infectious Diseases* 15 (12):1963–1969.

Bellaby, Ross. 2014. *The Ethics of Intelligence*: London: Routledge.

Belluck, Pam. 2009. "Webcast Your Brain Surgery? Hospitals See Marketing Tool." *The New York Times*, 24 May.

Bencivenga, Ermanno. 2000. *Hegel's Dialectical Logic*. Oxford: Oxford University Press.

Beres, Damon. 2015. "These High-Tech Shirts and Pants Can Help Protect Kids with Autism." *The Huffington Post*, 19 February 2015. www.huffingtonpost.com.au/entry/autism-gps-device_n_6705368.html?section=australia.

Bilton, Michael. 2003. *Wicked beyond Belief: The Hunt for the Yorkshire Ripper*. London: Harper Collins.

Blair, Irene V., Charles M. Judd, and Jennifer L. Fallman. 2004. "The Automaticity of Race and Afrocentric Facial Features in Social Judgments." *Journal of Personality and Social Psychology* 87 (6):763–778.

Bok, Sissela. 1989. *Secrets: On the Ethics of Concealment and Revelation*. Toronto: Vintage Books.

Bolton, John. 2013. "Edward Snowden's Leaks Are a Grave Threat to US National Security." *The Guardian*, 18 June.

BonJour, Laurence. 1985. *The Structure of Empirical Knowledge*. Cambridge, MA: Harvard University Press.

Bowcott, Owen, and Richard Norton-Taylor. 2016. "UK Spy Agencies Have Collected Bulk Personal Data Since 1990s, Files Show." *The Guardian*, 21 April.

Bowling, Ben, and Coretta Phillips. 2007. "Disproportionate and Discriminatory: Reviewing the Evidence on Police Stop and Search." *The Modern Law Review* 70 (6):936–961. doi: 10.1111/j.1468–2230.2007.00671.x.

Bowman, Sue. 2013. "Impact of Electronic Health Record Systems on Information Integrity: Quality and Safety Implications." *Perspectives in Health Information Management* 10 (Fall).

Boyle, Matthew. 2009. "Two Kinds of Self-Knowledge." *Philosophy and Phenomenological Research* 78 (1):133–164. doi: 10.1111/j.1933-1592.2008.00235.x.

Branch, P., A. Daley, and A. Henschke. 2015. "Expert Panel: Metadata Retention Report." *The Conversation*, 27 February. https://theconversation.com/expert-panel-metadata-retention-report-38168.

Brennan, Samantha. 2006. "Moral Lumps." *Ethical Theory and Moral Practice* 9 (3):249–263.

Brennan, Samantha. 2009. "Feminist Ethics and Everyday Inequalities." *Hypatia* 24 (1):141–159.

Brennan, Samantha. 2013. "Rethinking the Moral Significance of Micro-Inequities: The Case of Women in Philosophy." In *Women in Philosophy: What Needs to Change*, edited by Katrina Hutchison and Fiona Jenkins. Oxford: Oxford University Press.

Brey, Philip. 2005. "Artefacts as Social Agents." In *Inside the Politics of Technology: Agency and Normativity in the Co-Production of Technology and Society*, edited by Hans Harbers. Amsterdam: Amsterdam University Press.

Brockmole, James R., David Z. Hambrick, David J. Windisch, and John M. Henderson. 2008. "The Role of Meaning in Contextual Cueing: Evidence from Chess Expertise." *The Quarterly Journal of Experimental Psychology* 61 (12):1886–1896.

Brook, Andrew. 1998. "Unified Consciousness and the Self." *Journal of Consciousness Studies* 5:583–591.

Brunner, H. G., M. Nelen, X. O. Breakefield, H. H. Ropers, and B. A. van Oost. 1993. "Abnormal Behavior Associated with a Point Mutation in the Structural Gene for Monoamine Oxidase A." *Science* 262 (5133):578–580.

Buchanan, Allen, Dan W. Brock, Norman Daniels, and Daniel Wikler. 2000. *From Chance to Choice: Genetics & Justice*. 1st edn. Cambridge: Cambridge University Press.

Butler, Joseph. 2008. "Of Personal Identity." In *Personal Identity*, edited by John Perry, 99–106. Berkeley: University of California Press. Original edition, The Analogy of Religion.

Caldara, Roberto C. A., Bruno Rossion, Pierre Bovet, and Claude-Alain Hauert. 2004. "Event-Related Potentials and Time Course of the 'Other-Race' Face Classification Advantage." *Neuroreport* 15 (5):905–910.

Caldwell, H. K., and Young W. S. III. 2006. "Oxytocin and Vasopressin: Genetics and Behavioral Implications." In *Handbook of Neurochemistry and Molecular Neurobiology*, edited by Latja Abel and Ramon Lim, 573–607. Berlin: Springer.

Campbell, Mikey. 2015. "Apple Invents Ringstyle Wearable Device with Voice Control, Haptics, Cameras and More." *Apple Insider*, 01 October.

Campbell, Tom. 2006. *Rights: A Critical Introduction, Routledge Contemporary Political Philosophy*. London: Routledge.

Carlato, Daniel. 2008. "Brain Scans as Mind Readers? Don't Believe the Hype." *Wired Magazine*, 19th May.

Cassia, Viola Macchi, Dana Kuefner, Marta Picozzi, and Elena Vescovo. 2009. "Early Experience Predicts Later Plasticity for Face Processing: Evidence for the Reactivation of Dormant Effects." *Psychological Science* 20 (6): 853–859.

Chalmers, Alan Francis. 1999. *What Is This Thing Called Science?* 3rd edn. St Lucia: University of Queensland Press.

Chalmers, David. 2006. "Strong and Weak Emergence." In *The Re-Emergence of Emergence*, edited by Philip Clayton and Paul Davies. Oxford: Oxford University Press.

Chalmers, David John. 1996. *The Conscious Mind: In Search of a Fundamental Theory, Philosophy of Mind Series*. New York: Oxford University Press.

Chambers, Duncan, Paul Wilson, Carl Thompson, and Melissa Harden. 2012. "Social Network Analysis in Healthcare Settings: A Systematic Scoping Review." *PloS One* 7 (8): e41911.

Charness, Neil, Michael Tuffiash, Ralf Krampe, Eyal Reingold, and Ekaterina Vasyukova. 2005. "The Role of Deliberate Practice in Chess Expertise." *Applied Cognitive Psychology* 19 (2):151–165. doi: 10.1002/acp.1106.

Cheshire Jnr, William P. 2008. "Doing Small Things Well: Translating Nanotechnology into Nanomedicine." In *Nanoscale: Issues and Perspectives for the Nano Century*, edited by Nigel M. de S. Cameron and M. Ellen Mitchell, 315–336. Hoboken: John Wiley & Sons.

Churchland, Paul M. 1981. "Eliminative Materialism and the Propositional Attitudes." *The Journal of Philosophy* 78 (2):67–90.

Clark, Andy. 1997a. *Being There: Putting Brain, Body and World Together Again*. Cambridge: MIT Press.

Clark, Andy. 1997b. "The Dynamical Challenge." *Cognitive Science* 21 (4):461–481. doi: 10.1207/s15516709cog2104_3.
Clark, Andy. 2008. *Supersizing the Mind: Embodiment, Action and Cognitive Extension*. Oxford: Oxford University Press.
Clark, Andy, and David Chalmers. 1998. "The Extended Mind." *Analysis* 58 (1):7–19. doi: 10.1093/analys/58.1.7.
Clayton, Ellen Wright. 2005. "Informed Consent and Biobanks." *The Journal of Law, Medicine & Ethics* 33 (1):15–21.
Cocking, Dean, and Jeanette Kennett. 1998. "Friendship and the Self." *Ethics* 108 (3):502.
Cohen, Elliot D. 2010. *Mass Surveillance and State Control*. London: Palgrave Macmillan.
Coonan, Clifford. 2016. "Loan Sharks Demand Nude Photos as Collateral from Students." *The Irish Times*, 15th June, 2016. www.irishtimes.com/news/offbeat/loan-sharks-demand-nude-photos-as-collateral-from-students-1.2685631.
Costantini, Marcello, and Patrick Haggard. 2007. "The Rubber Hand Illusion: Sensitivity and Reference Frame for Body Ownership." *Consciousness and Cognition* 16 (2): 229–240.
Council for International Organizations of Medical Sciences. 2005. Pharmacogenetics: Towards Improving Treatment with Medicines. Geneva: Council for International Organizations of Medical Sciences (CIOMS).
Crane, T. 2001. "Intentional Objects." *Ratio* 14 (4):336–349.
Crompton, Malcolm. 2011. "Personal Communication." Canberra, 12 May.
Cudd, Anne. 2013. "Contractarianism." In Stanford Encyclopedia Of Philosophy, edited by Edward N. Zalta.
D'Agostino, Fred, Gerald Gaus, and John Thrasher. 2014. "Contemporary Approaches to the Social Contract." accessed 20/07/2016. http://plato.stanford.edu/archives/win2012/entries/contractarianism-contemporary/.
Daniels, Norman. 1979. "Wide Reflective Equilibrium and Theory Acceptance in Ethics." *The Journal of Philosophy* 76 (5):256–282.
Daniels, Norman. 1980. "Reflective Equilibrium and Archimedean Points." *Canadian Journal of Philosophy* 10 (1):83–103.
Daniels, Norman. 2008. *Just Health: Meeting Health Needs Fairly*. 1st edn. Cambridge: Cambridge University Press.
Darwall, Stephen L. 1977. "Two Kinds of Respect." *Ethics* 88 (1):36–49.
Dawkins, Richard. 2006. *The God Delusion*. London: Bantam Press.
de Haan, Willem. 2008. "Violence as an Essentially Contested Concept." In *Violence in Europe*, edited by S. Body-Gendrot and P. Spierenburg. Dordrecht: Springer.
DeCew, Judith. 2006. "Privacy." In Stanford Encyclopedia Of Philosophy, edited by Edward N. Zalta.
DeGrazia, David. 2005. *Human Identity and Bioethics*. Cambridge: Cambridge University Press.
Deikman, A. J. 1996. "I = Awareness." *Journal of Consciousness Studies* 3 (4):350–356.
Delgado, Mauricio R. 2008. "Fool Me Once, Shame on You; Fool Me Twice, Shame on Oxytocin." *Neuron* 58 (4):470–471.
Delmas, Candice. 2015. "The Ethics of Government Whistleblowing." *Social Theory and Practice* 41 (1):77. doi: 10.5840/soctheorpract20154114.
DeMarco, Joseph P. 1994. A *Coherence Theory in Ethics, Value Inquiry Book Series*. Amsterdam: Rodopi.
DeMarco, Joseph P. 1997. "Coherence and Applied Ethics." *Journal of Applied Philosophy* 14 (3):289–300. doi: 10.1111/1468–5930.00064.

DeMarco, Joseph P., and Paul J. Ford. 2006. "Balancing in Ethical Deliberation: Superior to Specification and Casuistry." *Journal of Medicine & Philosophy* 31 (5):483–497.
Deneubourg, J. L., and S. Goss. 1989. "Collective Patterns and Decision-Making." *Ethology Ecology & Evolution* 1 (4):295–311. doi: 10.1080/08927014.1989.9525500.
Denman, Donald. 1997. "Property and the Environment." In *The Idea of Property in History and Modern Times*, edited by Colin Kolbert. London: Churchill Press.
Dennett, Daniel Clement. 1991. "The Reality of Selves." In *Consciousness Explained*, xiii, 511 p. Boston: Little, Brown and Co.
Deutsch, Harry. 2009. "Relative Identity." In *The Stanford Encyclopedia of Philosophy*, edited by Edward N. Zalta.
Devine, Patricia G. 1989. "Stereotypes and Prejudice: Their Automatic and Controlled Components." *Journal of Personality and Social Psychology* 56 (1):5–18.
Devitt, Michael. 1990. "Meanings Just Aint in the Head." In *Meaning and Method: Essays in Honour of Hilary Putnam*, edited by George Boolos, 79–104. Cambridge: Cambridge University Press.
Dewan, Shaila. 2015. "Judges Replacing Conjecture with Formula for Bail." *The New York Times*, 26 June.
Dingle, Sarah. 2014. "Attorney-General George Brandis Struggles to Explain Government's Metadata Proposal." *ABC News*, August 7. www.abc.net.au/news/2014-08-07/brandis-explanation-adds-confusion-to-metadata-proposal/5654186.
Downing, Paul E., Yuhong Jiang, Miles Shuman, and Nancy Kanwisher. 2001. "A Cortical Area Selective for Visual Processing of the Human Body." *Science* 293 (5539):2470–2473. doi: 10.1126/science.1063414.
Drahos, Peter. 1996. "A *Philosophy of Intellectual Property*." Thesis (PhD), Dartmouth: Australian National University, 1997.
Drahos, Peter, and John Braithwaite. 2002. *Information Feudalism: Who Owns the Knowledge Economy?* London: Earthscan.
Dretske, Fred Irwin. 1981. *Knowledge and the Flow of Information*. Oxford: B. Blackwell.
Dworkin, Ronald. 1978. *Taking Rights Seriously*. Cambridge: Harvard University Press.
Eberhardt, Jennifer L., Phillip Atiba Goff, Valerie J. Purdie, and Paul Davies. 2004. "Seeing Black: Race, Crime, and Visual Processing." *Journal of Personality & Social Psychology* 87 (6):876–893.
Ebertz, Roger P. 1993. "Is Reflective Equilibrium a Coherentist Model?" *Canadian Journal of Philosophy* 23 (2):193–214.
Editorial. 2012. "The End of Privacy?" *The New York Times*, 14 July. www.nytimes.com/2012/07/15/opinion/sunday/the-end-of-privacy.html.
El Guindi, Fadwa. 1999. *Veil: Modesty, Privacy and Resistance, Dress, Body, Culture*. Oxford: Berg.
Ellis, Hadyn D., and Michael B. Lewis. 2001. "Capgras Delusion: A Window on Face Recognition." *Trends in Cognitive Sciences* 5 (4):149–156.
Ellsberg, Daniel. 2013. "Edward Snowden: Saving Us from the United Stasi of America." *The Guardian*, 10 June.
Elsabbagh, Mayada, Agnes Volein, Gergely Csibra, Karla Holmboe, Holly Garwood, Leslie Tucker, Sanya Krljes, Simon Baron-Cohen, Patrick Bolton, Tony Charman, Gillian Baird, and Mark H. Johnson. 2009. "Neural Correlates of Eye Gaze Processing in the Infant Broader Autism Phenotype." *Biological Psychiatry* 65 (1):31–38.
Endomondo. 2011. "Terms and Conditions." accessed 16 March 2012. www.endomondo.com/terms.
Endomondo.com. 2012. Endomondo Fact Sheet.

European Commission. 2010. A Comprehensive Approach on Personal Data Protection in the European Union. In *COM 609*, edited by European Commission.

European Data Protection Supervisor. 2001. Regulation (EC) No 45/2001.

Evans, Nicholas G. 2012. "Great Expectations." *Journal of Medical Ethics* 39:209–213.

Everett, Margaret. 2005. "The Social Life of Genes: Privacy, Property and the New Genetics." In *Information Ethics: Privacy, Property, and Power*, edited by Adam D. Moore, 226–250. Seattle: University of Washington Press.

Farrell, Henry. 2015. "Facebook Wasn't Great at Respecting Privacy in the First Place. It's Gotten Much Worse." *The Washington Post*, August 18. Accessed 11/01/2016. www.washingtonpost.com/blogs/monkey-cage/wp/2015/08/18/facebook-wasnt-great-at-respecting-privacy-in-the-first-place-its-gotten-much-worse/.

Farrell, Paul. 2016a. "Lamb Chop Weight Enforcers Want Warrantless Access to Australians' Metadata." *The Guardian*, 19 January.

Farrell, Paul. 2016b. "Privacy Commissioner Challenges Ruling Journalist Can't Access Own Phone Data." *The Guardian*, 11 February.

Farroni, Teresa, Gergely Csibra, Francesca Simion, and Mark H. Johnson. 2002. "Eye Contact Detection in Humans from Birth." *Proceedings of the National Academy of Sciences of the United States of America* 99 (14):9602–9605. doi: 10.1073/pnas.152159999.

Faunce, Thomas A., and Joel Lexchin. 2007. "'Linkage' Pharmaceutical Evergreening in Canada and Australia." *Australia New Zealand Health Policy* 4 (8):1–11.

Feinberg, Joel. 1985. *The Moral Limits of the Criminal Law*. Vol. 3: Harm to Self. New York: Oxford University Press.

Feng, Lu, Jiangang Liu, Zhe Wang, Jun Li, Ling Li, Liezhong Ge, Jie Tian, and Kang Lee. 2011. "The Other Face of the Other-Race Effect: An fMRI Investigation of the Other-Race Face Categorization Advantage." *Neuropsychologia* 49 (13):3739–3749.

Fiala, Andrew. 2006. "A Critique of Exceptions: Torture, Terrorism, and the Lesser Evil." *International Journal of Applied Philosophy* 20 (1):127–142.

First, Michael. 2005. "Desire for Amputation of a Limb: Paraphilia, Psychosis, or a New Type of Identity Disorder." *Psychological Medicine* 35:919–928.

FitBit. 2015. "FitBit." accessed 12/01/2016. www.fitbit.com/au/about.

Fitzgerald, Brian. 2003. "Theoretical Underpinning of Intellectual Property: 'I Am a Pragmatist but Theory Is My Rhetoric'." *Canadian Journal of Law and Jurisprudence* 16 (2):179–190.

Fletcher, George C., and Jens David Ohlin. 2008. *Defending Humanity: When Force Is Justified and Why*. Oxford University Press.

Flood, Alison. 2012. "Big e-Reader Is Watching You." *The Guardian (UK)*, 4 July. www.guardian.co.uk/books/2012/jul/04/big-ereader-is-watching-you.

Floridi, Luciano. 2002. "On the Intrinsic Value of Information Objects and the Infosphere." *Ethics and Information Technology* 4 (4):287–304.

Floridi, Luciano. 2004. "Information." In *The Blackwell Guide to the Philosophy of Computing and Information*, edited by Luciano Floridi. Oxford: Blackwell Publishing.

Floridi, Luciano. 2005a. "Is Semantic Information Meaningful Data?" *Philosophy and Phenomenological Research* 70 (2):351–370. doi: 10.1111/j.1933-1592.2005.tb00531.x.

Floridi, Luciano. 2005b. "The Ontological Interpretation of Informational Privacy." *Ethics And Information Technology* 7:185–200.

Floridi, Luciano. 2006. "Four Challenges for a Theory of Informational Privacy." *Ethics and Information Technology* 8:109–119.

Floridi, Luciano. 2008. "The Method of Levels of Abstraction." *Minds and Machines* 18 (3):303–329. doi: 10.1007/s11023-008–9113-7.

Floridi, Luciano. 2011a. *The Philosophy of Information*. Oxford: Oxford University Press.

Floridi, Luciano. 2011b. "Semantic Conceptions of Information." In *The Stanford Encyclopedia of Philosophy*, edited by Edward N. Zalta.

Fodor, Jerry A. 1983. *The Modularity of Mind: An Essay on Faculty Psychology*. Cambridge, MA: MIT Press.

Frankfurt, Harry. 2006. *Taking Ourselves Seriously and Getting It Right*, edited by Debra Satz. Stanford, California: Stanford University Press.

Frankfurt, Harry G. 1971. "Freedom of the Will and the Concept of a Person." *The Journal of Philosophy* 68 (1):5–20.

Frankfurt, Harry G. 1988. *The Importance of What We Care About: Philosophical Essays*. Cambridge: Cambridge University Press.

Freudenheim, Milt. 2009. "And You Thought a Prescription Was Private." *New York Times*, August 9.

Friedman, Batya, Peter H. Kahn, and Alan Borning. 2002. Value Sensitive Design: Theory and Methods. In *University of Washington Computer Science and Engineering Technical Report*: University of Washington.

Friedman, Batya, and Helen Nissenbaum, eds. 2007. "*Bias in Computer Systems*." Edited by John Weckert, *Computer Ethics*. Aldershot: Ashgate.

Friedman, Marilyn. 2000. "Autonomy, Social Disruption and Women." In *Relational Autonomy: Feminist Perspectives on Automony, Agency, and the Social Self*, edited by Catriona Mackenzie and Natalie Stoljar, 35–51. New York: Oxford University Press.

Friedman, Milton. 1970. "The Social Responsibility of Business Is to Increase Its Profits." *The New York Times Magazine*, September 13.

Funder, Anna. 2002. *Stasiland*. Melbourne: Text Publishing.

Garrett, Laurie. 1996. *The Coming Plague*. London: Penguin Books.

Garrett, Laurie. 2001. *Betrayal of Trust*. New York: Hyperion books.

Garrett, Laurie. 2012. "Flu Season." *Foreign Policy*, January 5.

Gelman, Andrew, Jeffrey Fagan, and Alex Kiss. 2007. "An Analysis of the New York City Police Department's 'Stop-and-Frisk' Policy in the Context of Claims of Racial Bias." *Journal of the American Statistical Association* 102 (479):813–823. doi: 10.1198/016214506000001040.

Gert, Bernard. 2004. *Common Morality: Deciding What to Do*. Oxford: Oxford University Press.

Gert, Bernard, Charles Culver, and Danner Clouser. 2006. *Bioethics: A Systematic Approach*. Oxford: Oxford University Press.

Gettier, Edmund L. 1963. "Is Justified True Belief Knowledge?" *Analysis* 23:121–123.

Gillies, Peter. 2009. "Colour in Branding – Asserting a Monopoly in a Colour for Marketing Purposes – The Cadbury – Darrell Lea Litigation." *International Trade and Business Law Review* 253 (12):253–265.

Glover, Jonathan. 1986. "It Makes No Difference Whether or Not I Do It." In *Applied Ethics*, edited by Peter A. Singer. Oxford: Oxford University Press.

Glover, Jonathan. 1988. *I: The Philosophy and Psychology of Personal Identity*. London: Allen Lane/ Penguin.

Glover, Jonathan, ed. 1990. *Utilitarianism and Its Critics*. New York: Macmillan Pub. Co.

Glover, Jonathan. 2000. *Humanity: A Moral History of the Twentieth Century*. New Haven, CT: Yale University Press.

Goodin, Robert E. 1985. *Protecting the Vulnerable: A Reanalysis of Our Social Responsibilities*. Chicago: University of Chicago Press.

Gosling, Angela, and Martin Eimer. 2011. "An Event-Related Brain Potential Study of Explicit Face Recognition." *Neuropsychologia* 49 (9):2736–2745.

Greenberg, Andy. 2012. *This Machine Kills Secrets: How Wikileaks, Cypherpunks and Hacktivists Aim to Free the World's Information*. New York: Penguin.
Greenwald, Glen. 2014. *No Place to Hide: Edward Snowden, The NSA, and the U.S. Surveillance State*. New York: Metropolitan Books.
Grice, H. P. 1957. "Meaning." *The Philosophical Review* 66 (3):377–388.
Griffin, James. 1986. *Well-Being: Its Meaning, Measurement and Moral Importance*. Oxford: Oxford University Press.
Griffin, James. 2008. *On Human Rights*. Oxford: Oxford University Press.
Griffiths, Paul E., and Karola Stotz. 2006. "Genes in the Postgenomic Era." *Theoretical Medicine and Bioethics* 27:499–521.
Guerrero, Alexander A. 2007. "Don't Know, Don't Kill: Moral Ignorance, Culpability, and Caution." *Philosophical Studies* 136:59–97.
Gutman, Amy. 1994. "Introduction to Examining Multiculturalism and the Politics of Recognition." In *Examining Multiculturalism and the Politics of Recognition*, edited by Amy Gutman, 3–24. Princeton, NJ: Princeton University Press.
Guzik, Keith. 2009. "Discrimination by Design: Predictive Data Mining as Security Practice in the United States' 'War On Terrorism'." *Surveillance and Society* 7 (1):1–17.
Habermas, Jurgen. 1994. "Struggles for Recognition in the Democratic Constitutional State." In *Multiculturalism: Examining the Politics of Recognition*, edited by Amy Gutman, 107–148. Princeton, NJ: Princeton University Press.
Habermas, Jurgen. 1995. "Reconciliation through the Public Use of Reason: Remarks on John Rawls's Political Liberalism." *The Journal of Philosophy* 92 (3):109–131.
Hackman, Rose. 2015. "Is the Online Surveillance of Black Teenagers the New Stop-and-Frisk?" *The Guardian*, 23 April.
Haidt, Jonathan. 2001. "The Emotional Dog and Its Rational Tail: A Social Intuitionist Approach to Moral Judgment." *Psychological Review* 108 (4):814–834.
Hanson, Norwood Russell. 1958. *Patterns of Discovery: An Inquiry into the Conceptual Foundations of Science*. London: Cambridge University Press.
Hardcastle, Valerie Gray, and C. Matthew Stewart. 2005. "Localization in the Brain and other Illusions." In *Cognition and the Brain: The Philosophy and Neuroscience Movement*, edited by Andrew Brook and Kathleen Akins, Cambridge; New York: Cambridge University Press.
Hardin, Garrett. 1968. "The Tragedy of the Commons." *Science* 162 (3859):1243–1248. doi: 10.1126/science.162.3859.1243.
Harding, Luke. 2014. *The Snowden Files: The Inside Story of the World's Most Wanted Man*. New York: Vintage Books.
Harmann, Gilbert. 1977. *The Nature of Morality: An Introduction to Ethics*. New York: Oxford University Press.
Haslanger, Sally. 2000. "Gender and Race: (What) Are They? (What) Do We Want Them to Be?" *Noûs* 34 (1):31–55.
Hauskeller, Christine. 2004. "Genes, Genomes and Identity. Projections on Matter." *New Genetics and Society* 23 (3):285–299.
Hearn, Louisa. 2010. "Google on Privacy: Change Your Name." *Sydney Morning Herald*, August 17.
Hegel, Georg Wilhelm Friedrich. 1967. *Philosophy of Right*. Translated by T. M. Knox. London: Oxford University Press.
Hegel, Georg Wilhelm Friedrich, and M. J. Inwood. 2007. *Hegel's Philosophy of Mind*. Translated by William Wallace and Arnold V. Miller. Oxford: Clarendon. Original edition, 1830.

Henschke, Adam. 2010. "Did You Just Say What I Think You Said? Talking about Genes, Identity and Information." *Identity in the Information Society* 3 (3):435–456.

Henschke, Adam. 2011. "Soft Biometrics the Next Step for Security Surveillance, According to Aussie Researchers." *The Australian*, 06/09/2011. www.theaustralian.com.au/higher-education/soft-biometrics-the-next-step-for-security-surveillance-according-to-aussie-researchers/story-e6frgcjx-1226130769980.

Henschke, Adam. 2012. "Making Sense of Animal Disenhancement." *NanoEthics* 6 (1):55–64. doi: 10.1007/s11569-012-0140-8.

Henschke, Adam. 2014. "Metadata and Privacy: Surveillance State or Business as Usual?" *The Conversation*, 12 November. https://theconversation.com/metadata-and-privacy-surveillance-state-or-business-as-usual-33949.

Henschke, Adam. 2015a. "AshelyMadison.Com: Fifty Shades of Grey Hat Hacking." *Ethics.org*, January 20. www.ethics.org.au/on-ethics/blog/july-2015-(1)/ashleymadison-com-fifty-shades-of-grey-hat-hacking.

Henschke, Adam. 2015b. "Ashley Madison: An Affair May Be Morally Wrong, But Can We Justify Vigilante Punishment Based on Sexual Morality?" *The Age*, 20th August. www.theage.com.au/comment/ashley-madison-an-affair-may-be-morally-wrong-but-can-we-justify-vigilante-punishment-based-on-sexual-morality-20150820-gj3pzv.html.

Henschke, Adam. 2015c. "Benign and Powerful: The Contradictory Language of Metadata Retention." *The Conversation*, March 2nd. https://theconversation.com/benign-and-powerful-the-contradictory-language-of-metadata-retention-38225.

Henschke, Adam. 2015d. "Opportunity Costs: Scarcity and Complex Medical Machines." In *Machine Medical Ethics*, edited by Simon Peter van Rysewyk and Matthias Pontier, 131–150. Dordrecht: Springer.

Henschke, Adam. 2015e. "We Should Care about Metadata and What Governments Do with It." *The Courier Mail*, 20 February. www.couriermail.com.au/news/opinion/we-should-care-about-metadata-and-what-governments-do-with-it/story-fnihsr9v-1227225953591.

Henschke, Adam. 2017. "The Internet of Things and Dual Layers of Ethical Concern." In *Robot Ethics*, edited by Patrick Lin, Keith Abney and Ryan Jenkins. Oxford: Oxford University Press.

Henschke, Adam, and Nicholas G. Evans. 2012. "Winning Well by Fighting Well: Probability of Success and the Relations between War's Ends and Warfighters' Roles." *International Journal of Applied Philosophy* 26 (2):149. doi: 10.5840/ijap201226212.

Hesketh, Ian. 2009. *Of Apes and Ancestors: Evolution, Christianity and the Oxford Debate*. Toronto: University of Toronto Press.

Hettinger, Edwin C. 1989. "Justifying Intellectual Property." *Philosophy and Public Affairs* 18 (1):31–52.

Heyman, Steven. 1991 "The First Duty of Government: Protection, Liberty and the Fourteenth Amendment." *Duke Law Journal* 41:507–571.

Hill, Kashmir. 2012. "How Target Figured Out a Teen Girl Was Pregnant Before Her Father Did." *Forbes*, February 16. Accessed 11/01/2016. www.forbes.com/sites/kashmirhill/2012/02/16/how-target-figured-out-a-teen-girl-was-pregnant-before-her-father-did/.

Hobbes, Thomas. 1968. *Leviathan*, edited by C. B. Machperson. Middlesex: Pelican Classics. Original edition, 1651.

Hochstein, Shaul, and Merav Ahissar. 2002. "View from the Top: Hierarchies and Reverse Hierarchies in the Visual System." *Neuron* 36 (5):791–804.

Honoré, Anthony (Tony) M. 1961. "Ownership." In *Oxford Essays in Jurisprudence: A Collaborative Work*, edited by Anthony Gordon Guest. London: Oxford University Press.

Hook, C. Christopher. 2008. "Nanotechnology and the Future of Medicine." In *Nanoscale: Issues and Perspectives for the Nano Century*, edited by Nigel M. de S. Cameron and M. Ellen Mitchell, 337–357. Hoboken: Wiley & Sons.

Househ, Mouwafa. 2013. "The Use of Social Media in Healthcare: Organizational, Clinical, and Patient Perspectives." In *Enabling Health and Healthcare through ICT: Available, Tailored, and Closer*, edited by Karen L. Courtney, Omid Shabetsari and Alex Kuo. IOS Press.

Hughes, Justin. 1988. "The Philosophy of Intellectual Property." *Georgetown Law Journal* 77:287–366.

Hume, David. 1985. *A Treatise of Human Nature*, edited by Ernest C. Mossner. London: Penguin. Original edition, 1739. Reprint, 1985.

Hunt, Elle. 2016. "Instagram Star Essena O'Neill: 'The Way It All Turned So Negative Just Numbed Me'." *The Guardian*, 05 January.

Hurka, Thomas. 2005. "Proportionality in the Morality of War." *Philosophy and Public Affairs* 33 (1):34–66.

Hursthouse, Rosalind. 1999. *On Virtue Ethics*. Oxford: Oxford University Press.

Inness, Julie C. 1992. *Privacy, Intimacy, and Isolation*. New York: Oxford University Press.

Jackson, Frank. 1991. "What Mary Didn't Know." In *The Nature of Mind*, edited by David M. Rosenthal. New York: Oxford University Press. Original edition, The Journal of Philosophy, LXXXIII, 5 (May 1986):291–295.

Jackson, Frank. 2003. "Mind and Illusion." In *Minds and Persons*, edited by Anthony O'Hear, 251–272. Cambridge: Cambridge University Press.

Jackson, Frank, and Philip Pettit. 2004. "In Defence of Folk Psychology." In *Mind, Morality and Explanation*, edited by Frank Jackson, Philip Pettit and Michael Smith, 13–35. Oxford: Oxford University Press.

Johnson, Bobbie. 2010. "Privacy No Longer a Social Norm, Says Facebook Founder." *Guardian UK*, January 11.

Johnston, Josephine, and Angela A. Wasunna. 2007. "Patents, Biomedical Research, and Treatments: Examining Concerns, Canvassing Solutions." *The Hastings Center Report* 31 (1):S2–S36.

Jones, Peter. 2006. "Toleration, Recognition and Identity." *Journal of Political Philosophy* 14 (2):123–143. doi:10.1111/j.1467–9760.2006.00246.x.

Jonsen, Albert R., and Stephen Edelston Toulmin. 1988. *The Abuse of Casuistry: A History of Moral Reasoning*. Berkeley: University of California Press.

Joyce, Richard. 2006. *The Evolution of Morality*. Cambridge: MIT Press.

Kagan, Shelly. 1989. *The Limits of Morality*. Oxford: Oxford University Press.

Kagan, Shelly. 1998a. *Normative Ethics, Dimensions of Philosophy*. Boulder: Westview Press.

Kagan, Shelly. 1998b. "Rethinking Intrinsic Value." *The Journal of Ethics* 2:277–297.

Kant, Immanuel. 1934. *Critique of Pure Reason*. Translated by J. M. D. Meiklejohn. London: Dent.

Kanwisher, Nancy. 2000. "Domain Specificity in Face Perception." *Nature Neuroscience* 3 (8):759–763.

Kasperbauer, T. J. 2015. "Psychological Constraints on Egalitarianism: The Challenge of Just World Beliefs." *Res Publica* 21 (3):217–234. doi: 10.1007/s11158-015–9284-z.

Kavka, Gregory S. 1983. "Hobbes's War of All against All." *Ethics* 93 (2):291–310.

Kennett, Jeanette, and Cordelia Fine. 2009. "Will the Real Moral Judgment Please Stand Up?" *Ethical Theory and Moral Practice* 12 (1):77–96. doi: 10.1007/s10677-008–9136-4.

Khaleeli, Homa, and Monday 8 August 2016 18.12 BST. 2016. "The Perils of 'Flying While Muslim'." *The Guardian UK*, 8th August.

Kharpal, Arjun. 2016. "Apple Vs FBI: All You Need to Know." *CNBC*, 29 March 2016. Accessed 20 August 2016. www.cnbc.com/2016/03/29/apple-vs-fbi-all-you-need-to-know .html.

Khatchadourian, Haig. 1968. "Common Names and 'Family Resemblances'." In *Wittgenstein: The Philosophical Investigations*, edited by George Pitcher, 205–230. Macmillan.

Kilcullen, David. 2016. *Blood Year: The Unvravelling of Western Counterterrorism*: Oxford University Press.

Kim, Jaegwon. 1999. "Making Sense of Emergence." *Philosophical Studies* 95:3–36.

Kim, Jaegwon. 2006. "Emergence: Core Ideas and Issues." *Synthese* 151 (3):547–559. doi: 10.1007/s11229-006-9025-0.

Kirsh, David, and Paul Maglio. 1994. "On Distinguishing Epistemic from Pragmatic Action." *Cognitive Science* 18 (4):513–549.

Kitcher, Philip. 2007. "Does 'Race' Have a Future?" *Philosophy & Public Affairs* 35 (4):293–317.

Kitcher, Philip. 2011. "Militant Modern Atheism." *Journal of Applied Philosophy* 28 (1). doi: 10.1111/j.1468–5320.2010.00500.x.

Kizza, Joseph Migga, and Jackline Ssanyu. 2005. "Workplace Surveillance." In *Electronic Monitoring in the Workplace: Controversies and Solutions*, edited by John Weckert, 1–18. Hershey: Idea Group Publishing.

Klein, Peter. 2011. Skepticism. In *Stanford Encyclopedia of Philosophy*, edited by Edward N. Zalta.

Koepsell, David. 2009. *Who Owns You? The Corporate Gold Rush to Patent Your Genes*. West Sussex: Wiley-Blackwell.

Kolers, Avery. 2003. "Cloning and Genetic Parenthood." *Cambridge Quarterly of Healthcare Ethics* 12 (04):401–410. doi: 10.1017/S0963180103124097.

Kolers, Avery, and Tim Bayne. 2001. "'Are You My Mommy?' On the Genetic Basis of Parenthood." *Journal of Applied Philosophy* 18 (3):273–285. doi: 10.1111/1468–5930.00194.

Kornell, Nate. 2009. "Metacognition in Humans and Animals." *Current Directions in Psychological Science* 18 (1):11–15. doi: 10.1111/j.1467–8721.2009.01597.x.

Korsgaard, Christine M. 1996. *The Sources of Normativity*. New York: Cambridge University Press.

Korsgaard, Christine M. 2009. *Self-Constitution: Agency, Identity, and Integrity*. Oxford: Oxford University Press.

Krigolson, Olav E., Lara J. Pierce, Clay B. Holroyd, and James W. Tanaka. 2008. "Learning to Become an Expert: Reinforcement Learning and the Acquisition of Perceptual Expertise." *Journal of Cognitive Neuroscience* 21 (9):1833–1840. doi: 10.1162/jocn.2009.21128.

Kroes, Peter. 2009. "Technical Artifacts, Engineering Practice, and Emergence." In *Functions In Biological and Artificial Worlds: Comparative Philosophical Perspectives*, edited by Ulrich Krohs and Peter Kroes. Cambridge: MIT Press.

Kveraga, Kestutis, Avniel S. Ghuman, and Moshe Bar. 2007. "Top-Down Predictions in the Cognitive Brain." *Brain and Cognition* 65 (2):145–168.

Kwek, Glenda. 2011. "Armageddon Super Virus Recipe: Keep Secret or Publish?" *Sydney Morning Herald*, December 6.

Kymlicka, Will. 1995. *Multicultural Citizenship: A Liberal Theory of Minority Rights*. Oxford: Clarendon Press.

Kymlicka, Will. 2002. *Contemporary Political Philosophy*. 2nd edn. Oxford: Oxford University Press.

Lauwereyns, Jan. 2010. *The Anatomy of Bias: How Neural Circuits Weigh the Options*. New York: Cambridge.

Le Grand, Richard, Philip A. Cooper, Catherine J. Mondloch, Terri L. Lewis, Noam Sagiv, Beatrice de Gelder, and Daphne Maurer. 2006. "What Aspects of Face Processing Are Impaired in Developmental Prosopagnosia?" *Brain and Cognition* 61 (2):139–158.

Lemos, Jakob de. 2007. Visual Detection and Emotional Response Detection and Display System, edited by U.S. Patent and Trademark Office USPTO. United States.

Lerner, Melvin. 1980. *The Belief in a Just World: A Fundamental Delusion*: Plenum Press.

Lester, Genevieve. 2016. *When Should State Secrets Stay Secret?* Cambridge: Cambridge University Press.

Lever, Annabelle. 2001. "Ethics and the Patenting of Human Genes." *Journal of Philosophy, Science and Law* 1 (1).

Levin, Sam. 2016. "A Beauty Contest Was Judged by AI and the Robots Didn't Like Dark Skin." *Guardian*, 8th September.

Levy, Neil. 2002. *Moral Relativism: A Short Introduction*. Oxford: Oneworld Publications

Levy, Neil. 2007. *Neuroethics: Challenges for the 21st Century*. Cambridge: Cambridge University Press.

Lewis, Michael, and Jeanne Brooks-Gunn. 1979. *Social Cognition and the Acquisition of Self*. New York: Plenum Press.

Ley, Susan. 2015. *Patients to Get New myHealth Record: $485m 'Rescue' Package to Reboot Labor's e-health Failures*. Minister For Health.

Locke, John. 1975. *An Essay Concerning Human Understanding*, edited by Peter. H. Nidditch, *Locke, John, 1632–1704. Works. 1975*. Oxford: Clarendon Press.

Locke, John, and Peter Laslett. 1963. *Two Treatises of Government*. Revised edn. New York: Mentor. Original edition, 1698.

Lockton, Vance, and Richard S. Rosenberg. 2005. "RFID: The Next Serious Threat to Privacy." *Ethics and Information Technology* 7 (4):221.

Lohr, Steve. 2014. "Unblinking Eyes Track Employees: Workplace Surveillance Sees Good and Bad." *New York Times*, 21 June 2014, Technology. Accessed 04/02/2016. www.nytimes.com/2014/06/22/technology/workplace-surveillance-sees-good-and-bad.html.

Lotan, Gilad, Erhardt Graeff, Mike Ananny, Devin Gaffney, and Ian Pearce. 2011. "The Revolutions Were Tweeted: Information Flows During the 2011 Tunisian and Egyptian Revolutions." *International Journal of Communication* 5 (31):1375–1405.

Louie, Janice K., Meileen Acosta, Kathleen Winter, Cynthia Jean, Shilpa Gavali, Robert Schechter, Duc Vugia, Kathleen Harriman, Bela Matyas, Carol A. Glaser, Michael C. Samuel, Jon Rosenberg, John Talarico, and Douglas Hatch. 2009. "Factors Associated with Death or Hospitalization Due to Pandemic 2009 Influenza A(H1N1) Infection in California." *JAMA: The Journal of the American Medical Association* 302 (17):1896–1902. doi: 10.1001/jama.2009.1583.

Lyon, David. 1994. *The Electronic Eye: The Rise of Surveillance Society. Minneapolis*: University of Minnesota Press.

Lyon, David. 2009. "Surveillance, Power, and Everyday Life." In *The Oxford Handbook of Information and Communication Technologies*, edited by Chrisanthi Avgerou, Robin Mansell, Danny Quah and Roger Silverstone. Oxford University Press.

Maas, Peter, and Megha Rajagopalan. 2012. "That's No Phone: That's My Tracker." *The New York Times*, 13 July. www.nytimes.com/2012/07/15/sunday-review/thats-not-my-phone-its-my-tracker.html?_r=0.

Macbeth, Steven W. Roland L. Fernandez, Brian R. Meyers, Desney S. Tan, George G. Robertson, Nuria M. Oliver, Oscar E. Murillo, and Mary P. Czerwinski. 2006. *Monitoring Group Activities*, edited by USPTO. United States: Microsoft Corporation.

MacIntyre, Alasdair C. 2008. *After Virtue: A Study in Moral Theory*. 3rd edn. Notre Dame: University of Notre Dame Press.

Mack, Arien. 2003. "Inattentional Blindness: Looking without Seeing." *Current Directions in Psychological Science* 12 (5):180–184. doi: 10.1111/1467–8721.01256.

Mackenzie, Catriona. 2000. "Imagining Oneself Otherwise." In *Relational Autonomy: Feminist Perspectives on Autonomy, Agency, and the Social Self*, edited by Catriona Mackenzie and Natalie Stoljar, 124–150. New York: Oxford University Press.

Mackenzie, Catriona, and Natalie Stoljar. 2000. "Introduction." In *Relational Autonomy: Feminist Perspectives on Autonomy, Agency, and the Social Self*, edited by Catriona Mackenzie and Natalie Stoljar, xi, 314 p. New York: Oxford University Press.

Mackie, David. 1999. "Personal Identity and Dead People." *Philosophical Studies* 95 (3):219–242.

MacKinnon, Catharine A. 1987. *Feminism Unmodified: Discourses on Life and Law*. Cambridge: Harvard University Press.

Malloy, Paul, Stephen Correia, Glenn Stebbins, and David H. Laidlaw. 2007. "Neuroimaging of White Matter in Aging and Dementia." *The Clinical Neuropsychologist* 21 (1):73–109.

Manson, Neil C., and Onora O'Neill. 2007. *Rethinking Informed Consent in Bioethics*. Cambridge, UK; New York: Cambridge University Press.

Marks, Jonathan H. 2006. "9/11 + 3/11 + 7/7 = ? What Counts in Counterterrorism?" *Columbia Human Rights Law Review* 37 (3):101–161.

May, Larry. 1996. *The Socially Responsive Self: Social Theory and Professional Ethics*. Chicago: University of Chicago Press.

May, Larry. 2010. "Complicity and the Rwandan Genocide." *Res Publica* 16:135–152. doi: 10.1007/s11158-010-9112-4.

McDougall, Bonnie S., and Anders Hansson. 2002. *Chinese Concepts of Privacy, Sinica Leidensia*. Leiden, Netherlands; Boston: Brill.

McNamara, Lawrence. 2009. "Counter-Terrorism Laws and the Media: National Security and the Control of Information." *Security Challenges* 5 (3):95–115.

McNeal, Gregory S. 2014a. "Facebook Manipulated User News Feeds to Create Emotional Responses." *Forbes*, 28 June. Accessed 11/01/2016. www.forbes.com/sites/gregorymcneal/2014/06/28/facebook-manipulated-user-news-feeds-to-create-emotional-contagion/.

McNeal, Gregory S. 2014b. "Controversy Over Facebook Emotional Manipulation Study Grows as Timeline Becomes More Clear." *Forbes*, June 30. Accessed 11/01/2016. www.forbes.com/sites/gregorymcneal/2014/06/30/controversy-over-facebook-emotional-manipulation-study-grows-as-timeline-becomes-more-clear/.

Meltzoff, A. N., and M. K. Moore. 1997. "Explaining Facial Imitation: A Theoretical Model." *Early Development and Parenting* 6 (3–4):179–192. doi: 10.1002/(sici)1099-0917(199709/12)6:3/4<179::aid-edp157>3.0.co;2-r.

Merges, R. P., and G. H. Reynolds. 2000. "The Proper Scope of the Copyright and Patent Power." *Harvard Journal on Legislation* 37:45–68.

Mill, John Stuart. 1971. "On Liberty." In *Utilitarianism, on Liberty, Essay on Bentham*, edited by Mary Warnock. London: The Fontana Library.

Mill, John Stuart. 1987. "Utilitarianism." In *Moral Philosophy – Selected Readings*, edited by George Sher. Fort Worth: Harcourt Brace College Publishers.

Miller, Joel. 2010a. "Stop and Search in England: A Reformed Tactic or Business as Usual?" *British Journal of Criminology* 50 (5):954–974. doi: 10.1093/bjc/azq021.

Miller, Seumas. 2010b. *The Moral Foundations of Social Institutions: A Philosophical Study*. Cambridge: Cambridge University Press.

Miller, Seumas, and Ian A. Gordon. 2014. *Investigative Ethics: Ethics for Police Detectives and Criminal Investigators*. Malden: Blackwell Publishing.
Miller, Seumas, and Michael J. Selgelid. 2006. "Ethical and Philosophical Considerations of the Dual-Use Dilemma in the Biological Sciences." *Science and Engineering Ethics* 13 (4):523–580.
Mishkin, Mortimer, Leslie G. Ungerleider, and Kathleen A. Macko. 1983. "Object Vision and Spatial Vision: Two Cortical Pathways." *Trends in Neurosciences* 6:414–417.
Mitchell, Sandra. 2004. "Why Integrative Pluralism?" *Emergence: Complexity & Organization* 6 (1):81–91.
Modood, T. 1998. "Anti-Essentialism, Multiculturalism and the 'Recognition' of Religious Groups." *Journal of Political Philosophy* 6 (4):378–399. doi: 10.1111/1467–9760.00060.
Mokrosinska, Dorota. 2014. "Privacy and the Integrity of Liberal Politics: The Case of Governmental Internet Searches." *Journal of Social Philosophy* 45 (3):369–389. doi: 10.1111/josp.12068.
Moor, James H. 2001. "The Future of Computer Ethics: You Ain't Seen Nothin' Yet!" *Ethics and Information Technology* 3 (2):89–91. doi: 10.1023/a:1011881522593.
Moor, James H. 2005. "Why We Need Better Ethics for Emerging Technologies." *Ethics and Information Technology* 7 (3):111–119.
Moore, Barrington. 1984. *Privacy: Studies in Social and Cultural History*. Armonk, NY: M.E. Sharpe; Distributed by Pantheon Books.
Moorhead, S. Anne, Diane E. Hazlett, Laura Harrison, Jennifer K. Carroll, Anthea Irwin, and Ciska Hoving. 2013. "A New Dimension of Health Care: Systematic Review of the Uses, Benefits, and Limitations of Social Media for Health Communication." *Journal of Medical Internet Research* 15 (4). doi: 10.2196/jmir.1933.
Moran, Richard. 2001. *Authority and Estrangement*. Princeton: Princeton University Press.
Moreno, Alvaro, and Arantza Etxeberria. 2005. "Agency in Natural and Artificial Systems." *Artificial Life* 11 (1–2):161–175. doi: 10.1162/1064546053278919.
Moreno, Alvaro, Jon Umerez, and Jesus Ibañez. 1997. "Cognition and Life: The Autonomy of Cognition." *Brain and Cognition* 34 (1):107–129.
Morgan, Lynn M. 2013. "The Potentiality Principle from Aristotle to Abortion." *Current Anthropology* 54 (S7):S15–S25. doi: 10.1086/670804.
Morozov, Evgeny. 2013. *To Save Everything Click Here: Technology, Solutionism and the Urge to Fix Problems That Don't Exist*. London: Penguin.
Morris, Steven. 2012. "Shopping Centre Tracking System Condemned by Civil Rights Campaigners." *The Guardian UK*, 04 January 2012. www.guardian.co.uk/business/2012/jan/04/shopping-centre-tracking-system-condemned/print.
Mueller, John, and Mark Stewart. 2011. *Terror, Security, and Money: Balancing the Risks, Benefits and Costs of Homeland Security*. Oxford: Oxford University Press.
Mueller, John, and Mark Stewart. 2016. *Chasing Ghosts: The Policing of Terrorism*. Oxford: Oxford University Press.
Mulgan, Tim. 2001. *The Demands of Consequentialism*. Oxford: Clarendon Press.
Muller, Sabine. 2009. "Body Integrity Identity Disorder (BIID) – Is the Amputation of Healthy Limbs Ethically Justified?" *The American Journal of Bioethics* 9 (1):36–43.
Murray, Sandra L. John G. Holmes, and Dale W. Griffin. 1996. "The Benefits of Positive Illusions: Idealization and the Construction of Satisfaction in Close Relationships." *Journal of Personality and Social Psychology* 70 (1):79–98.
Nagel, Thomas. 1975. "Review: Libertarianism without Foundations." *The Yale Law Journal* 85 (1):136–149.

National Institute of Standards and Technology. 2009. "NIST Test Proves 'The Eyes Have It' For ID Verification." accessed 06/11/2009. www.nist.gov/public_affairs/techbeat/tb2009_1103.htm#id.

National Science Foundation, and Department Of Commerce. 2003. Converging Technologies for Improving Human Performance: Nanotechnology, Biotechnology, Information Technology, and Cognitive Sciences, edited by Mihail C. Roco and William Sims Bainbridge: National Science Foundation and Department of Commerce,.

Neale, Stephen. 1992. "Paul Grice and the Philosophy of Language." *Linguistics and Philosophy* 15 (5):509–559.

Neisser, Ulric. 1979. "The Control of Information Pickup in Selective Looking." In *Perception and Its Development: A Tribute to Eleanor J. Gibson*, edited by A. D. Prick, 201–219. Hillsdale, NJ: Lawrence Erlbaum.

Netzer, Christian, and Nikola Biller-Andorno. 2004. "Pharmacogenetic Testing, Informed Consent and the Problem of Secondary Information." *Bioethics* 18 (4):344–360. doi:10.1111/j.1467–8519.2004.00401.x.

Nissenbaum, Helen. 2009. *Privacy in Context: Technology, Policy, and the Integrity of Social Life*. Stanford, California: Stanford Law Books.

Norman, Donald A. 2002. *The Design of Everyday Things*. New York: Basic Books.

Norris, Clive, and Michael McCahill. 2006. "CCTV: Beyond Penal Modernism?" *The British Journal of Criminology* 46 (1):97.

North, Douglass Cecil, and Robert Paul Thomas. 1973. *The Rise of the Western World: A New Economic History*. Cambridge: University Press.

Nozick, Robert. 1974. *Anarchy, State, and Utopia*. Oxford: Blackwell Publishing.

O'Connor, Timothy, and Hong Yu Wong. 2009. "Emergent Properties." In *The Stanford Encyclopedia of Philosophy*, edited by Edward N. Zalta.

Oakley, Justin, and Dean Cocking. 2001a. *Virtue Ethics and Professional Roles*. Cambridge: Cambridge University Press.

Oakley, Justin, and Dean Cocking. 2001b. "A Virtue Ethics Approach to Professional Roles." In *Virtue Ethics and Professional Roles*, 74–94. Cambridge: Cambridge University Press.

Okin, Susan Moller, Joshua Cohen, Matthew Howard, and Martha Craven Nussbaum. 1999. *Is Multiculturalism Bad for Women?* Princeton, NJ: Princeton University Press.

Olson, Eric T. 2010. "Personal Identity." In *The Stanford Encyclopedia of Philosophy*, edited by Edward N. Zalta.

Omand, David. 2010. *Securing the State*. Oxford: Oxford University Press.

Oshitani, Hitoshi, Taro Kamigaki, and Akira Suzuki. 2008. "Major Issues and Challenges of Influenza Pandemic Preparedness in Developing Countries." *Emerging Infectious Diseases* 14 (6):875–880. doi: 10.3201/eid1406.070839.

Ossorio, Pilar N. 2006. "About Face: Forensic Genetic Testing for Race and Visible Traits." *The Journal of Law, Medicine & Ethics* 34 (2):277–292. doi:10.1111/j.1748–720X.2006.00033.x.

Ossorio, Pilar N., and Troy Duster. 2005. "Race and Genetics: Controversies in Biomedical, Behavioral, and Forensic Sciences." *American Psychologist* 60 (1):115–128. doi: 10.1037/0003–066X.60.1.115.

Oxford Dictionaries Online. In *Oxford Dictionaries Online*: Oxford.

Parent, W. A. 1983. "Privacy, Morality, and the Law." *Philosophy and Public Affairs* 12 (4):269–288.

Parfit, Derek. 1971a. "On 'The Importance of Self-Identity'." *The Journal of Philosophy* 68 (20):683–690.

Parfit, Derek. 1971b. "Personal Identity." *The Philosophical Review* 80 (1):3–27.

Parfit, Derek. 1987. *Reasons and Persons*. Reprinted with corrections, 1987. edn. Oxford: Clarendon Press.

Parliamentary Joint Committee on Intelligence and Surveillance. 2015. *Advisory Report on the Telecommunications (Interception and Access) Amendment (Data Retention) Bill 2014*. Canberra: The Parliament of the Commonwealth of Australia.

Parrish, Julia K., Steven V. Viscido, and Daniel Grunbaum. 2002. "Self-Organized Fish Schools: An Examination of Emergent Properties." *The Biological Bulletin* 202 (3): 296–305.

Partridge, Emma. 2016. "$150,000 Facebook Post That Destroyed a Former Deputy Principal's Life." *The Age*, 8th August.

Patten, Alan. 1999. *Hegel's Idea of Freedom, Oxford Philosophical Monographs*. Oxford; New York: Oxford University Press.

Payne, B. Keith. 2001. "Prejudice and Perception: The Role of Automatic and Controlled Processes in Misperceiving a Weapon." *Journal of Personality and Social Psychology* 81 (2):181–192. doi: 10.1037/0022-3514.81.2.181.

Payne, B. Keith. 2005. "Conceptualizing Control in Social Cognition: How Executive Functioning Modulates the Expression of Automatic Stereotyping." *Journal of Personality and Social Psychology* 89 (4):488–503. doi: 10.1037/0022-3514.89.4.488.

Payne, B. Keith, Clara Michelle Cheng, Olesya Govorun, and Brandon D. Stewart. 2005. "An Inkblot for Attitudes: Affect Misattribution as Implicit Measurement." *Journal of Personality and Social Psychology* 89 (3):277–293. doi: 10.1037/0022-3514.89.3.277.

Peacock, A., Ke Xian, and M. Wilkerson. 2004. "Typing Patterns: A Key to User Identification." *Security & Privacy, IEEE* 2 (5):40–47.

Pearl, Mike. 2015. "Activists Say the LAPD's New Body Camera Program Is Full of Problems." *Vice*, 30 April.

Pelczar, Michael. 2000. "Wittgensteinian Semantics." *Nous* 34 (4):483–516.

Perrett, Roy W. 2000. "Taking Life and the Argument from Potentiality." *Midwest Studies in Philosophy* 24 (1):186–197. doi: 10.1111/1475-4975.00029.

Perry, John. 1978. A *Dialogue on Personal Identity and Immortality*. Indianapolis: Hackett Publishing Company.

Perry, John, ed. 2008a. *Personal Identity*. 2 edn. Berkeley: University of California Press.

Perry, John. 2008b. "The Problem of Personal Identity." In *Personal Identity*, edited by John Perry, 3–30. Berkeley: University of California Press.

Pettit, Philip. 1988. "The Consequentialist Can Recognise Rights." *The Philosophical Quarterly* 38 (150):42–55.

Pinkard, Terry P. 1988. *Hegel's Dialectic: The Explanation of Possibility*. Philadelphia: Temple University Press.

Pitcher, George, ed. 1968. *Wittgenstein: The Philosophical Investigations*: Macmillan.

Plassmann, Hilke, John O'Doherty, Baba Shiv, and Antonio Rangel. 2008. "Marketing Actions Can Modulate Neural Representations of Experienced Pleasantness." *Proceedings of the National Academy of Sciences* 105 (3):1050–1054. doi: 10.1073/pnas.0706929105.

Pogge, Thomas. 2005a. "Human Rights and Global Health: A Research Program." *Metaphilosophy* 36 (1/2):182–209.

Pogge, Thomas. 2005b. "World Poverty and Human Rights." *Ethics and International Affairs* 19 (1):1–7.

Pogge, Thomas. 2008. *World Poverty and Human Rights*. 2nd edn. Cambridge: Polity Press.

Pollard, Ruth. 2009. "Elite College Students Proud of 'Pro-Rape' Facebook Page." *Sydney Morning Herald*, November 9. www.smh.com.au/technology/elite-college-students-proud-of-prorape-facebook-page-20091108-i3js.html#moreRelatedCoverage.

Poon, Kai-Tak, and Zhansheng Chen. 2014. "When Justice Surrenders: The Effect of Just-World Beliefs on Aggression Following Ostracism." *Journal of Experimental Social Psychology* 52:101–112. doi: http://dx.doi.org/10.1016/j.jesp.2014.01.006.

Posner, Richard A. 2005. "Intellectual Property: The Law and Economics Approach." *The Journal of Economic Perspectives* 19 (2):57–73.

Pritchard, Duncan. 2004. "Epistemic Luck." *Journal of Philosophical Research* 29:193–222.

Putnam, Hilary. 1973. "Meaning and Reference." *The Journal of Philosophy* 70 (19):699–711.

Putnam, Hillary. 1975. "The Meaning of 'Meaning'." In *Minnesota Studies in the Philosophy of Science: Volume VII Language, Mind, and Knowledge*, edited by Keith Gunderson. Minneapolis: University of Minnesota.

Rachels, James. 1975. "Why Privacy Is Important." *Philosophy and Public Affairs* 4 (4): 323–333.

Radin, Margaret Jane. 1981. "Property and Personhood." *Stanford Law Review* 34 (5): 957–1016.

Ramli, David. 2011. "Peeping TomTom Sells Your Every Move." *The Australian Financial Review*, May 6. www.afr.com/p/business/technology/peeping_tomtom_sells_your_every_JdzlTffqhtoLHSPRGIvqoJ.

Rauschecker, Josef P., and Sophie K. Scott. 2009. "Maps and Streams in the Auditory Cortex: Nonhuman Primates Illuminate Human Speech Processing." *Nature Neuroscience* 12 (6):718–724.

Rawls, John. 1951. "Outline of a Decision Procedure for Ethics." *The Philosophical Review* 60 (2):177–197.

Rawls, John. 1971. *A Theory of Justice*. Original edn. Cambridge: Harvard University Press.

Rawls, John. 1985. "Justice as Fairness: Political Not Metaphysical." *Philosophy and Public Affairs* 14 (3):223–251.

Rawls, John. 1999a. "The Idea of an Overlapping Consensus." In *Collected Papers/John Rawls*, edited by Samuel Freeman, 421–448. Cambridge: Harvard University Press.

Rawls, John. 1999b. *The Law of Peoples: With, the Idea of Public Reason Revisited*. Cambridge, MA: Harvard University Press.

Rawls, John. 2001. *Justice as Fairness: A Restatement*, edited by Erin Kelly. Cambridge: The Belknap Press of Harvard University Press.

Rees, Christopher, and Debbie Heywood. 2014. "The 'Right to Be forgotten' or the 'Principle That Has Been Remembered'." *Computer Law & Security Review* 30 (5):574–578. doi: http://dx.doi.org/10.1016/j.clsr.2014.07.002.

Regan, T. 2004. *The Case for Animal Rights*. 3rd edn: Berkeley: University of California Press.

Reichlin, Massimo. 1997. "The Argument from Potential: A Reappraisal." *Bioethics* 11 (1):1–23. doi: 10.1111/1467–8519.00041.

Reiman, Jeffrey H. 1976. "Privacy, Intimacy, and Personhood." *Philosophy and Public Affairs* 6 (1):26–44.

Review Group on Intelligence and Communications Technologies. 2013. *Liberty and Security in a Changing World*. White House.

Reyburn, Hugh Adam. 1921. *The Ethical Theory of Hegel: A Study of the Philosophy of Right*. Oxford: Clarendon.

Ricketson, Sam, and Megan Richardson. 1998. *Intellectual Property: Cases Materials and Commentary*. 2nd edn. Sydney: Butterworths.

Rix, Mark. 2011. "Counter-Terrorism and Information: The NSI Act, Fair Trials, and Open, Accountable Government." *Continuum* 25 (2):285–297. doi: http://dx.doi.org/10.1080/10304312.2011.554059.

Robb, David, and John Heil. 2009. "Mental Causation." In *The Stanford Encyclopedia of Philosophy*, edited by Edward N. Zalta.

Roff, Heather M. 2013. "Killing in War: Responsibility, Liability, and Lethal Autonomous Robots." In *Routledge Handbook of Ethics and War: Just War in the 21st Century*, edited by Fritz Allhoff, Nicholas G. Evans and Adam Henschke. London: Routledge.

Rorty, Amélie, and David Wong. 1990. "Aspects of Identity and Agency." In *Identity, Character, and Morality: Essays in Moral Psychology*, edited by Owen J. Flanagan and Amélie Rorty, vii, 487 p. Cambridge, MA: MIT Press.

Rosen, Michael. 1982. *Hegel's Dialectic and Its Criticism*. Cambridge [Cambridgeshire]; New York: Cambridge University Press.

Ross, W. D. 1930. *The Right and the Good*. Oxford: The Clarendon Press.

Roxon. Nicola. 2010. *Healthcare Identifiers: Passed by Parliament edited by Health and Aging*. Canberra.

Royal United Services Institute. 2016. "Lone-Actor Terrorism." In *Countering Lone-Actor Terrorism Series*. London: Royal United Services Institute.

Russell, Bertrand. 1912. *The Problems of Philosophy*. London: Oxford University Press.

Safi, Michael. 2016. "The Takeover: How Police Ended Up Running a Paedophile Site." *The Guardian*, 13th July. Accessed 13 July. www.theguardian.com/society/2016/jul/13/shining-a-light-on-the-dark-web-how-the-police-ended-up-running-a-paedophile-site.

Salter, Michael, and Thomas Crofts. 2015. "Responding to Revenge Porn: Challenges to Online Legal Impunity." In *New Views on Pornography: Sexuality, Politics, and the Law*, edited by Comella Lynn and Shira Tarrant Praeger.

Scanlon, Thomas. 1975. "Thomson on Privacy." *Philosophy and Public Affairs* 4 (4): 315–322.

Scanlon, Thomas. 1976. "Nozick on Rights, Liberty, and Property." *Philosophy and Public Affairs* 6 (1):3–25.

Scanlon, Thomas Michael. 2000. *What We Owe Each Other*. Cambridge: Harvard University Press.

Scheffler, Samuel. 1993. *The Rejection of Consequentialism: Revised Edition*. 3rd edn. Oxford: Oxford University Press.

Scherer, Michael. 2012. "Inside the Secret World of the Data Crunchers Who Helped Obama Win." *Time*, 7 November. http://swampland.time.com/2012/11/07/inside-the-secret-world-of-quants-and-data-crunchers-who-helped-obama-win/.

Scott, Charity. 2008. "Belief in a Just World: A Case Study in Public Health Ethics." *Hastings Center Report* 38 (1):16.

Searle, John R. 1997. *The Mystery of Consciousness*. 1st edn. New York: New York Review of Books.

Searle, John R. 2008. "The Self as a Problem in Philosophy and Neurobiology." In *Philosophy in a New Century: Selected Essays*, viii, 201 p. Cambridge; New York: Cambridge University Press.

Selgelid, Michael J. 2005. "Module Four: Standards of Care and Clinical Trials." *Developing World Bioethics* 5 (1):55–72.

Selgelid, Michael J. and Christian Enemark. 2008. "Infectious Diseases, Secuirty and Ethics: The Case of HIV/AIDS." *Bioethics* 22 (9):457–465.

Selgelid, Michael J. and Eline M. Sepers. 2006. "Patents, Profits, and the Price of Pills: Implications for Access and Availability." In *The Power of Pills*, edited by Jillian C. Cohen, Patricia Illingworth and Udo Schuklenk. London: Pluto Press.

Selgelid, Michael J. 2009. "A Moderate Pluralist Approach to Public Health Policy and Ethics." *Public Health Ethics* 2 (2):195–205. doi: 10.1093/phe/php018.

Shamma, Shihab. 2008. "On the Emergence and Awareness of Auditory Objects." *PLoS Biol* 6 (6):e155.
Shannon, Claude Elwood, and Warren Weaver. 1949. *The Mathematical Theory of Communication*. Urbana: University of Illinois Press.
Sharpley, Christopher Francis, and Vicki Bitsika. 2010. "The Diverse Neurogeography of Emotional Experience: Form Follows Function." *Behavioural Brain Research* 215 (1):1–6.
Shoemaker, Sydney Sharpless. 1963. *Self-Knowledge and Self-Identity, Contemporary Philosophy*. Ithaca, New York: Cornell University Press.
Sieber, Joan E. 1998. "The Psychology of Whistleblowing." *Science and Engineering Ethics* 4 (1):7–23. doi: 10.1007/s11948-998-0002-5.
Siegler, Mark. 1994. "Confidentiality in Medicine – A Decrepit Concept." In *Contemporary Issues in Bioethics*, edited by Tom L. Beauchamp and LeRoy Walters, 179–131. Belmont: Wadsworth Publishing Company.
Simeone, Nick. 2014. Clapper: Snowden Caused 'Massive, Historic' Security Damage. U.S. Department of Defense.
Simons, Daniel. J., and Christopher. F. Chabris. 1999. "Gorillas in Our Midst: Sustained Inattentional Blindness for Dynamic Events." *Perception* 28 (9):1059–1074.
Singer, Peter W., and Allan Friedman. 2014. *Cybersecurity and Cyberwar: What Everyone Needs to Know*. Oxford: Oxford University Press.
Skene, Loane, and Scott Milkwood. 1997. ""Informed Consent" to Medical Procedures: The Current Law in Australia, Doctor's Knowledge of the Law, and Their Practices in Informing Patients." In *Health Care Law and Ethics*, edited by Leila Shotton, 69–92. Katoomba: Social Science Press.
Skuse, David. 2006. "Genetic Influences on the Neural Basis of Social Cognition." *Philosophical Transactions of the Royal Society B: Biological Sciences* 361 (1476):2129–2141. doi: 10.1098/rstb.2006.1935.
Smedley, Audrey, and Brian Smedley. 2005. "Race as Biology Is Fiction, Racism as a Social Problem Is Real: Anthropological and Historical Perspectives on the Social Construction of Race." *American Psychologist* 60 (1):16–26.
Smith, Gavin. 2015. *Opening the Black Box: The Work of Watching*: London: Routledge.
Smith, Michael. 1987. "The Humean Theory of Motivation." *Mind* 96 (381):36–61.
Smith, Michael. 1994. *The Moral Problem*. Malden: Blackwell Publishing.
Solove, Daniel. 2004. *The Digital Person: Technology and Privacy in the Information Age*. New York: New York University Press.
Solove, Daniel. 2008. *Understanding Privacy*. Harvard: Harvard University Press.
Sorensen, Roy 2009. "Vagueness." In *The Stanford Encyclopedia of Philosophy*, edited by Edward N. Zalta.
Sosa, Ernest, Jaegwon Kim, and Matthew McGrath. 2000. *Epistemology: An Anthology, Blackwell Philosophy Anthologies*. Malden, MA: Blackwell Publishers.
Spacks, Patricia Ann Meyer. 2003. *Privacy: Concealing the Eighteenth-Century Self*. Chicago: University of Chicago Press.
Sparrow, Robert. 2007. "Revolutionary and Familiar, Inevitable and Precarious: Rhetorical Contradictions in Enthusiasm for Nanotechnology." *NanoEthics* 1 (1):57–68. doi: 10.1007/s11569-007-0008-5.
Sporns, Olaf, Christopher J. Honey, and Rolf Kotter. 2007. "Identification and Classification of Hubs in Brain Networks." *PloS One* 2 (10):e1049.
Stempel, Jonathan. 2015. "NSA's Phone Spying Program Ruled Illegal by Appeals Court." *Reuters*, 7th May 2016. Accessed 20th September 2016. www.reuters.com/article/us-usa-security-nsa-idUSKBN0NS1IN20150507.

Sterba, James. 2005. *The Triumph of Practice over Theory in Ethics*. Oxford: Oxford University Press.

Sterelny, Kim. 1990. *The Representational Theory of Mind: An Introduction*. Oxford: Blackwell.

Sterelny, Kim. 2003. *Thought in a Hostile World: The Evolution of Human Cognition*, Hoboken: Blackwell Publishing.

Steup, Matthias. 2009. "The Analysis of Knowledge." In *Stanford Encyclopedia of Philosophy*, edited by Edward N. Zalta.

Stevens, Jacqueline. 2003. "Racial Meanings and Scientific Methods: Changing Policies for NIH-Sponsored Publications Reporting Human Variation." *Journal of Health Politics Policy and Law* 28 (6):1033–1088. doi: 10.1215/03616878-28-6-1033.

Straub, Jurgen. 2002. "Personal and Collective Identity: A Conceptual Analysis." In *Identities: Time, Difference, and Boundaries*, edited by Heidrun Friese and Aleida Assmann, 56–76. New York: Berghahn Books.

Strawser, Bradley Jay. 2010. "Moral Predators: The Duty to Employ Uninhabited Aerial Vehicles." *Journal of Military Ethics* 9 (4):342–368. doi: 10.1080/15027570.2010.536403.

Stroebe, Katherine, Tom Postmes, Susanne Tauber, and John Melissa. 2015. "Belief in a Just What? Demystifying Just World Beliefs by Distinguishing Sources of Justice." *PloS One* (March 2015). doi: 10.1371/journal.pone.0120145.

Stross, Randall. 2010. "When History Is Compiled 140 Characters at a Time." *New York Times*, May 1.

Surendran, Sankar, Kimberlee M. Matalon, Stephen K. Tyring, and Reuben Matalon. 2003. "Molecular Basis of Canavan's Disease: From Human to Mouse." *Journal of Child Neurology* 18 (9):604–610. doi: 10.1177/08830738030180090601.

Surendran, Sankar, Kimberlee Michals-Matalon, Michael J. Quast, Stephen K. Tyring, Jingna Wei, Ed L. Ezell, and Reuben Matalon. 2003. "Canavan Disease: A Monogenic Trait with Complex Genomic Interaction." *Molecular Genetics and Metabolism* 80 (1–2):74–80.

Sutton, Robbie M., and Elizabeth J. Winnard. 2007. "Looking Ahead through Lenses of Justice: The Relevance of Just-World Beliefs to Intentions and Confidence in the Future." *British Journal of Social Psychology* 46 (3):649–666. doi: 10.1348/014466606X166220.

Swami, Viren, and Adrian Furnham. 2008. "Is Love Really So Blind?" *The Psychologist* 21 (2):108–111.

Syal, Rajeev. 2013. "Abandoned NHS IT System Has Cost £10bn So Far." *The Guardian*, 18 September.

Tang, Paul C., and Thomas H. Lee. 2009. "Your Doctor's Office or the Internet? Two Paths to Personal Health Records." *New England Journal of Medicine* 360 (13):1276–1278. doi: 10.1056/NEJMp0810264.

Taylor, Charles. 1975. *Hegel*. Cambridge: Cambridge University Press.

Taylor, Charles. 1978. *Hegel and Modern Society*. Cambridge: Cambridge University Press.

Taylor, Charles. 1989. *The Sources of the Self: The Making of Modern Identity*. New York: Cambridge University Press.

Taylor, Charles. 1994a. "Multiculturalism and 'The Politics of Recognition': An Essay." In *Examining Multiculturalism and the Politics of Recognition*, edited by Amy Gutman, xi, 112 p. Princeton, NJ: Princeton University Press.

Taylor, Charles. 1994b. "The Politics of Recognition." In *Multiculturalism*, edited by Amy Gutman, xi, 112 p. Princeton, NJ: Princeton University Press.

Tegart, Greg W. J. 2010. *Smart Technology for Healthy Longevity*. Melbourne: Australian Academy of Technological Sciences and Engingeering.

The Human Rights Council. 2011. *Report of the Special Rapporteur on the Promotion and Protection of the Right to Freedom of Opinion and Expression*. Geneva: The Human Rights Council.

The World Bank. 2015. *Internet Users (Per 100 People)*. The World Bank.

Theodoridou, Angeliki, Angela C. Rowe, Ian S. Penton-Voak, and Peter J. Rogers. 2009. "Oxytocin and Social Perception: Oxytocin Increases Perceived Facial Trustworthiness and Attractiveness." *Hormones and Behavior* 56 (1):128–132.

Thielman, Sam. 2016. "Facebook Fires Trending Team, and Algorithm without Humans Goes Crazy." *The Guardian*, 29th August.

Thomson, Judith Jarvis. 1975. "The Right to Privacy." *Philosophy and Public Affairs* 4 (4):295–314.

Traynor, Ian, and Paul Lewis. 2013. "Merkel Compared NSA to Stasi in Heated Encounter with Obama." *The Guardian*, December 17. www.theguardian.com/world/2013/dec/17/merkel-compares-nsa-stasi-obama.

U.K. Government. 2006. *The National DNA Database*, edited by Parliamentary Office of Science and Technology. London: U.K. Parliament.

U.K. Government. 2012. Open Data White Paper: Unleashing the Potential, edited by Minister of State for Cabinet Office and Paymaster General. Whitehall: Controller of Her Majesty's Stationary Office.

Uniacke, Suzanne. 1996. *Permissible Killing: The Self-Defense Justification of Homicide*. Cambridge: Cambridge University Press.

United States District Court. 2003. *Greenberg* v. *Miami Children's Hospital Research Insititute, Inc.*: United States District Court, S.D. Florida, Miami Division.

United States District Court. 2006. *Washington University* v *William J. Catalona et al.*, edited by Eastern District of Missouri.

US Government. 1792. Fourth Amendment to the US Constitution.

van den Hoven, Jeroen. 1999. "Privacy and the Varieties of Informational Wrongdoing." *Australian Journal of Professional and Applied Ethics* 1:30–43.

van den Hoven, Jeroen. 2007a. "ICT and Value Sensitive Design." In *The Information Society: Innovation, Legitimacy, Ethics and Democracy in Honor of Professor Jacques Berleur s.j.*, edited by Philippe Goujon, Sylvian Lavelle, Penny Duquenoy, Kai Kimppa and Veronique Laurent, 67–72. Boston: Springer.

van den Hoven, Jeroen. 2007b. "Privacy and the Varieties of Informational Wrongdoing." In *Computer Ethics*, edited by John Weckert, 317–330. Aldershot: Ashgate Publishing.

van den Hoven, Jeroen. 2008. "Information Technology, Privacy and the Protection of Personal Data." In *Information Technology and Moral Philosophy*, edited by Jeroen van den Hoven and John Weckert, 301–321. Cambridge: Cambridge University Press.

van den Hoven, Jeroen, and Noemi Manders-Huits. 2006. "Identity Management and Moral Identification." *Algemeen Nederlands Tijdschrift Voor Wijsbegeerte* 98 (2):111–127.

van den Hoven, Jeroen, and Emma Rooksby. 2008. "Distributive Justice and the Value of Information: A (Broadly) Rawlsian Approach." In *Information Technology and Moral Philosophy*, edited by Jeroen van den Hoven and John Weckert, 376–396. Cambridge: Cambridge University Press.

van den Hoven, Jeroen, and John Weckert, eds. 2008. *Information Technology and Moral Philosophy*. Cambridge: Cambridge University Press.

van der Ploeg, Irma 1999. "The Illegal Body: 'Eurodac' and the Politics of Biometric Identification." *Ethics and Information Technology* 1 (4):295.

van Duijn, Marc, Fred Keijzer, and Daan Franken. 2006. "Principles of Minimal Cognition: Casting Cognition as Sensorimotor Coordination." *Adaptive Behavior* 14 (2):157–170. doi: 10.1177/105971230601400207.

Vandekerckhove, Wim. 2006. *Whistleblowing and Organizational Social Responsibility: A Global Assessment*: Ashgate.
Vandekerckhove, Wim, and David Lewis. 2012. "The Content of Whistleblowing Procedures: A Critical Review of Recent Official Guidelines." *Journal of Business Ethics* 108 (2):253–264. doi: 10.1007/s10551-011-1089-1.
Veltkamp, Martijn, Henk Aarts, and Ruud Custers. 2008. "Perception in the Service of Goal Pursuit: Motivation to Attain Goals Enhances the Perceived Size of Goal-Instrumental Objects." *Social Cognition* 26 (6):720–736.
Vizer, Lisa M., Lina Zhou, and Andrew Sears. 2009. "Automated Stress Detection Using Keystroke and Linguistic Features: An Exploratory Study." *International Journal of Human-Computer Studies* 67 (10):870–886.
Waddington, P. A. J., Kevin Stenson, and David Don. 2004. "In Proportion: Race, and Police Stop and Search." *British Journal of Criminology* 44 (6):889–914. doi: 10.1093/bjc/azh042.
Waldron, Jeremy. 1988. *The Right to Private Property*. Oxford: Clarendon Paperbacks.
Waldron, Jeremy. 2006. "Safety and Security." *Nebraska Law Review* 85 (3):454–507.
Waldron, Jeremy. 2009. "2009 Oliver Wendel Holmes Lectures: Dignity and Defamation the Visibility of Hate." *Harvard Law Review* 123:1596–2096.
Walsh, Patrick F., and Seumas Miller. 2015. "Rethinking 'Five Eyes' Security Intelligence Collection Policies and Practice Post Snowden." *Intelligence and National Security*. 1–24. doi: 10.1080/02684527.2014.998436.
Walzer, Michael. 1983. *Spheres of Justice: A Defense of Pluralism and Equality*. New York: Basic Books.
Wang, Y, OKW Ho, GQ Huang, and D Li. 2008. "Study on Vehicle Management in Logistics Based on RFID, GPS and GIS." *International Journal of Internet Manufacturing and Services* 1 (3):294–304.
Wansink, Brian. 2006. *Mindless Eating: Why Eat More Than We Think*. New York: Bantam Books.
Want, R. 2006. "An Introduction to RFID Technology." *IEEE Pervasive Computing* 5 (1):25–33.
Warren, Samuel D., and Louis D. Brandeis. 1890. "The Right to Privacy." *Harvard Law Review* 4 (5):193–220.
Weckert, John. 1986. "Putnam, Reference and Essentialism." *Dialogue: Canadian Philosophical Review/Revue Canadienne De Philosophie* 25 (03):509–521. doi: 10.1017/S0012217300020916.
Weckert, John, and Adam Henschke. 2009. "Computer Ethics and Applied Contexts." In *The Cambridge Handbook of Information and Computer Ethics*, edited by Floridi Luciano. Cambridge: Cambridge University Press.
Wensley, D. and M. King. 2008. "Scientific Responsibility for the Dissemination and Interpretation of Genetic Research: Lessons from the "Warrior Gene" Controversy." *Journal of Medical Ethics* 34 (6):507–509. doi: 10.1136/jme.2006.019596.
West, Caroline. 2012. "Words That Silence? Freedom of Expression and Racist Hate Speech." In *Speech and Harm: Controversies over Free Speech*, edited by Ishani Maitra and Mary Kate McGowan. Oxford: Oxford University Press.
Westin, Alan F. 1967. *Privacy and Freedom*. London: Bodley Head.
Wheeland, Matthew. 2016. "Four Ways Technology Will Change How We Commute in the Future." *The Guardian*, 17th August.
Whitmore, Andrew, Anurag Agarwal, and Li Da Xu. 2015. "The Internet of Things – A Survey of Topics and Trends." *Information Systems Frontiers* 17 (2):261–274.
Williams, Bernard. 1970. "The Self and the Future." *The Philosophical Review* 79 (2):161–180.

Williams, Bernard. 1981a. *Moral Luck*. Cambridge: Cambridge University Press.

Williams, Bernard. 1981b. "Persons, Character and Morality." In *Moral Luck: Philosophical Papers 1973–1980*. Cambridge: Cambridge University Press.

Williams, Bernard Arthur Owen. 1973. "A Critique of Utilitarianism." In *Utilitarianism: For and Against*. Cambridge: Cambridge University Press.

Williams, Michael. 1991. *Unnatural Doubts: Epistemological Realism and the Basis of Scepticism*. Oxford: Blackwell.

Wittenbrink, Bernd, Charles M. Judd, and Bernadette Park. 1997. "Evidence for Racial Prejudice at the Implicit Level and Its Relationship with Questionnaire Measures." *Journal of Personality & Social Psychology* 72 (2):262–274.

Wittgenstein, Ludwig. 1958. *Philosophical Investigations*. Translated by G. E. M. Anscombe. 2nd edn. Oxford: Blackwell.

Wittgenstein, Ludwig, Peter M. S. Hacker, and Joachim Schulte. 2009. *Philosophical Investigations*. Translated by G. E. M. Anscombe, P. M. S. Hacker and Joachim Schulte. Rev. 4th edn. Malden, MA: Wiley-Blackwell.

Wolf, Susan. 1994. "Comment on Multiculturalism and the Politics of Recognition." In *Examining Multiculturalism and the Politics of Recognition*, edited by Amy Gutman, 75–85. Princeton, NJ: Princeton University Press.

World Medical Association. 1964. *Ethical Principles for Medical Research Involving Human Subjects*, edited by World Medical Association. Helsinki: World Medical Association.

Wortley, Scot, and Akwasi Owusu-Bempah. 2011. "The Usual Suspects: Police Stop and Search Practices in Canada." *Policing and Society* 21 (4):395–407. doi: 10.1080/10439463.2011.610198.

Young, Garry. 2008. "Capgras Delusion: An Interactionist Model." *Consciousness and Cognition* 17 (3):863–876.

Zins, Chaim. 2007. "Conceptual Approaches for Defining Data, Information, and Knowledge." *Journal of the American Society for Information Science and Technology* 58 (4):479–493.

Index

Lightning Source UK Ltd.
Milton Keynes UK
UKHW020650021219
354600UK00017B/238/P

9 781107 570474